The Future of the Academic Journal

CHANDOS
PUBLISHING SERIES

Chandos' new series of books are aimed at all those individuals interested in publishing. They have been specially commissioned to provide the reader with an authoritative view of current thinking. If you would like a full listing of current and forthcoming titles, please visit our website www.chandospublishing.com or email info@chandospublishing.com or telephone +44 (0) 1223 891358.

New authors: we are always pleased to receive ideas for new titles. If you would like to write a book for Chandos, please contact Dr Glyn Jones on e-mail gjones@chandospublishing.com or telephone number +44 (0) 1993 848726.

Bulk orders: some organisations buy a number of copies of our books. If you are interested in doing this, we would be pleased to discuss a discount. Please email info@chandospublishing.com or telephone +44(0) 1223 891358.

The Future of the Academic Journal

EDITED BY
BILL COPE
AND
ANGUS PHILLIPS

Chandos Publishing
Oxford • Cambridge • New Delhi

Chandos Publishing
TBAC Business Centre
Avenue 4
Station Lane
Witney
Oxford OX28 4BN
UK
Tel: +44 (0) 1993 848726
Email: info@chandospublishing.com
www.chandospublishing.com

Chandos Publishing is an imprint of Woodhead Publishing Limited

Woodhead Publishing Limited
Abington Hall
Granta Park
Great Abington
Cambridge CB21 6AH
UK
www.woodheadpublishing.com

First published in 2009

ISBN:
978 1 84334 416 2

British Library Cataloguing-in-Publication Data.
A catalogue record for this book is available from the British Library.

Typeset by Domex e-Data Pvt. Ltd.
Printed in the UK and USA.

Contents

List of figures and tables

Figures

Tables

About the contributors

Claire Bird is Senior Publisher, Biosciences, at Oxford Journals. She joined Oxford Journals after graduating in molecular and cellular biochemistry from Oxford University in 2000. She is responsible for the management and development of Oxford Journals' molecular and computational biology list, which includes such journals as *Nucleic Acids Research* (NAR), *Human Molecular Genetics* and *Bioinformatics*. Claire has played a central role in Oxford Journals' open access experiments, including the transition of NAR to a fully open access model in 2005, and the launch of the company's optional open access initiative in the same year. She has authored or co-authored various articles and presentations on the subject.

Bill Cope is a Research Professor in the Department of Educational Policy Studies at the University of Illinois. He is the author or co-author of number a number of key and widely cited books in the fields of literacy and pedagogy, including *The Powers of Literacy* (Falmer Press, 1993), *Multiliteracies: Literacy Learning and the Design of Social Futures* (Routledge, 2000) and *New Learning: Elements of a Science of Education* (Cambridge University Press, 2008). From 2000 to 2003, he conceived and coordinated a major research project on digital authoring environments though RMIT University in Melbourne, Australia, 'Creator to Consumer in a Digital Age', funded by the Australian Government's Department of Industry. Dr Cope is also Director of Common Ground Publishing, a developer of hybrid open access/commercial academic publishing software, and a publisher of books and academic journals, based in the University of Illinois Research Park.

Iain Craig joined Blackwell Publishing, now Wiley-Blackwell, in 2005. He is a member of the Research & Analysis department based in Oxford, UK, and specializes in bibliometric analysis – including the citation performance and output of articles, authors, journals, research institutes and countries. Iain has written numerous articles on Impact Factors and citation analysis, including several published in peer-reviewed journals, and has spoken on the topic in a variety of settings, both to a publishing and academic audience. A graduate of the University of Edinburgh, his career in publishing began at Elsevier, Oxford, UK where he managed and commissioned a portfolio of journals, books and major reference works in the materials science, and latterly the organic chemistry subject areas.

J. Eric Davies is Honorary Visiting Research Fellow in the Department of Information Science at Loughborough University. From 1999 to 2007 he was Director of LISU, a national research and information centre concentrating on performance assessment of libraries and related cultural services, based at Loughborough University. His experience of professional library practice includes over 25 years in academic library management. He has been active in professional association affairs for many years and has served on the governing council of the Chartered Institute of Library and Information Professionals and chaired its Policy Development Committee. He is a Member of the Standing Committee of the Statistics and Evaluation Section of the International Federation of Library Associations and Institutions, and a member of the UK Government's Advisory Panel on Public Sector Information. He serves on the editorial boards of *Library Management* and *Evidence Based Library and Information Practice*.

Liz Ferguson joined Blackwell Publishing in August 2003 and is now Associate Publishing Director following the merger with Wiley's STM publishing division. She leads a multinational team publishing a growing list of more than 80 biological science journals, many of which belong to learned societies, federations and other non-profit organizations. Previously, Liz worked for a variety of publishers, including Lippincott Williams & Wilkins and Thomson Science, managing and developing a range of journals in clinical medicine. Her career in scholarly publishing started with Current Science in 1995 where she worked in an editorial role on a group of medical journals.

Karim Gherab-Martín is currently a visiting and teaching fellow in the Department of Philosophy, Harvard University. He has an MSc in theoretical physics and a PhD in philosophy of science and technology. He has worked as an IT consultant for telecom multinationals. He has also taught at the Autonoma University in Madrid, at the University of the Basque Country in Bilbao, and at Harvard University in Cambridge, MA. He is the author of *El Templo del Saber: Hacia la Biblioteca Digital*

Universal (published in English as *The New Temple of Knowledge: Towards a Universal Digital Library*, 2008). He has also coordinated a monographic in the periodical *Arbor*, entitled *Science and Culture on the Web* (2009).

José Luis González Quirós is Tenured Professor in the School of Telecommunications at Rey Juan Carlos University (Madrid). He has previously worked as Professor of Philosophy at Universidad Complutense, and as Vice Director of their summer courses, and has taught at the universities of Wyoming, Loyola University at Chicago, Veracruz and Lund. He is a member of the editorial staff for the journals *Revista de Libros*, *Nueva Revista* and *Revista Hispano Cubana* and founder and first director of the journal *Cuadernos de pensamiento político*. He is the author or co-author of 18 books and many articles. His works address a wide variety of topics which ultimately refer to matters of philosophy of mind, philosophy of politics and culture, as well as matters related to the creation and social assimilation of the technological revolution.

David Hakken is an anthropologist whose ethnography of information aims to understand the ways in which cultures and automated information and communication technologies mutually shape each other. His research has been grounded in England, Scandinavia, Upstate New York, Malaysia and China. His most current work is on open computing (especially free/libre and/or open source software) and knowledge networking. After 26 years in the State University of New York, in 2004 he began teaching social informatics in the new School of Informatics at Indiana University, promoting technologies that expand rather than undermine human capabilities. His book, *The Knowledge Landscapes of Cyberspace*, was published in 2003.

Stevan Harnad was born in Hungary, did his undergraduate work at McGill University and his graduate work at Princeton University. Currently Canada Research Chair in Cognitive Science at Université du Québec à Montréal and Professor in Electronics and Computer Science at Southampton University, UK, his research focuses on categorization, communication and cognition. Founder (1978) and Editor (till 2001) of *Behavioral and Brain Sciences*, he is Past President of the Society for Philosophy and Psychology, External Member of the Hungarian Academy of Science, and author and contributor to over 300 publications. The EPrints research team at Southampton University has been at the forefront in the critical developments in open access across the past decade.

Michiel van der Heyden is Head of Product Management for Elsevier Science & Technology's Department of Research Workflow Tools. He received his master's degree in industrial design engineering in 1996 from the Technical University of Delft, with a specialization in business and product development. He has been a founder/partner of a web company, designing and implementing internet applications for customers in the field of education and culture. He was Interim Head of the Central Public Services Department at the University Utrecht Library for two years. In this role his main focus was on the rapid changes caused by the growing interest in electronic information and new forms of rendering services. He was also responsible for new forms of information supply, the development and implementation of a marketing strategy, and the development of the digital university library.

Andrew Jakubowicz is Professor of Sociology at the University of Technology Sydney and Co-Director of the UTS Cosmopolitan Civil Societies Key Research Strength (Research Centre). He also is the Head of the Social and Political Change Academic Group. He has been published widely in the fields of cultural diversity, social policy, refugees, Jewish cultural studies, media sociology and new media. He coordinates the Making Multicultural Australia for the 21st Century website, which is produced in conjunction with state education and arts bodies around Australia. He also produces The Menorah of Fang Bang Lu website, which is an online documentary about the Jewish communities of Shanghai. He heads the Multimedia Interactive Research Environment research project, which seeks to re-centre the researcher as a creative subject between the silos of digital data collection and e-publishing. He also heads the online communities and human rights project at the not-for-profit Institute for Cultural Diversity.

Mary Kalantzis is Dean of the College of Education at the University of Illinois, Urbana-Champaign. Until 2005, she was Dean of the Faculty of Education, Language and Community Services at RMIT University in Melbourne, Australia, and President of the Australian Council of Deans of Education. She has been a Commissioner of the Australian Human Rights and Equal Opportunity Commission, Chair of the Queensland Ethnic Affairs Ministerial Advisory Committee and a member of the Australia Council's Community Cultural Development Board. With Bill Cope, she is co-author or editor of a number of books, including: *The Powers of Literacy* (Falmer Press, 1993), *Productive Diversity* (Pluto Press, 1997); *A Place in the Sun: Re-Creating the Australian Way of Life* (HarperCollins, 2000); *Multiliteracies: Literacy Learning and the Design* of *Social Futures* (Routledge, 2000); and *New Learning: Elements of a Science of Education* (Cambridge University Press, 2008).

Claire Kendall, MD, is a family physician in the Department of Family Medicine at the University of Ottawa and Co-Deputy Editor of *Open Medicine*. She is currently completing a master's degree in public health at the London School of Hygiene and Tropical Medicine.

Donald W. King is Distinguished Research Professor in the School of Information and Library Science, University of North Carolina at Chapel Hill. He is a statistician who has spent over 45 years describing and evaluating the information and communication landscape, and much of his research has involved scholarly communication. Along with Carol Tenopir, he has recently completed a longitudinal analysis over nearly 30 years of surveys of information-seeking and reading patterns of science journal readers. He has also conducted in-depth economic cost analyses of libraries and, to a lesser extent, publishing processes. He has co-authored 11 books and edited five others, and has authored about 60 journal articles and over 300 other formal publications. He has received a number of honours, including being named a Pioneer of Science Information, Chemical Heritage Foundation; being made a Fellow of the American Statistical Association; and receiving the Research Award and Award of Merit from the American Society for Information Science and Technology.

Sally Morris was the Chief Executive of the Association of Learned, Professional and Society Publishers (ALPSP) from 1998 to 2006; she was also Chair of the cross-industry Publishing Skills Group in the UK, President of the International Federation of Scholarly Publishers, and a member of the UK's Legal Deposit Advisory Panel. Since retiring at the end of 2006, she has taken on the role of Editor-in-Chief of the journal *Learned Publishing*, as well as offering consultancy on copyright and other aspects of scholarly publishing. Her publishing career started in the not-for-profit sector, at Oxford University Press. Before joining ALPSP she spent 25 years as a real publisher, including 11 years running a programme of 50 medical journals, and several years in charge of copyright and licensing for a large commercial publisher. She has degrees in English and medieval studies from the Universities of Cambridge and York, and is a member of the Chartered Institute of Management.

Sally Murray, MD, is Deputy Editor of *Open Medicine*, an independent open access medical journal, and was an Editorial Fellow at the *Canadian Medical Association Journal*. She has worked as a public health physician in various international health positions and is now a senior lecturer at Notre Dame University Australia.

Anita Palepu, MD, a general internist with special clinical and research interests in urban health, is Associate Professor of Medicine at the University of British Columbia and Michael Smith Foundation for Health Research Senior Scholar.

Michael A. Peters is Professor of Education in Educational Policy Studies at the University of Illinois and Adjunct Professor in the School of Art, Royal Melbourne Institute of Technology. His main research interests are in educational philosophy, theory and policy studies with a focus on the significance of both contemporary philosophers and the movements of poststructralism, critical theory and analytic philosophy to the framing of educational theory and practice. He is also interested in philosophical and political economy questions of knowledge production and consumption and constructions of the 'knowledge economy'. His major current projects include work on distributed knowledge, learning and publishing systems, and 'open education', including *Creativity and the Global Knowledge Economy*, with S. Marginson and P. Murphy (2009); *Open Education and Education for Openness*, with B. Rodrigo (2008); *Wittgenstein as Pedagogical Philosopher*, with N. Burbules and P. Smeyers, (2008); and *Truth and Subjectivity: Foucault, Education and the Culture of Self*, with T. Besley (2008).

Angus Phillips is Director of the Oxford International Centre for Publishing Studies and Head of the Publishing Department at Oxford Brookes University. He has degrees from Oxford and Warwick Universities, and many years' experience in the publishing industry including running a trade and reference list at Oxford University Press. He has acted as consultant to a variety of publishing companies, and trained publishing professionals from the UK and overseas in editorial, marketing and management. Angus is the author, with Giles Clark, of *Inside Book Publishing* (2008), and the editor, with Bill Cope, of *The Future of the Book in the Digital Age* (2006).

Martin Richardson has held a variety of positions at Oxford University Press (OUP) over the past 20 years. He is currently Managing Director of the Academic Books and Journals Divisions, where he is responsible for over 3,000 print and online publications across a broad range of subjects. OUP is keen to experiment with new ways of increasing dissemination of research and educational material by employing new technologies and business models. Under Martin's leadership, OUP began online journal publishing in the early 1990s and in 2000 launched the first of many online reference publications – the *Oxford English Dictionary*. In 2004, Oxford Scholarship Online was launched, providing a platform for the publication of OUP's extensive monograph programme. Martin has represented OUP on a number of publishing industry organizations, including the Association of Learned, Professional and Society Publishers, PLS and CrossRef. He is a regular speaker at conferences and has also published papers on various aspects of online publishing.

Joss Saunders commenced his copyright career in 1988 while lobbying for a national newspaper on the Copyright Bill as it passed through parliament. After some years litigating copyright and other intellectual property, he taught law in Poland, at Warsaw University. Since 1995 he has worked in Oxford, where he is a partner in the publishing law team of Blake Lapthorn solicitors, and has advised most of the major publishers in Oxford, as well as many national and international for-profit and not-for-profit publishers. He also works part-time for the international charity Oxfam. He lectures widely on copyright law for the Association of Learned and Professional Society of Publishers, the Publishers Training Centre, and for universities that offer publishing courses.

Sarah L. Shreeves is the Coordinator for the Illinois Digital Environment for Access to Learning and Scholarship, the institutional repository at the University of Illinois at Urbana-Champaign (UIUC). She has published and presented widely in areas focused on digital library interoperability and shareable metadata and was co-editor of a 2008 *Library Trends* issue on institutional repositories. Prior to coming to UIUC, Sarah worked for nine years in the MIT Libraries in Boston. She has a BA in medieval studies from Bryn Mawr College, an MA in children's literature from Simmons College, and an MS in library and information science from UIUC.

Pippa Smart is a research communication and publishing consultant, working for her own company, PSP Consulting. She has worked in academic and research publishing for over 20 years, in a variety of roles, including advising research publishers within the developing world and assisting them to develop more sustainable publishing models. She has been active within the Association of Learned, Professional and Society Publishers (ALPSP) for many years, especially in the development of their training support, and now runs a consulting business, researching and writing on publishing issues, negotiating co-publication agreements and running training courses.

Simon Smith is an exceptionally experienced technology lawyer with particular specialties in advising on intellectual property, competition and contract law for clients in the IT, electronic media and telecommunications industries. A frequent public speaker and writer, Simon has been described in the Legal 500 as 'simply outstanding'. He has a master's degree in intellectual property law, and joined Blake Lapthorn's publishing law team as a partner in 2005.

Carol Tenopir is a Chancellor's Professor at the School of Information Sciences at the University of Tennessee, Knoxville and Director of Research and Director of the Center for Information and Communication Studies, College of Communication and Information. She is the author of five books, including *Communication Patterns of Engineers* (IEEE/Wiley InterScience, 2004) and *Towards Electronic Journals* (SLA, 2000) with Donald W. King. Dr Tenopir has published over 200 journal articles, is a frequent speaker at professional conferences, and since 1983 has written the 'Online databases' column for *Library Journal*. Professor Tenopir holds a PhD degree in library and information sciences from the University of Illinois.

Kang Tchou did his MA thesis at Bucknell University on *Chinese Characters as Traveling Metaphors: In James Legge's The Book of Poetry and Canto LXXVII of Ezra Pound's Pisan Cantos*. His scholarly interests focus on China since 1850: political history, literature, cultural interaction between China and the West, and intellectual history. He is especially interested in the drama of China's development as it unfolds over 5,000 years and heads into the future. In particular, he is interested in the rapid expansion and diversification of modern Chinese intellectual life and in the successful adaptation of the Chinese language to thought, science and technology. He will be pursuing a doctorate in Chinese Studies at the Faculty of Asian and Middle Eastern Studies at Cambridge University.

Ale de Vries is Senior Product Manager for Platform & Content in the Academic & Government Products Group of Elsevier's Science & Technology division, which covers ScienceDirect, Scopus, Scirus and new product initiatives for the research community. His areas of responsibility are access management and authentication, content integration, interoperability and search engine partnerships. He is a frequent speaker and panellist on these subjects at conferences. Ale graduated with a degree in engineering management from Enschede University of Professional Education, and is an alumnus of IMD in Lausanne. His thesis project involved developing a strategic decision framework for developing network-enabled consumer services. He is an avid blogger and user of social media.

John Willinsky is Khosla Family Professor of Education at Stanford University. He directs the Public Knowledge Project at Stanford, Simon Fraser University and the University of British Columbia, which is researching systems for improving the scholarly and public quality of academic research. He is the author of the award-winning *Learning to Divide the World: Education at Empire's End* and *The Access Principle: The Case for Open Access to Research and Scholarship*, as well as a number of other books.

The contributors may be contacted via the editors as follows:

Dr William Cope
Research Professor
Department of Educational Policy Studies, College of Education
University of Illinois, Urbana-Champaign
326 Education
1310 S. Sixth Street, MC-708
Champaign, IL 61820
USA

E-mail: *billcope@illinois.edu*

Angus Phillips
Director
Oxford International Centre for Publishing Studies
2nd Floor, Buckley Building
Oxford Brookes University
Gipsy Lane Campus
Headington
Oxford OX3 0BP
UK

E-mail: *angus.phillips@brookes.ac.uk*

Preface

Why a book on the future of the journal? This book has its origins in our previous volume, *The Future of the Book in the Digital Age*, which was published in 2006. Our publisher, Glyn Jones, asked for a follow-up volume that would examine the academic journal. Given some time to think about the project, we decided that, yes, there would be mileage in such a book and that it would be worthwhile to pursue the idea. The next question was whether we could persuade authors to contribute. The previous volume had been based on a conference held in Oxford in 2005. This time we would have to start from scratch – although of course the present collection would make a fascinating conference.

We were fortunate to have the cooperation of the present set of contributors, some of the most important academic and commercial players in the field. We owe each of them a great debt of gratitude. The resulting collection is, we hope, an up-to-date and stimulating set of papers on different aspects of the scholarly journal and its future.

With contributions from leading academics and industry professionals, the book aims to provide an authoritative and balanced view of this fast-changing area. There are numerous views surrounding the future of journals and although the chapters we have contributed represent our own points of view, we were anxious in the selection of chapters to include a representative range of perspectives. We ourselves have backgrounds that embrace both publishing and academia. This book looks at a range of key topics that are of vital importance to academics and publishers alike, as well as librarians, members of learned and professional societies, and policy-makers. Will the journals business continue to grow? Open access initiatives still form a relatively small part of journals publishing, but will they become the norm? How do librarians, publishers and academics see the future for journals? Will other forms of access to knowledge, and different methods of scholarly communication, become more important? How will the academic journal be affected by public policy, changes in copyright law, and the views of learned societies and research bodies?

Bill Cope, Urbana-Champaign, Illinois, USA
Angus Phillips, Oxford, England
January 2009

Introduction

Bill Cope and Angus Phillips

The journal has a long history, stretching back to the seventeenth century. It lies at the heart of our system of scholarly communication and has stood the test of time. How then will it develop over the next few years and what changes can we predict with any degree of certainty? We hope the chapters in this volume provide some answers, drawing on the expertise of a range of academics and professionals. A prominent challenge to the present publishing structures is open access, which has begun to coexist with other publishing models and has support from both research bodies and universities. Will this become the dominant model of publication? There is of course an intimate connection between the journal article and the practice of scholarship. Are there also challenges to the established, linear process of the creation of knowledge? These may have major implications for academics, researchers, publishers, librarians and policy-makers.

The journal online

We can say, first of all, that the journal has gone online. Around 90 per cent of journals in English are now available online, and users expect to access articles in this way, whether at their place of work or study, or remotely from home. There is a growing trend of online-only journals and this will continue, providing cost savings to users' institutions and journal publishers. The proviso is that there is a significant cost involved for publishers in establishing platforms for online delivery, which has encouraged consolidation in the industry. For libraries, online access also reduces the need for shelf space to house journals in print form. Start-up journals may go online-only from their first issue. Online publication means that articles can be made available at different stages of their production, and that there is no need to wait to complete a journal issue before an article is published in its final form.

Philip Carpenter of Wiley-Blackwell writes:

> In STM, the migration of journals online is so advanced that the electronic version is effectively primary and print secondary. This is true in two senses. The online version is now commonly published ahead of print, an important factor when speed to publication is critical. Perhaps more significantly, the electronic article will often be richer than its print version, containing more data and certainly more functionality. (Carpenter, 2008)

Is online access creating a new dynamic among researchers, as proposed by James Evans (2008a)? Evans suggests that researchers are now citing a higher proportion of more recent articles and a narrower range of articles. He writes about his own article:

> I used a database of 34 million articles, their citations (1945 to 2005) and online availability (1998 to 2005), and showed that *as more journals and articles came online*, the actual number of them cited in research *decreased*, and those that were cited tended to be of more *recent* vintage ... Moreover, the easy online availability of sources has channelled researcher attention from the periphery to the core – to the most high-status journals. In short, searching online is more efficient, and hyperlinks quickly put researchers in touch with prevailing opinion, but they may also accelerate *consensus* and *narrow* the range of findings and ideas grappled with by scholars. (Evans, 2008b)

This immediately suggests disadvantages to the online journal, but there is no going back to the serendipity of browsing through print journals. Literature searches are most easily carried out online. The trend towards consensus may also reflect the nature of today's research. The sociologist Laurie Taylor is one who believes that today's research is dominated by a tick-box culture:

> There's been a real diminution in research freedom ... It's meant that a whole branch of anthropology and ethnography, where researchers spent two or three years with a group of people and came back with some inside story of their lives and culture, is now

almost impossible ... You get vapid little bits of research, which take six months to do and amount to little more than rejigging common sense, or you get people churning out orthodox research in areas approved of by the ESRC (Economic and Social Research Council) ... There's not much surprise in a lot of the research I come across now. It hugs the mainstream, because it doesn't have a licence to roam. (Taylor, 2008)

Open access

Hotly debated in recent years is the question of open access to journal articles. Supporters of open access maintain that research outputs are a public good, and should be freely available to all:

> Scholarship, and hence the content of scholarly journals, is a public good. A public good is one for which one consumer's use of the good is not competitive with, or exclusive of, another consumer's use of the same good. The classic illustration is national defense – some citizens cannot be defended without all being defended. But an illustration closer to home is a community's clear air – one resident's enjoyment of clean air does not interfere with another's enjoyment of the same 'good'. So too, one scholar's access to and benefit from the knowledge found in a scientific article published in a scholarly journal in no way limits another scholar's use of and benefit from that knowledge. (Edwards and Shulenburger, 2003: 12–13)

Support for open access is coming from both research bodies and academic institutions. For example, the Wellcome Trust asks that all research papers for which it has provided financial support are made freely available through PubMed Central (*www.pubmedcentral .nih.gov*). In February 2008, the Faculty of Arts and Sciences at Harvard University adopted a policy whereby faculty members must provide an electronic copy of each article so that it can be made freely available through an online repository.

Open access still forms a small part of the overall journals output, but it seems certain to grow in importance with the level of support it is receiving from funding bodies. It also serves to support the long tail of journals publishing – those niche journals which cannot survive as commercial publications. An author-pays model of publication will only work in disciplines, such as medicine, where there is sufficient funding available from research bodies or institutions. The green route of open access, self-archiving, does have the potential to undermine the traditional business model of journal publishing – subscriptions. If users expect to be able to find articles for free using a web search, will they cease to use their existing access routes for journals? We cannot give a definite answer to this question unless we can predict the systematic development of repositories which offer the kind of added value to be found in aggregated services from publishers and distributors. Up until now, most institutional repositories have not taken this approach, as commented on by the Ithaka report, *University Publishing in a Digital Age*:

> several librarians conceded to us that they are good at organizing information but lack expertise in choosing or prioritizing what merits publication. Libraries provide tools and infrastructure to support new forms of informal publishing, but these tend to be inward focused (towards the home institution) rather than externally focused (towards the best scholarship in a given discipline), limiting their appeal to users. As a result, institutional repositories so far tend to look like 'attics' (and often fairly empty ones), with random assortments of content of questionable importance. (Brown et al., 2007: 16)

Open access began as a movement in response to what were seen as excessive price increases by journals publishers. To many authors and users, open access is still not a big issue, as they have high levels of seamless access through their institution. It is important to remember that publishers can and do add value in journals publishing – whether through selection, quality control, editing, production, functionality, aggregation of similar and relevant content, linking, brand, entrepreneurship and business acumen. Even freely available content carries with it a certain level of cost. Joseph J. Esposito comments:

> When someone stubs a toe, there are always those who want to cut off the leg. This is the situation in scholarly communications today, where the predictable aches and pains of a mature industry have been met with a wild surgeon brandishing a saw. Prices are rising, therefore all information must be free. Publishers can and must be disintermediated and war declared on copyright. Reform peer review! Those who liberated the institutions' administrative buildings in their youth, will now free knowledge from the grubby

hands of commercial interests in their dotage. To further this agenda – which is extreme and at times seems like a violent eruption of emotion – members of the academy have at times found some strange bedfellows, most notably Google, a hard-driving commercial organization and darling of Wall Street. Is it possible that Google is being taken at its word when it declares, Don't be evil? (Esposito, 2007)

Scholarly communication

Research funding, academic advancement and traditional publishing all still rely on the foundations of the academic journal and monograph, but scholarly communication is changing. The system is global and increasingly based around communities that use a variety of collaborative tools, from social networking to virtual worlds. The journal article may be just one form of output from research. As can be seen from this book, there are a variety of responses. Repositories are accepting a wider range of media, including audiovisual clips and images, alongside documents. Journals now include a range of primary data and are reinventing themselves as subject portals. New collaborative tools are being created by researchers and commercial publishers.

As long as the journal remains important for the achievement of research funding and tenure, it will endure as a key component of scholarly communication. The Ithaka report said:

> while most provosts acknowledge flaws in the current credentialing system, they found it difficult to envision or embrace a clear digital alternative that meets their needs in making hiring, promotion and tenure decisions ... One provost opined, 'Am I supposed to give someone tenure based on what they've put on a blog?' (Brown et al., 2007: 18)

The increasing importance of the journal article in the humanities is also leading to an expansion of journal publishing in that area. By contrast there is a level of saturation in medicine and science, where the monograph has been much less important for a number of years.

The journal also remains important because of the key benefits it offers to the academic community and often to an audience outside, such as in the case of science journals. It is a vital tool for keeping up with knowledge. As Carol Tenopir says, 'scientists and social scientists read a lot. Scientists have always relied on reading the research of others to support their own work, but the amount that they read has often been grossly underestimated' (Tenopir, 2002: 112).

We are, however, looking at a new future for the journal as part of an overall network of knowledge creation and scholarly communication. We are moving away from a world in which a few producers generate content to transmit to a set of users. Instead, the world of knowledge creation has feedback mechanisms in place throughout. The end point is not a singular version of record, and our model of knowledge is like the beta version of new software – out there to be trialled and improved upon. Within this there are some fixed points – published and static journal articles – but the journey has become as important as the end result.

Chapter overview

The aim of this book is to provide a selection of chapters covering different aspects of the journal and its future. The book is divided into themed sections covering knowledge systems, the journals business, academic practices, the journal internationally, and digital transformations.

Bill Cope and Mary Kalantzis explore our knowledge system and examine the changes that are underway or likely to occur. They see the roots of this shift in technology, economics, a broadening of the sites of knowledge-making, geography and the globalization of knowledge, the rise of interdisciplinarity, and the growth of more collaborative systems. José Quirós and Karim Martin argue in favour of e-science — a new model which would democratize science. They pursue the notion of discourse as a constantly evolving entity, a beta version that gets gradually closer to scientific objectivity.

Angus Phillips provides an overview of business models in journals publishing. Experimentation with newer models carries on alongside the traditional use of subscriptions, while open access has both gold and green routes of publication. There is a strong correlation between the growth of journals and research spending. Carol Tenopir and Donald W. King chart the growth of journals publishing. They conclude that the growth in journal titles may slacken in a fully digital future, as the number of articles per title is not bound by any paper limitations.

Stevan Harnad, a well-known proponent of open access, argues that in the Gutenberg model of publishing, the costs of production and distribution required a toll-booth to be erected between the document and the user. By contrast, in the post-Gutenberg era of digital publishing, all published research articles will be openly accessible online, free for all would-be users worldwide.

Claire Bird and Martin Richardson describe a hybrid model of publishing, where subscription and open access coexist for the same journal title. Their experience at Oxford University Press suggests that a system of author-side payments may only be viable in certain disciplines, where authors have access to funds for publication.

Joss Saunders and Simon Smith provide a legal viewpoint, suggesting that copyright law alone is a cumbersome and ultimately ineffective mechanism to protect publishers' rights in a digital industry. Is it right that copyright exists in a journal article until 70 years after the author's death? They go on to suggest that publishers can use contract law as a flexible instrument to change their contracts to reflect demands for permanent access, open access or other threats and opportunities.

Iain D. Craig and Liz Ferguson look at the schemes used to rank journals. These are of interest to academics, publishers and policy-makers in higher education. Their examination of journal metrics covers the Impact Factor, download statistics, and newer, alternative measurements such as the h-index and eigenvector analysis.

Sarah Shreeves provides an overview of repositories and their likely impact on the future of the journal. Repositories, whether institutional or subject-based (disciplinary), typically provide open access to preprints and final manuscripts of accepted journal articles, among other material. She concludes that this area is a rapidly changing landscape subject to upheavals, reversals and sudden surges forward. Surveying the role of the library, J. Eric Davies finds there is less emphasis on the library as a place and more on it as a channel for a wide range of information. He suggests that the library offers the potential for becoming the neutral territory for the exchange of ideas and the development of plans for scholarly communication that involve all who are involved in the endeavour: authors, publishers, technologists, fund providers and readers.

Michael Peters provides an account of the political economy of academic publishing before focusing on education journals. Many e-journals are highly specialized with small groups of readers. This is the long tail of academic publishing, and the e-journal, especially with open journal, conference, archives and monograph systems, is an ideal vehicle for the specialized academic community.

John Willinsky, Sally Murray, Claire Kendall and Anita Palepu provide a case study of the launch of *Open Medicine*. This journal was born out of an example of editorial interference in medical publishing. They argue that it demonstrates how open access, in combination with open source publishing and management software, enables new journals to protect more readily the academic freedom of researchers and scholars.

There are three chapters which look at the journal internationally. Pippa Smart finds that journals published within the African continent strive to achieve the same as their counterparts within the developed world: to disseminate research findings and advance scientific knowledge. However, the majority of them struggle to exist due to economic and social factors that disable their operations, and their future is far from certain. David Hakken stresses the need for more collective, egalitarian means of scholarly communication. While new, computerized forms of journals hold out the promise of democratizing scholarly communication, he sees little reason to expect Asia to be in the forefront of this movement. Kang Tchou describes the recent development of the journal in China as a means of scholarly communication, and expresses the hope that scholars within the Chinese academy will choose to regard the academic journal as the refuge for the relatively free exchange of worthy ideas.

Michiel van der Heyden and Ale de Vries reveal how the publishing giant Elsevier is rethinking its business. They see it as important to break with the paradigm in which the journal and its article are the sole pivotal point of scholarly information, to create a world in which the academic journal is one element, albeit a key one, in an ecosystem of applications that are rich in both content and functionality, and that are deeply embedded in the daily lives of users. Andrew Jakubowicz argues that the web has not delivered an interactive environment for engagement with scholarly research that uses and is enlivened by multimedia; he proposes a model for a digital research and publishing project.

A coda to the volume is provided by Sally Morris. She suggests that while many are worrying about business models, open access and other issues in journals publishing – the spider in one corner – there is a real challenge facing all those who are involved in supporting the processes of scholarly communication – the tiger in the opposite corner. Researchers' very behaviour is being utterly transformed by the power of ICT. For example, there are informal and often bi-directional modes of communication through blogs, wikis and bookmarking sites, which are being adopted and adapted by the research community.

Bibliography

Brown, L., Griffiths, R. and Rascoff, M. (2007) 'Ithaka Report: University publishing in a digital age', available at: *http://www.ithaka.org/strategic-services/university-publishing* (accessed 13 March 2009).

Carpenter, P. (2008) 'Journals, science and the future of books in the humanities and social sciences', paper presented at A Challenge to the Book in Scholarship and Higher Education, Amsterdam, 13 October.

Edwards, R. and Shulenburger, D. (2003) 'The high cost of scholarly journals (and what to do about it)', *Change* 35: 10–19.

Esposito, J. J. (2007) 'The wisdom of Oz: The role of the university press in scholarly communications', *Journal of Electronic Publishing* 10(1).

Evans, J. (2008a) 'Electronic publication and the narrowing of science and scholarship', *Science* 321: 395–9.

Evans, J. (2008b) 'Research + web = more conformity, less diversity (at least, so far)', available at: *www.britannica.com/blogs/2008/08* (accessed 13 March 2009).

Taylor, L. (2008) Interviewed by Matthew Reisz, *Times Higher Education*, 13 November.

Tenopir, C. (2002) 'Electronic or print: are scholarly journals still important?', *Serials* 15: 111–15.

Part I
Knowledge systems

2

Signs of epistemic disruption: transformations in the knowledge system of the academic journal

Bill Cope and Mary Kalantzis

This chapter is an overview of the current state of scholarly journals, not (just) as an activity to be described in terms of its changing processes, but more fundamentally as a pivot point in a broader knowledge system. After locating journals in what we term the process of knowledge design, the chapter goes on to discuss some of the deeply disruptive aspects of the contemporary moment. These not only portend potential transformations in the form of the journal, but possibly also in the knowledge systems that the journal in its heritage form has supported. These disruptive forces are represented by changing technological, economic, distributional, geographic, interdisciplinary and social relations to knowledge. The chapter goes on to examine three specific breaking points. The first breaking point is in business models – the unsustainable costs and inefficiencies of traditional commercial publishing, the rise of open access and the challenge of developing sustainable publishing models. The second potential breaking point is the credibility of the peer-review system: its accountability, its textual practices, the validity of its measures and its exclusionary network effects. The third breaking point is post-publication evaluation, centred primarily on citation or impact analysis. We argue that the prevailing system of impact analysis is deeply flawed. Its validity as a measure of knowledge is questionable, in which citation counts are conflated with the contribution made to knowledge; quantity is valued over quality; popularity is taken as a proxy for intellectual quality; impact is mostly measured on a short timeframe; 'impact factors' are aggregated for journals or departments in a way that lessens their validity further; there is a bias for and against certain article types; there are exclusionary network effects; and there are accessibility distortions. Add to this reliability defects – the types of citation counted as well as counting failures and distortions – and clearly the citation analysis system is in urgent need of renewal. The chapter ends with suggestions intended to contribute to discussion about the transformation of the academic journal and the creation of new knowledge systems: sustainable publishing models, frameworks for guardianship of intellectual property, criterion-referenced peer review, greater reflexivity in the review process, incremental knowledge refinement, more widely distributed sites of knowledge production and inclusive knowledge cultures, new types of scholarly text and more reliable use metrics.

The knowledge business

These are some quantifiable dimensions of the academic and scholarly knowledge business: 'In 2004 … academic publishing in the Western world was dominated by 12 publishing corporations with combined annual sales of approximately $65 billion and employing in the order of 250,000 employees' (see Chapter 12). 'In 2006 the top ten STM [scientific, technical and medical] publishers took in 53 per cent of the revenue in the $16.1 billion [US] periodicals market' (see Chapter 10). Universities spend between 0.5 per cent and 1.0 per cent of their budgets on journals subscriptions (see Chapter 4). Morgan Stanley reports that academic journals have been the fastest-growing media subsector of the past 15 years (Morgan Stanley, 2002). An analysis of Ulrich's periodicals list shows that the number of scholarly journals increased from 39,565 in 2003 to 61,620 in 2008; of these, the number of refereed journals rose from 17,649 in 2002 to 23,973 in 2008. The number of articles per journal is up from 72 per annum in 1972 to 123 in 1995, and average length of an article increased by 80 per cent between 1975 and 2007 (see Chapter 5). Worldwide, approximately 5.7 million people work in research and development (R&D), publishing on average one article per year, and reading 97 articles per year. This average annual publication rate has stayed steady, and the dramatic increase in articles published in recent decades is attributable to increases in the number of R&D workers (Mabe and Amin, 2002).

And here are some of the qualitative dimensions of the business of academic and scientific knowledge-making: the process of publication is an integral aspect of the business of knowledge-making. Far from being a neutral conduit for knowledge, the publication system defines the social processes through which knowledge is made, and gives tangible form to knowledge. The message, of course, is by no means reducible to its medium. We take it for granted that there are knowledge referents external to knowledge representations, and that the representations are not ends in themselves. However, the representational media and the social norms of representation are as much the stuff of knowledge as the things those representations purport to represent.

This chapter takes the academic journal as its reference point because it is symptomatic of underlying knowledge systems. It looks at the academic journal in a moment of enormously unsettling, uncertain and perhaps also exciting times. We look at seismic stresses in the workings of the academic journal, and analyse these for signs of a deeper epistemic disruption – in the very ways we know.

But first, to define 'know'. What do we mean by specifically scientific, academic or scholarly knowledge? After all, people have a whole lot of ways of 'knowing' in everyday life, most of which do not have the credibility of peculiarly academic knowledge. Academic or scholarly knowledge has some extraordinary features. It has an intensity of focus and a concentration of intellectual energies greater than that of ordinary, everyday, commonsense or lay knowing. It relies on the ritualistic rigour and accumulated wisdoms of disciplinary communities and their practices. It entails, in short, a kind of systematicity that does not exist in casual experience. Husserl draws the distinction between 'lifeworld' experience and what is 'transcendental' about 'science' (Cope and Kalantzis, 2000a; Husserl, 1970). In these terms, the 'lifeworld' is everyday lived experience. The 'transcendental' of academic and scholarly knowledge stands in contradistinction to the commonsense knowing of the lifeworld, which by comparison is relatively unconscious and unreflexive. Academic and scholarly knowledge sets out to comprehend and create meanings in the world which extend more broadly and deeply than the everyday, amorphous pragmatics of the lifeworld. Such knowledge is systematic, premeditated, reflective, purposeful, disciplined and open to scrutiny by a community of experts. Science is more focused and harder work than the knowing in and of the lifeworld (Kalantzis and Cope, 2008).

The knowledge representation process is integral to the making of this peculiarly academic, scientific and scholarly knowledge. It is central to its business of epistemic design. This design process has three representational moments.

Available designs of knowledge

The first aspect is what we would call 'available designs' (Cope and Kalantzis, 2000b; Kress, 2000). The body of scholarly literature – the five million or so scholarly articles published each year, the (probably) hundred thousand books – is the tangible starting point of all knowledge work. These representational designs work at a number of levels – at one level as textual practices of describing, reporting on observations, clarifying concepts and arguing to rhetorical effect. They also represent intertextuality, at the level of bodies of knowledge, where no text sits alone but constantly draws upon and references other texts by way of conceptual distinction, or accretion of facts, or agreement on principle – among many of the possibilities that fuse a work into a body of knowledge. These representational designs are the fundamental ground of all academic and scholarly knowledge work. They give tangible form to fields of interest. In practical terms, there are two modes of availability for journal content: it is sold by commercial publishers or it is made available at no charge over the internet (open access).

Designing knowledge

The second aspect is the process of 'designing'. Available knowledge designs have a textual and intertextual morphology. These are the raw materials of already-represented knowledge or found knowledge objects. Designing is the stuff of agency, the things you do to know and the rhetorical representation of those things. It is also the stuff of communities of disciplinary practice. These practices involve certain kinds of knowledge representation – modes of argumentation, forms of reporting, descriptions of methods and data, ways of supplementing extant data, linking and distinguishing concepts, and critically reflecting on old and new ideas and facts. There is no knowledge-making of scholarly relevance without the representation of that knowledge. And that representation happens in a community of practice: with collaborators who co-author or comment upon drafts, with journal editors or book publishers who review manuscripts and send them out to referees, with referees who evaluate and comment, and then the intricacies of textual revision, checking, copy-editing and publication. Knowledge contents and the social processes of knowledge representation are inseparable.

The designed: new knowledge becomes integrated into a body of knowledge

Then there is a third aspect of the process, 'the (re)designed', when a knowledge artefact joins the body of knowledge. Private rights to ownership are established through publication. These do not inhere in the knowledge itself, but in the text which represents that knowledge (copyright) or through what the representation describes (patents). Moral rights to attribution are established even when default private intellectual property rights are forgone by attaching a 'commons' licence. On the other hand, even the most rigorous of copyright licence allows quoting and paraphrasing in the public domain for the purposes of the discussion, review and verification. This guarantees that a privately-owned text can be incorporated into a body of public knowledge and credited via citation. This is the point at which the process of designing metamorphoses into the universal library of knowledge, the repository of publicly declared knowledge, deeply interlinked by the practices of citation (see Chapter 3). At this point, the knowledge design becomes an 'available design', absorbed into the body of knowledge as raw materials for others in their design processes.

Of course, scholarly knowledge-making is by no means the only secular system of social meaning and knowing in modern societies. Media, literature and law all have their own design protocols. In this chapter, however, we want to focus specifically on the knowledge systems of science and academe as found in the physical sciences, the applied sciences and the professions, the social sciences, the liberal arts and the humanities. We are interested in their means of production of knowledge, where the medium is not the whole message but where the textual and social processes of representation nevertheless give modern knowledge its peculiar shape and form.

Forces of epistemic disruption

Our schematic outline of the knowledge representation processes – available designs/designing/the designed – could be taken to be an unexceptional truism but for the extraordinary social and epistemic instability of this moment. This chapter takes journals as a touchstone as it explores the dimensions of epistemic change – some well underway, others merely signs of things to come. Below are some of the roots of epistemic shift.

Technology

The most visible force of epistemic disruption is technological. We are going to start with this as the first item on our list of disruptions for its tangible obviousness, although not for its intrinsic epistemic disruptiveness. An information revolution has accompanied the digitization of text, image and sound and the sudden emergence of the internet as a universal conduit for digital content. But the information revolution does not in itself bring about change of social or epistemic significance. Academic publishing is a case in point. The internet-accessible PDF file makes journal articles widely and cheaply accessible, but its form simply replicates the production processes and social relations of the print journal: a one-way production process which ends in the creation of a static, stable text restricted to written language and static image. This change is not enough to warrant the descriptor 'disruptive'. The technological shift, large as it is, does not produce a change in the social processes and relations of knowledge production.

There is no deterministic relationship, in other words, between technology and social change. New technologies can be used to do old things. In fact, in their initial phases, new technologies are more often than not simply used to do old things – albeit, perhaps, more efficiently. At most, the technological opens out social affordances, frequently in ways not anticipated by the designers of those technologies. So what is the range of affordances in digital technologies that open new possibilities for knowledge-making? We can see glimpses of possible new and more dynamic knowledge systems, not yet captured in the mainstream academic journal. For instance, in contrast to texts replicating print and structured with typographic markup, we can envisage more readily searchable and data-mineable texts structured with semantic markup (Cope and Kalantzis, 2004). In contrast to knowledge production processes which force us to represent knowledge on the page, restricting us to text and static image, we can envision a broader, multimodal body of publishable knowledge with material objects of knowledge that could not have been captured in print or its digital analogue: datasets, video, dynamic models, multimedia displays. Things that were formerly represented as the external raw materials of knowledge can now be represented and incorporated within that knowledge. And in contrast to linear, lock-step modes of knowledge dissemination, we can see the potential for scholarly knowledge in the more collaborative, dialogical and recursive forms of knowledge-making already found in less formal digital media spaces such as wikis, blogs and other readily-accessible self-managed website-based content systems. Most journals are still making PDFs, still bound to the world of print-look-alike knowledge representation; but a reading of technological affordances tells us that we don't have replicate traditional processes of knowledge representation – digital technologies allow us to do more than that.

Economics

The second item on our list of potential disruptions is the economics of production. With the internet, we have got used to getting a wealth of information for free. Of course, it is not really free, because it takes human effort to create the content and physical infrastructure to manufacture, transmit and render the content – computers and storage devices and transmission networks. Actually, we have got used to a system of cross-subsidy, a kind of information socialism within a market economy. Wikipedia content is free because its authors donate their time and so must have other sources of income. Searching through Google is free because the company has copied other people's content without permission and without payment, and then makes a business out of a free service by putting advertising beside it. Open access academic journal content is free because universities value published output and pay salaries to academics to publish their work. This represents a profound shift in our expectations about the knowledge markets in which we have traditionally bought printed content. Now, when we reach a journal article on the internet to which we do not have subscription access and it costs $30 or $50 to view, this breaks the norm of information socialism to which the internet has accustomed us. The rise of open access journals is not the only symptom of resistance. (Brody et al., 2007, estimate that 15 per cent of academic journal articles are now open access.) Another symptom is the increasingly prevalent practice of posting preprints to discipline repositories. Informal pre-publication is eroding the significance of the post-publication text as both authors and readers find the immediacy of open discipline-based repositories more powerful and relevant than eventual publication (see Chapter 19). The ArXiv repository in high-energy physics is a case in point (Ginsparg, 2007). In some areas, conference proceedings are becoming more important than journal articles for their immediacy – computer science is a good example of this. In other areas, such as economics, where the world can change almost overnight, reports are becoming more important than journals. And, in almost every discipline, academic authors and increasingly the institutions for which they work are insisting upon the right to post their published articles to institutional repositories or personal websites, either in typeset or original manuscript form. More and more, academics are taking it upon themselves to do this, legally or illegally, with or without reference to the publishing agreements they have signed. For example, Bergstrom and Lavaty (2007) report using an internet search to turn up freely available versions of 90 per cent of articles in the top 15 economics journals. Similarly, Ginsparg (2007) reports that over one-third of a sample of articles from prominent biomedical journals were to be found at non-journal websites in 2003.

More distributed knowledge making

Next in our list of disruptions is a broadening of the sites of knowledge-making. Universities and conventional research institutes today face significant challenges to their historical role as producers of socially privileged knowledge. More knowledge is being produced by corporations than was the case in the past. More knowledge is being produced in hospitals, in schools, in lawyers' offices, in business consultancies, in local government, and in amateur associations whose members are tied together by common interest. More knowledge is being produced in the networked interstices of the social web, where knowing amateurs mix with academic professionals, in many places without distinction of rank. In these places, the logics and logistics of knowledge production are disruptive of the traditional values of the scholarly work – the for-profit, protected knowledge of the corporation; the multimodal knowledge of audiovisual media; and the 'wisdom of the crowd' which ranks knowledge and makes it discoverable through the internet according to its popularity. If one wanted to view these developments normatively, one could perhaps describe them as amounting to a democratization of knowledge. Or we could simply leave an empirical observation: knowledge is being made in more widely dispersed institutional sites.

Geographic inequities

Fourth in our list of disruptions is a geography of knowledge-making which unconscionably and unsustainably favours rich countries over poor, anglophone countries over non-English speaking, intellectual centres over peripheries. The situation does not yet show significant signs of changing, but surely it must. The situation of academic publishing in Africa is bleak, and the representation of articles published by Africa-based authors in the mainstream journals world dropped between 1995 and 2005 (see Chapter 14). Knowledge-making in China's 1,000 universities, even though they are going through a phase of burgeoning growth, has yet to reach the wider world of ideas (see Chapter 16). Meanwhile, some early signs of the globalization of knowledge-making are to be seen. Multinational authorship of journal articles is on the rise (see Chapter 19).

Interdisciplinarity

Fifth is the disruptive force of interdisciplinarity. Journals have traditionally been definers of disciplines or subdisciplines, delineating the centre and edges of an area of inquiry in terms of its methodological modes and subject matter. The epistemic modes that gave shape to the heritage academic journal are being broken apart today as we address the large tasks of our time – sustainability, globalization, diversity, knowledge or learning, to take just a few items on the contemporary intellectual agenda. Interdisciplinary approaches often need to be applied for reasons of principle, to disrupt the habitual narrowness of outlook of within-discipline knowledge work, to challenge the ingrained, discipline-bound ways of thinking that produce occlusion as well as insight. Interdisciplinary approaches also thrive in the interface of disciplinary and lay understandings. They are needed for the practical application of disciplined understandings to the actually-existing world. Robust applied knowledge demands an interdisciplinary holism, the broad epistemological engagement that is required simply to be able to deal with the complex contingencies of a really-integrated universe. Conventional discipline-defining journals are, in their essential boundary-drawing logic, not well suited to this challenge.

Knowledge-producing, symbol-making, participatory cultures

There is one final disruptive force, potentially affecting the social processes of knowledge-making themselves. If trends can be read into the broader shifts in the new, digital media, they stand to undermine the characteristic epistemic mode of authoritativeness associated with the heritage scholarly journal. The historical dichotomy of author and reader, creator and consumer is everywhere being blurred. Authors blog, readers talk back, bloggers respond. Wiki users read, but also intervene to change the text if and when they feel they should. Game players become participants in narratives. iPod users create their own playlists. Digital television viewers create their own viewing sequences. These are aspects of a general and symptomatic shift in the balance of agency in which a flat world of users replaces a hierarchical world of culture and knowledge in which a few producers create content to transmit to a mass of receivers (Cope and Kalantzis, 2007). What will academic journals be like when they escape their heritage constraints? There will be more knowledge collaborations between knowledge creators and knowledge users, in which user commentary can perhaps become part of the knowledge itself. Knowledge-making will escape its linear, lock-step, beginning-to-end process. The end point will not be a singular version of record – it will be something that can be re-versioned as much as needed. Knowledge-making will be more recursive, responsive, dynamic and above all, more collaborative and social than it was in an earlier modernity which paid greater obeisance to the voice of the heroically original author.

The above represents some of the potentially profound shifts that may occur in the knowledge regime, as reflected in the representational processes of today's academic journal. These shifts could portend nothing less than a revolution in the shape and form of academic knowledge ecologies. But for such change to occur, something may first have to break. Using our knowledge design paradigm, we will consider some specific fissures at three potential breaking points in today's academic knowledge systems: in the availability of designs of knowledge, in the design process, and in the ways we evaluate the significance of already-designed knowledge. At each of these knowledge-making moments we will examine points where fault lines are already visible, signs perhaps of imminent breaking points. We will examine open access versus commercial publishing (design availability), the peer-review system (designing) and citation counts as a measure of scholarly value (the designed).

Breaking point 1: how knowledge is made available

Academic knowledge today – manifest in the textual resources that frame scholarly work – is made available in two principal modes: at a price or for free.

Knowledge for sale

Some of the players in the pay-to-use mode are small publishers or associations which operate on an essentially self-sustaining model. However, the large journal publishers make up the bulk of the journals market. Holding a monopoly position on the titles of journals, they charge excessive prices to university libraries for subscriptions, usually enjoying high profit margins in the otherwise highly competitive media sector (Morgan Stanley, 2002). These profits are related in part to the artificial scarcity created by a system where prestige and authoritativeness attach to prestigious journals (see Chapter 3). Exploiting this position is particularly problematic when journal companies rely on the unpaid authoring and refereeing labour of academics – this is what gives a journal quality, not the mechanics of its production and distribution.

The prices of journals have risen rapidly over two decades. Between 1984 and 2001, during which time the consumer price index increased by only 70 per cent, the subscription rates of economics journals, for instance, rose 393 per cent, physics by 479 per cent and chemistry by 615 per cent (Edlin and Rubinfeld, 2004; McCabe et al., 2006). Journal prices increased 8 per cent in 2006 and over 9 per cent in 2007. The average subscription price of a chemistry journal in 2007 was $3,490, physics $3,103, engineering $1,919 and geography $1,086 (Orsdel and Born, 2006, 2008). In January 2006, the editor of the *Journal of Economic Studies* resigned in protest at his journal's $9,859 per annum subscription rate (Orsdel and Born, 2006).

Large publishing conglomerates have increased their subscription rates more than small academic publishers and nonprofits. On average in 2005, commercial publishers charged university libraries several times as much per page as nonprofit publishers (Bergstrom and Bergstrom, 2006). Bergstrom and McAfee created a value-for-money ranking system (*www.journalprices.com*) to analyse approximately 5,000 journals; according to their results, the six largest STM publishers mostly fall into the bad value category (74 per cent on average), while an extremely low percentage of titles from the nonprofits are rated as bad value (14 per cent) (Orsdel and Born, 2006). McCabe et al. (2006) found the average ratio of 2000–1990 prices for nonprofits and for-profits to be 2.03 and 3.77, respectively.

Commercial journal publishing, moreover, is increasingly dominated by a handful of multinational conglomerates – six publishers control 60 per cent of the scholarly journals publishing market (see Chapters 12–13). Elsevier controls 2,211 journals, Springer 1,574, Blackwell 863, and John Wiley 776 (McCabe et al., 2006). Blackwell and Wiley have since merged.

The result is what is often referred to as the 'journals crisis'. Libraries are simply unable to afford these price hikes. The average total library budget grew at only 4.3 per cent per annum between 1991 and 2002, or 58 per cent in total, while journal prices grew several times faster (Edlin and Rubinfeld, 2004). This has left less money for monograph purchases, journals from smaller publishers and new journal titles. The protests from libraries have been loud. In October 2007, the Max Planck Institute, a leading European research institute, cancelled its subscription to 1,200 Springer journals, not negotiating a new agreement until February 2008 (Orsdel and Born, 2008). As well as price hikes for subscriptions, 'bundling' of multiple titles has also had a negative effect, tending to squeeze small and non-commercial publishers out of library purchases. According to the Association of Research Libraries, between 1986 and 2000, libraries cut the number of monographs they purchased by 17 per cent, but the number of journal titles by only 7 per cent (Edlin and Rubinfeld, 2004).

It might have been expected that the move to electronic subscriptions would have allowed for a cheaper access option. However, a case study of ecology journals showed no reduction in prices for online-only journals (Bergstrom and Bergstrom, 2006). Discounts for online-only subscriptions average at only 5 per cent, and some of the largest publishers offer no discount at all (Dewatripont et al., 2006; Orsdel and Born, 2006). Publishers, in other words, are still basing their charges on the economics of traditional print publishing. Not only are their profits high; their cost structures are also high, reflecting perhaps a complacency which comes with their monopoly over prestige titles. The cost of producing an article is estimated to be about $3,400 for commercial journal publishers (Clarke, 2007). This is inexcusably high when the primary work of quality assessment and content development is with unpaid academic authors and peer reviewers. And for this high price, the publication process often remains painfully slow (compared, for instance, with the speed of new media spaces), and the final product is not particularly visible to internet search because it is hidden behind subscription walls.

Knowledge freely available

The open access rejoinder has been strident and eloquent. 'An old tradition and a new technology have converged to make possible an unprecedented public good' (Budapest Open Access Initiative, 2002). 'The internet has fundamentally changed the practical and economic realities of distributing scientific knowledge and cultural heritage' (Berlin Declaration on Open Access to Knowledge in the Sciences and Humanities, 2003). The open access claim that academic knowledge should be made freely available through the internet has been backed by cogent and at times impassioned argument (Bergman, 2006; Bethesda Statement on Open Access Publishing, 2003; Kapitzke and Peters, 2007; Peters et al., 2008; Willinsky, 2006a, 2006b). John Willinsky speaks of the 'access principle': 'A commitment to the value and quality of research carries with it a responsibility to extend the circulation of such work as far as possible and ideally to all who are interested in and who might profit by it' (Willinsky, 2006a: xii). And in the words of Stevan Harnad:

> some think the most radical feature of post-Gutenberg journals will be the fact that they are digital and online, but that would be a much more modest development if their contents were to continue to be kept behind financial firewalls, with access denied to all who cannot or will not pay the tolls ... [T]he optimal and inevitable outcome – for scientific and scholarly research, researchers, their institutions and funders, the vast research and development industry, and the society whose taxes support science and scholarship and for whose benefits the research is conducted – will be that all published research articles will be openly accessible online, free for all would-be users webwide. (see Chapter 6)

These arguments have been supported by practical initiatives to build open access infrastructure. Prominent among these are the Open Journals System software created by the US-Canadian Public Knowledge Project (*http://pkp.sfu.ca/*) and the DSpace open access repository software led by MIT (*http://www.dspace.org/*). The online Directory of Open Access Journals (*http://www.doaj.org/*) indexes many thousands of open access journals, and Open J-Gate (*http://www.openj-gate.com*) lists over a million open access articles. The Open Archives Initiative (*http://www.openarchives.org*) develops and promotes metadata standards to facilitate the accessibility of open access content.

Open access also now comes in many hues. In addition to 'core open access journals' (Clarke, 2007), there are many somewhat qualified varieties of access, including delayed open access, in which articles are made freely available after a period of time, and hybrid open access journals, in which some authors or the sponsors of their research may choose to pay an additional fee to have their article available for free (see Chapter 7). Moreover, some 67 per cent of journals allow some form of self-archiving in repositories (see Chapter 10), and these are colour-coded by the Sherpa Romeo initiative as green (can archive preprint and post-print), blue (can archive final draft post-refereeing), yellow (can archive pre-refereeing draft), and white (archiving not permitted) (*http://www.sherpa.ac.uk/romeo/*).

Meanwhile, a succession of institutional mandates now support one variety of open access or another. In December 2007, the US National Institutes of Health (NIH), which dispense some $29 billion in grants resulting in some 80,000 articles annually, required grantees to provide open access to peer-reviewed articles within one year of publication. In January 2008, the European Research Council announced that grant recipients must post articles and data within six months of publication. There has also been action at the university level. In 2007, Harvard University's Faculties of Arts and Sciences voted unanimously to require faculty to retain rights to post copies of published articles on the university's institutional repository. In the same year, 791 universities in 46 European countries voted unanimously to require open access to the results of publicly-funded research (Orsdel and Born, 2008). In October 2008, the Association of American Universities and the Association of Research Libraries issued a 'call to action' for US universities to take responsibility for the free, online dissemination of research content. These trends, concludes Peter Suber (2007), point powerfully in favour of a shift to open access.

In this context, repositories of various sorts are growing rapidly, both at an institutional level and by discipline (see Chapter 10). By 2007, there were one million articles in PubMed Central, developed by the US National Library of Medicine (*http://www.pubmedcentral.nih.gov/*), while the ArXiv repository in physics, mathematics, computer science, quantitative biology and statistics (*http://arxiv.org/*) contained half a million articles (Ginsparg, 2007). Meanwhile, Research Papers in Economics now contains over half a million items (*http://repec.org/*). To a significant degree, the development of these repositories involves the migration of content, legally and sometimes illegally, which has already been published or which is subsequently published in commercial journals (Bergstrom and Lavaty, 2007; Ginsparg, 2007).

The shift to open access scholarly journals is paralleled in many areas of cultural production and intellectual work in the era of new digital media. Yochai Benkler (2006) speaks of a burgeoning domain of 'social production' or 'commons-based peer production' in which 'cooperative and coordinate action carried out through radically distributed, nonmarket mechanisms that do not depend on proprietary strategies'. As computers and network access have become cheap and ubiquitous, 'the material means of information and cultural production in the hands of a significant fraction of the world's population'. Benkler considers this to be no less than 'a new mode of production emerging in the middle of the most advanced economies in the world', in which 'the primary raw materials in the information economy, unlike the industrial economy, are public goods – existing information, knowledge and culture'. Benkler describes:

> [the] emergence of a substantial component of nonmarket production at the very core of our economic engine – the production and exchange of information ... suggests a genuine limit on the extent of the market ... [and] a genuine shift in direction for what appeared to be the ever-increasing global reach of the market economy and society in the past half century. (Benkler, 2006: 18–19)

Wikipedia is a paradigmatic case of this social production. Print encyclopaedias were big business. For many households in the era of print literacy, this paper monster was their largest knowledge investment. Encyclopaedia entries were written by invited, professional experts. Wikipedia, by contrast, is free. It is written by anyone, knowledge professional or amateur, without pay and without distinction of rank. Academic knowledge does not fit the Wikipedia paradigm of social production and mass collaboration in a number of respects, including the non-attribution of authorship and the idea that any aspiring knowledge contributor can write, regardless of credentials. For the moment, however, we want to focus on the unpaid, non-market mode of production, a cornerstone of the case for open access journals.

Culture and information are taken out of the market economy in the paradigm of social production by theoretical fiat of their unique status as non-rivalrous goods or goods where there is no marginal cost of providing them to another person. Lawrence Lessig quotes Thomas Jefferson:

> He who receives an idea from me, receives instruction himself without lessening mine; as he who lights his taper at mine, receives light without darkening me. That ideas should freely spread from one to another over the globe, for the moral and mutual instruction

of man, and improvement of his condition, seems to have been peculiarly and benevolently designed by nature. (Lessig, 2008: 290)

In a similar manner, John Willinsky quotes economist Fritz Machlup: 'If a public or social good is defined as one that can be used by additional persons without causing any additional cost, then knowledge is such a good of the purest type' (Willinsky, 2006a: 9). Non-rivalrous goods are like the lighthouse, providing guidance to all ships equally, whether few or many ships happen to pass (Willinsky, 2006b). Michael Peters quotes Joseph Stiglitz: 'Knowledge is a public good because it is non-rivalrous, that is, knowledge once discovered and made public, operates expansively to defy the normal law of scarcity that governs most commodity markets' (Peters et al., 2008: 15). Lessig concludes:

> The system of control we erect for rivalrous resources (land, cars, computers) is not necessarily appropriate for nonrivalrous resources (ideas, music, expression) ... Thus a legal system, or a society generally, must be careful to tailor the kind of control to the kind of resource. ... The digital world is closer to the world of ideas than the world of things. (Lessig, 2001: 95, 116)

The peculiar features thus ascribed to knowledge, culture and ideas become the basis for a new and burgeoning 'gift economy' outside of the market (Raymond, 2001). Bauwens describes the consequent development of a 'political economy of peer production' as the 'widespread participation by equipotential participants', a 'third mode of production' different from for-profit or public production by state-owned enterprises. 'Its product is not exchange-value for a market, but use-value for a community of users ... [who] make use-value freely accessible on a universal basis, through new common property regimes' (Bauwens, 2005). Again, the sites of academic knowledge production are not like this in some important respects, for they are primarily not-for-profit or state-owned spaces, and they do not by and large use or need to use the new common property regimes to which Bauwens refers.

However, one thing does carry over from the case for a political economy of peer-to-peer production, and that is the idea that knowledge should be free. With this comes a series of common assumptions about the nature of non-market motivations. In the domain of social production, social motivations displace monetary motivations (Benkler, 2006: 93–4). Or, in Opderbeck's words, 'Traditional proprietary rights are supposed to incentivize innovation through the prospect of monopoly rents. The incentive to innovate in a purely open source community, in contrast, is based on "reputational" or "psychosocial" rewards' (Opderbeck, 2007). Translated into academe, Willinsky argues that 'the recognition of one's peers is the principal measure of one's contribution to a field of inquiry'. Less charitably, he calls this is an 'ego economy' driven by 'the necessary vanity of academic life' (Willinsky, 2006a: 20–2).

There are, however, some serious theoretical difficulties with these ideas of social production and non-rivalrous goods, and we will consider these before returning to the question of the alternative ways in which scholarly journals can be made and made available. On the question of 'social production', this new economy is also a kind of anti-economy. For its every inroad, it removes the economic basis for knowledge and culture-making as a form of employment. Tens of thousands of people used to work for encyclopaedia publishers, even if some of the jobs, such as that of the proverbial door-to-door salesperson, were less than ideal. Everybody who writes for Wikipedia has to have another source of income. What would happen to the global scholarly publishing industry if academics assumed collective and universal responsibility for self-publishing, an industry that in 2004 was reported to support 250,000 employees worldwide, with a $65 billion turnover (Peters, 2007)? What would happen to scholarly associations and research institutes which have historically gained revenue from the sale of periodicals and books? An ironic consequence of a move to social production would, in the much-trumpeted era of the knowledge or creative economy, be to value knowledge-making and creativity at zero, when coal and corn still cost whatever they do per tonne. How do knowledge workers eat and where do they live? Without doing away with the market entirely, we are consigning a good deal of knowledge work to involuntary volunteerism, unaccountable cross-subsidy, charity or penury. We know from experience the fate of workers in other domains of unpaid labour, such as the unpaid domestic work of women and carers. Making it free means that it is exploited. In the case of the knowledge economy, the exploiters are the likes of Google who take the unpaid work of social producers and make a fortune from it.

And on the distinction between rivalrous and non-rivalrous goods, the key theoretical problem is to base one's case on the circumstantial aspects of knowledge consumption rather than the practical logistics of knowledge production. Rivalrous and non-rivalrous goods equally need to be made. They cost their makers labour time, time which otherwise could be spent making buildings or food. Ostensibly non-rivalrous goods also need physical spaces, as well as tools, storage devices and distribution networks, all of which have to be made by people who need buildings and food. In these fundamental respects, knowledge or cultural goods are not so different from any other goods. In fact, knowledge and material domains are not so neatly separable. Buildings and food have design in them (and when we go to architects and restaurants we are in part purchasing intellectual property). Equally, all cultural products have to be made, delivered and rendered materially.

From this perspective, in this era of the new, digital media, we might be witnessing no more than one of the old marvels of industrial capitalism – a technology that improves productivity. In the case of knowledge-making, the efficiencies are so great – print encyclopaedias vs Wikipedia, celluloid movies vs digital movies posted to YouTube, PDF journal articles vs print journals – that we get the impression that the costs have reduced to nothing. But they have not. They have only been lowered. We have become too dazzled by the reduction in costs to notice the costs we are now paying. So low are these costs in fact that we can even afford to make these cultural products in our spare time, and not worry too much about giving away the fruits of our labours to companies who have found ways to exploit them in newly-emerging information markets. Knowledge is a product of human labour and it needs human labour to make it available. There can never be zero costs of production and distribution of knowledge and culture, in theory or empirically. At most, there are productivity improvements. Far from ushering in a new mode of production, the driving force is more of the same engine that over the past few centuries has made capitalism what it is.

So how do we move forward? In the most general of terms, there are two options. The first is socialism in all sectors. If knowledge and culture are to be free, so coal and corn or buildings and food must be if we are not to advantage the industries of the old economy over those of the new, to consign knowledge and culture work selectively to the gift economy. The second is to build an economics of self-sustainable, autonomous cultural production, where there is space for small stallholders (publishers, musicians, writers, knowledge workers) or where the cross-subsidies are transparent and explicit – including the economics of academic socialism in an otherwise mixed economy.

Returning now the particularities of scholarly journals, no doubt the excessive cost of commercial journal content represents both profiteering on the part of the big publishers and lagging inefficiencies when they have not re-tooled their fundamental business processes for the digital era. Clarke (2007) estimates that the production cost of a commercial journal article is $3,400, compared with $730 for an open access article.

On the other hand, however, open access publishing is bedeviled by problems of resourcing. Where does the $730 come from to produce the open access article? Without some kind of fee structure, open access publishing has to rely on academic volunteerism or cross-subsidy by taxpayers or fee-paying students who support the university system. Willinsky (2006a: 191) speaks lyrically of a return to the days when authors worked beside printers to produce their books. However, academics do not have all the skills or resources to be publishers. Having to be an amateur publisher adds another burden to an already-challenging job. Nor is playing amateur publisher necessarily the best use of time that could otherwise be devoted to research, writing and teaching. There is a lot of work in publishing. Someone has to provide the labour time. That time always comes at a direct or indirect cost. The problem with this ethereal 'reputational' economy is not that it is without costs, but that it shifts its costs often silently and unaccountably to places not well equipped to bear those costs or to evaluate effective and efficient resource use.

Sometimes open access publishing is forced to develop alternative, quasi-commercial funding mechanisms – in the form of author publication fees, 'memberships' and institutional subsidies. For example, the Public Library of Science charges a $1,500 author fee, while Springer will make an article available in open access for an author fee of $3,000 (Willinsky, 2006a: 1, 5). One could argue that the economic basis for this kind of open access knowledge system is a kind of socialism for the affluent – if you work as a professor in a big, well-resourced research university, you can afford to fund the publication of your article. You may also be able to donate some of your time to publishing, or have funding for graduate assistants who can do the publishing work. There are, in other words, key questions about the sustainability, equity and in fact the openness, of open access business models.

Towards sustainable scholarly publishing

To develop an economics of sustainability for academic knowledge systems, it is important to make some distinctions. These are not like other content creation spaces in the new media in some important respects. They are not like Wikipedia or YouTube insofar as universities are systems of public resourcing and elaborate cross-subsidy which already fund the idea-generation process. They are not like peer-to-peer production insofar as these particular knowledge workers are paid to be such by the public or not-for-profit private institutions that support their salaries. To this extent, involvement in the publication process is justifiable. It is a very small step to build funding for specific publication media and services into the infrastructure of universities. This, in fact, may be a new role for university libraries and rejuvenated university presses.

Lightweight, self-sustaining publication funding models can possibly be created in this space. Given today's digital infrastructure costs there is no reason why subscription fees should be so high, or author publication fees, or per-article purchase prices. How many academics would pay (say) $10 per year for journal access and publication alerts? How many academics would pay (say) $100 for rapid peer-review and publication? How many students would as willingly pay $1 for an article as they do for a song in the iTunes store? The key to today's journals impasse may be to develop low-cost digital infrastructures and self-sustaining business models.

Breaking point 2: designing knowledge credibly

The system of peer review is a pivotal point in the knowledge design process: the moment at which textual representations of knowledge are independently evaluated. Until this point, knowledge work is of no formal significance beyond the private activities of a researcher or intellectual. Peer review is required as a critical step towards their knowledge becoming socially validated, confirmed as knowledge-of-note and made more widely available.

Critical to our argument about modern knowledge systems is that it is representations of knowledge which are being evaluated, not something that might itself be called knowledge. Knowledge is not simply made of the stuff that happened in the laboratory, or what was found in the archive, or what transpired in social observation. Rather, it is what a scholar tells us has happened or was found or transpired. And, adding a further layer of abstraction of representation away from referent, the person and context of the scholar at the point of evaluation is removed through double-blind review. The text is examined simply as that – as a representation – and the reviewer interpolates hypothetical connections between the representations and possible referents. The referee does not know the identity of the author, and thus the location of their work, their interests or motivations. All the referee is working with as they evaluate a knowledge representation is what the text itself reveals.

Here are some of the characteristic features of the peer-review system. A journal editor receives a manuscript. They examine the text in order to decide on referees whose expertise, as shown by what they have already published, may be relevant to the content of the article to be reviewed. Referees are selected because they are qualified to review – in fact, often more qualified than the editor – and this judgment is based on the fact that the referee publishes into a proximal discourse zone. The key question is not whether they have relevant substantive knowledge so much as whether they will be able to understand the text. Refereeing also spreads the work around, creating a more distributed knowledge system than one that is publisher and editor-centric. The identity of the author is removed, and the text sent to more than one referee. Referees are asked to declare conflicts of interest of which the journal editor may be unaware – if they happen to be able to identify the author, or if they cannot give a work a sympathetic hearing because their understandings are diametrically opposed, for instance. The key motif of good refereeing, one of its intertextual tropes in fact, is independence and impartiality, an aura of reading a text for its intellectual merit alone, without prejudice to politics or paradigms or personal opinion. The referee promises not to disclose the paper's contents before publication, or to disclose their identity as a referee. After reading the text, they might recommend publication without qualification, or rewriting based on their suggestions, or rejection of the paper. Whatever their judgment, referees should support their recommendations with a cogent rationale and, if the recommendation is to rewrite, specific advice. Nor do referees of a particular work know of each other's identity; consequently, they cannot conspire to agree on the worth of a text. Multiple referees are sought in order to corroborate recommendations, in case, for instance, one referee's judgment transpires to be unsound. When there are conflicting opinions among the referees, the editor may weigh the assessments of the referee reports or, if uncertain, send the text out to more referees.

Prototypes of these textual practices predate the rise of the modern academic journal. In the domain of Islamic science, Ishap bin Ali Al Rahwl (854–931) in the 'Ethics of a Physician' discussed a procedure whereby a physician's notes were examined by a council of physicians to judge whether a patient had been treated according to appropriate standards (Meyers, 2004; Spier, 2002). In his *New Organon*, the scientific method of Francis Bacon included a process akin to peer review in which a reader of scientific speculations would patiently reconstruct the scientist's thoughts in order to reach the same judgment and thus prove the veracity of the scientist's claim (Bacon, 1620). There are, in other words, conceptual precursors to peer review in older textual practices.

Pre-publication peer review in a form more recognizable today began to evolve as a method of scientific knowledge validation from the seventeenth century, starting with Oldenberg's editorship of the *Philosophical Transactions of the Royal Society* (Biagioli, 2002; Guédon, 2001; Peters, 2007; Willinsky, 2006a). However, institutionalization of peer review processes did not become widespread until the twentieth century, either as a consequence of having to handle the increasing numbers of articles or in order to find appropriately qualified experts as areas of knowledge became more specialized (Burnham, 1990). A more dispersed peer-review process in which referees had a degree of independence from the journal editor was not widely applied until after the photocopier became readily accessible from the late 1950s (Spier, 2002).

There is some evidence, however, that we may be experiencing a period of decline in peer review, in part for the most practical of reasons. In the forms in which it has been practised in conventional publishing processes, peer review is slow. This is one of the principal reasons why repositories have been growing rapidly – as a site for faster publication of scholarly content. It is estimated that only 13 per cent of material in institutional repositories has been peer-reviewed (see Chapter 10). In the physics community, for instance, the ArXiv repository has become tremendously important. ArXiv does not arrange or require peer review, and preprints published there may or may not be subsequently submitted for peer review. To be able to post content at ArXiv, all you need is the endorsement of a current contributor, a process of some concern insofar as it creates a kind of private club in which the substantive scholarly criteria for membership are not explicitly spelt out. The repository's founder, Paul Ginsparg, also speaks of 'heuristic screening mechanisms' which include the worryingly vague admonition, 'of refereeable quality' (Ginsparg, 2007). The processes and criteria by which the unacceptability of content is determined by 'moderators' are not spelt out.

Speed of publication in the digital era is one factor that is reducing the significance of peer review in today's knowledge systems. However, there are four, more fundamental flaws in the process, each of which is less defensible in the era of digital communications: the discursive features of the heritage peer-review process; the textual forms being assessed; the validity of its measures; and its network effects.

Accountability in pre-publication processes

First, to take the discursive features of the peer-review process, these track the linearity and post-publication fixity of text manufacturing processes in the era of print. Peer review is at the pre-publication phase of the social process of text production, drawing a clear distinction between pre and post-publication at the moment of commitment to print. Pre-publication processes are hidden in confidential spaces, leading to publication of a text in which readers are unable to uncover the intertextuality, and thus dialogue, that went into this aspect of the process of knowledge design. The happenings in this space remain invisible to public scrutiny and thus unaccountable. This is in most part for practical reasons – it would be cumbersome and expensive to make these processes public. In the digital era, however, the incidental recording of communicative interchanges of all sorts is pervasive and cheap, inviting in cases of public interest (of which knowledge-making would surely be one) that these be made part of the public record or at least an independently auditable confidential record.

Then, in the post-publication phase, there is very little chance for dialogue that can have an impact upon the statement of record, the printed article, beyond later publication of errata. Reviews, citations and subsequent articles may reinforce, revise or repudiate the content of the publication of record, but these are all new publications, equally the products of a linear textual workflow. Moving to PDF as a digital analogue of print does very little to change this mode of textual and knowledge production.

Key flaws in this knowledge system are the lack of transparency in pre-publication processes, lack of metamoderation or audit of referee reports or editor–referee deliberations, and the relative closure of a one-step, one-way publication process. If we posit that greater reflexivity and dialogue will make for more powerful, effective and responsive knowledge processes, then we have to say that we are yet exploit the affordances of digital media to the full. Sosteric (1996) discusses Habermas's ideal speech situation in which both interlocutors have equal opportunity to initiate speech, there is mutual understanding, there is space for clarification, interlocutors can use any speech act, and there is equal power over the exchange. In each of these respects, the peer-review process is less than ideal as a discursive framework. There are power asymmetries, identities are not revealed, dialogue between referee and author is prevented, the arbiter-editor is unaccountable, consensus is not necessarily reached, and none of these processes are open to scrutiny on the public record.

We can see some of what may be possible in the ways in which the new media integrally incorporate continuous review in their ranking and sorting mechanisms – from the simple ranking and viewing metrics of YouTube to more sophisticated moderation and metamoderation methods at web publishing sites such as the web-based IT news publication, Slashdot (*http://slashdot.org/moderation.shtml*). Social evaluations of text that were practically impossible for print, are now easy to do using digital media. Is it just habits of knowledge-making practice that prevent us moving in these directions? What about setting up a more dialogical relation between authors and referees? Let the author speak to referee and editor, with or without identities revealed: How useful did you find this review? If you did, perhaps you might acknowledge a specific debt? Or do you think the reviewer's judgment might have been clouded by ideological or paradigmatic antipathy? Such dialogues are much of the time closed by the current peer-review system, and at best the author takes on board some of the reviewer's suggestions in the rewriting process, unacknowledged. Tentative experiments in open peer review, not too unlike post-publication review in a traditional publishing workflow, have been designed to grant greater recognition to the role of referees and create greater transparency, to discourage abusive reviews and to reduce the chances of ideas being stolen by anonymous reviewers before they can be published (Rowland, 2002). Why should referees be less honest in their assessments when their identities are revealed? They may be just as honest. In fact, the cloak of anonymity has its own discursive dangers including non-disclosure of interests, unfairly motivated criticisms and theft of ideas. In the new media, too, reviewers can be ranked by people whose work has been reviewed, and their reviews in turn ranked and weighted for their credibility in subsequent reviews. This is roughly how trusted super-author/reviewers emerge in Wikipedia. There could also be multiple points of review, blurring the pre and post-publication distinction. Initial texts can be published earlier, and re-versioning can occur indefinitely. In this way, published texts need not ossify, and the lines of their development may be traced because changes are disclosed in a publicly accessible record of versions. These are some of the discursive possibilities that digital media allow, all of which may make for more open, dynamic and responsive knowledge dialogue, where the speed of the dialogue is not slowed down by the media in which it is carried.

Textual practices

The second major flaw in the traditional peer-review process, and a flaw that need not exist in the world of digital media, is in the textual form of the article itself. Here is a central contradiction in its mode of textuality: the canonical scholarly article speaks in a voice of empirical transparency, paradigmatic definitiveness and rhetorical neutrality – this last oxymoron capturing precisely a core contradiction, epistemic hypocrisy even. Indeed, the textual form of the article abstracts knowledge away from its reference points. The article does not contain the data; rather it refers to the data or suggests how the author's results could be replicated. The article is not the knowledge, or even the direct representation of knowledge – it is a rhetorical re-presentation of knowledge. From a practical standpoint, this has to be the case for print and print lookalikes. But in the digital world, there is very little cost in presenting full datasets along with their interpretation, a complete record of the observations in point alongside replicable steps-in-observation, the archive itself alongside its exegesis. In other words, referees in the era of digital recording are not limited to reviewing the knowledge representation, but come a good deal closer to the world to which those representations point in the form of immediate recordings of that world. This can occur multimodally through the amalgamation of datasets, static image, moving image, and sound with text – captions, tags and narrative glosses. There are no page constraints (shape and textual form) or page limits (size and extent) in the digital record. This changes the reviewer's relationship with the knowledge itself, making them more able to judge the relations between the purported knowledge and its textual forms, and for this reason also more able to make a contribution to its shaping as represented knowledge. This would also allow a greater deal of transparency in the dialectics of the empirical record and its interpretation. It may also lead to a more honest separation of represented data from the interpretative voice of the author, thus creating a more open and plausible environment for empirical work. In a provocative and widely cited article, John Ioannidis (2005) argues that 'most published research findings are false'. Exposing data would invite critical reinterpretation of represented results and reduce the rates and margins of error in the published knowledge record.

Peer-review measures

A third major flaw in the heritage peer-review process is its validity. What does the peer-review system purport to measure? Ostensibly it evaluates the quality of a contribution to knowledge (Jefferson et al., 2002; Wager and Jefferson, 2001). But precisely what are the rubrics of knowledge? In today's review system these are buried in the under-articulated depths of initiation to peer community. Mostly, review is just a three-point scale – accept, accept with revisions, reject – accompanied by an open-ended narrative rationale. In the review text, the tropes of objectivity can hide, although none too effectively at times, a multitude of ideological, paradigmatic and even personal agendas. These are exacerbated by the fact that referees operate under a cloak of anonymity. There are times, moreover, when the last person who you want to review your work, the last person who is likely to be 'objective', is someone in a proximal discourse zone (Judson, 1994). For these reasons, the texts of peer review and the judgments that are made, are often by no means valid. One possible solution to this problem is to develop explicit, general knowledge rubrics at a number of subdisciplinary, disciplinary and metadisciplinary levels, and require that referees defend the validity of their judgments against the criteria spelt out in the rubrics. This would also have the incidental benefit of making the rules of the epistemic game explicit, and in so doing more accessible to network outsiders ... which brings us to the fourth major flaw in the peer-review system: its network effects.

Network effects

Peer-review pools generally work like this. A paper is sent to a journal editor. The editor is the initial gatekeeper, making a peremptory judgment of relevance to the area of knowledge and the quality of the work. Having passed this hurdle, the editor chooses suitable reviewers. This choice can reflect content or methodological expertise. But it can also be a choice of friends and enemies of ideas, positions and paradigms – another point of potential closure in the knowledge process. Given that referees are not paid, the bias amongst those who accept the task will be broadly established in any context where they owe something to the patronage of the editor or they are friends of the editor and stand in some kind of relation of reciprocal obligation. If the author has returned to them reviews that they consider to be unfair or plain wrong, they have no-one to whom they can appeal other than the editor of the journal who selected the referees in the first place – there are no independent adjudication processes, and more broadly, no processes for auditing the reliability of the journal as a knowledge validation system (Lee and Bero, 2006). The overall logic of such a system is to create self-replicating network effects in which a distributed system in fact becomes a system of informal, unstated, unaccountable power (Galloway and Thacker, 2007). Journals come to act like insider networks more than places where knowledge subsists on its merits, or at least that is the way it often feels to outsiders. Their tendency, then, is to maintain consensus, control the field, suppress dissent, reinforce the disciplinary ramparts, and support institutional and intellectual inertia (Horrobin, 1990). The practical effect is to exclude thinkers who, regardless of their merit, may be from a non-anglophone country, or teach in a liberal arts college, or who do not work in a university, or who are young or an early-career researcher, or who speak to an innovative paradigm, or who have unusual source data (Stanley, 2007). The network effect, in other words, is to exclude a lot of potentially valuable knowledge work conducted in rich knowledge spaces.

Finally, open access publishing does not necessarily reduce these points of closure in scholarly knowledge-making. The question of the cultural and epistemic openness of a knowledge system is a completely different one to the economics of its production. In fact, as we have seen, open access may even be accompanied by greater closure, in which even the heritage peer-review system, whatever its defects, is eroded, to be replaced by fewer, more powerful and even less accountable gatekeepers. On the other hand, there are no reasons why self-sustaining business models might not be open in an epistemic sense. In fact, reputational economies can be more viciously closed than commercial ones because they are driven by purely ideological interests. Ironically, cultural systems grounded in material sustainability often operate in practice with less ideological prejudice. Moreover, open access journals by and large perpetuate the print analogue workflow of PDF, with all its intrinsic deficiencies as an open knowledge system. It is important, in other words, not to mix discussions of business models, the technologies that are used and the epistemic conditions of openness – the latter does not necessarily correlate with the former two. New resourcing models and technologies can as be closed as old ones from an epistemic point of view.

Breaking point 3: evaluating knowledge, once designed

On a time dimension, knowledge is an iterative thing. Knowledge workers read the texts of others as reference points for their own knowledge work – to find out what has already been discovered and thought, and to determine which questions still need to be addressed. This is the basis of 'progress' in science and the evolution of frames of thinking. On a structural dimension, and for all the rhetorical heroism of discovery and analytical voice, knowledge is a social product. 'Standing on the shoulders of giants' was Isaac Newton's famous expression. This is why there is a deep and intrinsic intertextuality to formal knowledge representations: this question arises from that (citation); this method comes from here (citation); this idea or discovery builds on that (citation); this idea or discovery corroborates that (citation); this idea or discovery contradicts that (citation). The interplay of intellectual debt and new intellectual contribution is at the heart of scholarly work (Grafton, 1997). Integrating one's work into a body of knowledge requires a rhetorical play between this text and that (citation).

Citation analysis or bibliometrics has emerged over the past half-century as a principal measure for ranking the value of a published piece. The more people who have cited an author and their text, it is assumed, the greater the contribution to knowledge of that author and that text. This thinking was refined in the work of Eugene Garfield in the 1950s and in the company he founded in 1961, the Institute for Scientific Information, now owned by the multinational media company, Thomson-Reuters (see Chapter 9). To undertake citation counts, you need to count all the citations made in every article. Garfield's Science Citation Index, now renamed Web of Science, or Web of Knowledge (*http://www.isiwebofknowledge.com/*) when the social sciences and humanities are included, has since found competitors, principally Elsevier's Scopus (*http://www.scopus.com*), CiteSeerX (*http://citeseerx .ist.psu.edu*), and Google Scholar (*http://scholar.google.com*) (Harzing and Wal, 2008; Kousha and Thelwall, 2007; Norris and Oppenheim, 2007; Schroeder, 2007).

The Thomson Web of Knowledge way of calculating the value of a scholar's work is as follows: count the number of citations during this year to articles you have published in the two preceding years and divide this by the total number of articles you have published in these two years (Meho, 2007). This, in other words, is a measure of the average number of citations your publications get in the two years after you have published. If it takes more than two years to get citations for your article, they are not counted. More recently, physicist Jorge Hirsch has invented the h-index, where $h = 5$ when you have published five articles in your career which have received five citations, or 20 if you have 20 articles cited on average 20 times. This measure is designed to evaluate whole careers and value scholars who have produced consistently highly-cited articles (see Chapter 9). With the rise of online journals, another increasingly used 'impact' metric is download counts, or the number of times an article is accessed by users (see Chapter 11). Standards for the measurement of downloads have been established by the not-for-profit COUNTER organization (*http://www.projectcounter.org/*).

These are the principal systems of counting used to evaluate the worth of a knowledge-worker's output, and aggregated to determine quality of a journal or an academic department. They are poor measures indeed. We will use the two canons of assessment theory to interrogate the bases of citation measures: their validity and their reliability (Pellegrino et al., 2001). A valid assessment is one where the evidence collected can support the interpretative burden placed upon it. The assessment in, other words, measures what it purports to measure. A reliable assessment will consistently produce the same results when repeated in the same or similar populations. The assessment, in other words, is not fraught by inaccuracy in its implementation. Citation counts and impact factors fail on both criteria.

To evaluate the validity of citation counts, we need to start with the question of what we want to measure: the value of a scholar's work and their contribution to knowledge for the purposes of career evaluation, or assessing the intellectual quality of a journal or department. Some fundamental problems are described below.

The purposes of knowledge-making

All citation counts do is measure the number of mentions of a text. The ultimate utility of knowledge – actual impact – is on the broader social world, not the self-enclosed world reciprocal naming, which is a peculiar characteristic of academic networks. Citation counts measure academic network positions but not necessarily the ultimate social utility of knowledge, its originality in contributing to new knowledge, or its implications and its consequences in terms of anticipated or unanticipated applications (Browman and Stergiou, 2008).

Quantity valued over quality

Although citation counts and impact factors factor the total number of publications into their denominators, numerical evaluation of academic work is still powerfully connected to the total number of articles. This produces a culture of 'no thought unpublished', 'salami publishing' of one idea at a time, and 'honorary authorship' where additional authors are added for at times relatively marginal association with a work. Increasing your total number of publications increases your visibility, which increases the chance that you will get cited. However, numbers of any sort – publication counts, citation counts or impact factors – may turn out to be a lazy shortcut in promotion, hiring or departmental review – a metric with which you think you can evaluate a body of publications without having to read them (Simons, 2008).

Devaluing lightly-cited articles

If 90 per cent of cited articles are lightly cited, does it mean they have no value (Browman and Stergiou, 2008)? An article may demonstrate the strength of analysis or synthesis or data collection capacities of an active researcher. It may clarify their thinking. It might demonstrate their research competence and clarity of thinking. It may flow into their teaching, or be read by students and others, whom it may influence. Articles may be read and used without citation, contributing to one's background knowledge of a field. Download metrics at least come closer actual use in the sense of readership, but they do not say whether the paper was actually read, or whether the downloaded item was the one the reader was looking for, or whether people come back to the same article multiple times rather than download and store (see Chapter 9).

Is popularity a valid measure of knowledge?

Perhaps most seriously, citation is not about the actual intellectual quality or social impact of a text; it is about the extent to which an author and a text have been noticed or positioned themselves to be noticed. To take some cultural analogies and according to the same logic, you would have to choose the largest circulation magazine at a news stand, the best-selling novel in a bookstore, the hit song or CD album, or the movie with the biggest box office takings. Just because any of these things is popular, does not mean that it is the best quality measured in terms of the cultural canons of the domain, nor that it has the most profound social impact. There are small magazines which deal with specialist areas of interest, great novels which have not reached a mass readership, brilliant music that fits into genres without mass appeal and innovative movies which never leave the art house but deeply influence their genre. In fact, without being elitist, we could argue that the most innovative and influential works are not wildly popular, especially in the first instance. They often operate in small, specialized discourse spaces. In this sense, a powerful and knowledge-making work is more likely to be 'unpopular'. Popularity, in fact, is as often as not a sign that something is derivative, stooping to a lowest common denominator to reach a wide market or tainted by promotional and positional effects. Following are some of the effects of a popularity measure of knowledge. It values work which has hooks designed to reach a broader academic audience. It values work which is fashionable and reflects conventional wisdoms over work which is innovative and unconventional. It values large fields over small (in larger fields, such as medicine, there are more things to cite, and more people who can cite you, than in smaller fields, such as zoology). Cambridge biologist Peter Lawrence offers advice to the cynical citation-needing academic: 'Choose the most popular species; it may be easier to publish unsound but trendy work on humans than an incisive study on a zebrafish' (Lawrence, 2007).

Limiting impact to a short timeframe

The Thomson-Reuters Impact Factor only counts citations in the two years after an article is published. As Lawrence (2007) points out, 'truly original work usually takes longer than two years to be appreciated – the most important paper in biology of the 20th century was cited rarely for the first ten years'.

Aggregated impact factors

Each year, Thomson-Reuters ranks impact factors at the level of whole journals, or at least the 9,000 journals it has selected to be worthy of such a measure (Simons, 2008). Citation counts are often aggregated as a proxy for journal, departmental or university 'impact'. This adds another layer of invalidity to the citation counts at the article or author level. The quality of authors and their papers, in other words, is evaluated by the impact of the journals in which they publish and the departments or universities to which they belong. This is even lazier than citation counts themselves. 'Without exception', says Stevan Harnad, none of these metrics can be said to have face validity' (Harnad, 2008). Averaged values for journals or departments can be highly influenced by a few blockbuster articles in a particular two-year stretch. As Phillip Campbell, editor of *Nature*, has said:

> our own internal research demonstrates how a high journal impact factor can be the skewed result of many citations of a few papers rather than the average level of the majority, reducing its value as an objective measure of an individual paper. (Campbell, 2008)

According to Campbell, 89 per cent of *Science*'s impact factor in 2004 was generated by just 25 per cent of its papers. As for the 75 per cent whose impact was relatively low, and thus who did *Nature* a disserve if the journal is to be judged by its impact factor, 'they were in disciplines with characteristically low citation rates per paper like physics, or with citation rates that are typically slow to grow, like the Earth sciences, or because they were excellent (e.g. visionary) but not "hot"' (Campbell, 2008).

The logic of popularity as reflected in citation counts can influence an editor's decisions – they will be more likely to choose your paper if it has features which make it more likely to enhance their journal's impact factor. Journal impact factors can also be skewed by editors who, during the review process, suggest the inclusion of additional citations from the journal to which the author is submitting (see Chapter 9). After all, it is in the interest of the author publishing in that journal that its impact factor be raised, and citing other articles in that journal will do just that. Furthermore, a high impact factor as measured by citation metrics may be more the product of promotional power and positioning in the marketplace than the quality of knowledge (Bornmann et al., 2008). This market-popularity logic creates a closed circle in which market visibility breeds market visibility.

As an aside, another frequently used quantitative measure of journal quality is its rejection rate. The higher the rejection rate, it is assumed, the better the quality of the published article. However, not only does a high rejection rate add a level of arbitrariness to the review process – the mild reservations of one reviewer working for a journal with a high rejection rate might lead to rejection of an excellent work. Rejection rate measures reduce journal quality to the contingencies of supply and demand. In the digital era, anything that meets a certain standard can readily be published. There are no fixed limits in the supply of publishing space as there were in the era of print journals – the denominator in this equation. On the other hand, the size of the numerator is no more than a function of the size of a field. Of course, journals with names as expansive as *Science* and *Nature* and with infrastructures that assure wide public exposure will have high rejection rates. But small fields may produce consistently excellent work, a high proportion of which should be published. Why should a low rejection rate cast aspersions on a journal in a specialist field?

Bias favouring some genres of article

Review articles, which overview a body of research, are much more likely to be cited than new research and new thinking. Review articles are also more likely to be cited than the articles upon which they rely for their syntheses (Bornmann et al., 2008; Meho, 2007; Simons, 2008). Citing a review article dispenses with the need for long reference lists, a particularly important thing when word or page limits have been set (Pauly and Stergiou, 2008). Journal editors have noticed the relative impact of review articles, which explains their sixfold increase between 1991 and 2006 (see Chapter 9). Longer articles get cited more when they cover a broader range of issues. More authors correlates with wider citation (Bornmann et al., 2008).

Network effects

The citation system rewards people who can forcefully work networks and find their way into journals with wider circulation, thus rewarding academic entrepreneurship ahead of intellectual content. It creates a citation barter system in which authors feel they need to mention friends, patrons, and people to whom they own a positional debt (Lawrence, 2007). You dutifully quote leaders in the field, and you don't confront contrasting views and results openly in case the people you mention might be your reviewer or a friend of your reviewer, and also not to get people off-side who might cite you. It is a good idea to quote people who are heavily cited in the hope that they might notice you and cite you, thus enhancing your visibility. In other words, citation metrics measure social power dynamics which are not necessarily related to criteria of intellectual quality and social impact (Bornmann et al., 2008; Lawrence, 2007). 'Creative discovery is not helped by measures that select for tough fighters and against more reflective modest people', concludes Peter Lawrence (2008). This is a system that works against women, people from non-anglophone countries, people with ideas and data that do not mesh well with the conventional wisdoms of those who dominate a field.

Besides, the academic star system which the citation system supports, based as it is on the mass-media logic of popularity rankings, is peculiarly poorly suited to a new media environment in which knowledge and cultural creation are more broadly distributed. In this sense, citation-popularity rankings track the logic of the old media world, which valued economies of scale.

Accessibility distortions

Studies show that open access publishing doubles research impact (see Chapter 6). Repeated studies lauding the positive effects of open access come to similar conclusions (Brody et al., 2007; Willinsky, 2006a). From a knowledge system point of view, this only means that increased citations are the product of easier accessibility. It does not mean that the knowledge they contain has necessarily had a higher impact. In hybrid open access journals, research shows that open access articles can generate between 25 per cent and 250 per cent more citations than articles which are not freely available (Orsdel and Born, 2006). This means that people who can afford to pay open access author fees get more cited for their investment. In fact, electronic access generally may only serve to accentuate a herd mentality. Examining a database of 34 million articles between 1945 and 2005, Evans (2008) shows that as more articles are made accessible online, either through open access or commercial subscription, the articles and journals cited have tended to be fewer and more recent. His explanation? Scholars are becoming more influenced by one another's choices of citation than a close reading of the texts on their merits. As a consequence, fields hasten to consensus and conformity.

As to the reliability of citation counts, this is explored below.

Self and negative citation

Is citation a measure of the value of a paper? The simple assumption is that citation denotes positive impact, and the more citations are better. But not when it is self-citation. Not when it is negative citation. Not when popularity is in fact notoriety. Perspectives which may in the general view of the field be wrong-headed and extreme may be few, but they are regularly used as straw people or paradigmatic reference points when attempting to position one's argument in an ostensibly balanced way against the range of interpretative alternatives. For instance, a small number of anti-immigration academics who work in the field of immigration studies are more regularly cited because they represent the only mentionable counterpoints in a field which is by and large populated by people who are sympathetic to immigration. The impact factors of the anti-immigration folks will be greater simply because theirs is a minority position within the field, not necessarily because their position is intellectually more defensible. Notwithstanding their impact factor, the anti-immigration views are not in fact more influential because the rest of the field only cites them in order to disagree with them. They serve as a rhetorical foil, but for this they are rewarded citation counts. And what happens when you don't cite a source but cite a source which cites a source – such as a review article or the literature section in a regular article – thus failing to give credit to the origins of an idea or the original source of an idea or data? What happens when a much-cited piece proves to be wrong? 'Your paper may ... have diverted and wasted the efforts of hundreds of scientists, but [the impact factor] will still look good on your CV and may land you a job' (Lawrence, 2007). And what about stuff that you don't cite but which has influenced you greatly, or that you deliberately don't cite because you don't want to support the person or position or be seen to be supporting them, or don't cite because the work although of general influence is not directly relevant to your subject at hand?

Have the articles even been read?

A study of ecology papers by Todd and Ladle (2008) showed that only 76 per cent of cited articles supported the claim being made for them by the author making the citation. Todd and Ladle's further study of misprinted citations shows that perhaps only 20 per cent of cited papers are read, indicating that people are citing citations rather than sources they have read. The increasing reliance on meta-analyses and review articles exacerbates this problem, particularly when the secondary article cites source articles uncritically, as if their findings were correct (Todd and Ladle, 2008).

Failures to count correctly

The citation counting system is riddled with elementary inaccuracies. Incorrectly referenced items may be as high as one-third, lowering the chance of a citation being counted (Todd and Ladle, 2008).

'Homographs' occur frequently when initials are used instead of whole first names – in the reference lists as well as citation databases – which leads to a failure to distinguish scholars who have the same last name and initial (Meho, 2007). Citations are also more likely to be counted when they are in English or when an author has a conventional English name (Harzing and Wal, 2008). When the editor of *Nature* went to analyse the impact factor attributed to the journal by Thomson-Reuters Web of Knowledge, he concluded, 'Try as we might, my colleagues and I cannot reconcile our own counts of citable items in *Nature*' (Campbell, 2008).

What's counted is what counts

The Thomson-Reuters databases include a limited number of journals, mostly English language from North America and Europe (Meho, 2007). They only count citations in these journals. How are these selected? On the basis of some general criteria of no particular relevance to impact and intellectual quality, such as timeliness of publication, and some highly-subjective criteria such as the stature of the members of the editorial board (*http://scientific.thomson.com/free/essays/selectionofmaterial/journalselection/*). A librarian colleague of ours e-mailed Thomson to ask about their selection processes, and their answer was 'All journal evaluations are done solely by Thomson staff. We do receive recommendations for journals from researchers but they have no part in the evaluation process.' Given that impact factor ratings generate impact (the apparent prestige of a journal for authors and respectable citability for readers), this is an indefensibly opaque process. Given Thomson-Reuters' position in the world of academic publishing, it could also be regarded without too much suspicion as a case of the fox guarding the chicken coop. For all its touted open-ness, Google Scholar may be little better. In response to a query by a scholarly publisher as to why its 20 or so journals had not yet been indexed despite years of requests, the Google e-mail respondent simply replied: 'we are currently unable to provide a time frame for when your content will be made available on Google Scholar'.

To the extent that they work at all, citation counts work for some fields better than others

In molecular biology and biochemistry, for example, 96 per cent of citations are to journal articles and the Web of Knowledge database covers 97 per cent of cited articles, resulting in a 92 per cent coverage of the field. However, in the humanities and arts, only 34 per cent of citations are to journal articles, of which only 50 per cent are counted in the Web of Knowledge, producing a mere 17 per cent coverage (see Chapter 9). Meanwhile bibliometrics, despite its name, completely ignores books, and thus favours disciplines in which more journal articles are published over those where books are also a significant publication venue. Butler (2008) concludes that for most disciplines in the social sciences and humanities, standard bibliometric measures cannot be supported. Moreover, citation practices vary. Bornmann et al. report on research by Podlubny which estimates that one citation in mathematics is equivalent to 15 in chemistry and 78 in clinical medicine, practically precluding analyses across fields (Bornmann et al., 2008).

Citation counts are a function of field size

If you work in a small field (such as a rare medical condition, finely-specified disability, localized knowledge, small culture, minority interest, or technical specialty), you will have fewer things to cite and fewer people who can cite you. Yet the knowledge may be just as important and have a great impact within that area of knowledge. Low citation count, then, will be a function of the size of the field, not the impact of your work (Lawrence, 2008).

Framing knowledge futures

If today's knowledge systems are broken in places and on the verge of breaking in others, what, then, is to be done? Below, we present an agenda for the making of future knowledge systems which may optimize the affordances of the new, digital media.

Sustainable scholarly publishing

Beyond the open access/commercial publishing dichotomy, there is a question of resourcing models and sustainability. Academics' time is not best spent as amateur publishers. The key question here is how to build sustainable resourcing models which neither require cross-subsidy of academics' time, nor the unjustifiable and unsustainable costing and pricing structures of the big publishers. The challenge is to develop new business models, either in the form of academic socialism (institutional support for publishing by libraries or university presses paid for by government or institutions) or lightweight commercial models which do not charge unconscionable author fees, subscription rates or per-article purchase prices.

Guardianship of intellectual property

How does one balance academics' and universities' interest in intellectual property with the public knowledge interest? The 'gift economy' also supports a 'theft economy' in which private companies profit from the supply of content provided at no charge. Google copies content, mostly without permission and always without payment, and makes money from advertising alongside this content. The October 2008 settlement between Google and the Author's Guild, which distributes revenues from books Google has scanned in a number of US libraries, may create as many new problems as it solves older ones (Albanese, 2008). The key question here is how to establish an intellectual property regime which sustains intellectual autonomy, rather than a 'giveaway' economy which undervalues the work of the academy. Moreover, journal articles and scholarly monographs do not need to have one or other of the 'free' copyright licences upon which many of the new domains of social production depend, such as the Creative Commons licence (Lessig, 2001) that underwrites Wikipedia or the General Public License (Stallman, 2002a, 2002b; Williams, 2002) that locks free or open source software and its derivatives into communal ownership (Fitzgerald and Pappalardo, 2007). This is because authors are strongly named in academic knowledge regimes – the credibility of a work is closely connected to the credentials of an author, and copyright strengthens this claim to credibility. Furthermore, the imperatives of attribution and 'moral rights' are rigorously maintained through academic citation systems. A (re)user of copyrighted knowledge, conversely, has extraordinary latitude in 'fair use', quoting and paraphrasing for the purposes of review and criticism (see Chapter 8). A version of 'remix culture', to use Lessig's portrayal of the new world of digital creativity (Lessig, 2008), has always been integral to academic knowledge systems. However, to the extent that it is essential to build on the work of others, this is already built into conventional copyright regimes (Cope, 2001).

Moreover, private author-ownership is integral to academic freedom, where authors in universities are allowed to retain individual ownership of copyright of published works, but not the rights to patents or course materials (Foray, 2004). This is also why many open access journals retain traditional copyright licences. Moreover, academics are not necessarily good stewards of these copyrights, when for instance they hand over these rights for no return to commercial publishers who subsequently sell this self-same content back to the institution for which they work, and at monopoly prices. As universities take a greater interest in content production in the regime of academic socialism, they should in all probability take a greater interest in copyright, whether that be libraries managing repositories or university presses publishing content, which they can then make available for free or sell at a reasonable price.

Criterion-referenced review

What does it mean to do high-quality intellectual work? Rather than unstructured commentary, we should require referees to consider multiple criteria, and score for each: the significance of questions addressed, setting an intellectual agenda, rigour of investigation, originality of ideas, contribution to understanding, practical utility – these are some criteria that emerged in research as part of the UK Research Assessment Exercise (Wooding and Grant, 2003). Or, with a more practical text focus, we might ask referees to address systematically clarity of thematic focus, relationships to the literature, research design, data quality, development or application of theory, clarity of conclusions and quality of communication. Or, with an eye to more general knowledge processes, we might ask referees to evaluate a report of intellectual work for its specifically experiential, empirical, categorical, theoretical, analytical, critical, applicable and innovative qualities (Kalantzis and Cope, 2008). Clear disciplinary and metadisciplinary criteria will increase referees' accountability and give outsiders an equitable opportunity to break into insider networks.

Greater reflexivity and recursiveness in the peer-review process

Digital technologies and new media cultures suggest a number of possibilities for renovation of the knowledge system of the scholarly journal. Open peer review where authors and referees know each other's identities, or blind reviews that are made public, may well produce greater accountability on the part of editors and referees, and provide evidence of and credit the contribution a referee has made to the reconstruction of a text (see Chapter 3). Reviews could be dialogical, with or without the reviewer's identity declared, instead of the unidirectional finality of an accept/reject/rewrite judgment. The referee could be reviewed – by authors, moderators, or other third-party referees, and their reviews weighted to provide their accumulated, community-ascribed value as a referee. In addition, whether review texts and decision dialogues are on the public record or not, they should be open to independent audit for abuses of positional power.

A fluid process of incremental knowledge refinement

Instead of a lock-step march to a single point of publication, then a near-irrevocable fixity to the published record, a more incremental process of knowledge recording and refinement is straightforwardly possible in the digital era. This could even end the distinction between pre-publication refereeing and post-publication review. Re-versioning would allow initial, pre-refereeing formulations to be made visible, as well as the dialogue that contributed to rewriting for publication. Then, as further commentary and reviews come in, the author could correct and reformulate, thus opening the published text to continuous improvement.

More integrative, collaborative and inclusive knowledge cultures

Instead of the heroic author shepherding a text to a singular moment of publication, the 'social web' and interactive potentials intrinsic to the new media point to more broadly distributed, more collaborative knowledge futures. What has been called Web 2.0 (Hannay, 2007), or the more interactive and extensively sociable application of the internet, points to wider networks of participation, greater responsiveness to commentary, more deeply integrated bodies of knowledge and more dynamic, reflexive and faster-moving knowledge cultures.

More widely distributed sites of knowledge production

The effect of a more open system would be to open entry to the republic of scholarly knowledge for people currently outside the self-enclosing circles of prestigious research institutions and highly-ranked journals. Make scholarly knowledge affordable to people without access through libraries to expensive institutional journal subscriptions, make the knowledge criteria explicit, add more accountability to the review process, allow all-comers to get started in the process of the incremental refinement of rigorously validated knowledge, and you will find new knowledge – some adjudged to be manifestly sound and some not – emerging from industrial plants, schools, hospitals, government agencies, lawyers' offices, hobbyist organizations, business consultants and voluntary groups. Digital media infrastructures make this a viable possibility.

Globalizing knowledge production

Approximately one-quarter of the world's universities are in the anglophone world. However, the vast majority of the world's academic journal articles are from academics working in anglophone countries. A more comprehensive and equitable global knowledge system would reduce this systemic bias. Openings in the new media include developments in machine translation and the role of knowledge schemas, semantic markup and tagging to assist discovery and access across different languages. They also speak to a greater tolerance for 'accented' writing in English as a non-native language.

New types of scholarly text

J. C. R. Linklider (1965) wrote of the deficiencies of the book as a source of knowledge and imagined a future of 'procognitive systems'. He was anticipating a completely new knowledge system. That system is not with us yet. In the words of Jean-Claude Guédon (2001), we are still in the era of digital incunabula. Escaping the confines of print look-alike formats, however, expansive possibilities present themselves. With semantic markup, large corpora of text might be opened up to data-mining and cybermashups (Cope and Kalantzis, 2004; Sompel and Lagoze, 2007; Wilbanks, 2007).

Knowledge representations can present more of the world in a less mediated form in datasets, images, videos and sound recordings (Fink and Bourne, 2007; Lynch, 2007). Whole disciplines traditionally represented only by textual exegesis, such as the arts, media and design might be formally brought into academic knowledge systems in the actual modalities of their practice (see Chapter 18). New units of knowledge may be created, at levels of granularity other than the singular article of today's journals system – fragments of evidence and ideas contributed by an author within an article (Campbell, 2008), and curated collections and mashups above the level of an article, with sources duly credited by virtue of electronically tagged tracings of textual and data provenance.

Reliable use metrics

More and better counting is needed if we are to evaluate reliably the impact of published scholarly work. We need to review, not Thomson-selected citations or unreliably collected Google citations, but *every* citation. We could ask authors to tag for the kind of citation (agreement, distinction, disagreement, etc.) We could collect download statistics more extensively and consistently. We could ask readers to rate articles, and weight their ratings by their rater-ratings. We could ask for a quick review of every article read, and record and rate the breadth and depth of a scholar's reading or a reader's rating credentials. We could harvest qualitative commentary found alongside citations.

Reliable use measures

Instead of shortcuts to reading, we could ask scholarly evaluators to read whole texts alongside author exegeses and independent assessment of the impact of their ideas (Lawrence, 2008; Wooding and Grant, 2003). What did this research or these ideas actually do in a field? Instead of the dubious numerical proxies, we would ask the question directly – what was the actual impact of this intellectual work on the world?

If it is the role of the scholarly knowledge system to produce deeper, broader and more reliable knowledge than is possible in everyday, casual experience, what do we need to do to deepen this tradition rather than allow it to break, a victim to the disruptive forces of the new media? The answers will not only demand the development of new publishing processes. They will entail require the construction of new knowledge systems.

This inevitably leads us to an even larger question: how might renewed scholarly knowledge systems support a broader social agenda of intellectual risk-taking, creativity and innovation? How is renovation of our academic knowledge systems a way to address the heightened expectations of a 'knowledge society'? And what are the affordances of the digital media which may support reform?

Whatever the models that emerge, the knowledge systems of the near future could and should be very different from those of our recent past. The sites of formal knowledge validation and documentation will be more dispersed across varied social sites. They will be more global. The knowledge processes they use will be more reflexive and so more thorough and reliable. Knowledge will be made available more quickly. Through semantic publishing, knowledge will be more discoverable and open to disaggregation, reaggregation and reinterpretation. There will be much more of it, but it will be much easier to navigate. The internet provides us these affordances. It will allow us to define and apply new epistemic virtues. It is our task as knowledge workers to realize the promise of our times and to create more responsive, equitable and powerful knowledge ecologies.

Bibliography

Albanese, A. (2008) 'Harvard slams Google settlement; others react with caution', *Library Journal*, available at: *http://www.libraryjournal.com/article/CA6610115.html* (accessed 1 September 2008).

Bacon, F. (1620) 'The New Organon', available at: *http://www.constitution.org/bacon/nov_org.htm*.

Bauwens, M. (2005) 'The political economy of peer production', *CTheory*, available at: *http://www.ctheory.net/articles.aspx?id=499* (accessed 1 September 2008).

Benkler, Y. (2006) *The Wealth of Networks: How Social Production Transforms Markets and Freedom*, New Haven, CT: Yale University Press.

Bergman, S. S. (2006) 'The scholarly communication movement: highlights and recent developments', *Collection Building* 25: 108–28.

Bergstrom, C. T. and Bergstrom, T. C. (2006) 'The economics of ecology journals', *Frontiers in Ecology and Evolution* 4: 488–95.

Bergstrom, T. and Lavaty, R. (2007) 'How often do economists self-archive?', available at: *http://repositories.cdlib.org/ucsbecon/bergstrom/2007a/* (accessed 1 September 2008).

Berlin Declaration on Open Access to Knowledge in the Sciences and Humanities (2003) Available at: *http://oa.mpg.de/openaccess-berlin/berlindeclaration.html* (accessed 1 September 2008).

Bethesda Statement on Open Access Publishing (2003) Available at: *http://www.earlham.edu/~peters/fos/bethesda.htm* (accessed 1 September 2008).

Biagioli, M. (2002) 'From book censorship to academic peer review', *Emergences: Journal for the Study of Media & Composite Cultures* 12: 11–45.

Bornmann, L., Mutz, R., Neuhaus, C. and Daniel, H.-D. (2008) 'Citation counts for research evaluation: standards of good practice for analyzing bibliometric data and presenting and interpreting results', *Ethics in Science and Environmental Politics* 8: 93–102.

Brody, T., Carr, L., Gingras, Y., Hajjem, C., Harnad, S. and Swan, A. (2007) 'Incentivizing the open access research web: publication-archiving, data-archiving and scientometrics', *CTWatch Quarterly*, available at: *http://www.ctwatch.org/quarterly/articles/2007/08/incentivizing-the-open-access-research-web/* (accessed 1 September 2008).

Browman, H. I. and Stergiou, K. I. (2008) 'Factors and indices are one thing, deciding who is scholarly, why they are scholarly, and the relative value of their scholarship is something else entirely', *Ethics in Science and Environmental Politics* 8: 1–3.

Budapest Open Access Initiative (2002) Available at: *http://www.soros.org/openaccess/read.shtml* (accessed 1 September 2008).

Burnham, J. C. (1990) 'The evolution of editorial peer review', *Journal of the American Medical Association* 263, available at: *http://jama.ama-assn.org/cgi/content/abstract/263/10/1323* (accessed 1 September 2008).

Butler, L. (2008) 'Using a balanced approach to bibliometrics: quantitative performance measures in the Australian research quality framework', *Ethics in Science and Environmental Politics* 8: 83–92.

Campbell, P. (2008) 'Escape from the impact factor', *Ethics in Science and Environmental Politics* 8: 5–7.

Clarke, R. (2007) 'The cost profiles of alternative approaches to journal publishing', *First Monday* 12, available at: *http://www.uic.edu/htbin/cgiwrap/bin/ojs/index.php/fm/article/view/2048/1906* (accessed 1 September 2008).

Cope, B. (2001) 'Content development and rights in a digital environment' in B. Cope and R. Freeman (eds) *Digital Rights Management and Content Development, Vol. 2.4: Technology Drivers Across the Book Production Supply Chain, From the Creator to the Consumer*, Melbourne: Common Ground, pp. 3–16.

Cope, B. and Kalantzis, M. (2000a) *Multiliteracies: Literacy Learning and the Design of Social Futures*, London: Routledge.

Cope, B. and Kalantzis, M. (2000b) 'Designs for social futures' in B. Cope and M. Kalantzis (eds) *Multiliteracies: Literacy Learning and the Design of Social Futures*, London: Routledge, pp. 203–34.

Cope, B. and Kalantzis, M. (2004) 'Text-made text', *E-Learning* 1: 198–282.

Cope, B. and Kalantzis, M. (2007) 'New media, new learning', *International Journal of Learning* 14: 75–9.

Dewatripont, M., Ginsburgh, V., Legros, P. and Walckiers, A. (2006) *Study on the Economic and Technical Evolution of the Scientific Publication Markets in Europe*, Brussels: European Commission.

Edlin, A. S. and Rubinfeld, D. L. (2004) 'Exclusion or efficient pricing? The "big deal" bundling of academic journals', available at: *http://repositories.cdlib.org/blewp/art167/* (accessed 1 September 2008).

Evans, J. A. (2008) 'Electronic publication and the narrowing of science and scholarship', *Science* 321: 395–9.

Fink, J. L. and Bourne, P. E. (2007) 'Reinventing scholarly communication for the electronic age', *CTWatch Quarterly*, available at: *http://www.ctwatch.org/quarterly/articles/2007/08/reinventing-scholarly-communication-for-the-electronic-age/* (accessed 1 September 2008).

Fitzgerald, B. and Pappalardo, K. (2007) 'The law as cyberinfrastructure', *CTWatch Quarterly*, available at: *http://www.ctwatch.org/quarterly/articles/2007/08/the-law-as-cyberinfrastructure/* (accessed 1 September 2008).

Foray, D. (2004) *The Economics of Knowledge*, Cambridge MA: MIT Press.

Galloway, A. R. and Thacker, E. (2007) *The Exploit: A Theory of Networks*, Minneapolis, MN: University of Minnesota Press.

Ginsparg, P. (2007) 'Next-generation implications of open access', *CTWatch Quarterly*, available at: *http://www.ctwatch.org/quarterly/articles/2007/08/next-generation-implications-of-open-access/* (accessed 1 September 2008).

Grafton, A. (1997) *The Footnote: A Curious History*, London: Faber and Faber.

Guédon, J.-C. (2001) 'In Oldenburg's long shadow: librarians, research scientists, publishers, and the control of scientific publishing', available at: *http://www.arl.org/resources/pubs/mmproceedings/138guedon.shtml* (accessed 1 September 2008).

Hannay, T. (2007) 'Web 2.0 in science' *CT Watch Quarterly*, available at: *http://www.ctwatch.org/quarterly/articles/2007/08/web-20-in-science/* (accessed 1 September 2008).

Harnad, S. (2008) 'Validating research performance metrics against peer rankings', *Ethics in Science and Environmental Politics* 8: 103–7.

Harzing, A.-W. K. and Wal, R. van der (2008) 'Google Scholar as a new source for citation analysis', *Ethics in Science and Environmental Politics* 8: 61–73.

Horrobin, D. F. (1990) 'The philosophical basis of peer review and the suppression of innovation', *Journal of the American Medical Association* 263, available at: *http://jama.ama-assn.org/cgi/content/abstract/263/10/1438* (accessed 1 September 2008).

Husserl, E. (1970) *The Crisis of European Sciences and Transcendental Phenomenology*, Evanston, IL: Northwestern University Press.

Ioannidis, J. P. A. (2005) 'Why most published research findings are false', *PLoS Med* 2: 696–701.

Jefferson, T., Wager, E. and Davidoff, F. (2002) 'Measuring the quality of editorial peer review', *Journal of the American Medical Association* 287: 2786–90.

Judson, H. F. 1994. 'Structural transformations of the sciences and the end of peer review', *Journal of the American Medical Association* 272: 92–4.

Kalantzis, M. and Cope, B. (2008) *New Learning: Elements of a Science of Education*, Cambridge: Cambridge University Press.

Kapitzke, C. and Peters, M. A. (2007) *Global Knowledge Cultures*, Rotterdam: Sense.

Kousha, K. and Thelwall. (2007) 'Google Scholar citations and Google Web/URL citations: a multi-discipline exploratory analysis', *Journal of the American Society for Information Science and Technology* 58: 1055–65.

Kress, G. (2000) 'Design and transformation: new theories of meaning' in B. Cope and M. Kalantzis (eds) *Multiliteracies: Literacy Learning and the Design of Social Futures*, London: Routledge, pp. 153–61.

Lawrence, P. A. (2007) 'The mismeasurement of science' *Current Biology* 17: 583–5.

Lawrence, P. A. (2008) 'Lost in publication: how measurement harms science', *Ethics in Science and Environmental Politics* 8: 9–11.

Lee, K. and Bero, L. (2006) 'What authors, editors and reviewers should do to improve peer review', available at: *http://www.nature.com/nature/peerreview/debate/nature05007.html* (accessed 1 September 2008).

Lessig, L. (2001) *The Future of Ideas: The Fate of the Commons in a Connected World*, New York: Random House.

Lessig, L. (2008) *Remix: Making Art and Commerce Thrive in the Hybrid Economy*, New York: Penguin Press.

Linklider, J. C. R. (1965) *Libraries of the Future*, Cambridge, MA: MIT Press.

Lynch, C. (2007) 'The shape of the scientific article in the developing cyberinfrastructure', *CTWatch Quarterly*, available at: *http://www.ctwatch.org/quarterly/articles/2007/08/the-shape-of-the-scientific-article-in-the-developing-cyberinfrastructure/* (accessed 1 September 2008).

Mabe, M. A. and Amin, M. (2002) 'Dr Jekyll and Dr Hyde: author-reader asymmetries in scholarly publishing', *Aslib Proceedings* 54: 149–57.

McCabe, M. J., Nevo, A. and Rubinfeld, D. L. (2006) 'The pricing of academic journals', available at: *http://repositories.cdlib.org/blewp/art199/* (accessed 1 September 2008).

Meho, L. I. (2007) 'The rise and rise of citation analysis', *Physics World* 20: 32–6.

Meyers, B. (2004) 'Peer review software: has it made a mark on the world of scholarly journals?', available at: *http://www.editorialmanager.com/homepage/resources.html* (accessed 1 September 2008).

Morgan Stanley (2002) *Scientific Publishing: Knowledge Is Power*, London: Morgan Stanley Equity Research Europe.

Norris, M. and Oppenheim, C. (2007) 'Comparing alternatives to the Web of Science for coverage of the social sciences' literature', *Journal of Informetrics* 1(2): 161–9.

Opderbeck, D. W. (2007) 'The penguin's paradox: the political economy of international intellectual property and the paradox of open intellectual property models', *Stanford Law & Policy Review* 18, available at: *http://papers.ssrn.com/sol3/papers.cfm?abstract_id=927261* (accessed 1 September 2008).

Orsdel, L. C. Van and Born, K. (2006) 'Periodicals price survey 2006: journals in the time of Google', *Library Journal*, available at: *http://www.libraryjournal.com/article/CA6321722.html* (accessed 1 September 2008).

Orsdel, L. C. Van and Born, K. (2008) 'Periodicals price survey 2008: embracing openness', *Library Journal*, available at: *http://www*

.libraryjournal.com/article/CA6547086.html?q=periodicals+price+survey+2008 (accessed 1 September 2008).

Pauly, D. and Stergiou, K. I. (2008) 'Re-interpretation of 'influence weight' as a citation-based index of new knowledge (INK)', *Ethics in Science and Environmental Politics* 8: 75–8.

Pellegrino, J. W., Chudowsky, N. and Glaser, R. (2001) *Knowing what Students Know: The Science and Design of Educational Assessment*, Washington, DC: National Academies Press.

Peters, M. A. (2007) *Knowledge Economy, Development and the Future of Higher Education*, Rotterdam: Sense Publishers.

Peters, M. A., Marginson, S. and Murphy, P. (2008) *Creativity and the Global Knowledge Economy*, New York: Peter Lang.

Raymond, E. (2001) *The Cathedral and the Bazaar: Musings on Linux and Open Source by an Accidental Revolutionary*, Sebastapol, CA: O'Reilly.

Rowland, F. (2002) 'The peer-review process', *Learned Publishing* 15: 247–58.

Schroeder, R. (2007) 'Pointing users toward citation searching: using Google Scholar and Web of Science', *Libraries and the Academy* 7: 243–8.

Simons, K. (2008) 'The misused impact factor', *Science* 322(5899): 165.

Sompel, H. Van de and Lagoze, C. (2007) 'Interoperability for the discovery, use, and re-use of units of scholarly communication', *CTWatch Quarterly*, available at: *http://www.ctwatch.org/quarterly/articles/2007/08/interoperability-for-the-discovery-use-and-re-use-of-units-of-scholarly-communication/* (accessed 1 September 2008).

Sosteric, M. (1996) 'Interactive peer review: a research note', *Electronic Journal of Sociology*, available at: *http://socserv.socsci.mcmaster.ca/EJS/vol002.001/SostericNote.vol002.001.html* (accessed 1 September 2008).

Spier, R. (2002) 'The history of the peer-review process', *Trends in Biotechnology* 20: 357–8.

Stallman, R. (2002a) *Free Software, Free Society*, Boston, MA: GNU Press.

Stallman, R. (2002b) 'The GNU Project', available at: *http://www.gnu.org/gnu/thegnuproject.html* (accessed 1 September 2008).

Stanley, C. A. (2007) 'When counter narratives meet master nparratives in the journal editorial-review process', *Educational Researcher* 36: 14–24.

Suber, P. (2007) 'Trends favoring open access', available at: *http:// www.ctwatch.org/quarterly/articles/2007/08/trends-favoring-open-access/* (accessed 1 September 2008).

Todd, P. A. and Ladle, R. J. (2008) 'Hidden dangers of a "citation culture"', *Ethics in Science and Environmental Politics* 8: 13–16.

Wager, E. and Jefferson, T. (2001) 'Shortcomings of peer review in biomedical journals', *Learned Publishing* 14: 257–63.

Wilbanks, J. (2007) 'Cyberinfrastructure for knowledge sharing', available at: *http://www.ctwatch.org/quarterly/articles/2007/08/ cyberinfrastructure-for-knowledge-sharing/* (accessed 1 September 2008).

Williams, S. (2002) *Free as in Freedom: Richard Stallman's Crusade for Free Software*, Sebastapol CA: O'Reilly.

Willinsky, J. (2006a) *The Access Principle: The Case for Open Research and Scholarship*, Cambridge MA: MIT Press.

Willinsky, J. (2006b) 'The properties of Locke's common-wealth of learning', *Policy Futures in Education* 4: 348–65.

Wooding, S. and Grant, J. (2003) 'Assessing research: the researchers' view', Joint Funding Bodies' Review of Research Assessment, UK, available at: *http://www.ra-review.ac.uk/reports/* (accessed 1 September 2008).

3

Arguments for an open model of e-science

José Luis González Quirós and Karim Gherab

The road to digital scientific literature

The open access movement advocates free access to scientific publications. Some followers of the movement support the obligation to provide open access to all articles where the research has been supported by public funds (Harnad, 2006: 75; Sale, 2006: 94). The basic inspiration behind this movement is the idea that digital technology permits us to somehow get back the spirit that infused the origins of modern science – a dialogue between scientists without mediation or obstacles. The enormous development of science has required the presence of market entities capable of promoting, storing and distributing the growing mass of scientific information, but together with its undeniable advantages, this system has also created a good number of problems of all kinds, not least of which is the cost.

Following a series of meetings of open access promoters, there have been a number of public statements and recommendations which have set the standard of open access initiatives up to now. Two roads have been identified to reach the dream of full open access: the 'golden' road and the 'green' road (Guédon, 2004 316). The 'golden' road would have the journals themselves digitize their past and present publications, so that the electronic versions could be available at no cost to anyone wishing to read them. The 'green' road calls for scholars to store – or self-archive – their (usually) peer-reviewed pieces, in digital format, in institutional repositories, as the final step in their research efforts.

There are various issues related to self-archiving, including the fear of scholars not being given due credit, the violation of copyright laws (Harnad, 2006: 79), the need to make archiving mandatory (Harnad, 2006: 75; Sale, 2006: 94; also House of Commons, 2004: 93), and the use of incentives (Guédon, 2006: 32–3) to get scholars to store their work in institutional repositories. These are important issues to consider when thinking of open access projects involving digital repositories, whether institutional or subject-based.

It is quite understandable that publishers are reluctant to relinquish the subscription business model. As it is, they have managed to set in motion a model which is both efficient and profitable, and they cannot see clear reasons to let go of it, particularly when some of the reasons given by open access advocates may seem somewhat immature. But it is not just a question of economic interest. There are also scholarly interests involved. Current developments represent a very serious challenge to the established order; however, it should not be forgotten that this order is the result of many years' work and experience. In order to keep generating income on the 'golden' road, commercial journals have turned to the 'author-payment' model (House of Commons, 2004), in which the author who wishes for open access to their work (or usually, the institution funding this work) must pay the journal a certain amount: in the case of Springer Open Choice Program (see *http://www.springer.com/open+choice?SGWID=0-40359-0-0-0*), that amount may be as much as US$3,000 (Bailey, 2006: 24).

On the other hand, publishers, including the Royal Society of London (2005), warn that the 'green' road may include non peer-reviewed papers – a fundamental problem within our contemporary understanding of science. (It should be pointed out that, although itself a nonprofit entity, the Royal Society publishes an income-producing journal, the revenues of which are used to finance its inner functioning, as well as to prepare reports, offer scholarships, fund research and give awards.) Nevertheless, several prototypes of peer review have been tested since 1996 (Harnad, 1996), and presently there are proposals for several models of open peer-review (Swan, 2006: 6), a review model that shows the reviewers' objections online so that everybody can see them and comment or suggest what they see fit, until finally the reviewers reach a decision in the traditional way. The supporters of digital repositories mention other advantages of self-archiving scientific publications (Hajjem et al., 2005; Harnad and Brody, 2004; Kurtz and Brody 2006: 49; Lawrence, 2001).

A growing number of open access advocates think that 'golden' road and 'green' road are but stages on two paths leading to the same destination, in which journals will end up as a kind of file repositories, with a great number of added services.

Open access: from linguistic and disciplinary monopoly to the pluralism of languages and cultures

Any way you may look at it, the system of prestigious journals generates an artificial scarcity with undesirable effects. To demand a careful selection of what is published is not the same thing as holding that only the pieces that can be fitted into a finite number of prestigious journals deserve to be published. A hierarchical ranking of journals has a number of advantages, as it gives them financial autonomy and stimulates competitiveness, but it seems undeniable that in a context of fast-moving research, the preservation of such a system will force the exile to limbo, or the publication in low-impact journals, of pieces that in a period of less abundance of original work would undoubtedly have deserved a better fate. The Malthusian character of the system would be defendable if there were no alternatives, but it becomes absurd when there are other ways to publicize what does not fit into a system with obvious physical and functional limitations.

The existence of much more open publication repositories increases the possibilities of research and multiplies the significance of science. It could be argued that the proliferation of places in which science can be published will increase all kinds of risks, such as fraud, publication of irrelevant texts, etc. It is undoubtedly true that such risks exist, and would increase. But it is precisely an increase in risk, not a creation of new risks. For indeed, as we know, the traditional system of scientific publication, for all its virtues, is not free from these problems. We must trust that the various communities and institutions that will develop the new electronic repositories and journals will put in place adequate review and control systems, to compensate for the abovementioned increase in risk. But above all, we must be confident that by taking advantage of digital systems of search and recognition, the visibility of new contributions will be enormously enlarged.

Not only is this the case for prestigious journals in English relating to well-established research fields; such moves might have really decisive repercussions in other research sectors, such as journals in other languages (as significant as Russian, French, Spanish, Chinese or

German), in less established fields of research, and in the social sciences, humanities and interdisciplinary studies. All of these have in common a rather marginal situation, in contrast to the massive rock of more established, classical scientific research.

Many of the venues in which the work carried out in these sectors gets published are virtually inaccessible journals with a limited, local impact, and so cannot become a part of the 'Great Conversation' (to use an expression similar to Oakeshott's, so often mentioned by Rorty). The new digital scene cannot be a 'balm of Fierabras' (the magic ointment often mentioned in *Don Quixote*, which could supposedly heal any wound, similar to the American 'snake oil'), but it is clear that it will offer very interesting possibilities to publications that, as things are today, are stillborn in the presses (as Hume thought had they happened with the first edition of his *Treatise*).

For this kind of work, the system of digital publication may have substantial advantages: its abundance, accessibility and immediacy will significantly increase the impact of each publication. To give but one example, Mendel's writings probably would not have had to wait for years to be discovered by a curious biologist, had they appeared in a digital medium.

Granted, the abundance of voices makes for great noise. But that noise is already with us and does not seem likely to stop; nor does it seem reasonable to try to stop it. What the growth and maturity of new digital publication systems will provide is a new means to handle that noise, a new way to listen. Good indexes, by names and by subjects, will permit us to find easily what may interest us in that new ocean of knowledge. And a new system of reading records, critical notes, experts' opinions and so on, will inform us on what may be of interest for us in a much richer and more pluralistic way than the traditional system does.

As could be expected, the new technological systems, the digital universe, will give us a portrait of the research world much more like its contemporary reality than that suggested by the traditional system of great journals. Great journals have reached the limits of the printed world, which anyway will always end up as an encyclopaedic image of knowledge, a systematic portrait. The ideal image of that kind of representation is the interpretation of science offered by positivism, the Archimedean conception of science – tiered, hierarchical and reductive.

Such an idea of science may be defined by Sellars (1966: v, ix): 'Science is the measure of all things, of what is that it is, and of what is not that it is not'. This way of describing science requires that its written presentation be a figure of perfect geometry, in an intelligible, harmonic space with no room for error or dispute: science measures and decides, and there is no more to be said. There is some sociological translation of this in a hierarchical academy, in which honours are given through equally objective and precise methods, such as indexes of impact, awards and honours of all kinds, etc. It is of course an exaggeration, to say the least, and anyway it is a portrait that may have been a faithful representation of science in the beginning years of the last century, but certainly has nothing in common with our current world. Galison and Hacking, among others, have called attention to these kinds of new developments, this new diversity of science. Galison writes:

> I will argue this: science is disunified, and – against our first intuitions – it is precisely the disunification of science that brings strength and stability. This argument stands in opposition to the tenets of two well-established philosophical movements: the logical positivists of the 1920s and 1930s, who argued that unification underlies the coherence and stability of the sciences, and the antipositivists of the 1950s and 1960s, who contended that disunification implies instability. (Galison, 1997: 781)

On the other hand, as Hacking has argued, in our contemporary world:

> the ideal of science does not have to lead towards the majestic unity that the positivists dreamed of. It leads instead, as our very image of life does, to a plethora of research programmes and scientific projects, all competing among themselves. It is the image that science offers when it is observed most closely, with greatest attention to its development, as opposed to focusing on an idealistic image of excellence and purity. (Hacking, 1983: 218)

This ebullient image of current scientific activity, and even more, of contemporary discussion at all levels of rational thinking, no longer fits within the narrow limits of a printed universe. Digital technology may offer us a much truer image of the very complex reality of contemporary research, thinking and debate. Today it may seem we are entering chaos, and the preservation of what orderly spaces we have inherited may appear sensible, but there are no real grounds for fear. History shows that technological revolutions always appear as threats but end up settling as opportunities. It falls to institutions, scholars and companies to perfect the instruments needed to create the necessary order, and to take advantage of all the possibilities that the new publication systems offer, to allow an unprecedented enlarging of our perspectives, so that formless noise will permit us to hear the polyphony of new forms of knowledge, new science. It will be a new and powerful melody which will encompass contributions from places seemingly very distant from the centres of debate, publications in all languages, texts conceived in new and suggestive cultures, in different disciplinary matrices which at present we cannot even imagine.

Although the history of human discoveries shows an amazing variety of situations and resources around the creation of any fruitful knowledge, the tendency to systematize what we know with certainty invites us to do a logical reconstruction of the history of discoveries, which very often is far from looking anything like what really happened. It is not easy to exclude the notion of coincidence, chance, when looking at the course of human progress. Therefore, it is very likely that there have been as many lost occasions, at the very least, as casual successes; many findings that stayed beyond the reach of our hands due to sheer chance, unhappy chances in these cases.

This kind of speculation, by the way, goes against the impression that so many and such different thinkers have had at times, that we already know practically all there is to know. Historians tell us Aristotle was convinced of it. Closer to us, a century ago, physicists even thought the pretension of finding new fields could damage the dignity of science. Not long ago, for very different reasons, it became fashionable to talk about the 'end of science'. In any case, what we carry on our shoulders is so much that in many fields we move with difficulty. Digital technology can help us to carry that burden.

In many respects, science is a system, but for its creators it is, and should be, a nest of problems. Only as acquired knowledge can science be logically organized. It is a very important task, though perhaps secondary. The movement of time demands that we keep improving the looks of what may be called *normal science*, established knowledge. Be that as it may, it is a very restrictive view of that conquered territory to present it as ground on which we may travel easily, with the help of an organized set of sufficient, orderly and consistent plans. No matter how orderly, acquired science is a ground that can never be travelled without surprises. As a living, active city, science goes time and again back on its steps, buries its ruins and explores new avenues, institutions and constructions. Added to the conquest of what is yet unknown, this is highly problematic and demands arduous work. A static description of science, organized as an ideally perfect system, far from a growing city, might present the image of an abandoned graveyard. Good science is always an invitation to reconsider problems, to state them anew, to think for ourselves. As Feynman (1999: 24) liked to repeat, in science 'what is most interesting is that which does not fit, the part that does not work as expected'.

This kind of mismatch between what was expected and what surprisingly happens appears mainly when scientists work – as they do most of the time – in hitherto unknown fields, which they explore with the instruments discovered in other pursuits. Still, this kind of surprise abounds also when one goes back on what was supposed to be said, or on what is taken for granted, for common doctrine, and attempts to trace those ideas to their source. For that purpose, it is essential to have easy access to the relevant texts, in order to be able to compare what is written in them with what it is said they say. Such a return to the sources is a very interesting experience, especially important in the disciplines of the spirit, to use the old German term.

Digital technology can of course improve our access to any kind of sources, with hardly any restrictions, and it will permit us to enjoy, in a very short time, an immensely rich variety of sources that, though usually forgotten, are full of interest and opportunities for a great many studies. Besides this, the new technological environment may offer scholars an approach emphasizing the problems more than the system, revision more than confirmation, diversification more than methodological and disciplinary orthodoxy. A digital environment furthers a number of hybridizing processes which now and then may produce some monstrosity, but will also surely make for the existence of new viable and exciting variations.

Work with multidisciplinary sources, always fertile and innovative, will become a possibility, much more real than it has been up to now. Digital repositories are sure to offer many occasions to renew our thinking, and will help strengthen the tendency to learn from what others are doing, to listen to what others are saying, and to attempt hitherto unthinkable partnerships. The tree of knowledge grows and becomes more complex. Thanks to the new communications systems, we may accelerate the processes of multidisciplinary diversification and enrichment that are already beginning; we may more easily break through ideological bounds, language, space and time barriers, to get closer to the reality of a new Tower of Babel, where at long last we will be able to understand each other.

Strange as it may seem, objections to the presumed advantages of storing knowledge in new ways are almost as old as writing itself. Today, as we face an explosive expansion of the available information, as well as the breakdown of the rule-system developed during the nineteenth and twentieth centuries to rank and organize publications, and to index them for their preservation and use, the same objections appear again from those who try to discredit the possibilities for innovation that the use of digital technologies will bring. Such elitist thinking opposed first writing and then printing. Indeed, it echoes Don Quixote's madness. In *Vida de Don Quijote y Sancho* (I, XI), Unamuno's Quixote says, 'How true, Sancho, is what you say: that through reading and writing madness came into this world'. Likewise, in *El libro de arena*, Borges writes that 'the printing press ... is one of the greatest evils for man, because it has tended to multiply unnecessary texts'. These represent testimonies of a well-known reluctance which now reappears and tries to renew its arguments in the face of the new technological possibilities.

The Popperian model of knowledge

Trying to avoid the withering of critical spirit that the excessive self-complacency of neo-positivism might bring, the greatest wisdom of Popper's post-positivism lies in affirming that together with the objectiveness of knowledge, there must always be the tentativeness of conjecture, and that from a logical standpoint, scientific activity is best understood as an attempt to disprove ill-established beliefs, rather than as an attempt – inevitably very weak – to confirm more or less eternal, indisputable (presumed) truths. In an ideal (that is, simplified) presentation of science, Popper underlined that our efforts to understand reality are, as to their epistemic value, mere conjectures, and that the canonical scientific spirit should seek not to verify them – a goal we must in principle consider unreachable, as there is always something new, a beyond – but to test them through their courageous exposure to what the Austrian philosopher called 'falsification'. This means that conjectures should be contrasted through experimentation, analyses, debates, etc., that is, put through an ideally rational competition with alternative possibilities, taking care that opportunistic arguments or language traps do not undermine or undervalue circumstances and details that may be unfavourable. This is not to say, obviously, that the real activity of researchers should always follow the Popperian model: the reality of research is much richer, more complex and diverse than any program, no matter how reasonable. This presentation of science as a model inviting to heterodoxy, or at least not forbidding it, must be completed with another Popperian idea which calls for the value of objectivity and introduces equilibrium in the logic of the research system. This idea consists in assuming that the whole universe of conjectures, propositions, empirical data, arguments, disprovals, etc. forms an ideal whole that nobody can encompass totally, due both to the immensity of the sub-wholes that form it and to our own intellectual limitations. Still, that whole is an ideal frame of reference which allows us to place each document in a specific place. That place is indeed very poorly described if we refer to it through a merely thematic analysis. The fact is that any document has a plurality of meanings, it may be read in many ways, but ideally, all of them may somehow find their place in a logical universe such as Popper's World III.

This Popperian model describes very well the logical possibilities of the links between texts that digital technology permits. Any text is a specific theoretical choice among the myriad of existing possibilities, in order to say something consistent about some specific assumptions. There is never only one form to express that meaning, but, as it usually happens in research work, a network of relevant opinions (a well-catalogued network in a digital environment) will allow us to place the decisive points through the convergence of readers' judgments, critical reflections and text quotations. This logical model will be digitally captured in a series of tags, which may be grouped as the classic descriptions of the printed publication world have been grouped so far. However, these tags will be a lot less conventional, and a lot richer, than traditional cataloguing ones (González Quirós and Gherab Martín, 2006).

All comments about an interesting text may be used to tag its digital form, and will allow us to read any text in a much richer and enlightening context. The strong numerical identity of a digital text makes it possible to attach to it any number of texts to clarify and qualify it, without confusing readers. Any digital text may aspire to be a critical edition. Readers, colleagues, critics, scholars of all kinds, and librarians prepared to understand texts, will be able and forced to produce new alternative descriptions, and to perfect the contour of their cataloguing as they see fit.

The Popperian model of World III offers us an epistemological frame apt for any kind of discourse, and in the end will lead us to new forms of reading and writing science (González Quirós, 2008). To get there is not a matter of sheer technology, as practically all the necessary technology is already available. What is needed is to improve our institutions and to learn to manage the new systems with all the guarantees that may be necessary. When all of this starts to become a neatly defined reality, critical and sufficient readings of any text will be possible in easier and more complete ways, besides making access to any work much simpler and cheaper, as is already happening. And these advantages will allow researchers to concentrate on what really matters, in contributing something new and relevant.

Scholarly journals and e-science

The term 'e-science' was coined in the UK, together with a Grid computing project launched toward the end of last century. The Grid infrastructure was born as an answer to the need to develop distributed computing, to deal with the constant increase in data generation by the projects of so-called Big Science. The reason is sufficiently explained by Foster (2002: 42–3): the ratio of increase in storage, network and computing power was doubled every 12, 9 and 18 months, respectively. As the generation of data by Big Science and the computing needs relating to its simulations were pushing existing technological capacity to its limits, the obvious strategy was to take advantage of the fast technological progress of communication networks to make storage easier and, above all, to increase computing power.

Nowadays the 'term e-science is used to represent the increasingly global collaborations – of people and of shared resources – that will be needed to solve the new problems of science and engineering' (Hey and Trefethen, 2003: 809). It is then admissible to think of including digital libraries and repositories, as well as e-journals, as components to be added to those already considered typical of e-science, understood as Grid – that is, computers, databases, scientific instruments, sensors, ontologies, semantic webs, web services, computing and data visualization programs, and so on.

Journals are increasingly directing their readers to web pages in which researchers publicize the details of their experimental data. *Nature*, for instance, is already demanding that researchers attach such details through its website. But with the size some scientific instruments and experiments are reaching (especially in Big Science), the rate of growth of the mass of data to be collected and processed is really dazzling.

Where will all this data be stored? It used to be easy to include in a journal a bunch of data with a couple of graphs attached. Today, with Big Science, not only it would be absurd to include the enormous amount of data, but it would be possible to allow the readers of electronic journals to construct their own graphs, thanks to visualization programs available through web services. In a way, this step of providing the data through the web and letting users create their own graphs, instead of giving them to the reader as a finished product, shows the transformation of the kind of contents journals will have to provide in a not distant future: instead of products, they will offer online services, in accord with the progress of a service-oriented web, instead of an object-oriented web.

Electronic journals should therefore have access to the databases where the experimental results are, and to different kinds of online computing and visualization services, that is, web-based applications. These tools are offered by the Grid technology, using increasing numbers of web services interfaces, programs that electronic journals infrastructures should be able to seek and retrieve through internet. For this, electronic journals must adapt their computing resources to the Grid protocols of exchange and interoperability. This is because 'computing, storage and software are no longer objects that we possess, but utilities to which we subscribe' (Foster, 2002: 47).

Naturally, it would be financially impossible for journals to provide storage and long-term curation for the enormous amassing of data coming out of Big Science projects. These projects (as, for instance, CERN) collect data and store information in data warehouses and data marts, before the data can be consulted through graphic visualization programs (histograms, etc.), or used to carry out various simulations. In view of this, the best option for journals would probably be to make visualization tools available to researchers, or at least to offer easy access through their published stories, either to the sources where the relevant information is stored, or to data-mining services, to look for patterns or sequences that may be of interest. The adaptation of journals to the open protocols of the Open Archive Initiative, and of Grid, will then make it easy for authors (and readers) to link with the original data, the images or simulations they want to show. In addition, it will allow researchers to access data not only online, but also on time. Members who are leading large projects in the Grid community are aware of this possibility, and are betting on a future convergence:

> In addition, scientific research in many fields will require the linking of data, images and text so that there will be a convergence of scientific data archives and text archives...
>
> Scholarly publishing will presumably eventually make a transition from the present situation – in which the publishers own the copyright and are therefore able to restrict the group of people who can read the paper – to a model in which they are funded not

> for the paper copy but for providing a refereeing service and a curated electronic journal archive with a permanent URL. (Hey and Trefethen, 2003: 819)

> Ultimately, we can imagine a future in which a community's shared understanding is no longer documented exclusively in the scientific literature but is documented also in the various databases and programs that represent – and automatically maintain and evolve – a collective knowledge base. (Foster, 2005: 817)

Our Popperian model of World III may be interpreted along the lines of these forecasts. But a touch both epistemological and pragmatic must be added. Journals must become a crossroad of disciplines, a place where ideas and experimental data converge. Each idea and each relevant set of data will have its specific place in the Popperian jungle, so that future science historians will be able to evaluate minutely the extent to which a new set of experimental data was the cause of a change in theory, or a larger mutation, or even what we often term, somewhat metaphorically, a revolution. Future historians may also be able to evaluate more precisely any existing contrary influence. A growing interaction between online texts, data and simulations will show how science works. The interaction between theoretical changes and changes due to the 'independent life' of experiments will be easier to see if both are combined on the internet under the umbrella of an adequate epistemological model. Quite independently from the kind of publications the future may bring, any epistemological model should be open and all publications should find their inspiration in that ever-adapting model that the progress of the various disciplines will deliver.

Journals as innovation in assembly

How could the Popperian model, whose physical representation might be reasonably exercised by digital repositories, be made compatible with the preservation of the advantages that scholarly journals offer? Our proposal aims to make both perspectives compatible, and advocates using journals to the limit, in order to get from them the best they can offer. For that, we propose that any given piece may be reprinted by as many journals as may deem it necessary. Let us suppose that a digital repository publishes a mathematician's article presenting a new method to solve a differential equation that happens to be useful to approach problems both in astrophysics and in molecular biology. In this case, the piece should be published simultaneously in interested mathematics journals, and in astrophysics and molecular biology journals that may detect the news. This can be done in two ways:

- The first is to have the journals themselves detect new developments that might be of interest to their readers. For this, they would have to invest in efficient search and retrieval technologies, as well as trust in the action of their network of (scholarly) experts, who in a way would act as hunt-beaters, looking for potentially interesting pieces to publish. In a way, journals should invest both in automatic tools (technological infrastructure) and in an effective social network of scholars (human infrastructure), who will substitute for the current roles of referees.

- The second is to have the author give their piece directly to the journal, provided the former knows the potential impact of this work on other specific disciplines – not very likely, but still possible. In this case, traditional referees would act their usual way, with the difference that other referees might be doing the same work for other competing journals. Far from being a disadvantage, this would make for competition and some pressure to make the right choice.

The aim is to transform the way journals work, so that picking pieces would no longer be their main task – this would sooner or later be done reasonably well by the repositories – but to present integrating discourses focused on a problem to be solved. As opposed to an amalgam of pieces, a discourse has a specific aim. It presents a story both plural in its examples and integrated in its arguments, consistent in their ordering. The order of the pieces and their mutual interdependence will have clear reasons, and the success of the discourse will depend on the coherence of its contents. In other words, the aim of journals must be to decrease the entropy generated by digital repositories (whether institutional or disciplinary), and decrease the noise to the point where the researcher can 'hear' the essence of the message: a coherent, well expressed, and orderly discourse, with its pros and cons (if there are any), seeking to privilege knowledge above the mere selection of information. It is a formidable challenge, but the weapons offered by digital technology are also admirable.

In such a way, as several journals may offer the same pieces, the researcher will look in them for the underlying discourse, the unified discourse that the editorial board has prepared. That is, the reader will look for a 'photograph' of the present state of the art on some specific problem related to his/her discipline. And there is no doubt that the best strategy to get the best portrait of a specific branch of science is to have the best group of experts – a reliable editorial board.

Scholars will reward the journals whose editorial boards gather experimental data, graphs, articles and comments related to the solution of common problems, forming optimal discourses on a specific issue. By taking them to the limit of their possibilities, these journals will give the best of themselves in this digital era, an era we have yet barely entered.

The value of the pieces published in journals, then, will be not just the work of filtering and selecting done by the peers, but the relations and the correct ordering that the editors may bring to them. Given that space is not a limitation in the digital world – unlike the world of printed journals – then any electronic journal will be able to use and reuse pieces or the critiques of them as many times as it wants, should it benefit the discourse. Of course, peer review of each piece can be done by the traditional method, or else be open to new and more democratic proposals with the help of computing tools. Still, it will be the editorial board's responsibility to present an epistemological construct in agreement with objectivity and the current state of the question for the different chapters of normal science.

This reuse of scientific pieces by journals is what we call the *recycling industry*, or *secondary market*. This is a method that Tim O'Reilly, who has popularised the expression 'Web 2.0', has called 'innovation in assembly', by analogy with other industries in which value has shifted to the integration of components. Such is the case with older initiatives, such as PC making, or more recent initiatives such as Open Source, or the projects for web services where the scientific version is often known as 'Service-Oriented Science' (Foster, 2005); for further examples, see Gherab (2008). In his 'What is Web 2.0?', O'Reilly explains 'innovation in assembly' as follows:

> When commodity components are abundant, you can create value simply by assembling them in novel or effective ways. Much as the PC revolution provided many opportunities for innovation in assembly of commodity hardware, with companies like Dell making a science out of such assembly, thereby defeating companies whose business model required innovation in product development, we believe that Web 2.0 will provide opportunities for companies to

beat the competition by getting better at harnessing and integrating services provided by others. (O'Reilly, 2005)

Just as O'Reilly sees in Web 2.0 a promising future for companies, we believe our proposal opens the doors to a new way to improve the contents of academic journals, a new scientific communication which, to borrow O'Reilly's felicitous expression, will lead us to Science 2.0. No doubt, the resemblance to his arguments is not just in the terms, but arises from the fact that our idea of Science 2.0 shares several of the characteristics which are pushing to success many projects faithful to the principles of Web 2.0: accessibility, openness to participation, immediacy, innovation in assembly, competitiveness, social networks, technological infrastructure, recommendation techniques, and even the notion of discourse as a constantly-evolving entity, a kind of beta version that supposedly is getting ever closer to the desired scientific objectivity.

It is not clear how these changes could be introduced in sectors in which copyright and patents still play a crucial role for the industries involved. It is the case with the music, cinema, publishing, applied chemistry and medical industries, and there is a similar problem with disciplines such as applied biology or chemistry. Nevertheless, the sociology of science teaches us that the values of science, and the goods scientists trade, are essentially different from those of such sectors. The *good* scientists trade is none other that the search for *truth*, and their currency is the articles they publish. The *ethos* of science, as pointed out by Robert K. Merton (1973: 270), is composed of universalism and 'communism', among other things. Besides, scientists gain more prestige as the impact they have on their peers grows, and the only way for it to grow is through having their articles abundantly read and cited. Scientists will therefore not complain if their articles are published by several journals at the same time. On the contrary, they will be delighted. Furthermore, they will probably want to modify their texts to adapt them to the various kinds of readers they will be addressing. We will go into this question with more detail below.

Digital repositories as trading zones

We have spoken of reusing articles freely, but a word about how we think repositories should be organized is in order. To a certain extent, the digital repositories network is a physical representation of the Popperian model, a materialization of an abstract ideal that the recording of science should attempt to reach. We think that the concept of trading zone, introduced by Peter Galison (1997: 803–44) with regard to another issue and at a somewhat different moment, is a good way to see how digital repositories should be organized.

Galison talks about zones of trade, of exchange, between different scientific cultures, and borrows notions from anthropology to show the way in which a technical sub-language emerges, a kind of pidgin, which allows those cultures to understand each other and negotiate. These cultures are not necessarily different disciplines: they could be both part of the same discipline, for instance, theoreticians, experimenters and instruments-designers in the field of particles physics. After some time, new disciplines are born with more perfect languages, the creoles, which are cultural sub-products of the pidgins. These subcultures will eventually evolve their own journals, their scientific societies, their awards, their university courses, PhD programmes, etc.

Galison points to the statistical Monte Carlo method as the unifying element, the *pidgin/creole* that allowed scientists of such distant fields as meteorology, nuclear physics, computer science, and chemistry, to understand each other after the end of the Second World War, in order to reach a specific goal: to build the hydrogen bomb. The techniques of the Monte Carlo method became a trading zone, a space in which the scientists exchanged knowledge. What is more, the simulations that scientists came in time to develop with Monte Carlo methods, to forecast the consequences of the explosions – no doubt an unmanageable task with the differential equations of traditional mathematics – started to be perceived by many of the participants as real facts, that is, as if simulations were not mere representations, but somehow the true metaphysics beyond the curtains of the senses. The Monte Carlo method was harvesting successes in various disciplines and allowed scientists to jump more easily from one disciplinary field to another.

Digital repositories are gradually shaped by the participants' interventions, and become trading zones when scholars of different subcultures exchange files. They are a daily meeting point for the exchange of knowledge, with different sections for different kinds of products. They are markets in which scholars deposit, following specific self-archiving protocols, the products they want to show their peers. To create a link – a citation – to some article stored in a repository becomes a form of purchase: 'I buy you this idea', if it is a theoretical piece; 'I buy you these empirical results', in the case of experimental results (for instance, a database or a graph); or 'I buy you this instrument', if the object of interest is a new instrument, or a computing algorithm able, for example, to calculate or simulate a specific fold of a protein.

Citation indexing has become essential as a basic metrical element in the attempt to develop a science of science (scientometrics), but they are only one special case among the myriad marks and tags scholars can use to trade. Many of them are yet to be discovered, but others have already become subjects of study; for example, to count the number of downloads of an article from the internet. We would like to suggest for digital repositories the use of open tags, already abundantly used by successful projects in Web 2.0. Instead of following a hierarchical structure, like a taxonomy, the web is witnessing a sort of network-tagging, non-hierarchical but highly interdisciplinary, that has come to be known as 'folksonomy'. On the basis of the same principles used by the web, though more cautiously as science is one realm in which truth still has an almost incalculable value, we propose that articles stored in digital repositories be not tagged simply with metadata selected by the article's author, but that any number of scholars, in the same discipline or in others, may add tags as they see fit.

In this way, any specific article could be tagged in different languages from various disciplines, some seemingly very distant. Nowadays, a scientist who writes an article has to prepare an abstract and a set of keywords to go with it. When writing the abstract, the scientist knows very well who he is addressing, and takes care to use the appropriate language, with its familiar rhetoric, in order to capture the attention of the desired readers. Likewise, when choosing the keywords, he will employ terms and expressions typical of the specific discipline, a jargon he knows is used and will be easily recognized by his peers. And yet, that jargon may be hard to understand for a scholar from another discipline, or even from a different subculture within the same discipline. In many cases, the jargon of an academic community evolves very quickly, often depending on the degree and rate of progress in their discipline, perhaps in connection with new ideas, new phenomena or new instruments.

If we allow a scholar of discipline B to introduce new tags, with keywords more akin to his field, in an article written by a scholar from discipline A, we are making it easier for scholars of B to retrieve that article. Of course, we could create security belts so that in the first perimeter only the author can tag; in the second perimeter only scholars in field A can add keywords; in a third circle scholars of disciplines C and D – disciplines quite close in their practices, beliefs and goals – may be allowed to tag; next, fields E, F and G could have access, and so on to encompass all disciplines. In a way, this model will leave a trace of the epistemological development of science. Just as the Monte Carlo method simulations were seen as metaphysical representations of the problems the scientists were dealing with, the model of digital repositories we propose is a kind of simulation of the social relations activities conducted by scientists, a representation of interdisciplinary exchange of knowledge.

In fact, tags would become a sort of pidgin in those trading zones, a limited language which, given time, might become a kind of creole if a new discipline were to emerge from this market in which new ideas, languages, metaphors, techniques, practices, rules and beliefs have been traded. The aim of this 'mercantile exchange' is to solve specific problems, and the means used is the coordination of actions in an e-agora where interdisciplinary exchanges will be significantly easier than they are now.

Digital technology is highly malleable and will permit us to build any architecture we deem most adequate for the epistemological collaboration model we are trying to design. We might, for instance, give more weight to a tag edited by a recognized specialist, or we could open a full fan of different weights, depending on who is tagging, from what discipline the tagger comes, and so on, somehow like Google's PageRank gives more weight to the more reliable nodes (or websites). Combinations are potentially infinite and the choice will depend on our good judgment. Still, we must bear in mind that the choice of every key expression that tags an article will certainly be not just an epistemic decision, but will be explicitly or implicitly conditioned by a bunch of values, beliefs, wishes, etc. Some of the problems that plague printed journals will reappear, only differently, because the amount of information is vastly larger and the technological tools available are much better.

The role of journals will be precisely to eliminate the background noise, to decrease entropy. Focusing on problems instead of disciplines, the mission of scientific journals will be to watch over the presentation of an integrating discourse aimed at solving a specific concrete problem, if necessary including in their pages (printed or, preferably, electronic) articles, graphs and animation from various disciplines. To put it briefly, they should publish a coherently ordered selection of the state of the art on a given problem.

Continuing with the mercantile analogy, the repositories would be primary markets, and journals would play a more sophisticated role by selecting from that primary market the products best adapted to the deeper demands of their readers; a more demanding, competitive and expert market in their field. The journals would sell goods manufactured to certain specifications, and with a high level of quality. Paradoxical as it may seem, they would at once address the general public and be more selective. Furthermore, they would have great prescriptive value, as a primary market that is not integrated to the value chain would tend to be sterile, and would disappear.

In this way, the delay in the dissemination of results among the experts could be avoided, although the presentation of those results to the global village would surely fall to the great journals, which therefore would still have a great political value, because they would still manage the information able to attract the attention of large sectors of public opinion, and as a consequence, of businessmen and politicians. But the difference with what happens today would still be enormous. The risk of ignoring really valuable work would be greatly reduced, as would be the temptation to include mere 'big names'. Journals would stake their prestige almost on every number. Literally anyone can get into that secondary market, because the raw matter is abundant and cheap, and there would be great competition between new prescriptors and older, well-known prescriptors. If this set of changes would come to pass, we would undoubtedly witness a real institutional mutation, a new defeat to the mandarins, made possible by the powerful increase of basic science and the gigantic progress in the information distribution systems. Science would be democratized from below, and would become more international and more competitive. The significance and visibility of research would be enhanced, and its social influence would expand without jeopardizing the reliability and the honesty of its work.

Bibliography

Bailey Jr, C. W. (2006) 'What is open access?', in N. Jacobs (ed.) *Open Access: Key Strategic, Technical and Economic Aspects*, Oxford: Chandos Publishing, pp. 13–26.

Foster, I. (2002) 'The Grid: a new infrastructure for 21st century science', *Physics Today*, February, pp. 42–7.

Foster, I. (2005) 'Service-oriented science', *Science* 308: 814–17.

Galison, P. (1997) *Image and Logic. A Material Culture of Microphysics*, Chicago, IL: University of Chicago Press.

Gherab, K. (2008) 'Writing science in the 21st century: from technologies of recommendation to industries of innovative reuse', *The International Journal of Technology, Knowledge and Society* 4(6): 113–20.

Guédon, J. C. (2004) 'The "green" and "gold" roads to open access: the case for mixing and matching', *Serials Review* 30: 315–28.

Guédon, J. C. (2006) 'Open access: a symptom and a promise', in N. Jacobs (ed.) *Open Access: Key Strategic, Technical and Economic Aspects*, Oxford: Chandos Publishing, pp. 27–38.

González Quirós, J. L. (2008) 'La reinvención de las bibliotecas', *Revista de Occidente* 308: 81–95.

González Quirós, J. L. and Gherab Martín, K. (2006) *El templo del saber: hacia la biblioteca digital universal*, Barcelona: Deusto. [Published in English as *The New Temple of Knowledge: Towards a Universal Digital Library*, Altona, VIC: The University Press – Common Ground Publishing, 2008.]

Hacking, I. (1983) *Representing and Intervening. Introductory Topics in the Philosophy of Natural Science*, Cambridge: Cambridge University Press.

Hajjem, C., Harnad, S. and Gingras, Y. (2005) 'Ten-year cross-disciplinary comparison of the growth of open access and how it increases research citation impact', *IEEE Data Engineering Bulletin* 28: 39–47.

Harnad, S. (1996) 'Implementing peer review on the net: scientific quality control in scholar electronic journals', in R. Peek and G. Newby (eds) *Scholarly Publishing: The Electronic Frontier*, Cambridge, MA: MIT Press, pp. 103–18.

Harnad, S. (2006) 'Opening access by overcoming Zeno's paralysis', in N. Jacobs (ed.) *Open Access: Key Strategic, Technical and Economic Aspects*, Oxford: Chandos Publishing, pp. 73–86.

Harnad, S. and Brody, T. (2004) 'Comparing the impact of open access (OA) vs non-OA articles in the same journals', *D-Lib Magazine*, available at: *http://www.dlib.org/dlib/june04/harnad/06harnad.html* (accessed 27 February 2009).

Hey, T. and Trefethen, A. (2003) 'The data deluge: an e-Science perspective', in A. F. Berman, G. Fox and A. J. G. Hey (eds) *Grid Computing: Making the Global Infrastructure a Reality*, Chichester: John Wiley and Sons, pp. 809–24.

House of Commons – Science and Technology Committee (2004) *Scientific Publications: Free for all?*, Tenth Report of Session 2003–04, Volume I: Report, London: Stationery Office.

Kurtz, M. and Brody, T. (2006) 'The impact loss to authors and research', in N. Jacobs (ed.) *Open Access: Key Strategic, Technical and Economic Aspects*, Oxford: Chandos Publishing, pp. 45–54.

Lawrence, S. (2001) 'Free online availability substantially increases a paper's impact', *Nature*, available at: *http://www.nature.com/nature/debates/e-access/Articles/lawrence.html* (accessed 27 February 2009).

Merton, R. K. (1973) *The Sociology of Science: Theoretical and Empirical Investigations*, Chicago, IL: University of Chicago Press.

O'Reilly, T. (2005) 'What is Web 2.0? Design patterns and business models for the next generation of software', available at: *http://www.oreillynet.com/lpt/a/6228* (accessed 27 February 2009).

Royal Society (2005) 'Royal Society warns hasty "Open Access" moves may damage science', available at: *http://www.royalsoc.ac.uk/news.asp?id=3881* (accessed 27 February 2009).

Sale, A. (2006) 'Researchers and institutional repositories', in N. Jacobs (ed.) *Open Access: Key Strategic, Technical and Economic Aspects*, Oxford: Chandos Publishing, pp. 87–98.

Sellars, W. (1963) *Science, Perception and Reality*, London: Routledge and Kegan Paul.

Swan, A. (2006) 'Overview of scholarly communication', in N. Jacobs (ed.) *Open Access: Key Strategic, Technical and Economic Aspects*, Oxford: Chandos Publishing, pp. 3–12.

Part II
The journals business

4

Business models in journals publishing

Angus Phillips

Journals publishing is big business. The total value of the journals market in 2006 was estimated as £7 billion (Richardson, 2007). Globally there are around 23,700 peer-reviewed journals available, 1.92 million researchers producing articles, and 1.59 million new articles are published each year (RIN, 2008). Between 0.5 and 1 per cent of expenditure by universities is on journals. This chapter examines the current business models in journal publishing, from subscription to newer, open access models, and analyses the dynamics of this profitable and fast-moving area of publishing. Examining how the business models are evolving will also shed light on the future of the journals business.

The characteristics of the journals business

Journals have traditionally been a highly profitable sector of publishing. Whereas there is often considerable uncertainty over how many copies of a book will be sold, journals sold on subscription exhibit a high degree of reliability for sales forecasting as well as predictable cash flows. For example, as *The Economist* has said, 'If a company owns the must-read title in, say, vibrational spectroscopy, it has a nice little captive market' (5 December 2001). Fixed costs tend to be higher than in other publishing sectors and, given that it takes time to establish a journal's reputation, this means that the period necessary for a journal to break even can extend up to five to seven years. However, the feature of high fixed costs also underpins the sector's profitability as once those costs are exceeded, the profit margins can be extremely healthy. Typical margins can exceed 30 per cent.

Journals are also less price-sensitive than some other forms of publishing. According to a Morgan Stanley research report on the industry:

> The scientific journal business is characterised by relatively inelastic demand, with individual journals generally having a strong following within their particular niche ... since 1986 the average price of a journal has risen by 215 per cent while the number of journals purchased has fallen by only 5.1 per cent. (Morgan Stanley, 2002: 2)

This has also been noted by Page et al. (1997: 281), who write: 'it appears that the price of a journal has only a very small effect on the sales of that journal'. A reflection of the sector's overall profitability is that journal publishers tend to be bought and sold for relatively high multiples of the sales revenues. For example, Eric de Bellaigue (2004: 222) describes Cinven and Candover's acquisition of Wolters Kluwer's academic publishing assets (with a multiple of four times sales) in 2002 as 'a vindication of the attractions of a business that is cash generative, judged to be relatively immune to economic fluctuations'.

Another characteristic of the journal business is that many companies have moved towards a service model as opposed to a product model. Subscribers have 24/7 access, remote access, sophisticated search facilities, and access to aggregated content. Online publication means that publishers know who their customers are and can measure levels of satisfaction with the service offered, whereas previously with print publication they dealt with key intermediaries such as the subscription agents.

Journal publishers also have to offer an efficient service to their authors. Typically, neither authors nor the reviewers of individual papers receive payments for their contributions to journals. Editors of high-status journals may be paid and/or receive a contribution to their office costs. Traditionally, page charges have been paid by authors, although this practice is less common than previously.

It is estimated that around 90 per cent of journals in English are now available online: 84 per cent of journals in the humanities and social sciences, and 93 per cent of scientific, technical and medical (STM) titles (Cox and Cox, 2006). Many libraries still prefer to have print copies as well as online access, partly for security of archiving, but over time there has been movement towards online-only subscriptions. Users now expect this form of access, and with libraries keen to save on shelf space, there are benefits to all parties. It has been estimated that 'the profitability of a customer improves by 15 per cent as they transfer from paper and on-line subscriptions (most pay for both currently) and opt for just on-line access' (Morgan Stanley, 2002: 2). In the UK the issue is clouded by the addition of VAT to online products but not to print/online combined products.

The lifecycle of a journal

There are risks to the launch of a new journal and it may take several years for a new journal to break even. At present the area of humanities and social sciences is seen as attractive for the launch of new journals, with some parts of the sciences seen as relatively saturated. A new journal concentrating on a smaller subject area may spin off from a title with broader coverage. A strong brand (*Nature* is a good example) may help the launch of other titles. Ulrich's data for the period from 2000 to 2004 show that 1,925 new STM journals were launched, of which 1,850 were still active in the spring of 2007 (Amin, 2008). According to data from 2005 to May 2007, a total of 1,256 STM journals were launched. The top ten publishers accounted for 56 per cent of the journals started in this period; in total 120 publishers were involved in journal launches.

Typically it may take five years for a journal to become profitable – cover its costs – and longer to provide a return on the initial investment. Break-even is taking longer to achieve than previously, with the average period having increased from three to five years to five to seven years, as it takes longer to establish new titles in the market (Bannerman, 2008). 'The third year is often a critical milestone in terms of both sufficient subscriber growth and high quality article submissions to enable publishers to assess the title's likely success or failure' (EPS, 2006: 56).

Edlin and Rubinfeld comment on the concentration of ownership in the industry and the development of the so-called 'Big Deal': 'Bundling can be seen as a device that erects a strategic barrier to entry. At a simple level of analysis, the Big Deal contracts leave libraries few budgetary dollars with which to purchase journals from new entrants' (Edlin and Rubinfield, 2005: 441). There are definite advantages to bundling in terms of the range of journals offered, but in the view of librarians, it then becomes difficult to vary or withdraw titles (Fowler, 2008). In universities, courses may change or even be dropped from the course portfolio, but under the terms of the institutions' agreement with publishers, the journals portfolio cannot easily be altered to match these changes. Withdrawing the whole bundle would be deeply unpopular, as the journals have entered the catalogue and users expect these titles to be available. In any case, libraries are not immediately able to adopt new journals as it takes time to alter their budgets. Taking on a new journal often means cancelling an existing subscription. The open access model does provide a way to break into a market with a new title, and this advantage can be mimicked by publishers offering new titles for free within a larger bundle for the first two years. But librarians are faced with another difficulty regarding open access journals – which ones should they catalogue? How much time and expense should be invested in this process?

Journals are typically reviewed five years after launch to assess their long-term viability. They will be assessed on their intellectual health – e.g. usage rates, impact factors, rejection rates – as well as their financial health. Those journals which are made available as part of bundled deals, in addition to separate subscriptions, may be able to survive on a circulation of a few hundred.

Pricing

The price of an individual journal when newly published will be set in line with the market, for example competing titles. The publisher has to adopt the most effective strategy to get the title established and build market share. Over time, however, what happens to journals pricing? If demand is price-inelastic – less sensitive to price changes – then publishers can simply push up prices in response to cost pressures and maintain their profitability.

According to the 2008 Research Information Network report:

> The journal market is, in economic terms, unusual in that the reader in the faculty or corporation may select or recommend the titles that are acquired, without having to bear directly the cost of acquisition. So the purchase is made by the library, which has the budget, but is driven by the requirements of its readers. Price signals do not reach the ultimate consumer – the reader. In such an environment, pricing is generally geared closely to the cost of producing the journal. (RIN, 2008: 16)

As institutions have opted to buy bundles of journals, they have become interested in the value gained from a subscription, such as the number of titles included and the terms of access. Publishers would argue that increased value has been provided as titles are bundled together, page extents have increased, and search functions have been greatly improved. Overall, journals are much more readily available. A journal that would have been bought by about 500 libraries in the early 1990s is now available in about 7,000 libraries (Campbell, 2008).

The journals industry saw large price increases up to the turn of the last century:

> throughout the 1980s and 1990s, the prices of journals were increased year on year well above the rate of inflation. The increases were particularly dramatic in what is broadly described as the STM (scientific, technical and medical) field, but the cost of journal subscriptions has increased significantly in the social sciences and humanities as well. (Thompson, 2005: 99)

Tenopir and King (2000) report that the average price of a journal was $284 in 1995 compared with $39 in 1975, over seven times higher; when adjusted for inflation, this represents a 2.6-fold price increase.

More recently, journal prices in the UK rose by 39 per cent between 2000 and 2006, while inflation during this period was 16 per cent. 'On average, periodical prices have risen faster than inflation in the UK; however this is a very crude measure, taking no account of the relative value in terms of journal size or quality' (White and Creaser, 2007: 4). Niche journals tend to have higher prices (arising from a lower subscriber base); higher circulation journals will have lower prices and are more likely to have advertising income.

There are pricing variations between disciplines, reflecting differences in funding and the necessity for scientific researchers to have the latest research. Table 4.1 shows price differences between a selection of academic disciplines.

Consolidation among the publishers in the journals market, and the price inelasticity of the market, have given publishers considerable power to raise their prices. By way of response, the development of library consortia has strengthened the hands of the purchaser in any negotiation over pricing. Price increases on bundles may be capped for a certain period. The open access debate has also cast a spotlight on journals pricing and the value offered. When considering the value to their institutions of bundles or site licences, librarians now have a greater set

Table 4.1 Journal pricing by discipline

Subject	Average price per title ($)	Change in price 2004–2008 (%)
Chemistry	3,490	35
Physics	3,103	30
Biology	1,810	40
Astronomy	1,671	32
Mathematics & Computer Science	1,411	27
Business & Economics	897	32
Political Science	541	48
Law	275	39
Language & Literature	221	39
Music	161	60

Source: Van Ordsel and Born (2008).

of metrics at their disposal, including usage rates. The variation in journal pricing between commercial publishers (higher) and non-profit publishers (lower) has been documented, but as King and Alvarado-Albertorio (2008: 262) note, this does not take account of the value given by the bundled deals put together by the large commercial publishers. Examining the price of an individual journal has become less relevant if it is a title that is commonly available as part of a bundle. Publishers would prefer to concentrate on other measures, such as the average price of each download by a user, which has been falling as usage has risen sharply. At Elsevier, the average price paid per article download in 2008 was around $2.00 (Amin, 2008).

Cost structure

The costs of publishing a journal can be divided into fixed and variable elements. The fixed elements, which will not vary according to the number of subscribers, include editing, the costs of peer review, typesetting and the costs of an online platform. At the Canadian not-for-profit publisher, NRC Research Press, the costs of copy-editing rose by 160 per cent between 1986 and 2001, and the costs of peer review by 117 per cent (Holmes, 2004). At Taylor & Francis, their fastest-growing cost line is payments back to the academic community, to support office and other costs for journal editors. This has risen faster with the increased use of full economic costing by universities (Bannerman, 2008). Some publishers have achieved cost savings by outsourcing the production route to external suppliers, perhaps in India, which carry out a variety of activities including copy-editing, typesetting and project management. Variable costs, which are dependent on the number of subscriptions to a journal, cover the printing and mailing of print copies and any extra costs associated with additional electronic subscriptions. With online delivery, variable costs tend to be lower (partly because the cost of printing, if any, is shifted to the end user), but the fixed costs are significant. An online environment requires skilled IT staff, an enhanced sales function, and customer service that supports 24/7 delivery. Again at NRC Research Press, five support staff were taken on over time as the publisher moved to electronic delivery; extra to this comes the purchase (and replacement) cost of hardware and software. It is reported that ScienceDirect, the online platform from Elsevier, cost around £200 million to establish (Clarke, 2007).

In journals publishing, the proportion of fixed costs is high, with estimates of between 60 and 80 per cent. Over the long term this is likely to lead to higher profits, once a title has become established. But if the number of subscribers starts to fall, there is a greater risk of a loss being made, and prices have to rise. Fixed costs are independent of the business model.

Fixed costs are also called first-copy costs and there has been much discussion over their level per article. This has become important to the debate over open access and the level of fee that needs be charged in the author-pays model of publication. There are differing estimates for the level of first-copy costs from between $250 to $2,000 per publisher article – up to around $4,000 or even $8,000 (King, 2007; Wellcome, 2004). The variations can be explained by a number of factors. For example, the costs of peer review will be higher in a high-quality journal with a high rejection rate (up to and exceeding 90 per cent). Again, high-quality journals will have higher editorial and administrative costs, and each issue may include more editorial copy, comment and news. Most recently, the RIN report suggested a figure of £1,136 for the average first-copy publishing cost (rising to £2,331 if the non-cash costs of peer review are included; RIN, 2008: 35).

By moving to purely online delivery, obviating the costs of print publication, the costs of publication will be reduced. A JISC study of learned society publishers revealed a likely reduction in cost per page from £144 to £97 for an average article length of 9.8 pages (2004 figures from Waltham, 2006: 96). For some journals struggling to remain viable, this is a possibility. But the market may still expect print publication as there is the problem of archiving:

> Until librarians are convinced that the archiving problem has been satisfactorily solved, many will continue to insist on receiving hard copies of each issue as well as access online and the economies that could be achieved by moving entirely into an online environment – both in terms of production costs and in terms of shelf space – will not be realized. (Thompson, 2005: 323)

Some markets, for example Australia, are more receptive to online-only publication; the situation in the UK is complicated by the VAT applicable to digital but not print products (Bannerman, 2008).

Subscription model

The predominant business model in journal publishing remains one of subscription. The majority of subscriptions are taken out by institutions rather than individual subscribers, and there has been a steady decline in the take-up of individual subscriptions, which are price-sensitive (Tenopir and King, 2000). The major development in recent years has been the bundling of subscriptions together – to offer digital access to a number of titles – and the availability of site licences to institutions. This has provided subscribers with a range of content, and publishers have sought to add value to these bundles by increasing the number of titles and pages available. Bundles have been described as 'a near ubiquitous feature of the research library collection' (Hahn, 2006). In 2006, 93 per cent of US research libraries held bundles with at least one of the top five publishers, and three publishers (Wiley, Elsevier and Springer) had over 70 per cent market penetration. In this market, 82 per cent of bundles were acquired through consortia. The subscription model has the considerable benefit for the publisher of predictable advance income. For the subscriber working within a fixed budget there is also a predictable cost – in comparison with a pay-per-view model, for example.

Yet Toby Burrows talks of bundling as a 'Faustian bargain' with a trade-off between access to a higher number of journals and greater rigidity in the system. He writes:

A recent survey of members of the Association of Research Libraries (ARL) shows very clearly what the trade-offs have been. Multi-year contracts are common, with 76% of those in the survey extending for three years or more. Nondisclosure agreements are also frequent, with 61% of libraries having signed at least one such agreement, forbidding them to discuss the terms and prices of the contract. Bans or limitations on cancellations during a contract are also common, with only 3% of agreements allowing the libraries complete freedom to cancel titles and clear evidence that titles in bundles are being protected during cancellation projects. (Burrows, 2006)

Could extra elements of flexibility within the bundled contracts be attractive to libraries, or will their users simply expect that the list of titles can only continue to expand?

Alternative business models

What alternatives are there to the traditional subscription model for journals? Some publishers already operate pay-per-view (PPV) services and this can provide useful additional income. In theory, increased online access should mean there is less need for users to purchase articles individually, but this market remains healthy. Users searching on Google may come across articles not readily available to them and decide they are worth the one-off purchase. For most publishers this income will rarely exceed 10 per cent of revenues – as Ian Bannerman (2008) has commented: 'We are not quite in iTunes territory'. But could a more systematic PPV model enable libraries and other institutions to monitor usage rates of journals and assess better which journals should be kept and which should be weeded out? Would it be a welcome antidote to the continuous growth of journal collections? Or does the subscription model continue to win out for its predictability? JISC-sponsored trials in 2006 looked at the possibilities of PPV. The final report concluded:

A pricing model which simply applies a fixed charge for every fulltext article downloaded by users across an institution presents far too much risk and uncertainty in terms of library budgeting. It has been shown in the trials that overall annual expenditure can be very significantly higher compared with using more traditional pricing models. (JISC Collections, 2007: 13)

Advertising is another source of income for some journals. A prominent scientific journal such as *Nature* has the ability to command substantial revenues, but for most publications the opportunities are more limited. None of the leading publishers have advertising revenues that exceed 9 per cent of total income (Outsell, 2007: 4). This has the advantage of shielding journals from the dips in advertising income that affect the fortunes of the magazine market, for example. But as online advertising revenues grow, are there new opportunities for journal publishers? Subject portals could potentially attract advertising revenues, although the level of income will vary according to the discipline. OncologySTAT (*www.oncologystat.com*) is an online resource from Elsevier in the area of cancer care. Access is free once a user has registered, and revenues come from online advertising, sponsorship and education grants. Some are doubtful about the possibility of simply transferring print advertising online.

With journals moving steadily towards online-only publication, there remains the option of print-on-demand to provide additional revenues or to aid start-up journals. Themed collections of journal articles may be given ISBNs and published in print or as PDF downloads. Publishers such as Hindawi use print-on-demand to lower the investment risk of starting up new journals. (Wilson-Higgins and Bernhardt, 2008)

Other innovative ideas include the use of Second Life by *Nature*, which has a presence in the virtual world and is marketing virtual meeting rooms and conference facilities, and inviting sponsorship.

Open access

The arrival of open access has formed a significant challenge to the status quo in journals publishing, forming a threat to the reliable business models of journals publishers. Open access can be viewed as a profound philosophical challenge or, as Sally Morris states in Chapter 19, just another business model. Experimentation with open access continues by both new entrants and the established players. On the face of it, a not-for-profit model should lead to lower costs. There are lower transaction costs involved, even if under the author-pays model, payments have to be collected from authors (with the risk of bad debts). Although a surplus may be required to supply investment funding, there is not the necessity to provide a return for the owners of the company. In terms of the income that open access journals attract, this can come from the authors, their institutions, or the relevant research funding bodies. The attraction of author payments as a business model is that break-even should come much sooner, rather than having to wait for a title to command sufficient subscriptions. An author-payment model may, however, put off some contributors, and as Claire Bird comments:

> The journal business model is therefore turned on its head, from 'reader-side payment' to 'author-side payment'. It seems immediately clear that this kind of model may only be viable in certain disciplines where authors have access to funds for publication. (Bird, 2008)

There are a number of variations on open access, from the 'gold' route (funding from a research body or the author's institution) to the 'green' route (the author self-archives the article, as preprint or postprint, in a subject-based or institutional repository). Although some journals may be fully open access, commercial publishers are commonly operating hybrid models, through which the author can pay for open access on publication, with their article appearing alongside content that is not open access. There may be a discount on the payment from the author if they are based at an institution with a subscription to the journal. The subscription price of the journal may also be reduced as open access content increases. It is estimated that less than 1 per cent of peer-reviewed articles are presently published in open access journals under the author-pays model. There are other forms of open access, including delayed open access (around 6 per cent of articles), which is common in society journals, and open archiving (around 7 per cent) (Amin, 2008).

Most commentators think it is too early to say how effective the open access model will become. There is evidence of falls in income for publications that go fully open access, and this has persuaded many publishers to opt for the sponsorship model – authors can pay for open access at the time of publication. As open access journals become more successful, it is entirely possible that their costs will rise accordingly with the costs of peer review.

If most authors decide not to go down the open access route, is it due to lack of funds or their uncertainty over what to some appears to be vanity publishing? Mary Waltham (2006: 124) comments on the uptake of open access: 'Within certain disciplines there may be some resistance to shifting to a producer pays model because of enduring scholarly traditions and/or questions of quality'. The research company Outsell comments on the open access business model:

> a useful way to think about open access publishing is to consider it in the context of a basic shift in business models that is mandated by a move from a journal economy of scarcity (the print world) to a journal economy of plenty (the online world) ... the very nature of the new media has begun to assert itself, and everything, including the subscription business model, is in question as completely new players flood the market with free content, new forms of content, advertising-supported business models, and unique ways of creating content that bypass many traditional processes. (Outsell, 2006: 3)

Traditional publishers would respond that in the face of this flood of free content, it is ever-more important for branded, peer-reviewed journals to offer quality assurance to their authors and readers.

Future of business models

For the moment, the most sustainable business model for journals remains subscription. Advertising does not form a significant source of revenue and it poses difficulties for publishers who wish to move to online-only delivery, as the business may not simply transfer online. Pay-per-view does not offer the budgetary reliability of the subscription model, whether to the publisher or the customer. Costs can be reduced by moving to electronic-only publication, and this will be a growing trend, as can be seen with new journal start-ups. Johnson and Luther predict that:

> As the opportunity cost of continuing to invest in print becomes too great, online will be the growing focus of publishing processes. Except for top-tier, broad circulation titles – which sometimes are used more like magazines – surviving printed editions may become mere add-ons available via print-on-demand. (Johnson and Luther, 2007: 2)

Open access models have a number of variants. There remain questions about the financial sustainability of these models. Commercial publishers have experimented with hybrid models but their success remains limited. There is no doubt, however, that open access can provide marketing benefits, for example to aid market penetration for a new journal or to encourage usage of subscription journals. Berkeley Electronic Press has found that allowing non-subscribers to read articles for free as guests helps to drive sales of subscriptions, with guest access accounting for 75 per cent of their subscription sales. In order to access the free content, guests have to fill in a short form which allows the publisher to inform their library of their interest in the journal (Perciali, 2008). Open access publication also serves to support the long tail of journals publishing – those niche journals which cannot survive as commercial publications.

A possible future trend is a reversal of the bundling model or at least the offer of greater flexibility by publishers. When licensing e-books, librarians are keen to avoid a similar structure, preferring to go with a particular platform and then choosing which titles are relevant.

Theodore Bergstrom asked why profits remain high in the journals industry:

> There is free entry to the journal publishing industry. Libraries are not compelled to subscribe to expensive journals, and scholars are not compelled to write for them, referee for them, or edit for them. Why has competition not driven profits to zero? (Bergstrom, 2001: 189)

Part of the answer, as he himself acknowledges, is the strong reputation of the established journals: authors prefer to publish in them, and scholars and professionals want their institutions to subscribe to them. This is reflected in the time it takes to establish a new journal and for it to become profitable. Bergstrom argues that the 'academic community is stuck in an equilibrium where it will continue to pay huge rents to owners of commercial journals' (Bergstrom, 2001: 192).

How will open access affect business models? An increase in self-archiving, for example, might lead to a diminished demand for subscriptions if students and researchers can find articles from other sources. Beckett and Inger (2006), surveying librarians internationally, found that only 38 per cent believe that publishers should not worry about libraries cancelling subscriptions because of repositories. The open access model has certainly provided a challenge to the equilibrium in the industry, but so far has not fundamentally shaken its structure. It is certainly less of an option in subject areas which are not so well funded, for example in the arts and humanities. Many publishers assert that the health of the journals industry is a reflection of the commercial discipline and entrepreneurship within the industry. The continued consolidation of the journals market suggests that this remains an attractive sector of publishing, and that larger players can benefit from growing even bigger. Further growth can be anticipated with the strength of newer markets such as China and India. Publishers will increase their profitability if they can spread the relatively high fixed costs of journals publishing over a larger number of titles – this is a driver for further acquisitions. In the area of pricing, the industry has moved away from pricing and selling a physical product (in print form) towards pricing a service on the basis of the value offered to journal users. Customers also have a fuller set of metrics with which to negotiate. With better data available to customers, commercial publishers are finding it harder simply to increase prices to increase profits and they have to prove that they are offering greater value for money.

Publishers continue to experiment with new business models:

> Experimenting with business models might accomplish two goals for STM publishers – generating incremental revenue from users, and acting as a valuable marketing tool. In an age of technological innovation, to be seen to experiment is to be seen as competitive and moving forward. It is, of course, also a defensive measure, as declining subscriptions threaten to force publishers away from traditional revenue channels. (Outsell, 2007: 34)

What if the unit of currency ceases to be the journal and becomes something else? Timo Hannay, Head of Web Publishing, Nature Publishing Group highlights an issue critical for all publishers:

> how to create viable business models that don't involve charging for content (whether readers or authors). That's not because I believe it's necessarily going to become impossible to charge readers, but it won't always be the optimal (or even a viable) business model, especially for collaborative online services, so we need other options. In short, we need to get much better at monetizing traffic. (Hannay, 2007)

In conclusion, a variety of business models and continued experimentation are desirable for the health of the sector. As Brown et al. have written about academic publishing:

> Different economic models will be appropriate for different types of content and different audiences. It seems critical to us that there

continues to be a diverse marketplace for publishing a range of content, from fee-based to open access, from peer reviewed to self-published, from single author to collaboratively created, from simple text to rich media. This marketplace should involve commercial and not-for-profit entities, and should include collaborations among libraries, presses and academic computing centres. (Brown et al., 2007: 4)

Bibliography

Amin, M. (2008) Director, Academic Relations, Elsevier, interviewed by the author, 3 June.

Bannerman, I. (2008) Managing Director, Journals, Taylor & Francis, interviewed by the author, 4 July.

Beckett, C. and Inger, S. (2006) *Self-Archiving and Journal Subscriptions: Co-existence or Competition?*, An International Survey of Librarians' Preferences, Publishing Research Consortium Summary Paper.

Bergstrom, T. C. (2001) 'Free labor for costly journals?', *Journal of Economic Perspectives* 15: 183–98.

Bird, C. (2008) 'Oxford Journals' adventures in open access', *Learned Publishing* 21(3): 200–8.

Brown, L., Griffiths, R. and Rascoff, M. (2007) *University Publishing in a Digital Age*, Ithaka Report.

Burrows, T. (2006) 'Brave New World or plus ça change?: Electronic journals and the academic library', *Australian Academic and Research Libraries* 37: 170–8.

Campbell, R. (2008) Quoted in 'Give me an "E"', *Information World Review*, 8 October.

Clarke, R. (2007) 'The cost profiles of alternative approaches to journal publishing', *First Monday* 12(2).

Cox, J. and Cox, L. (2006) *Scholarly Publishing Practice 2005*, Association of Learned and Professional Society Publishers.

de Bellaigue, E. (2004) *British Book Publishing as a Business since the 1960s: Selected Essays*, London: British Library.

Edlin, A. S. and Rubinfeld, D. L. (2005) 'The bundling of academic journals', *American Economics Review* 95: 441–6.

Electronic Publishing Services (EPS) (2006) *UK Scholarly Journals: 2006 Baseline Report*.

Fowler, C. (2008) Subject Librarian, Oxford Brookes University, interviewed by the author, 6 October.

Hahn, K. (2006) 'The state of the large publisher bundle: findings from an ARL member survey', *ARL Bimonthly Report*, April.

Hannay, T. (2007) Interviewed by John Dupois in 'Confessions of a science librarian', available at: *http://jdupois.blogspot.com* (accessed 13 March 2009).

Holmes, A. (2004) 'Publishing trends and practices in the scientific community', *Canadian Journal of Communication* 29(3): 359–68.

JISC Collections (2007) *JISC Business Model Trials*, 12 June, available from: *www.jisc-collections.ac.uk*.

Johnson, R. K. and Luther, J. (2007) *The E-Only Tipping Point for Journals: What's ahead in the Print-to-Electronic Transition Zone*, Association of Research Libraries.

King, D. W. (2007) 'The cost of journal publishing: a literature review and commentary', *Learned Publishing* 21(2): 85–106.

King, D. W. and Alvarado-Albertorio, F. M. (2008) 'Pricing and other means of charging for scholarly journals: a literature review and commentary', *Learned Publishing* 21(4): 248–72.

Morgan Stanley Equity Research (2002) 'Scientific publishing: knowledge is power', available from: *www.econ.ucsb.edu/~tedb/Journals/morganstanley.pdf* (accessed 17 February 2009).

Outsell (2007) *Scientific, Technical and Medical Information: 2007 Market Forecast and Trends Report*.

Page, G., Campbell, R. and Meadows, J. (1997) *Journal Publishing*, Cambridge: Cambridge University Press.

Perciali, I. (2008) 'Journals at bepress: new twists on an old model', *Learned Publishing* 21(2): 116–22.

Richardson, P. (2007) *Publishing Market Profile: The United Kingdom*, Publishers Association.

Research Information Network (RIN) (2008) *Activities, Costs and Funding Flows in the Scholarly Communications System in the UK*, available from: *http://www.rin.ac.uk*.

Tenopir, C. and King, D. W. (2000) *Towards Electronic Journals: Realities for Scientists, Librarians, and Publishers*, Special Libraries Association.

Thompson, J. B. (2005) *Books in the Digital Age*, Cambridge: Polity Press.

Van Orsdel, L. C. and Born, K. (2008) 'Periodicals price survey 2008: embracing openness', *Library Journal*, 15 April.

Waltham, M. (2006) 'Learned society business models and open access', in Neil Jacobs (ed.) *Open Access: Key Strategic, Technical and Economic Aspects*, Oxford: Chandos, pp. 121–9.

Wellcome Trust (2004) 'Costs and business models in scientific research publishing', available at: *http://www.wellcome.ac.uk/About-us/Publications/Reports/Biomedical-science/WTD003185.htm* (accessed 17 March 2009).

White, S. and Creaser, C. (2007) *Trends in Scholarly Journal Prices 2000–2006*, LISU.

Wilson-Higgins, S. and Bernhardt, B. (2008) 'Printing and shipping publications on-demand', paper presented at XXVIII Charleston Conference, 7 November.

5

The growth of journals publishing
Carol Tenopir and Donald W. King

Introduction

For the last 60 years, scholarly journals have witnessed unprecedented growth, controversy and change. Since the late 1940s, the number of scholarly journals has increased sharply, with hundreds of new titles and new topics being introduced each decade. Beginning in the late 1960s and especially since the 1990s, the form of journals has been transformed into digital versions that speed both access and delivery of articles to readers and provide enhanced functionality. E-journals are now more popular with libraries and readers than their print counterparts, although both forms continue to coexist for a majority of titles. This combination of more titles and more widespread availability in both print and electronic formats has engendered lively debates in the library, publishing and scholarly communities, and has kept scholarly journals at the forefront in discussions of the promise and problems with traditional forms of scholarly communication channels.

Profound changes to the look, functionality and publishing rhythms of the scholarly journal are outside the scope of this chapter and are covered elsewhere in this volume. Some of the changes in electronic publishing emphasize the unit of scholarly *article* rather than the unit of journal *title*. In this chapter, the unit of analysis is mostly the scholarly journal *title*, each of which is made up of many individual articles as well as some non-article material such as letters to the editor, book reviews, calendars of events, etc. It will be up to others to speculate whether or not the journal title, typically made up of issues that include articles and non-article content, will thrive. This chapter is based on the assumption that it will, although with increased digital functionality and the capability of being easily separated into smaller components, such as articles or parts of articles, through search and display. Some characteristics of articles are included here, but within the context of the journals that publish them.

A historical perspective

To truly understand the growth of journal publishing in the twentieth and twenty-first centuries, a brief history of journal publishing will help, as the history of journals stretches back much further than the middle of the twentieth century, the starting point of many discussions. For a more detailed history of scholarly journals, see Houghton (1975), Kronick (1976), Meadows (1998) and Tenopir and King (2000).

The history of modern scholarly journals is generally traced back to the seventeenth century, with the first scholarly journal believed by most to be *Le Journal des Sçavans* ('Journal of the Experts'), founded by Denis de Sallo in France in January 1665. The first journal issue shared some characteristics with a modern journal – it had ten articles, some letters, and notes, for example – but it was only 20 pages long and covered information on many different topics. The founding and development of *Le Journal des Sçavans* corresponded to the budding practice of sharing discoveries and ideas through correspondence between scholars, the rise of scientific societies, and the concomitant development and growth of newspapers. Indeed, this first journal was a new type of news organ for the scholarly community, including such newsworthy topics as obituaries of luminaries, abstracts of books, reports of legal decisions, and summaries of a range of developments on topics or issues thought to be of interest to educated men. The title was later changed to *Journal des Savants* and published as a literary magazine (Houghton, 1975; Tenopir and King, 2000).

Others point to *Philosophical Transactions of the Royal Society of London* as the first truly modern journal (Meadows, 1998; Price, 1975). Launched in March 1665 as a monthly periodical, *Philosophical Transactions* provided a means for members of the Royal Society of London to distribute the results of their scientific experiments and achieve a wider distribution of Royal Society lectures. The first issue is now available in digital form through JSTOR, along with the complete run, and the early issues are certainly more accessible and likely to have been read more in the past few years than they were in their first 300 years.

Whether it was *Le Journal des Sçavans* or *Philosophical Transactions* that earned the title of first modern journal, the growing pace of experimental science and the desire to share ideas and results more widely and efficiently than personal letters, hand copyists or books allowed, by the late seventeenth century, the scientific journal was 'a solution whose time had come' (Tenopir and King, 2000, 56).

According to Houghton (1975) and Garrison (1934), by the end of the seventeenth century there were between 30 and 90 scientific and medical journals being published worldwide, with a total of 755 journal titles by the end of the eighteenth century. Price (1975: 164) puts the number of titles at 'about one hundred by the beginning of the nineteenth century, one thousand by the middle, and some ten thousand by 1900'. Journal titles and the professional societies that often sponsored them began to move from broad coverage of all issues that might interest the educated man, to specialization.

Scientific specialization was reflected both in the birth of new journals that covered a narrower or more focused topic and in the 'twigging' of existing broad journals into narrower, more specialized topics. Influential thinkers in the history of science point to the growth of specialized journal publishing as a reflection of the development of scientific thought. Kuhn (1970), for example, who described the formation of scientific paradigms and paradigm shifts in his *Structure of Scientific Revolutions*, stated that the formation of specialized journals (along with the creation of specialized societies and a role in the curriculum for the new ideas) demonstrates the acceptance of a new paradigm in science.

The specialization of science continued through the nineteenth and twentieth centuries, and the importance of journals to scholars as both readers and authors persisted. Derek de Solla Price (1963) famously plotted the growth of the number of journals from 1665 through 2000 (Figure 5.1). He discussed the exponential growth curve that would lead to nearly a million journal titles by 2000 if the historical rate of growth continued. His calculations showed the number of titles doubling every 15 years, increasing by a power of ten in 20 years, and by a factor of 1,000 in 150 years.

According to Price (1975: 169), 'in the three hundred years which separate us from the mid-seventeenth century, this represents a factor of one million'. Price (1975: 169) likens the growth in the number of journals to 'a colony of rabbits breeding among themselves and reproducing every so often'. Price (1975: 170) suggests there is something about scientific discoveries that engenders this rabbit-like

Figure 5.1 Total number of scientific journals and abstract journals founded worldwide, 1665–2000

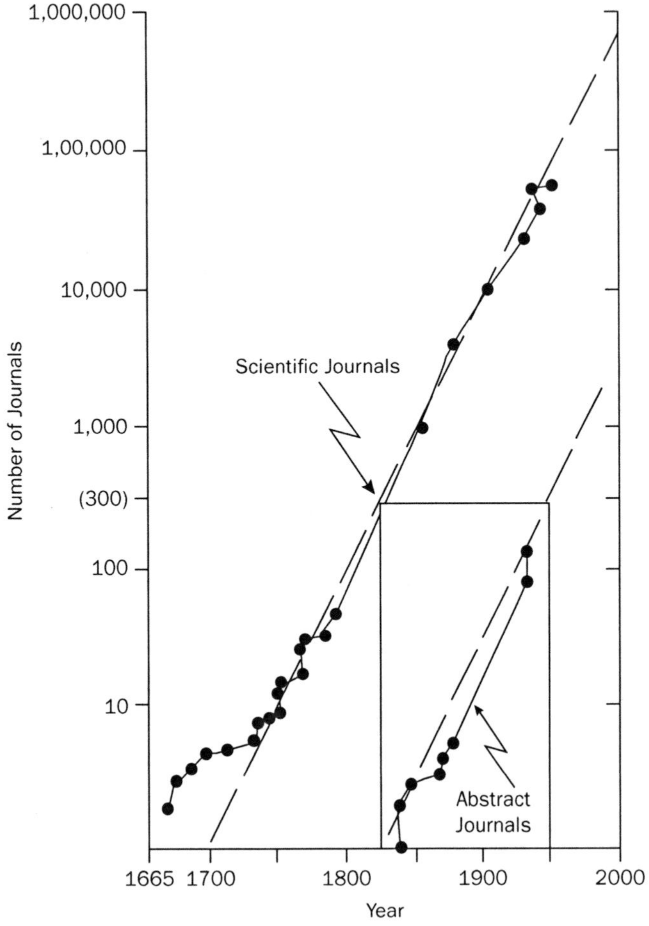

Source: Price (1963, 1975); reprinted in Tenopir and King (2000).

behaviour, as each new 'advance generates a series of new advances at a reasonably constant birth rate, so that the number of births is strictly proportional to the size of the population of discoveries at any given time'. Based on this, he concludes that:

the number of journals has been growing so that every year about one journal in twenty, about 5 per cent of the population, has a journal-child – a quotient of fecundity that is surely low enough to be reasonable but which must inevitably multiply the population by ten in each succeeding half-century. (Price, 1975: 170)

Price's calculations do not account for discontinued journals, however, and although new titles have undoubtedly arisen more quickly than obsolete titles have been discontinued, so the actual growth in total journal titles may be somewhat lower (Houghton, 1975; Kronick, 1976; Meadows, 1998). His disclaimer that he is plotting the 'number of journals founded (not surviving) as a function of date' (Price 1975: 166) is also not entirely accurate, as he plots the total cumulative number of journals each year, not just those newly founded each year. He also seems to confuse periodicals with scholarly journals. Price's assertion that 'according to the World List of Scientific Periodicals, a tome larger than any family Bible, we are now well on the way to the next milestone of a hundred thousand such journals' (Price, 1975: 164), almost certainly includes trade journals and other non-peer reviewed titles. The following section gives further consideration to such problems with counting.

Price identified the relationship between new discoveries in science and the twigging (or parenting) of journal titles. He also found the relationship between the growth in the number of journal titles, the growth rate of individual journal articles, and the corresponding growth rates of the number of abstract journals. He showed that the number of articles also follows the same exponential growth as the number of scientific journals. As author productivity has remained fairly constant over time, Price speculated that growth in the numbers of scientific journals and scientific articles is closely tied to, and increases in tandem with, the number of scientists.

Price also showed that, from 1830 through the early 1960s, about one abstracts journal was created for every 300 journal titles. Abstracts journals are founded due to an impending crisis of information overload – as the number of journal articles increases, scholars cannot hope to read every article that may be potentially relevant in their field. As Price anticipated, this remains a problem. He even called the then new method of 'electronic sorting' 'no more than a palliative and not the radical solution that the situation demands. It can only delay the fateful crisis by a few paltry decades' (Price, 1975: 168). Modern 'electronic sorting' search engines have solved the problem of finding the ever-increasing amount of scholarly information. As anticipated by Price, the challenge today is finding the best or most relevant information from among the myriad of articles.

Recent growth in number of titles

It is surprisingly difficult to come up with an accurate number of how many scholarly journals currently exist, let alone model how that number has changed over time. Mabe (2003), Tenopir (2004) and Morris (2007) all have struggled with the best way to reconcile the differences in number of titles estimated by Price, Tenopir and King, and others. If Price's curve had remained constant, there would have been close to a million titles by 2000.

King, McDonald, Roderer (1981), Tenopir and King (2000) and Mabe (2003) have shown that the growth in journal titles, journal articles, research and development (R&D) workers, and R&D expenditures in the USA are all correlated (see Figure 5.3 and later discussion). Although there remains a correlation between the number of scientists and the number of journal titles, as demonstrated by Price, Price's curve has flattened. The number of scientists continued to increase through the 1990s, but by 2000 we most certainly did not have his predicted million journal titles. This discrepancy is most likely due to the increase in the average number of articles published each year per journal title (Tenopir and King, 2000).

King, McDonald and Roderer (1981) estimated that there were a total of 4,447 US-based journals in 1977, compared with their estimate of over 57,400 titles worldwide (Figure 5.2). Using the same method of counting only those titles with a US presence, Tenopir and King (1997, 2000) estimated that the number of US-based journal titles had increased to 6,771 by 1995, a figure that is remarkably close to the prediction by King et al. (1981) that there would be 7,000 US-based journal titles by 1999. These relatively low numbers did not include any titles that did not have a US editorial office. In today's international publishing world, this way of counting no longer makes sense.

At the other extreme, Meadows and Singleton (1995) estimated that there were approximately 70,000 to 80,000 scholarly journals worldwide. (Earlier estimates by Meadows (1993, 1998), ranged from 10,000 journals in 1951 to 71,000 in 1987.) These high numbers seem reasonable when compared with King et al.'s 1977 estimate of 57,400 titles worldwide, but both may be an over-count if we restrict the picture to scholarly peer-reviewed journals. These estimates most likely include other types of periodical, such as some non-peer reviewed magazines or trade journals and perhaps even newsletters, in addition to peer-reviewed journals.

Ulrich's Periodical Directory, published since 1932, is probably the best source for monitoring the number and growth in number of periodical

| Figure 5.2 | Total number of scientific and technical journals in the USA, 1839–2000 (predicted after 1978) |

Source: King, McDonald and Roderer (1981); reproduced with permission.

titles and offers a level of consistency over time. Ulrich's 300,000 titles include all types of serial, not just scholarly journals. The directory also contains discontinued or forthcoming titles in addition to actively published titles. Searches in the online versions can be restricted to academic/scholarly journals, refereed journals, or titles that are coded as either or both. Searches can also be restricted to active titles, avoiding the problem of counting dead or inactive titles for which Price was criticized. Using Ulrich's as the basis for monitoring the growth and number of journals has the advantage of being replicable and consistent.

Although it offers consistency, there are also problems associated with relying on Ulrich's. Almost certainly it does not include every single scholarly journal title available in the world today, particularly those published by small publishers and that are not in English or that do not provide an English-language abstract. Guédon (2008) observes that estimates based on Ulrich's 'tend to yield lower numbers' because Ulrich's 'aims at a specific clientele largely made up of librarians from rich countries. It selects what it thinks is of potential interest for potential buyers' (Guédon, 2008: 43). Morris (2007: 299) points out that Ulrich's is 'entirely reliant on the information supplied by the publishers of the journals listed therein. New journals are often not listed immediately. There can therefore be no hard-and-fast guarantees as to the completeness, currency, or accuracy of that information'. In addition, within the records for the journals that are included in Ulrich's, Jacso (2001) has documented serious 'errors of omission' or incompleteness of fields in some of the journal title records such as Library of Congress subject headings.

Still, Ulrich's is the best and most consistent source we have to estimate actual journal growth over time. Mabe (2003: 191) justifies his choice to use Ulrich's by saying 'only Ulrich's attempts to cover all serial publications and to classify them by a number of criteria. Ulrich's also has the undeniable advantage of being available in a readily researchable CD-ROM format as well as online'. Mabe used the CD-ROM version for his searches; all of the searches presented below are from the online version of UlrichsWeb. As the web version is completely updated weekly, retrospective searches are not possible. All of the older data presented here were collected on the date indicated.

Searches of UlrichsWeb in 2003 through 2008 show the growth in journal titles over time. (see Table 5.1). How many journals there are depends very much on the search strategy (as demonstrated by Morris, 2007), so several Boolean search strategies are presented below. To eliminate one of the abovementioned problems with Price's data, searches were in all cases restricted to 'active' titles only – that is, those that were currently being published at the time of the search.

It is worth noting that designations in Ulrich's rely on publishers self-reporting the information accurately. As reported by Tenopir (2004), one Ulrich's editor has acknowledged that publishers are not necessarily consistent in understanding the difference between academic/scholarly or refereed. According to the Ulrich's FAQ:

> The term refereed is applied to a journal that has been peer-reviewed. Refereed serials include articles that have been reviewed by experts and respected researchers in specific fields of study including the sciences, technology, the social sciences, and arts and humanities. (*http://www.ulrichsweb.com/ulrichsweb/faqs.asp*)

Table 5.1   Growth in number of journals according to UlrichsWeb, May 2002 to February 2008

	May 2002	February 2003	October 2004	June 2006	October 2007	February 2008
Active (all)	n/a	175,639	193,299	204,808	216,405	219,774
Active AND online	30,564	33,393	37,533	48,788	55,795	56,885
Active AND academic/ scholarly	n/a	39,565	45,614	54,052	60,288	61,620
Active AND refereed	22,835	23,231	21,802	23,187	23,758	24,059
Active AND academic/ scholarly AND refereed	16,925	17,649	21,532	22,788	23,658	23,973
Active AND online AND refereed	n/a	12,575	11,722	14,338	15,441	15,668

Using a slightly different strategy with Ulrich's CD-ROM, Mabe (2003) obtained a figure of 14,694 active academic/scholarly *and* refereed periodicals in the summer of 2001 (that is, active titles coded with both designations). His strategy is closest to line five in Table 5.1 (17,649 in February 2003). The main difference in Mabe's strategy, however, is the use of the Boolean ANDNOT to eliminate titles containing one of several type indicators, including audiocassette, bibliography, Braille, broadsheet and 20 other similar designations. (Differences between other variations in strategy or whether the web, Dialog or CD-ROM version of Ulrich's is searched are discussed by Morris, 2007.)

Going a step further, Mabe has also recalculated the annual collective growth rate of journals since 1665 using a logarithmic scale (see Figure 5.3 for an updated version of his 2003 chart). Allowing for a few exceptions, such as immediately after the Second World War, his findings suggest that:

> for most of the last three centuries, the growth rate of active peer reviewed scholarly and scientific journals has been almost constant at 3.46% per annum. This means that the number of active journals has been doubling every 20 years. (Mabe, 2003: 193)

Figure 5.3 Active refereed scholarly/academic journal title growth since 1665 (log scale)

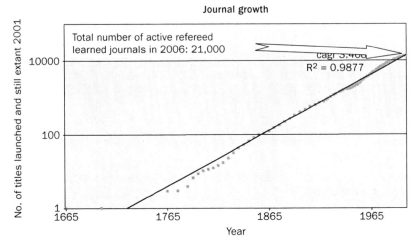

Journal growth

Total number of active refereed learned journals in 2006: 21,000

cagr 3.46d
$R^2 = 0.9877$

Source: Updated from Mabe (2003), through personal correspondence with Mabe; reproduced with permission.

Changes in number of articles and length of articles

On average, journals are publishing more articles each year, whether or not they publish them in issues. Counting growth in journal titles is still important for those who deal in a world of titles and the commodity of the entire journal as a unit, including publishers, scholarly societies and librarians. Journal titles remain important to scholars as well, especially for authorship, current awareness reading and assessment of relevance and quality (Nicholas et al., 2005, 2006; Tenopir and King, 2007). When conducting research or reading for other purposes, however, the article as a unit is more important than the journal as a whole.

Björk et al. (2008) have attempted to measure how many scholarly articles are published yearly and how many of those are available in open access. Working from Ulrich's and the Thomson Scientific (ISI) citation databases, they estimate that from 23,750 journals published in 2006, the total number of peer-reviewed journal articles was approximately 1,350,000. (Incidentally, about 19.4 per cent of those articles were available through some variety of open access by early 2008.) They found that non-ISI title journals publish on average 26.7 articles per title per year, while ISI titles publish 111.7 articles per title per year.

Tenopir and King (2000) have reported an average of 123 articles published yearly per title in US-based science and social science journals. This number excludes humanities journals, but includes social sciences, engineering, medicine and all sciences.

Bjork et al. (2008) believe that their calculation of the total number of journal articles published yearly is in line with the estimate by Elsevier (2004) that 1.2 million articles are published yearly in peer-reviewed journals by publishers in science, technology and medicine. Bjork et al.'s numbers also include social sciences and humanities.

Although co-authorship has increased in most fields over time, the productivity of authors has remained relatively constant, at approximately one article per year per author and approximately two in science (Tenopir and King, 2000). The relationship that exists between the number of R&D workers and the number of journal titles can also be found between R&D workers and the number of journal articles (see Figure 5.4). Although not every researcher publishes, as the number of R&D workers increases, so do the numbers of authors and articles (Mabe, 2003; Tenopir and King, 2000).

As part of a National Sciences Foundation (NSF) project entitled 'Statistical Indicators of Scientific and Technological Information Communication,' King Research, Inc. observed characteristics of science journals published in the USA. These characteristics were tracked

Figure 5.4   **Growth rates of R&D workers versus journals and articles**

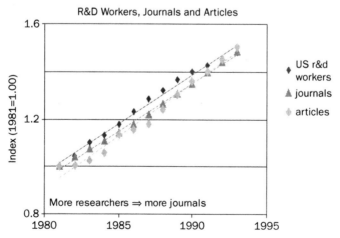

Source: Figure 4 in Mabe (2003) and presented at CIBER course on electronic publishing, 2004; reproduced by permission of author.

annually from a sample of journals observed in libraries from 1960 to 1977 and 1985, and later at the University of Tennessee, School of Information Sciences in 1990 and 1995 (in 1990 also under NSF contract). The results were categorized by nine fields of science designated by NSF during the first observations. Basic data included number of titles, type of publisher, price, circulation, etc. Sub-samples of issues and articles produced such journal characteristics as issues, articles, article pages, non-article pages, proportion of graphics pages, authors (and their affiliation), and number of citations. 'Science journals' is defined as a primary vehicle for communicating information and research results, often employing peer review or refereeing process to aid in screening and editorial control. 'Science journals' does not include trade journals. Some of these results were published by Tenopir and King (1997, 2000, 2004).

The King Research, Inc. studies found that in 1960 there were 2,815 science journals based in the USA with 208,300 articles, or an average of 74 articles per journal. The growth of US science journals is shown in Table 5.2.

Between 1985 and 1995, the growth trend in the number of journals based in the USA seemed to dampen substantially, while the number of articles continued to grow at a healthy rate. It may be that the cost of starting new journals and the financing necessary to fund journals until they become profitable (or at least break even) have encouraged publishers to increase the size of journals rather than start new ones. It can typically take as many as six years for a new journal to break even, requiring about $50,000 in investment just to keep it going during that time (Page et al., 1997; Tenopir and King, 2000).

As the number of articles per journal title increases, presumably the rate of growth in number of new titles can slow somewhat, remembering that the total growth of journals and journal articles has paralleled the

Table 5.2 Growth of science journals based in the USA, 1965–1995

Year	No. journals	Increase over previous decade (%)	No. articles	Increase over previous decade (%)	Articles per journal
1965	3,010	–	217,400	–	72
1975	4,175	38.7	353,700	62.7	85
1985	5,750	37.7	546,000	54.4	95
1995	6,771	17.8	832,800	52.5	123

Source: Tenopir and King (1997); King et al. (1981).

concomitant growth of R&D workers for many years (Mabe, 2003; Tenopir and King, 2000). Another calculation that is relevant to information overload, but may or may not be relevant to the growth in number of titles or articles, is the change in the average length of the articles published. Bringing up to date the calculations of article length in 1975 by King et al. (1981) and in 1995 by Tenopir and King (1997), Table 5.3 shows that the average length of article increased 80 per cent

Table 5.3 Average article length of US science articles, 1975–2007

Year	Average article length (no. pages)	Change (%) 1975–2007	Change (%) 1995–2007
1975	7.41	80	–
1995	11.66	–	14
2007	13.35	–	–

Table 5.4 Average article length in 1995 and 2007

Field	Average article length (no. pages) 1995	Average article length (no. pages) 2007	Change (%) 1995–2007
Physical sciences	8.51	9.05	+6
Mathematics	16.29	20.01	+23
Computer sciences	11.80	14.41	+22
Environmental sciences	14.03	14.38	+2
Engineering	11.23	10.21	–9
Life sciences	10.74	9.98	–7
Psychology	15.45	13.39	–13
Social science	24.16	15.31	–37
Other sciences/ multi-sciences*	6.92	11.43	+65
All fields (weighted)	11.66	13.35	+14

Source: Data obtained from samples of approximately 50 journals from each field. The average article length across all fields is a weighted average of the individual fields, with weight factors based on the size of journal populations in Ulrich's as of 19 October 2008. *Other sciences and multi-sciences include other fields of science such as the information sciences, library science and multi-science publications such as Science and Nature.

in the 32-year period from 1975 to 2007, with the great majority of that growth coming between 1975 and 1995.

Journal article length is somewhat dependent on subject field. Table 5.4 shows that although there have been large percentage changes in length, both positive and negative, during the 12-year period before 2007, the net effect has been a regression toward the mean length across all fields. While in 1995 the difference between the field with the longest article and the field with shortest articles was 17.2 pages, by 2007 this range had narrowed to 11 pages.

Online journals

As shown in Table 5.1, many scholarly journals are still only available in print. Of the approximately 24,000 refereed journal titles active in February 2008, 65 per cent (15,668) are listed in Ulrich's as being available online. This does not mean they are only online – a majority are still available in both paper and e-versions. In 2004, just 4,600 journal titles in Ulrich's were only available electronically (online or CD-ROM) (Tenopir, 2004). The 65 per cent of journals available in some e-versions includes all subject disciplines. Estimates of online availability of STM titles are much higher – 90 per cent according to publishing consultant John Cox (2007).

The discrepancy between estimates may also be due to factors other than subject discipline, as defining 'online' is not as easy as it might be. 'Online' in the strictest sense means that the entire journal is available in digital form, including all articles, editorial content and other non-article content. The fully online journal can truly and completely replace any print counterpart, and online versions often contain more articles and more content than a corresponding print version. Online in a less restrictive sense might mean that articles are available online, either directly from the publisher as an online journal or as separate articles within a database of articles.

An even less restrictive definition might mean that the publisher allows open access publishing, so that some articles may be available online from a variety of sources, including subject or institutional repositories, author websites, article databases, etc. This last category, often called the 'green' road of open access publishing, includes approximately 11.3 per cent of the 1.3 million articles published in 2006, according to Bjork et al. (2008).

The growth of electronic journals

Electronic journal growth has increased exponentially over the last decade. Of particular interest are full-text online periodicals, which have grown dramatically since the early 1990s. The *Fulltext Sources Online* directory (Glose, 2008), which has tracked the online availability of journals, magazines, newspapers, news transcripts and other periodicals over time, shows a dramatic increase, particularly in the last ten years. Although it includes all types of periodicals and not just scholarly journals, the directory is a useful source when estimating online availability of periodical titles. As of July 2008, *Fulltext Sources Online* included nearly 40,000 periodical titles that are available in whole or part online. The growth of entries in this directory is one way to monitor the growth in online periodicals, as growth in the directory can be assumed to mirror the growth of online sources (Figure 5.5). This 40,000 figure is best compared with the 56,885 online active titles reported by UlrichsWeb (Table 5.1), which is just 26 per cent of all active periodical titles.

Scholarly journals are much more likely to be available in electronic form. A survey of publishers in 2003 by John Cox Associates, Ltd. estimated that 75–83 per cent of scholarly journals were available online in whole or in part, with the highest percentage in the sciences (Cox, 2004). That same source now estimates over 90 per cent (Cox, 2007). Although the exact number of e-only journals is difficult to estimate, in

Figure 5.5 Growth in periodical titles

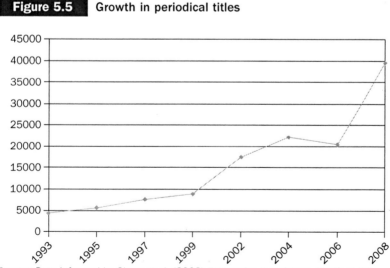

Source: Data informed by Glose et al. (2008) *Fulltext Sources Online*, Medford, NJ: Information Today.

part because we are still in a world where many journals are published in both print and electronic forms, the availability of journal articles in electronic form has obviously greatly increased. Of print and electronic refereed journal titles, 65 per cent of UlrichsWeb's active refereed titles are online as of February 2008, up from 54 per cent in February 2003 (Table 5.1). As at June 2008, the Directory of Open Access Journals (*www.doaj.org*) includes over 3,400 titles, up from just over 800 in 2003.

Predictions for the future

Although the rate of growth has not matched Price's prediction, the number of journal titles will almost certainly continue to increase for the immediate future. At a fairly steady growth rate of 3.4 per cent (Mabe, 2003) with some ups and downs, journals have shown remarkable consistency in their growth, even as the number of articles and average length of articles continues to increase for most subject disciplines. Societal factors, such as the decrease in the number of R&D workers or the amount of national spending on R&D, would slow the growth of journal titles. This may certainly happen in selected countries, but is unlikely to occur on the worldwide scale that encompasses scholarship and research. The publication of journals may shift to different nations and new economic models may take hold.

The focus on the digital article rather than the digital journal as a unit for search and retrieval will have some impact on future growth in the number of journals. Article authoring remains constant at between one and two articles per author per year, and the number of authors continues to increase. The pressure to publish in peer-reviewed journals remains high in academic circles worldwide, however. Most academic authors who choose to put their scholarship on their own websites or in article repositories still publish a copy in a peer-reviewed journal. For now, this creates alternative ways to get to the same work, rather than replacing journal titles.

A more likely disruption to the centuries of growth in the number and size of journals is the growth in these alternatives to journals. Electronic distribution of articles, separated from their journal home, is possible and becoming common. Web search engines serve as locator for articles housed in subject or institutional repositories. Most of these articles are still tied to their corresponding publication in a journal, but the desirability of this in the future is questioned by some. If journal prices continue to increase, the number of journal titles continues to grow, and readers and libraries perceive they can access a majority of the information needed from repositories, licence prices (or willingness to pay the fees of fee-based open access journals) may decrease and some journals may not survive.

Whether this is a negative or positive outcome is debated by many, but one thing is certain. Journals have served a purpose to scholars as both readers and authors for over 300 years and their growth reflects the growth of science, scholarship, and research and development. A disruption to their pattern of growth would reflect a major change in the way science is disseminated.

At present, e-journals are mostly digital versions of printed journals and as such have still not realized their full potential. Journal and article functionality that breaks the bonds of the printed page has emerged slowly in the last several decades, but now seems to be picking up momentum. The pace of these changes (which began with citation linking within and between articles, links to external data sets, e-publication of individual articles without waiting for an entire issue, and virtual personalized issues) will almost certainly increase and will greatly influence the future of the journal.

Judging from the past, the journal will remain important even as it is transformed with additional digital functionality. Links to and from data sets, the incorporation of more social networking features such as reader-assigned subject tagging, and the inclusion of automated ways to identify high-impact or high-quality articles are just some of the features that will be incorporated into journal systems. Most require a substantial investment on the part of journal publishers and authors, which means we will not see every function in every journal. The primary purposes of the peer-reviewed journal – to publish, disseminate and archive high-quality research results – will survive amidst the changes that technology enables in scholarly communication. The number of journals required to do so and the growth rate of new titles may slacken in a fully digital future, as the number of articles per title is not bound by paper limitations.

Acknowledgments

The authors wish to acknowledge the assistance of University of Tennessee graduate students Lei Wu, Liuyan Yang and Amy Love, and in particular William (Ben) Birch, who conducted the calculations of journal article length and journal growth.

Bibliography

Björk, B.-C., Roos, A. and Lauri, M. (2008) 'Global annual volume of peer reviewed scholarly articles and the share available via different open access options', paper presented at the International Conference on Electronic Publishing, Toronto, 25–7 June.

Cox, J. (2004) *House of Commons Science and Technology Committee: Tenth Report, Session 2003–2004*, Appendix 27, available at: *http://www.publications.parliament.uk/pa/cm200304/cmselect/cmsctech/399/39902.htm#evidence* (accessed 21 October 2008).

Cox, J. (2007) 'Can the past thirty years tell us about the next decade? A personal review of the recent and future history of the journal', paper presented at the annual conference of the United Kingdom Serials Group, Warwick, 16–18 April, summarized in *UKSG Serials E-News* 143, available at: *http://www.ringgold.com/uksg/si_pd.cfm?Pid=10&Articleid=3057&XSection=Business&issueno=143* (accessed 25 May 2008).

Elsevier (2004) 'Responses to the questions posed by the Science and Technology Committee', available at: *http://www.elsevier.com/authored_news/corporate/images/UK_STC_FINAL_SUBMISSION.pdf* (accessed 25 May 2008).

Garrison, F. H. (1934) 'Medical and scientific periodicals of the seventeenth and eighteenth centuries', *Bulletin of the History of Medicine* 2: 285–341.

Glose, M. B., Currado, T. D. and Elliott, T. (eds) (2008) *Fulltext Sources Online*, Medford, NJ: Information Today, Inc., twice yearly.

Guédon, J.-C. (2008) 'Mixing and matching the green and gold roads to open access: Take 2', *Serials Review* 34: 41–51.

Houghton, B. (1975) *Scientific Periodicals: Their Historical Development, Characteristics and Control*, Hamden, CT: Linnet Books & Clive Bingley.

Jacso, P. (2001) *Content Evaluation of Databases*, Englewood, CO: Libraries Unlimited.

King, D. W., McDonald, D. D. and Roderer, N. K. (1981) *Scientific Journals in the United States: Their Production, Use, and Economics*, Stroudsburg, PA: Academic Press.

Kronick, D. A. (1976) *A History of Scientific and Technical Periodicals: The Origins and Development of the Scientific and Technological Press, 1665–1790* (2nd edn), Metuchen, NJ: Scarecrow Press.

Kuhn, T. S. (1970) *Structure of Scientific Revolutions* (2nd edn, enlarged), Chicago, IL: University of Chicago Press.

Mabe, M. (2003) 'Growth and number of journals', *Serials* 16: 191–97.

Meadows, A. J. (1993) 'Too much of a good thing? Quality versus quantity', In H. Woodward and S. Pilling (eds) *International Serials Industry*, Aldershot: Gower, pp. 24–7.

Meadows, A. J. (1998) *Communicating Research*, London and San Diego, CA: Academic Press.

Meadows, A. J. and Singleton, A. (1995) 'Introduction', in F. Rowland, C. McKnight and J. Meadows (eds) *Project Elvyn: An Experiment in Electronic Journal Delivery*, London: Bowker Saur, pp. 15–36.

Morris, S. (2007) 'Mapping the journal publishing landscape: How much do we know?', *Learned Publishing* 20: 299–310.

Nicholas, D., Jamali, H., Huntington, P. and Rowlands, I. (2005) 'In their very own words: authors and scholarly journal publishing', *Learned Publishing* 18: 212–20.

Nicholas, D., Jamali, H. and Rowlands, I. (2006) 'On the tips of their tongues: authors and their views on scholarly publishing', *Learned Publishing* 19: 193–203.

Page, G., Campbell, R. and Meadows, J. (1997) *Journal Publishing*, Cambridge: Cambridge University Press.

Price, D. J. de Solla (1963) *Little Science, Big Science*, New York: Columbia University Press.

Price, D. J. de Solla (1975) *Science since Babylon* (enlarged edn), New Haven, CT: Yale University Press.

Tenopir, C. (2004) 'Online databases: Scholarly online journals; how many?' *Library Journal* 129: 32.

Tenopir, C. and King, D. W. (1997) 'Trends in scientific scholarly journal publishing in the United States', *Journal of Scholarly Publishing* 23: 135–70.

Tenopir, C. and King, D. W. (2000) *Towards Electronic Journals: Realities for Scientists, Librarians, and Publishers,* Washington, DC: Special Libraries Association.

Tenopir, C. and King, D. W. (2007) 'Perceptions of value and value beyond perceptions: measuring the quality and value of journal article readings', *Serials* 20: 199–207.

6

The post-Gutenberg open access journal

Stevan Harnad

Some think the most radical feature of post-Gutenberg journals will be the fact that they are digital and online, but that would be a much more modest development if their contents were to continue to be kept behind financial firewalls, with access denied to all who cannot or will not pay the tolls. This chapter will show how the optimal and inevitable outcome – for scientific and scholarly research, researchers, their institutions and funders, the vast research and development industry, and the society whose taxes support science and scholarship and for whose benefit the research is conducted – will be that all published research articles will be openly accessible online, free for all would-be users webwide.

The classical learned journal

To understand the journal of the future, however, we must first understand the journal of the present. This chapter is exclusively about *refereed journals*, not about trade journals, magazines or newsletters. These journals publish only peer-reviewed scientific and scholarly research. According to Ulrich's, there are about 25,000 of them, publishing about 2.5 million articles per year, across all disciplines and in all languages. There are, however, some uncertainties about Ulrich's classification scheme and about the average article-count for journals that are not indexed by Thompson-Reuters ISI (ISI journals average somewhat over 100 articles per year). With this in mind, Bjork et al. (2008) make a lower estimate of 23,750 journals and 1.35 million articles per year.

Refereed journals have the following properties:

1. *Peer review*: Every article published in these journals is first sent, by a qualified specialist editor or editorial board, to experts specialized in its subject matter. These experts are called 'referees' or 'peers' and are invited to review the submitted manuscript, determine whether its subject matter and quality are potentially suitable for publication in the journal in question, and if so, to indicate what corrections and revisions (if any) need to be made so that it meets that journal's established quality standards for acceptance. Both the referees and the authors are answerable to the editors, who select which referee recommendations are binding, and who judge whether a revised draft has satisfied the recommendations. The editors and the journal title are in turn answerable to the journal's usership in establishing and maintaining the journal's quality standards. In most fields there are a number of journals, varying horizontally in terms of their focus and subject matter, and vertically in terms of their selectivity and quality standards, as maintained by the rigour of their peer review (Harnad, 1998a).

2. *Document production*: All articles that a journal accepts for publication are copy-edited (to varying degrees) and then marked up for publication – formerly only as print on paper, but nowadays most journals also generate a digital document online.

3. *Access provision*: The journals provide access to their products, the journal articles, by selling (and in various ways delivering access through) annual subscriptions to the print edition or licences to the online edition. Journals often also sell single issues, online or on paper, or even single articles (the 'pay-to-view' model). Although it varies by field, most journals make ends meet through institutional subscriptions and licences. Individual subscriptions exist too, but they are not what sustains the market for most journals.

4. *Archiving*: Both print and paper editions have to be stored and preserved. Individual subscribers do what they want with their personal copies, but institutional libraries (as well as national deposit libraries) are responsible for the archival storage of print editions of journals. For the online edition there is still some inconsistency about who owns and preserves what, but both the libraries and the publishers are currently involved in storing and preserving both the print and the digital documents.

5. *Copyright*: Providing peer review, generating the final document, providing access to it online and on paper, and storing and preserving it,

all have costs, most of them borne by the publisher. The customers – the libraries – also bear some of the storage and preservation costs for the paper and online edition they have purchased, but we will focus on publisher costs. The peers referee for free, but we will be focusing particularly on the costs of *implementing* peer review (processing submissions, selecting referees, adjudicating the referee reports, and adjudicating the revisions, including any editorial input). In order to cover all their publishing costs (1–4), many journal publishers require the transfer of copyright from the author to the publisher to make it the exclusive vendor. This means no rival publisher can sell the same articles, and even the authors have to request permission from the publisher to reuse their own published writing in their own further publications.

Four of these five properties are also shared with other forms of publication; peer review, however, is unique to scientific and scholarly journal publishing (although some scholarly and scientific monographs may sometimes also be refereed by consultant specialists as rigorously as some journal articles). There are online editions of books, but they have not yet become as prevalent and as widely used as online versions of articles. The essential common point is that copyright is transferred to publishers so that they can recover their costs and make a profit.

Publishing for income vs publishing for impact

What, besides peer review itself, distinguishes the 2.5 million articles published every year in the world's 25,000 peer-reviewed journals from everything else that is published? It is the unusual nature of the authorship of those journals. The authors are all scientific and scholarly researchers, and none of them publish their articles for the sake of earning royalty income or fees from their sale. They publish them for one reason, and one reason only: so that their work will be read, used, applied and built upon by their fellow researchers worldwide. This is called 'research impact'. It is for the sake of research impact that researchers publish their findings instead of just putting them in a desk drawer (or not doing research at all). It is for the sake of research impact that their institutions and funders mandate that researchers should 'publish or perish'. It is for the sake of research impact that citizens support research with their taxes. And it is research impact that drives scientific and scholarly research progress (Harnad, 2001a).

Trade publishing

It is useful to contrast the special case of refereed research journals with most of the rest of the printed word. The authors of trade books do not write for research impact. Nor do the authors of newspaper articles and magazines. They write for fees or royalty income. Even the writers of scientific and scholarly textbooks – although they are often the authors of journal articles wearing other hats – write for royalty revenue rather than research impact. Some scholarly monographs – in fields where the publish-or-perish mandate puts more weight on publishing books than on publishing journal articles – have a mixed agenda and will probably follow the same pattern as journals, eventually; but for now, because of the true costs of print-based publication and distribution, scholarly monographs are still reliant on the trade publishing model.

And what is the trade publishing model? That the publisher tries to recover costs and make a fair profit by selling access to the joint product: the author's writing plus the publisher's editing, quality control, copy-editing, markup, and the generation and distribution of the text as print on paper. This is why copyright is transferred to publishers: so they can make good on their investment, sharing their profit with their authors.

Gutenberg toll-access

That, at least, was the picture in the Gutenberg era: the true costs of print production and distribution required a toll-booth to be erected between the document and the user. Access was sold, with publisher and author taking a share of the admission receipts. Writing, after all, was a trade, a way of earning a living, and so was publishing. Writers and publishers were no more interested in giving away their products than any other producer of any other good or service is.

How has the post-Gutenberg era of digital documents and online access changed that? In principle, authors can now *give away* their writing, if they wish to (and can afford to). This is presumably what bloggers are doing. But despite all we are hearing about open source, open content, open access and Creative Commons licensing, both the writing and the publishing *trades* are still proceeding apace, pretty much as they had before. And this is largely because there remains a need to put bread on the table. The fact that it has recently become possible for authors to give away their writing in digital form on a global scale does not mean that most of them *wish* to do so (Harnad et al., 2000).

Reprint requests and author give-aways

The authors of peer-reviewed journal articles, however, present an exception. Not only have they never sought or received income from the sales of their articles, but even back in Gutenberg times these special authors had had the practice of mailing, at their own expense, free copies (reprints) of their articles to any would-be user who requested them. The reason, again, was research impact. Researchers do not earn their revenue from selling their articles but from having them widely read, used and cited. The publish-or-perish reward system of academia is not based merely on a brute publication count. Measures of impact are counted as well, chief among them being *citations*. For scholars and scientists, their employment, salaries, promotion, tenure, funding, prizes and prestige all depend on the degree of uptake and usage of their research findings.

Access barriers and impact barriers

For this special kind of author (the would-be give-away author), the access barriers of Gutenberg publishing – having to transfer copyright to the publisher and then let the publisher deny access to those who could not or would not pay – were always anathema, because *access barriers are impact barriers*. Yet these give-away authors had no choice but to enter into this "Faustian bargain" (not with the devil, but with Gutenberg's costly mechanism of access-provision and its resulting cost-recovery needs) as the inescapable price of having any research impact at all (beyond what they could manage by hand-mailing manuscripts) (Harnad 1994).

The post-Gutenberg galaxy

Impact-barriers were inescapable – until the post-Gutenberg era of digital documents and online access provision (Harnad, 1990, 1991). For as soon as it became technically possible, these give-away authors began making their research papers (before and after refereeing) accessible free for all, first through e-mail, then by 'self-archiving' them online (Harnad, 1995, 2001b) in order to make them open access in 'anonymous ftp' archives, then on personal or central websites, and most recently in their own research institutions' interoperable, Open Access

Initiative (OAI) compliant institutional repositories (Tansley and Harnad, 2000) so they can be harvested and jointly searched through search engines such as OAIster, Citeseer, Citebase, Google Scholar and Google (Hitchcock et al., 2002). Studies have now repeatedly demonstrated that making articles open access doubles their citation impact (Brody et al., 2006; Hajjem et al., 2005; Harnad and Brody, 2004; Lawrence, 2001).

Open access (and almost open access)

The status quo in 2008 is that about 15 per cent of the 2.5 million peer-reviewed articles published annually are spontaneously being made open access by their authors. This will soon be changing, however, as universities and research institutions as well as research funders worldwide are extending their publish-or-perish mandates to mandate that the access to and the impact of those 2.5 million published articles should be maximized through author self-archiving (Harnad et al., 2003). Over 65 universities and funders worldwide (including Harvard and the US National Institutes of Health) have already mandated open access self-archiving (see the Registry of Open Access Repository Material Archiving Policies, ROARMAP). Over 90 per cent of journals have already adopted a 'full-green' or 'pale-green' open access policy, 63% of them endorsing the immediate self-archiving by their authors, of their own final refereed drafts, in their own open access institutional repositories (see ROMEO) (Harnad et al., 2004).

For the 32 per cent of (pale-green) journals that endorse only unrefereed preprint self-archiving and still embargo open access to the refereed draft (for 6–12 months or more) and the 5 per cent who do not endorse any version being made open access at all, immediate research usage and impact needs can nevertheless be fulfilled almost immediately. For any institutional repository deposit that is inaccessible (because access to it is set as 'closed access' instead of open access, owing to publisher restrictions), the institutional repositories have a button that allows any would-be user to click to send an instant 'e-mail e-print request' to the author, who need only click to have the e-print instantly e-mailed to the requester by the repository software. This is not yet 100 per cent open access: only 63 per cent open access + 37 per cent almost-open access. But as open access and open access mandates and the resulting usage and impact grow, author and user pressure will ensure that the optimal and inevitable outcome – 100 per cent green open access – will soon follow.

Once all articles are made open access through author self-archiving, and all journals are fully green with regard to open access, what next? What has been described so far has either already happened or is about to happen with high probability. But beyond that point – the point that provides the barrier-free access, usage and impact that research and researchers need – we enter into the realm of speculation about the future of journal publishing, copyright and peer review. Although it is not possible to predict the outcome with any confidence, it is possible to anticipate the main contingencies.

Universal green open access may eventually make subscriptions unsustainable

In and of itself, universal green open access self-archiving simply means that any researcher whose institution cannot afford subscription access to the publisher's print or online edition of the journal in which a particular article happens to appear can henceforth access the author's refereed final draft online for free. No one knows how long the demand for the print edition or the publisher's proprietary PDF will continue to cover the costs of journal publishing. It has to be noted, however, that producing a print edition and the publisher's PDF itself costs money; thus, if and when the demand for the publisher's print and PDF versions should vanish, so will all the costs associated with print and PDF: the author's peer-reviewed, accepted final draft, self-archived in his institution's OAI-compliant institutional repository, will become the official, canonical draft, and expenses (2–4) above (document production, access provision and archiving) will either have vanished or been offloaded onto the author and the distributed network of open access institutional repositories. As a consequence, there will no longer be any need to transfer copyright to the publisher (5), nor to block access, usage and reuse. Journals will have eliminated products and services for which there is no longer a demand, cutting costs and downsizing so that their only remaining expense will be the cost of implementing peer review (Harnad, 2001a).

Gold open access publishing

How much does it actually cost to implement peer review? The author provides the text and the revisions for free. The peers review for free. But a qualified editor must select the referees and adjudicate the referee reports and the revisions, and the online correspondence must be managed and coordinated. Currently, the cost per paper of implementing peer review has been estimated to be between $200–500 per accepted paper (if one factors the cost of rejected papers into the cost of accepted papers) (Doyle, 2001). There is a model for recovering this cost. It has already been tested for much higher costs – in fact the full gamut of costs of current journal publication, from $1,500 per paper for publishing online-only to $3,000 or more if the print edition is included. Here, instead of the user-institution paying the publisher a subscription fee for a *product* – the incoming journal – the author-institution pays the publisher a publication fee for a *service* – publication – per outgoing article. This is called the 'gold' open access publishing cost-recovery model (Harnad, 1997a, 1998b, 1999).

There are already over 3,000 gold open access journals – journals that make their own articles freely accessible online. Not all of them charge for publication – in fact, the majority still make ends meet through subscriptions or subsidies. But a significant number are sustaining themselves purely by charging author-institution publication fees. The problem is that with over 90 per cent of all 25,000 refereed journals still being subscription-based, the funds for paying institutional gold open access publication fees are currently committed to paying for institutional subscription fees. But if and when the availability of universal green open access were ever to eliminate the demand for the publisher's official version, on paper and online, making subscriptions unsustainable, then simple arithmetic shows that institutions would have at least three times as much annual windfall savings from their incoming journal subscription cancellations as they would need to pay the publication costs for their own outgoing articles – if all they had to pay for was peer review (Harnad, 2001a, 2001b).

In other words, there is currently already enough institutional money changing hands to sustain current publication costs through subscriptions. If journals downsized to become just peer-review service-providers, institutions would save far more than enough money to pay for it.

Would pay-to-publish lower peer-review standards?

Some have expressed the concern that if author-institutions pay to publish, then peer-review standards will decline, as journals lower acceptance standards in order to have more papers to publish. To a degree, something like this is already the case with subscription journals. There is a quality hierarchy: on the high end are the journals with high standards of quality and high selectivity, and on the low end are journals that are virtually vanity presses, accepting almost everything submitted. These quality differences are known to all researchers, on the basis of the journals' track records (and often also their citation impact factors). As such, publishing in a journal with low quality standards not only has less prestige – hence less 'publish-or-perish' value for the *author*'s career (e.g. in performance evaluation), but *users* also know the journals' track records for quality, and avoid the journals whose contents are not reliable, which again is not good for authors, shopping for a journal that users will read and cite.

None of this will change with the journal's cost-recovery model. With gold open access publishing, it is the author-institution that pays for publication instead of the user-institution, but it is the peers who referee. Hence the journals that authors will most want to publish in, and that users will most want to use, will continue to be the journals with the track record for high-quality peer-review standards (and high usage and impact metrics).

Improving the efficiency of peer review

If anything, the cost of peer review will go down once open access prevails. Not only will more and more authors be making their papers available even before they are refereed, as preprints (the way many physicists and computer scientists have been doing for years), allowing pre-refereeing commentary to improve their quality and thereby reduce the burden on the referees, but the online medium will also make it easier for editors to pick referees and to distribute the refereeing load more evenly (Harnad, 1996, 2008).

Peer feedback after posting instead of peer filtering before publishing?

Some have made even more radical predictions, suggesting that refereeing (hence journals) will disappear completely once open access prevails, and that ad lib peer commentary will replace answerable peer review as the means of quality control. Having umpired a peer-reviewed open peer commentary journal for a quarter of a century (Harnad, 1978, 1982), I am quite familiar with the difference between advance peer review, and post hoc peer commentary, and I am sceptical that the latter can replace the former (Harnad, 1997b, 1998a).

The critical difference is *answerability*. An author is answerable to the editor for meeting the referees' recommendations. With post hoc commentary, whether or not to meet commentators' recommendations is entirely up to the author. Furthermore, it is not at all clear whether self-appointed commentators are likely to be the qualified 'peers' in the way the editor-selected and answerable journal referees are. Nor is it clear whether raw, unfiltered drafts, along with self-appointed vetters' comments will yield a literature that researchers can navigate and use, allowing them to judge what is and is not reliable enough to be worth investing their finite time to read, or to risk their even more precious time and effort to try to use and build upon. Not to mention that it is not clear what will play the role of the journal's name and prior track record for tagging quality in a world with just self-posted preprints and self-posted comments (the author's name and track-record?).

The post-Gutenberg journal: optimal and inevitable for research and researchers

Post-Gutenberg peer review will be far more powerful and efficient, but it will still be the natural, answerable, expert-based quality-control system for research findings that deserves to retain the name 'refereed journal'. What will really distinguish post-Gutenberg journal publication will be that it is openly accessible to all users webwide and an integral part of a global open research web, on which research data, research papers before and after peer review, open peer commentary, research metrics and data-mining will allow scholarly/scientific collaboration, interactivity and productivity at a speed, scope and scale that were unthinkable in the Gutenberg era (Harnad, 2003; Shadbolt et al., 2006).

Bibliography

Björk, B-C, Roos, A. and Lauri, M. (2008) 'Global annual volume of peer reviewed scholarly articles and the share available via different open access options', paper presented at ElPub 2008, Open Scholarship: Authority, Community and Sustainability in the Age of Web 2.0, Toronto, 25–27 June, available at: *http://www.oacs .shh.fi/publications/elpub-2008.pdf* (accessed 1 September 2008).

Brody, T., Carr, L., Gingras, Y., Hajjem, C., Harnad, S. and Swan, A. (2007) 'Incentivizing the open access research web: publication-archiving, data-archiving and scientometrics', *CTWatch Quarterly* 3(3), available at: *http://eprints.ecs.soton.ac.uk/14418/* (accessed 1 September 2008).

Brody, T., Harnad, S. and Carr, L. (2006) 'Earlier web usage statistics as predictors of later citation impact', *Journal of the American Association for Information Science and Technology (JASIST)* 57(8): 1060–72, available at: *http://eprints.ecs.soton.ac.uk/10713/* (accessed 1 September 2008).

Doyle, M. (2001) 'Peer-review alternatives for preprints, mechanisms', paper presented at the CERN Workshop on the Open Archives Initiative (OAI) and Peer Review Journals in Europe (OAI1), Geneva, 22–4 March, available at: *http://eprints.rclis.org/archive/00000921* (accessed 1 September 2008).

Hajjem, C., Harnad, S. and Gingras, Y. (2005) 'Ten-year cross-disciplinary comparison of the growth of open access and how it increases research citation impact', *IEEE Data Engineering Bulletin* 28(4): 39–47, available at: *http://eprints.ecs.soton.ac.uk/11688/* (accessed 1 September 2008).

Harnad, S. (1978) 'Editorial', *Behavioral and Brain Sciences* 1(1), available at: *http://www.ecs.soton.ac.uk/~harnad/Temp/Kata/bbs .editorial.html* (accessed 1 September 2008).

Harnad, S. (ed.) (1982) *Peer Commentary on Peer Review: A Case Study in Scientific Quality Control*, New York: Cambridge University Press.

Harnad, S. (1990) 'Scholarly skywriting and the prepublication continuum of scientific inquiry', *Psychological Science* 1: 342–3, available at: *http://cogprints.org/1581/* (accessed 1 September 2008).

Harnad, S. (1991) 'Post-Gutenberg galaxy: the fourth revolution in the means of production of knowledge', *Public-Access Computer Systems Review* 2(1): 39–53, available at: *http://cogprints.org/1580/* (accessed 1 September 2008).

Harnad, S. (1995) 'I. Overture: The Subversive Proposal' and passim, in: A. Okerson and J. O'Donnell (eds) *Scholarly Journals at the Crossroads; A Subversive Proposal for Electronic Publishing*, Washington, DC: Association of Research Libraries, available at: *http://www.arl.org/sc/subversive/* (accessed 1 September 2008).

Harnad, S. (1996) 'Implementing peer review on the net: scientific quality control in scholarly electronic journals', in: R. Peek and G. Newby (eds) *Scholarly Publishing: The Electronic Frontier*, Cambridge MA: MIT Press, pp. 103–18, available at: *http://cogprints.org/1692/* (accessed 1 September 2008).

Harnad, S. (1997a) 'How to fast-forward serials to the inevitable and the optimal for scholars and scientists', *Serials Librarian* 30: 73–81, available at: *http://cogprints.org/1695/* (accessed 1 September 2008).

Harnad, S. (1997b) 'Learned inquiry and the net: the role of peer review, peer commentary and copyright', *Learned Publishing* 11(4): 283–92, available at: *http://cogprints.org/1694/* (accessed 1 September 2008).

Harnad, S. (1998a) 'The invisible hand of peer review', *Nature [online]*, 5 November, available at: *http://cogprints.org/1646/* (accessed 1 September 2008).

Harnad, S. (1998b) 'On-line journals and financial fire-walls', *Nature* 395(6698): 127–8, available at: *http://cogprints.org/1699/* (accessed 1 September 2008).

Harnad, S. (1999) 'Free at last: the future of peer-reviewed journals', *D-Lib Magazine* 5(12), available at: *http://cogprints.org/1685/* (accessed 1 September 2008).

Harnad, S. (2001a) 'For whom the gate tolls?' Published as: Harnad, S. (2003) 'Open access to peer-reviewed research through author/institution self-archiving: maximizing research impact by maximizing online access', in: D. Law and J. Andrews (eds) *Digital Libraries: Policy Planning and Practice*, Surrey: Ashgate Publishing, pp. 63–98; available at: *http://cogprints.org/1639/* (accessed 1 September 2008).

Harnad, S. (2001b) 'The self-archiving initiative', *Nature* 410: 1024–5, available at: *http://cogprints.org/1642/* (accessed 1 September 2008).

Harnad, S. (2003) 'Back to the oral tradition through skywriting at the speed of thought', in: J.-M. Salaün and C. Vendendorpe (eds) *Les défis de la publication sur le web: hyperlectures, cybertextes et méta-éditions*. Paris: Presses de l'enssib, available at: *http://www.interdisciplines.org/defispublicationweb/papers/6* (accessed 1 September 2008).

Harnad, S. (2008) 'Post-Gutenberg peer review: the invariant essentials and the newfound efficiencies', available at: *http://users.ecs.soton.ac.uk/harnad/Temp/peerev.pdf* (accessed 1 September 2008).

Harnad, S. and Brody, T. (2004) 'Comparing the impact of open access (OA) vs non-OA articles in the same journals' (Japanese translation), *D-Lib Magazine* 10(6), available at: *http://eprints.ecs.soton.ac.uk/10207/* (accessed 1 September 2008).

Harnad, S., Varian, H. and Parks, R. (2000) 'Academic publishing in the online era: what will be for-fee and what will be for-free?' *Culture Machine* 2, available at: *http://cogprints.org/1700/* (accessed 1 September 2008).

Harnad, S., Carr, L., Brody, T. and Oppenheim, C. (2003) 'Mandated online RAE CVs linked to university eprint archives: improving the UK Research Assessment Exercise while making it cheaper and easier', *Ariadne* 35, available at: *http://www.ariadne.ac.uk/issue35/harnad/* (accessed 1 September 2008).

Harnad, S., Brody, T., Vallieres, F., Carr, L., Hitchcock, S., Gingras, Y. Oppenheim, C., Stamerjohanns, H. and Hilf, E. (2004) 'The access/impact problem and the green and gold roads to open access', *Serials Review* 30, available at: *http://eprints.ecs.soton.ac.uk/10209/* (accessed 1 September 2008).

Hitchcock, S., Brody, T., Gutteridge, C., Carr, L., Hall, W., Harnad, S., Bergmark, D. and Lagoze, C. (2002) 'Open citation linking: the way forward', *D-Lib Magazine* 8(10), available at: *http://eprints.ecs.soton.ac.uk/7717/* (accessed 1 September 2008).

Lawrence, S. (2001) 'Online or invisible?' *Nature* 411(6837): 521, available at: *http://citeseer.ist.psu.edu/online-nature01/*.

Shadbolt, N., Brody, T., Carr, L. and Harnad, S. (2006) 'The open research web: a preview of the optimal and the inevitable', in N. Jacobs (ed.) *Open Access: Key Strategic, Technical and Economic Aspects*, Oxford: Chandos, pp. 195–205; available at: *http://eprints.ecs.soton.ac.uk/12453/* (accessed 1 September 2008).

Tansley, R. and Harnad, S. (2000) 'Eprints.org software for creating institutional and individual open archives', *D-Lib Magazine* 6(10), available at: *http://www.dlib.org/dlib/october00/10inbrief.html#HARNAD* (accessed 1 September 2008).

7

Publishing journals under a hybrid subscription and open access model

Claire Bird and Martin Richardson

Introduction

As a department of the University of Oxford, Oxford University Press has a strong imperative to explore any publishing model that might further the dissemination of research. In 2004 this led us to embark on a series of open access publishing initiatives, with the aims of testing the demand from researchers for open access, and exploring how open access models might coexist alongside subscription-based models.

Most informed participants understand that the costs of validating and disseminating research output must be covered somehow. Without the possibility of charging for access through subscriptions or licences, a common approach under an open access model is to cover publishing costs primarily through author-side payments. The journal business model is therefore turned on its head, from 'reader-side payment' to 'author-side payment'. It seems immediately clear that this kind of model may only be viable in certain disciplines where authors have access to funds for publication. An understanding of the differences between disciplines was therefore another important aim of our experiments.

Overview of 'Oxford Open' models

Our experiments with open access are grouped together under the 'Oxford Open' brand and can be divided broadly into two types: full open access models, where the entire journal is open access immediately upon publication; and optional open access models, where authors can decide whether or not to pay for immediate open access to their article. The latter gives rise to a hybrid journal made up of a variable combination of open and subscription access content. In each case, we aim to obtain the revenue needed by each journal for open access publication through author-side charges.

Nucleic Acids Research (NAR) is the largest journal owned and published by Oxford Journals. It provides an example of a traditional subscription-based journal that has made the transition to full open access; significant funds now come from author-side charges. Since 2005, all new NAR content has been made freely available online immediately on publication.

Our experiences in transitioning NAR to a fully open access model are documented elsewhere (Bird, 2008; Richardson and Saxby, 2004).

Optional open access

In July 2005 we launched an optional open access model for approximately 20 journals, across a range of disciplines (see *www.oxfordjournals.org/oxfordopen*). Since then, we have followed suit with further titles, including many published on behalf of learned societies; at the time of writing, about one-third of our journals (70 titles) are part of the initiative. Echoing the NAR institutional membership model, we decided to offer significant discounts on the charge payable for optional open access for corresponding authors based at institutions with an online subscription to the relevant journal. This adds value to the institutional subscription under the hybrid open access model. Further discounts are available for authors based in developing countries.

Optional open access charges are currently the same for the majority of the participating journals, though in future it is possible that we may need to introduce different rate bands taking into account each journal's cost structure and the level of uptake that each title is experiencing.

Uptake

Across the 65 journals offering the 'Oxford Open' option in 2007, overall uptake was around 7 per cent, which was similar to the uptake in 2006. Table 7.1 shows that the average uptake was highest in the life sciences (approximately 11 per cent), a predictable result given that the

| Table 7.1 | | Uptake of the 'Oxford Open' option by subject area 2007 | | |

Subject area	No. of journals	Articles published	Open access articles	Open access uptake (%)
Medicine	30	5,799	289	5
Life sciences	19	3,609	388	11
Social sciences and humanities	13	598	14	2
Mathematics	3	614	29	5
Total	65	10,620	720	7

open access movement has a higher profile here than in the other subject areas and funding is usually greatest in the life sciences. Average uptake for the participating medical and mathematics journals was 5 per cent in 2007, and 2 per cent for participating social science and humanities titles. Access to funding to cover open access charges is likely to be limited in the latter areas.

These averages mask the fact that for a handful of large journals in molecular and computational biology, uptake is considerably higher than the average, while many journals are experiencing little or no uptake.

For example, *Bioinformatics* is a well-established journal; it published its 24th volume in 2008 and publishes around 600 articles each year. Computational biology is a booming area and open access is a particularly hot topic in this community. In a 2004 survey, we asked the journal's authors whether they would choose to pay for optional open access. Of the 901 respondents who answered this question, 44 per cent said 'yes'. Forty-two per cent said 'no', because they did not have the necessary funds, while the remaining 14 per cent said 'no', although they would have funds available for this. These results encouraged us to make *Bioinformatics* one of our first titles to introduce optional open access. In 2007, *Bioinformatics* experienced open access uptake of 24 per cent which, while higher than for other participating journals, is still lower than might have been expected from the survey response. In 2008, open access uptake for this journal increased slightly to 27 per cent of articles.

Overall, the majority of authors are based at institutions with online access to *Bioinformatics*, and therefore pay the discounted rates. For example, in 2006, 87 per cent of authors choosing the open access option for *Bioinformatics* were eligible for the reduced subscriber rates.

Effect on subscription prices

When we launched the optional 'Oxford Open' model we promised our library customers that the online subscription prices of participating journals would be adjusted in future years, taking into account the percentage of content published under the author-side payment open access model. Our standard policy is to price the online-only (and print-only) subscriptions to our journals at 95 per cent of the combined (print and online) price. In the case of journals with 'Oxford Open' uptake, we apply a further discount to the online-only price for the following year, based on the amount of open access content published in the previous year. In 2008, the average online-only price increase for the 28 Oxford journals with open access uptake in 2006 was just 1.7 per cent – much lower than the average increase of 6.9 per cent across all our titles.

Because pricing is dependent on many factors, including variations in page extent and exchange rate adjustments, as well as open access uptake in previous years, open access adjustments do not always result in an actual price decrease from one year to the next; they may simply reduce the necessary price increase. However, when all factors are taken into account, eight 'Oxford Open' titles saw an absolute reduction in price from 2007 to 2008, and a further five journals have seen reductions in subscription price in 2009, due to increased open access uptake (see Table 7.2). As yet, it is

Table 7.2 Open access uptake and the effect on 2008 online-only price

OA uptake, 2006 (% pages)	No. journals	Actual price change, 2008 vs. 2007 (%)	Effective price reduction* due to open access (%)
0	26	+8	0
1–5	20	+3	−2
6–10	6	0	−8
11–12	2	−3	−18†

* Measured vs. our normal pricing model
† These two journals had a −9 per cent online price adjustment in 2007 due to open access uptake in 2005

too early to say what impact these price reductions will have on the number of subscriptions, or whether there might be a 'tipping point' in open access uptake, beyond which subscription attrition might accelerate, but we are of course watching this closely.

Usage and citation

To determine whether open access can be shown to have an impact on online usage, we have been working with CIBER (University College London, Centre for Publishing) looking at trends for both NAR and the optional 'Oxford Open' journals. The report concludes that the significant increase in online usage experienced by NAR in recent years can largely be attributed to the opening up of the journal to search engines, although the move to full open access may have increased usage by a further 7–8 per cent (Nicholas et al., 2006). The CIBER group is currently analysing usage data for open access and non-open access articles in optional 'Oxford Open' journals with significant uptake, to see whether further conclusions can be drawn.

There is still considerable controversy about whether open access publication leads to higher citations. A study undertaken for us in 2006 by LISU, based at Loughborough University, was inconclusive with respect to citations in three of our journals publishing open access articles (Creaser, 2006). A recent report by Phil Davis et al. (2008), who looked at open access studies articles published in 11 journals published by the American Physiological Society, concluded that there was no evidence of a citation advantage for open access articles in the first year after publication, although the study did find that open access articles were associated with 89 per cent more full-text downloads than subscription access articles in the first six months after publication. This is in contrast to reports of increased citation impact by, for example, Hajjem et al. (2005).

Practicalities

Along with valuable insights into the views and behaviours of our authors, and the potential impact of open access on journal finances, we have also learnt a great deal about the practicalities of implementing author-side payment open access models.

The following is not intended to be an exhaustive list, but journals considering experimenting with author-side payment open access for the first time may find it helpful to consider these areas:

- *Defining what is meant by open access*: It is widely accepted within the open access community that open access means more than simply free access. Peter Suber has written extensively on this in his SPARC Open Access Newsletter (Suber, 2007). When we refer to open access content at Oxford Journals we mean that the content is not only freely available online, but also free to reuse for non-commercial purposes, without the need to seek permission. We make a clear distinction between 'free access' content (for example, content previously published under subscription that we choose to make free 12 or 24 months after publication) and 'open access' content published under the open access author licence. Other publishers may however define open access differently. As such, journals need to decide what they mean by open access and ensure that this is clear to authors and readers.

- *The open access licence*: 'Oxford Open' content is published under the above terms with a Creative Commons Attribution Non-Commercial License (see *http://creativecommons.org/licenses/by-nc/2.0/uk/*). It was not essential that we moved to Creative Commons licensing for our open access content. However, the Creative Commons approach brings certain benefits, in particular the terms of reuse are immediately available to the user and the machine-readable element (incorporated into the article tagging) helps search engines and other applications to identify a work by its licence terms. Creative Commons is increasingly being seen as the standard licensing approach for open access content, and is recognized by the open access community.

- *Timing of payment*: From the beginning of our open access experiments we felt it was very important to keep the open access decision and payment process separate from the editorial review process. Therefore, for optional 'Oxford Open' journals, authors make their decision about open access after manuscripts have been accepted for publication. We believe that it is very important to retain editorial independence and for authors to be reassured that their open access decisions will not influence editorial decisions.

- *When an author changes his or her mind*: We have also placed great emphasis on ensuring that open access options for authors are clear and widely promoted. However, authors may not always understand the charges involved, or may simply change their mind down the line after selecting open access on their author licence form. Under the optional model, our policy in these instances is to revert to the normal subscription model if we are able; for example, if the article has been published online ahead of print under our 'advance access' model, but not yet in an issue, we can replace the article with a 'closed access' version showing a standard (non-open access) copyright line. However, if the article has already been published in an issue of the journal in its final definitive form, we do not reverse the open access status of the article after this point. If this is the case, we must then decide whether to pursue payment of the author-side charges, and this will depend on the individual circumstances of the case.

Conclusions

The hybrid subscription/open access model that we have described here has worked well for us since it was introduced three years ago. It has enabled us to offer our authors the choice of whether to pay for their articles to be made available open access, and has also enabled us to ensure that our subscribers are paying only for non-open access material. So far our experience suggests that models funded exclusively by author-side charges seem unlikely to be viable across all of the disciplines in which we publish, so we foresee a future of diverse models, ranging across full open access, optional open access, delayed free access (for example, where journal content is made freely available 12 months after publication), subscription access, and every combination in between, depending on the requirements of the community which each journal serves.

Acknowledgment

This chapter is an abridged and updated version of 'Oxford Journals' adventures in open access: from reader-side payment to author-side payment' by Claire Bird, which was originally published in *Learned Publishing*, Vol. 21, No. 2 (April 2008).

Bibliography

Bird, C. (2008) 'Oxford Journals' adventures in open access: from reader-side payment to author-side payment', *Learned Publishing* 21: 200–8.

Creaser, C. (2006) 'Evaluation of open access journal experiment: Stage 2 interim data' in 'Assessing the impact of open access – preliminary findings from Oxford Journals', available at: *http://www.oxfordjournals .org/news/oa_report.pdf* (accessed 2 March 2009).

Davis, P. M., Lewenstein, B. V., Simon, D. H., Booth, J. G. and Connolly, M. J. L. (2008) 'Open access publishing, article downloads, and citations: randomised controlled trial', *BMJ* 337: a568.

Hajjem, C., Harnad, S. and Gingras, Y. (2005) 'Ten-year cross-disciplinary comparison of the growth of open access and how it increases research citation impact', *IEEE Data Engineering Bulletin* 28: 39–47.

Nicholas, D., Huntington, P. and Jamali, H. R. (2006) 'The impact of open access publishing on use and users' in 'Assessing the impact of open access – preliminary findings from Oxford Journals', available at: *http://www.oxfordjournals.org/news/oa_report.pdf* . (accessed 2 March 2009).

Richardson, M. and Saxby, C. (2004) 'Experimenting with open access publishing', *Nature*, available at: *http://www.nature.com/nature/focus/ accessdebate/12.html* (accessed 2 March 2009).

Suber, P. (2007) 'Open access overview', available at: *http://www.earlham .edu/~peters/fos/overview.htm* (accessed 2 March 2009).

8

The future of copyright: what are the pressures on the present system?

Joss Saunders and Simon Smith

Plagiarism and piracy may always be with us, and are the plagues of publishing. Modern copyright law has been with us for three hundred years, and the past can teach us much about the future. We have moved a long way from the early years of modern copyright, when one of the punishments for copyright infringement in France was death by strangling. Today's law is more subtle. Litigation, border controls, police and trading standards all have a part to play, as they have for many years. But most commentators agree that the last 20 years have thrown up new challenges. It is a sad fact that the law lags some way behind industry standards and practices. As legal advisers to journal publishers, we have had to struggle to adapt old legal tools to new and evolving problems. In this chapter we aim to share our learning from the last 20 years of advising publishers on these challenges, and to apply some of the lessons of the recent as well as the more distant past to addressing the pressures that publishers face in looking at the future of copyright and their business models and practices. We propose a flexible use of the law of contract to protect publishers against some of the biggest risks.

Journals publishing is an international business, but copyright law differs from country to country. In particular, although the laws of the USA and the UK are both based on the common law system, there are important differences between them which lead to conflict. Google's library digitization programme is a clear example of the difference, as fair use in the USA is a wider concept than fair dealing in the UK (or indeed, the European Union more widely), enabling Google in the USA to digitize works without the publishers' permission, when their European counterparts operate in a more legally restricted environment.

Likewise, the European database right has no equivalent in the USA. Even plagiarism is treated differently by the two systems. As solicitors qualified in England and Wales, the authors of this chapter write from the perspective of the laws in force in the UK, but in practice many of the challenges can be addressed by appropriately worded contracts, whether those are subject to the laws of England, the laws of particular US states (New York, Massachusetts and California often being the most popular), or indeed any of the other numerous legal systems around the world.

This chapter first addresses three current challenges (digitization, user-generated content and hyperlinking), then explores how the law of contract can be used to solve new problems as they emerge. We conclude with an examination of the evolving criminal law of copyright infringement.

Throughout, it is important to balance the tension between copyright law and contract law. While the former is a creature of statute, the latter owes its success to the market. The two are closely linked. Copyright is the essential subject matter of any licence for the journal or individual articles in it. Copyright law also helps to create the criminal law sanctions for infringement of copyright. We will address the considerable protection afforded by contract law later. For now, we should recognize that other statutory and regulatory interventions are also important in protecting the rights in a journal. The contributing author's reputation is protected throughout the copyright-related mechanism of moral rights in most countries of the world (with the significant exception of the USA). Other protection for publishers is provided through the typographical right, the database right, trade mark law, and the law of passing off or unfair competition. These rights (with the exception of the typographical right) were not primarily developed for the benefit of publishers, but have been successfully adopted and used by publishers. Regulatory issues also have an important bearing in subject-specific areas, such as the publication of clinical trial results and restrictions on the reuse of clinical data through data exclusivity.

The value of the database right has been much discussed, but since the 2005 case of *British Horseracing Board Ltd and others v William Hill Organization Ltd*, when the European Court of Justice ruled that the betting chain William Hill was not infringing the right when it reused sectors of the British Horseracing Board's database of race information to commercial ends, the weight of opinion has moved against overreliance on the right. It still has value in cases where the compilation of the database itself (as opposed to the underlying data) has been expensive and/or time-consuming. By contrast, trade mark rights have been enjoying a renaissance, and this is set to continue in the publishing world. More and more publishers are replying on trade marks for titles, series and characters. As authors like Beatrix Potter come out of copyright, the trade marks in their creations become the most valuable right that remains.

While copyright law is under heavy pressure as a result of the internet, laws on fair dealing and the pressures of Google and other internet businesses, trade marks, which can be registered, are relatively easy to protect and not subject to the fair dealing exemptions, offer an effective tool in the major markets to protect the authors' and publishers' rights as they indicate the authenticity and credentials of the origination of the work. Trade mark rights are regularly pirated, but enforcement is often easier than for copyright, with the trade mark registration certificate carrying significant value. It is not surprising that lawyers are increasingly asked both by publishers and authors to register trade marks to protect their rights.

It is safe to predict that in a contribution to a book on the future of the journal, this chapter will contain material that is out of date before it is published. Rather than focus on today's technologies, we address the challenge by considering the underlying legal principles from the cases in relation to digitization and fair dealing, user-generated content and hyperlinks, and use the way the law has struggled to keep up as a lens to look into the future.

Under current UK legislation, there is no infringement of copyright if material is used in the process of criticism, review or reporting, or is copied for the purposes of research or private study (so-called 'fair dealing'). However, these provisions, and other parts of UK copyright law which are designed to give certain special exemptions to educational establishments, will not assist within the context of a full-scale back-copy digitization project; the right to do this remains with the copyright owner. This is fine from a publisher's point of view if it is the publisher that owns the copyright, but where copyright is retained, in the case of a journal, by the learned society or by the individual authors, then the job of obtaining the necessary rights for a digitization project can be lengthy and daunting. To avoid such problems in the future, the use of any well-drafted journal publication agreement, picking up all electronic, digitization and back-copy rights, will be vital.

There is also the issue of the ability of the publisher to grant long-term access to a digitized archive. The market in the UK has moved sufficiently that large academic organizations are now insisting on obtaining perpetual access to back copies of journals, and as a result publishers are faced with the problem of not only obtaining copyright permission for digitization but also making sure that that permission allows the publisher to grant long-term, and often perpetual, access to its customers. On the face of it, this appears to be an exceptionally wide right, but in the light of what we have said elsewhere in this chapter, one must question the economic value of copyright works which, although still protected by the laws of copyright, have little economic value themselves due to their age and diminishing relevance. Are learned societies giving up much when they grant such apparently wide-ranging rights? Great care must be taken, however, as there are strange and ancient rules regarding 'perpetual' rights under English law, but again, a well-drafted journal publication agreement will deal with these issues.

In late 2007, a number of online content providers including academic publishers adopted the Automated Content Access Protocol (ACAP) to regulate internet access to copyright content by way of search engines. The protocol provides a framework that allows online publishers to set out access and use policies using coding that search engine crawlers can be programmed to understand, resulting in search engine mechanisms being able to comply with a publisher's access policies. Major players including Reed Elsevier and the British Library have been involved with ACAP. On the other hand, Google has not adopted the protocol, and indeed has expressed doubts over the effectiveness of such an approach.

The interactive nature of digital media brings with it new challenges to existing copyright law and those who need to establish new contractual mechanisms within it. In the case of the printed publication, while it is possible to annotate an individual copy, a reader is unable to amend the publication as a whole as seen by the rest of the world. Blogging and other interactive mechanisms permit – indeed encourage – users to submit their own comments and amendments to publications online so that a work becomes a living entity which changes on a daily, if not hourly, basis. This new world brings exciting new possibilities for publishers, but also considerable dangers. What if, as now frequently happens, the user takes content from one site and incorporates it in his or her own upload to another site? And what if the owner of that site appears to know full well what is going on but, at the very least, turns a blind eye? It is precisely this that is alleged by Viacom in the litigation it commenced against YouTube in early 2007. In its submission to the court, Viacom alleged that YouTube users had uploaded 160,000 clips from television programmes owned by Viacom and these clips had been viewed 1.5 million times. Viacom claimed damages of US$1 billion. The *Viacom International, Inc. et al. v Youtube, Inc. et al.* case was still ongoing in March 2009.

In October 2008, Google settled (subject to court approval) its high-profile disputes in the USA with the Authors Guild Inc, the Association of American Publishers, and various major US publishers. The legal actions centred on Google's scanning and digitization of books in copyright from US libraries. Having copied the entire text of these books, Google then made extracts available on its Google Book Search service. Central to the lawsuit was whether what Google was doing was protected as fair use under US copyright law. The settlement will allow any publisher (including UK publishers) and/or author whose books have been digitized by Google potentially in breach of US copyright to claim royalties/fees from Google. Google will set up the Book Rights Registry (in effect a sort of collecting society) to manage any claims.

UK rights holders (publishers and authors) whose books may have been digitized by Google are advised to register with the Book Rights Registry to claim their entitlement as soon as the US court approves the settlement. Under international copyright law, any books published in the USA by UK publishers or distributed in the USA should potentially benefit, as will the works of UK authors. As such, the settlement potentially applies to many UK publishers and authors.

Under US law, the Digital Millennium Copyright Act 1998 permits an online service provider without actual knowledge of specific infringing postings to promptly remove those postings once it is made aware of the infringing material and thereby escape liability, and in the Viacom case it is up to Viacom to prove that YouTube knew full well what was going on. In its defence, YouTube points out that its terms and conditions of use, with which all users are meant to comply, requires users not to post infringing material, and the site also incorporates a copyright infringement notification procedure under which copyright owners can alert YouTube to infringing activities. Viacom claims that these steps do not go far enough to exculpate YouTube from liability.

A similar position exists in the UK under the Electronic Commerce (EC Directive) Regulations 2002, which relieve internet service providers that are acting as mere conduits or hosting third-party information, the details of which they have no actual knowledge of, from liability if the information they host or transmit infringes third-party copyright. However, as is the case in the Viacom litigation in the USA, it is far from clear whether this legislation exempts user-generated content aggregators such as YouTube in the same way as it does in the case of more 'traditional' internet service providers.

In late 2007, a number of online content providers including CBS, Fox, Microsoft and (of particular note) Viacom adopted *The Principles for User Generated Content Services*, which are designed to be 'a comprehensive set of guidelines to help user generated content services and content creators work together towards their collective goal of bringing more content to more consumers through legitimate channels' (see *http://www.ugcprinciples.com*). YouTube (owned by Google) is conspicuous by its absence from involvement with these new principles.

Another feature of online publishing that simply did not exist before the advent of the internet is that of hyperlinks. The ability to link dynamically to related content wherever it may be held in an electronic system has vastly improved efficiency of information and knowledge dissemination, but, as ever, there is a darker side, as the relevant technology permits not only simple linking (a link from one website to another that is obvious to the user), but also so-called 'deep linking' (which takes the user to a specified part of a website, bypassing a homepage and possibly anything that identifies the owner of the website), and 'framing' (which permits a website to display content from another website within a frame, thus giving the illusion that the content is controlled by the owner of the first website). This first came to judicial notice in the UK in the 1996 Scottish case of *Shetland Times Limited v Dr Jonathan Wills and Another*, in which it was alleged that the website of one local newspaper had 'framed' content from the website of a rival local newspaper. Claims of copyright infringement and passing off were made, but were ultimately settled before the court could give a judgment on whether such activity actually infringed any rights.

Why it takes a long time to change copyright law, and how contract law comes to the rescue

Copyright law is based on legislative solutions and international treaties. That is a main reason why change is slow, and the future challenges legislators to react more swiftly to changing copyright practices. In the twentieth century, major copyright change came after lengthy consultations, with significant UK Copyright Acts passed in 1911, 1956 and 1988. However, the pace of change has picked up since 1988, and although in the UK the Copyright, Designs and Patents Act 1988 remains the foundation of the legislation, it has been amended frequently to take into account changes such as the European database right, the European Copyright Directive, the extension of the duration of copyright, the World Intellectual Property Organization internet treaties, increased performers' rights, and the list continues. In the USA, the biggest changes were brought when the country finally joined the international Berne Convention on copyright, and later with the Digital Millennium Copyright Act.

Due to the international nature of digital copyright, however, it is increasingly necessary for the rules to be agreed at an international level. This inevitably means that the process takes longer, and that it is hard to make changes quickly to reflect technical change. Within Europe, the fact that copyright law is to a large extent harmonized by the 2001 Copyright Directive means that any change has to be agreed by a diplomatic process that now involves 27 different countries. In 2008, the UK has discussed changes to the fair dealing legislation, but change is hampered by the fact that the list of fair dealing exemptions is a closed list, with 21 permitted exceptions to copyright set out in the Copyright Directive. The UK cannot amend its copyright legislation to add to the list without first agreeing a change through the 27-nation European Union. An example of the problem is that the UK Copyright Act permitted the copying of abstracts of scientific and technical journals (section 60, Copyright, Designs and Patent Act 1988), but the European Copyright Directive does not recognize this as a permitted use, with the result that while analogue copying of abstracts is still permitted under the Directive's so-called grandmother clause (which states that use that was permitted before the Directive may continue in analogue form), digital copying of abstracts is now anomalous and at risk of challenge in the European courts. Any clarification of the right of abstract publishers to reproduce digital copies of abstracts is now dependent on the European diplomatic process.

European copyright law also brings together the common law tradition which has long governed UK and Irish publishing contracts, and the civil law tradition based on the Code Napoleon which prevails in continental Europe. One of the main tensions here is that the civil law tradition tends to be more favourable to authors (for example the French *droit d'auteur* puts the author at the heart of publishing, whereas the English term *copyright* implies the economic right to make copies, which often vests in the publisher). So when the Copyright Directive sought to harmonize European copyright law, there was at best a partial harmonization, with different rules in force regarding the transfer of copyright, and different scope for countries to opt in to different types of fair dealing exceptions to copyright. Thus, for example, educational privileges differ from country to country.

Likewise at the wider international level, copyright law is now addressed by the World Trade Organization in the Trade Related Aspects of Intellectual Property Rights (TRIPs) agreement, and is subject to the all-or-nothing approach to treaty reform that has resulted in a deadlocked Doha Round of Trade Talks. Copyright becomes dependent on agreement on trade concessions and agricultural reform. A similar difficulty in getting unanimity at the Berne Convention level led to an entirely separate treaty framework in the UN Copyright Conventions of 1996. But it is hard to see how a new body can be set up every time an existing treaty body becomes deadlocked.

The relative inflexibility of copyright law can be seen in the way that it deals with particular types of work. The UK Copyright regime, for example, defines literary works and then applies, in the main, the same rules to everything that falls within that definition. The standard length of copyright protection under UK law for any literary work extends to the end of the 70th year after the death of the author of that work, the rationale for this being to protect the interests not only of the author, but also of his family for two generations. This general principle was established in the nineteenth century to protect the families of great authors. But for copyright to exist in a journal article until 70 years after the author's death seems almost ludicrous; indeed the same can be said about almost any literary copyright work with the exception of those few works that earn significant income.

A study by Rufus Pollock of Cambridge University has set out a balance between the benefits to society from quicker access to copyright material measured against the cost to individuals of losing their rights. This suggested that the optimal length of copyright would be about 14 years. However, such an approach ignores the huge value of major works such as those by the Irish writer James Joyce, whose works remain under copyright protection until 2011 and whose estate has been vigorous in recent years in protecting that copyright in a number of jurisdictions.

Should there be different periods of protection for different types of work? Should there be some form of automatic compulsory licence for academic works which kicks in, say, after a 12-month period following first publication? In practice one sees more and more policies being imposed by the funders of academic research which require free or discounted dissemination of academic articles after an initial embargo period, that period usually running for either 12 or 18 months. The recently published US National Institutes of Health policy is but one example of this trend.

What is the reaction of publishers to be? Clearly one possible reaction is to adapt existing publishing contracts to the new regime, as is being imposed by those who, ultimately, hold the purse-strings for academic research. Adaptation of policies will also be driven by pressures from the publishers' main customers, academic institutions themselves. Maintaining an effective control based solely on a strict interpretation of copyright law for the entire period of copyright protection is simply no longer tenable in today's marketplace.

There is clear evidence, highlighted in much of what we have said above, to show that copyright law alone is a cumbersome and ultimately ineffective mechanism to protect publishers' rights in a rapidly evolving digital industry. The use of contract law, on the other hand, permits the rapid adoption of new business models tailored to this ever-changing landscape, and licensing mechanisms can be used to impose higher charges for early access to new academic thinking, lower charges for access to material which may be regarded by users as simply background reading, with perhaps special access rights granted to funders or groups of users who are sponsored by those funders.

It must be noted that contract law, at least in the USA and Europe, is not dependent on legislative change. It is an incredibly flexible instrument that adapts to change on a daily basis. Journal publishers can change their contracts to reflect demands for library substitution, permanent access, open access, or other threats and opportunities, without waiting for new legislation. In the USA, the software industry and indeed the music industry rely on licences (which are contracts) to argue that digital content is not a physical product subject to rules on the sale of physical goods, but instead is a service. The 'first copy doctrine' contained in section 109(a) of the US Copyright Act 1976 provides 'the owner of a particular copy ... lawfully made ... or any other person authorized by such owner, is entitled, without the authority of the copyright owner, to sell or otherwise dispose of the possession of that copy'. This would in theory permit a copy of software to be resold, with the loss of licensing income to the publisher. Publishers have argued that their content is not sold subject to the rules in section 109, but is licensed, and because a licence is flexible, it can contain restrictions on reuse. This is helpful for journal subscription models, and means that journal licences can be updated regularly to deal with new technical threats (like devices that circumvent copyright control software), without waiting for legislation to outlaw particular forms of circumvention.

Broadly, the USA and UK adopt the principle of freedom of contract to enable publishers to include whatever terms they like in their licences and other contracts. However, publishers need to be increasingly aware of the residual powers of intervention of the courts and other authorities. These powers tend to be more intrusive in Europe. For example, the UK's Unfair Contract Terms Act 1977 and recent European consumer protection legislation makes individual consumer licences (such as a licence for individual journal subscribers) subject to certain tests that are designed to protect the individual against what are sometimes seen as exploitative corporates. The best-known of these rules in Europe are those rules on the free movement of goods, which are at the heart of the territorial rights debate in the book trade. British publishers have argued that they need to hold European rights in books they publish in the UK, because otherwise the American publisher can export copies to France or other European Union countries, and then lawfully resell them in the UK, as no contract is allowed to restrict the sale of a book (or other goods) that have lawfully been placed on the market in any territory of the European Union (as extended by the European Economic Area agreements, including Norway). US publishers by contrast argue that this is an unjustified land grab by UK publishers. The most recent manifestation of this in the digital world is the argument by US publishers that they should have world rights to digital exploitation of traditional print products, for example e-books. The result of this would be that if a print product is subject to territorial restrictions, and the digital product is not, then the print publisher will end up marketing a product and seeing the benefits accrue to a competing digital publisher.

The criminal law

No review of the future of copyright would be complete without an examination of the criminal penalties on infringers, even if in practice publishers do not often see prosecutions for infringement, and certainly not as much as the music and film industries, which regularly threaten infringers with criminal sanctions. The law treats deliberate copyright infringement as a crime. The UK Intellectual Property Office (2007) has estimated that intellectual property crime costs the UK £9 billion a year, and that the figure is likely to grow in future. Of course, this includes trade-marked and patented goods. Much of the infringement relates to online sales, and copyright is particularly susceptible to online infringement through digital distribution.

Under current UK legislation, the making of infringing copies of copyright works for sale or hire, the distribution of infringing copies in the course of a business or to the extent that this prejudicially affects the rights of the copyright owner, and the importation of infringing copies into the UK other than for private or domestic purposes, all carry criminal penalties of up to six months imprisonment and/or a maximum fine of £5,000. Those penalties can, in each case, be increased up to ten years imprisonment and/or an unlimited fine in the more serious cases that are dealt with on indictment. However, these offences are clearly mostly relevant to the 'physical world' and less so to the online environment.

The *Gowers Report on Intellectual Property* is the first such wide-ranging report on intellectual property law in the UK in two decades. Much of the report looks at the consequences of the advent of the digital revolution. With respect to criminal law, the report notes that although criminal sanctions for copyright infringement were expressly extended to online content in 2003 (with a new offence of communicating a copy to the public by electronic transmission in the course of a business or to an extent prejudicially affecting the copyright owner), the relevant maximum penalty remained two years imprisonment rather than ten years imprisonment. The report therefore recommends extending the maximum penalty for online commercial infringement of copyright to ten years imprisonment.

In practice, however, the use of criminal law sanctions is rare. In many cases publishers and other rights owners want to be able to act quickly in order to close down infringing activity, and several mechanisms such as injunctions and other interim court orders available from the civil courts tend, on the whole, to provide more effective mechanisms than those involving law enforcement agencies who arguably do not see copyright infringement in the same serious light as the other criminal offences they tend to deal with. While the criminal law is a useful backup, underlining the threat which society wishes to pose to those who unlawfully profit from the intellectual works of others, it is likely always to be the civil courts that remain at the forefront of the battle against copyright infringement. It is noteworthy, of course, that the civil courts enforce contractual rights, and this reality supports the authors' contention that it is to contractual mechanisms, as much as the underlying statute law, that publishers and other rights holders need primarily to look in order to fashion and protect their evolving business models in the digital age.

Conclusion

The pressures on the current system will continue to grow, as new technologies emerge. The law will continue to fail to keep up, as legislators lag behind the technology. It will be all the more important for publishers, through their business practices, to continue to adapt to cybercrime and to new entrants who challenge existing models of copyright exploitation. In this process of adaptation, contract law has a vital role to play, and forward-looking publishers will not only use contract law to protect their rights, but will also develop their licences and other modes of exploitation to take advantage of the new commercial opportunities that will arise.

Bibliography

HM Treasury (2006) *Gowers Review of Intellectual Property*, London: Stationery Office.

IP Crime Group (2007) *Intellectual Property Crime Report 2007*, Newport: UK-IPO.

Pollock, R. (2008) *Forever Minus a Day? Theory and Empirics of Optimal Copyright Term*, Cambridge: University of Cambridge Faculty of Economics, Cambridge.

9

Journals ranking and impact factors: how the performance of journals is measured

Iain D. Craig and Liz Ferguson

Why rank journals?

There are many ways in which a journal may be ranked, such as surveying the opinions of the individuals who read them, or using empirical measurements based on the numbers of citations or downloads of the journal's articles. Before considering any of these ranking mechanisms in detail, however, it is worth dwelling on why we would wish to rank journals in the first place.

Estimates of the number of peer-reviewed journals in current circulation vary considerably, but a recent article places the number at around 23,000 (Morris, 2007). With readers having limited time to search and read the literature and libraries having limited financial resources to acquire journal content, some form of value judgment is required to provide focus. Assigning a numerical ranking to a journal (e.g. citations per article, cost per ranking unit, or downloads per article) allows for ready comparisons between titles with similar aims and scope. These average measures encapsulate one or more characteristics of the journal and, depending on which perspective you are viewing from, enable the individual to focus their finite resources better.

An additional reason to rank journals is related to the increasing desire to rank individuals, research groups, and even institutions by the quantity and quality of their output in peer-reviewed journals. While this practice is ill-advised due to the problems of extrapolating the average journal quality to the individual articles which are published in those journals, a number of current schemes nevertheless do just that. More sophisticated schemes will investigate the quality of individual articles themselves rather than rely on the bulk average; however, the use of journal quality as a proxy for author quality has the benefit of convenience, being far less labour-intensive than collecting individual citation scores for each article.

From a publisher's perspective, we are interested in pursuing activities which maximize the quality and visibility of our journals, ensuring they reach as many interested users as possible, and are attractive to potential authors seeking to publish their highest-quality research. To this end, scoring highly in various systems of ranking is crucially important to the long-term success of a journal.

Conventional measurement types

Methods of ranking journals can be qualitative, quantitative, or a combination of elements of both. With the emergence of online journal content platforms and the availability of increasing computational power, quantitative methods have largely asserted dominance over the qualitative methods. This is not to say that quantitative methods are intrinsically better than qualitative methods; it is more a function of the ease with which data can be acquired and analysed. According to Lehmann (2006), 'Institutions have a misguided sense of the fairness of decisions reached by algorithm; unable to measure what they want to maximize (quality), they will maximize what they can measure'.

Certain subject disciplines lend themselves particularly well to quantitative methods such as citation analysis. Other disciplines, particularly the arts and humanities, are less well suited to evaluation by citation analysis (see *Subject-specific citation differences* in this chapter). Qualitative judgments as to the relative merits of different journals are much more prevalent in these subjects than in the sciences, for example.

Citation linkages

The most common form of quantitative measurement is based upon citation linkages, whereby two documents, A and B, are linked when document B cites document A by means of a reference to document A in its bibliography. This type of citation linkage is largely understood to be a means of substantiating and building upon previous work, although there are numerous alternative reasons why an author may cite previous work (Case and Higgins, 2000), including criticising previous work or conforming to social hierarchical mechanisms. Despite these possible alternative reasons for the presence or absence of a citation, the interpretation of a citation-based analysis typically relies on the assumption that citations are provided for positive reasons.

Counting the citation linkages between documents requires a well-structured citation index. A citation index allows a user to navigate from an article, both backwards to previous work and forwards to work which has referenced the article in question. While not inventing the concept of citation indexing, Eugene Garfield can be credited with commercializing the process and applying it to the scholarly communication process. Garfield (1955) describes the concept of his citation index, and in 1961 the Institute of Scientific Information (ISI), the company he founded, launched the Science Citation Index. For many decades, the standards in citation indexing were the ISI citation indexes (now part of Thomson-Reuters and collectively known as Web of Science). In recent years new citation indexes have emerged, such as Scopus (*http://www.scopus.com*), CiteSeerX (*http://citeseerx.ist.psu.edu*) and GoogleScholar (*http://scholar.google.com*).

The main differences between Scopus and Web of Science are related to the breadth and depth of coverage (how many journals they cover over how many years), but they operate on the same principles: receiving a defined set of journal articles and their references directly from the publisher, initially as print-copy for scanning and optical character recognition (OCR) and latterly as an e-feed. In this way, Scopus and Web of Science capture and index bibliographic metadata for a selected group of high-quality titles, allowing them to match citing references to target articles with a high degree of accuracy.

GoogleScholar and CiteSeerX operate using an autonomous citation indexing principle, whereby indexing robots look for scholarly material by trawling the internet, including the major journal content hosted on delivery platforms (such as Wiley InterScience, ScienceDirect, etc), centralized subject repositories such as arXiv, institutional repositories, or even researchers' personal webpages. Once the robots have identified suitable content, indexing algorithms extract bibliographic metadata and citing references, and these are matched to existing articles in their database.

In addition to the standard document B cites document A citation, other forms of citation-based linkages are possible, such as bibliographic coupling (Kessler, 1963) where two documents cite a common third document (document C) or co-citation studies (Marshkova, 1973; Small, 1973) which measure the number of times documents A and B are cited together in subsequent literature.

Bibliographic coupling and co-citation studies of the journal literature have until recently been small-scale studies and largely confined to the academic realm of scientometrics because of the need to have access to the underlying raw citation data. However, the same principles can be applied to any collection of documents. The advent of institutional and subject-based repositories, which make their metadata readily available for harvesting, mean that these measurements are becoming more commonplace.

Subject-specific citation differences

Researchers communicate research outputs of different subject areas in different ways. Some predominantly use journals, while others use a much broader range of media such as monographs, book chapters, working papers, reference works, handbooks and conference proceedings. This has dramatic consequences on the application and validity of journal-based citation analysis in different disciplines.

In Table 9.1, the first column, 'Importance of journals', describes the proportion of references within ISI indexed journals which refer to other journals (Moed, 2005). The data set consists of the references of original articles and reviews published in the ISI indexes during 2002, with only references to items from 1980 onwards being considered. In molecular biology and biochemistry, 96 per cent of references are to other journal articles, whereas in the humanities and arts only 34 per cent of references are to other journal articles. A citation analysis based on journal citations will, therefore, capture much more of the research communication in molecular biology and biochemistry than it will in the humanities and arts.

The ISI citation indexes provide variable coverage of different subject areas, with some areas being better represented than others. The column headed 'ISI coverage of journal literature' in Table 9.1 indicates the proportion of references to articles in journals indexed by ISI, and therefore visible in any citation analysis. The journal coverage is highest in molecular biology and biochemistry and lowest in the humanities and arts.

Multiplying the importance of journals by the journal coverage provides a value for the effective ISI coverage of the totality of research communication in that particular subject area. In the humanities and arts, only 34 per cent of communication is via journal articles and only 50 per cent of those journal articles are indexed in ISI. This gives an overall coverage value of 17 per cent.

This combination of the significance of journal communication and the actual coverage of the journal literature indicates that the questions

Table 9.1 Importance and coverage of different subjects in ISI citation indexes (based on references in articles and reviews published during 2002)

Discipline	Importance of journals (%)	ISI coverage of journal literature (%)	Overall ISI coverage (%)
Molecular biology and biochemistry	96	97	92
Biological sciences related to humans	95	95	90
Chemistry	90	93	84
Clinical medicine	93	90	84
Physics and astronomy	89	94	83
TOTAL ISI	84	90	75
Applied physics and chemistry	83	89	73
Biological sciences ~ animals and plants	81	84	69
Psychology and psychiatry	75	88	66
Geosciences	77	81	62
Other social sciences ~ medicine and health*	75	80	60
mathematics	71	74	53
Economics	59	80	47
Engineering	60	77	46
Other social sciences†	41	72	29
Humanities and arts‡	34	50	17

Source: Reproduced with kind permission of Springer Science and Business Media.
*Includes public environment and occupational health, nursing, sport sciences.
†Includes sociology, education, political sciences, and anthropology.
‡Includes law.

which can be answered through citation analysis vary greatly between subject areas. Perhaps even more importantly, they will vary between different citation indexes, such as Web of Science, Scopus, GoogleScholar, CiteSeerX etc.

Finally, these differences will also vary over time. The data reported in Table 9.1 are taken from an examination of the ISI citation indexes in 2002. Since then, coverage has increased, most notably with the October 2008 integration of the ISI proceedings indexes. Longitudinal comparisons need to be undertaken with the knowledge that coverage is not fixed, but is constantly in motion.

Citation distributions

The distribution of citations to articles follows a skewed rather than normal distribution, i.e. a small number of items are exceptionally highly cited, with the majority of items being seldom cited. A study of biomedical journals reported that:

> Fifteen per cent of a journal's articles collect 50% of the citations, and the most cited half of the articles account for nearly 90% of the citations. Awarding the same value to all articles would therefore tend to conceal rather than to bring out differences between the contributing authors. (Seglen, 1992)

The findings of this research are borne out by Wiley-Blackwell's recent internal analysis of a sample of journals across a number of diverse subject areas (S. Chong, personal communication, 2008). The analysis examined articles and reviews published in 2004, with citation counts from publication to April 2008, i.e. between 4.25 and 3.25 years from publication. The proportion of articles which contributed 50 per cent of the total citations received in that period were recorded and plotted in Figure 9.1.

A consequence of this skewed distribution is that average values tend to be highly influenced by the presence or absence of a handful of

Figure 9.1 Percentage of articles published in 2004 which account for 50 per cent of citations in the following 3.25–4.25 years

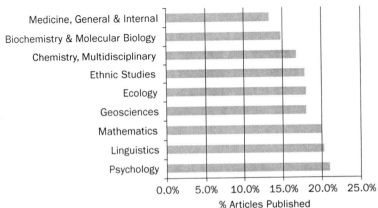

highly-cited items from one year to the next. The implication is that consideration should be given to the type of statistical method or test that is applied when examining sets of citation data. Non-parametric methods will, in many cases, be more appropriate than their parametric counterparts.

Journal citation reports

The most common journal aggregated citation-based measurement in use today is the Impact Factor, which is published annually by ISI as a component of its Journal Citation Report (JCR). But the Impact Factor is not the only measurement that is provided in the JCR, and some of the other measurements, such as Total Citations, Cited Half-Life and Immediacy Index, provide valuable information at the journal level. Measurements aggregated to the level of the subject category provide useful benchmarking values or rankings.

The Impact Factor

The Impact Factor is a measure of the average number of citations to the articles contained within a given journal. This calculation is based on the citations originating from the journal subset indexed in ISI's Web of Science, approximately 9,000 of the 23,000 journals estimated to be in existence (Morris, 2007). In practice, only those journals which appear in either the Science or Social Science citation indexes will receive an Impact Factor.

The Impact Factor imposes some special restrictions on the calculation of this average, limiting it to citations during a defined period of time, to articles published in a second defined period of time. The definition of the 2008 Impact Factor is provided by:

$$\frac{\text{Citations in 2008 to all items from 2006 and 2007}}{\text{Number of 'source items' from 2006 and 2007}}$$

The Impact Factor was created by Garfield in the early 1960s as a measure to select new journals to add to his growing Science Citation Index. By aggregating author-level citation data to the level of the journal, he could determine which journals were most commonly cited. For a fuller historical explanation of the origins of citation indexing and the Impact Factor, see Bensman (2007). Journals which Garfield identified as heavily cited but not indexed at that time were then added to the citation index. Garfield noted that a relatively small core of journals were responsible for the majority of citations, and this allowed him to cost-effectively cover a large proportion of cited articles, without necessarily indexing the entire corpus of research. In an essay currently available on the Thomson-Reuters website, this inner core of journals is highlighted:

> ...an analysis of 7,528 journals covered in the 2005 JCR® revealed that as few as 300 journals account for more than 50% of what is cited and more than 25% of what is published in them. A core of 3,000 of these journals accounts for about 75% of published articles and over 90% of cited articles. Furthermore, this core is not static. Its basic composition changes constantly, reflecting the evolution of scholarly topics. (Testa, year unknown)

The suitability of the Impact Factor as a measure of journal quality has been thoroughly debated (e.g. Seglen, 1997) and we do not propose to revisit old arguments here. Suffice to say, despite the noted shortcomings, the Impact Factor is a powerful metric, perhaps the pre-eminent metric, in the author, library and research funding community, and although it is frequently used in an inappropriate manner, it cannot be dismissed.

Total Citations

While the average citation per article calculation that is the Impact Factor mitigates for the effects of journal size, it has a tendency to favour review journals which typically publish a relatively small number of highly-cited articles (although see *Reviews* in this chapter). The Total Citations measure provides a broader perspective by counting citations from all citing articles from the current JCR year to all previous articles (from any year) in the journal in question. Such a metric will obviously highlight the larger, higher-quality, journals. In theory, as the journal's total output, and hence citeable material, can only ever increase from year to year, the Total Citations value should also increase from year to year. In practice, however, obsolescence of the literature occurs (see *Cited Half-Life* in this chapter), with material becoming less likely to be cited the older it becomes. This, to a degree, keeps in check the year-on-year rise of the Total Citation figure.

Cited Half-Life

An article's citation distribution over time can be monitored and characterized. Taking an idealized article, the citations per period will typically rise over time to a maximum. This maximum is dependent on the inherent quality of the article, the subject area (medical sciences will reach a peak more rapidly than social sciences), and the type of document (short communications will typically see an earlier peak than original research articles). From this peak it will then drop off, again at a rate dependent on quality, subject area, and the type of article.

The Cited Half-Life value characterizes the age distribution of citations to a journal, giving an indication of the rate of obsolescence. The Cited Half-Life as defined by ISI in the JCR is the median age of the papers that were cited in the current year. For example, a Cited Half-Life in JCR 2008 of 6.0 years means that of the citations received by the journal from all papers published in 2008, half were to papers published between 2003 and 2008.

The desired value for a Cited Half-Life varies depending on the journal. A long Cited Half-Life for a journal can be interpreted as meaning longevity in articles and a journal that serves an archival purpose, whereas a short Cited Half-Life can indicate articles which are on the cutting-edge but quickly rendered obsolete by the pace of change in the subject area. Both of these qualities are desirable for different reasons.

Immediacy Index

The Immediacy Index is an indication of how rapidly citations to a journal take place, and is calculated as the ratio of the number of citations received in the current year, to the number of source items published in the current year. Within-year citations indicate that the research is being rapidly built upon, which is a desirable outcome for any journal.

Subject aggregated data

Since JCR 2003 (published summer 2004), ISI have produced data aggregated to the level of the subject category in addition to the journal-specific values mentioned above. These data allow for benchmarking against peer journals, and enhance the usability of the journal-specific data. The data provided at a subject level include: Total Citations, median Impact Factor, aggregate Impact Factor, aggregate Immediacy

Index, aggregate Citing Half-Life, aggregate Cited Half-Life and total articles.

By comparing, for example, the change in a journal's Impact Factor over time against the change in the median or aggregate Impact Factor over the same period, one can determine whether changes at a journal level are to do with the quality of the articles within the journal itself, or merely a reflection of an overall trend at the subject level. This is particularly useful when explaining step-changes in Impact Factor across a group of journals.

One note of caution should be sounded when performing longitudinal analysis of the journals in the JCR: the ISI journal universe is constantly in flux. The net change in the number of titles is positive, but journals cease, merge and split, while some are simply dropped as they no longer fulfil the selection criteria as research trends evolve over time. Conversely, new journals and occasionally new subjects are added to better reflect the current status of research. This change in the composition of the indexes, and hence the JCR, means that care needs to be taken when interpreting data to ensure that the observed result is a true result, and not simply an artefact of the evolving composition of the index.

Using JCR metrics in promoting journals

There exist in the JCR a number of metrics that can be used to rank journals. The choice of one particular metric over another depends on the message to be conveyed, and the ranking of the journal in each of the metrics. For instance, a large journal without a particularly high Impact Factor may be ranked highly by Total Citations, and so may adopt that as its unique selling point in marketing messages.

Ultimately, journal editors and publishers are competing in a crowded world for the attention of readers and potential authors. Marketing messages are prepared and distributed which make use of a variety of metrics, with the intention of appealing to as many potential authors as possible and with the intention of improving those metrics in the future.

Author behaviour and journal strategies

Increasingly, the academic and financial success of a researcher is tied to their ability to publish in high-impact journals. In some instances, this imperative results in journal submission choices being made not due to the journal's suitability in terms of the article content and the audience to be served, but simply because it has an Impact Factor above a certain value. This strategy is clearly misguided, as simply appearing in a journal with a high Impact Factor does not guarantee that an article will receive any more citations than if it had appeared in a journal with a much lower Impact Factor (though that assumption cannot be tested). Nor does it follow that an individual article will receive the average number of citations that previous articles have received, due to the skewed distribution of citations in a journal's articles. The 2005 CIBER study of more than 5,500 authors (Rowlands and Nicholas, 2005) clearly illustrates the importance of the Impact Factor in publication decisions: the Impact Factor was the third most important reason (after reputation and readership) for authors to select a journal for submission of their most recent paper. A survey carried out by Wiley-Blackwell into the submission behaviours of early-career authors identified the same trend, though interestingly it was slightly less pronounced than in more experienced researchers (L. Ferguson, personal communication, 2007).

Impact Factors and rankings are a regular agenda item for journal editorial board meetings for the reasons outlined above. The Impact Factor has a substantial effect on author behaviour when choosing where to publish and most editors believe, with justification, that a good Impact Factor and the high ranking it brings is one of the strongest drivers of high-quality submissions. This notion is supported by data made available by the editors of *Aging Cell*, published by Wiley-Blackwell, a young journal in a growing field (Figure 9.2). Data on manuscript submissions have been recorded in six-month periods, and

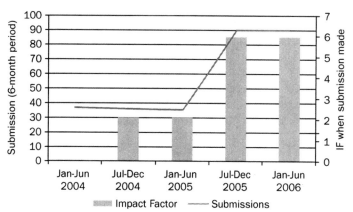

Figure 9.2   Manuscript submissions in six-month periods versus Impact Factor for the journal *Aging Cell*

are plotted alongside the Impact Factor held by the journal at the point the manuscript was submitted.

The Impact Factor of *Aging Cell* increased from 2.118 to 5.960 between JCR 2005 and 2006. Comparing the level of submissions in the six-month period before the rise to the submissions once the new, higher, Impact Factor was published, the journal received approximately 150 per cent more submissions than in the previous period.

A number of strategies are available to an editor who wishes to improve the likelihood of their journal gaining a good Impact Factor. Some approach these with more enthusiasm than others.

Review articles

Review articles typically attract more citations on average than primary research articles (see for example Moed et al., 1996; Peters and Van Raan, 1994). The effect of this can be seen in ISI Impact Factor listings, with many subject categories topped by review journals.

There is however some evidence of journal-specific effects here. Average citation rates of review and research articles in *New Phytologist*, for example, show marked differences, while the review and regular research articles in *Journal of Urology* and *Alimentary Pharmacology and Therapeutics* exhibit less pronounced differences (Figure 9.3).

One explanation for these differences is the nature of the review articles themselves. 'Review' is a catch-all term for numerous different document types, ranging from a full comprehensive review, to a

Figure 9.3a Average number of citations (to end April 2008) to regular and review articles published in *New Phytologist*, 2004–2006

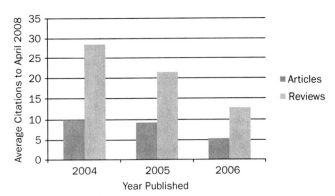

Figure 9.3b Average number of citations (to end April 2008) to regular and review articles published in *Journal of Urology*, 2004–2006

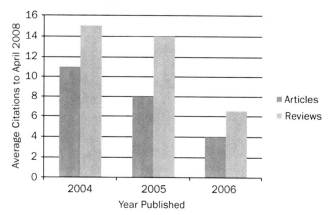

Figure 9.3c Average number of citations (to end April 2008) to regular and review articles published in *Alimentary Pharmacology and Therapeutics*, 2004–2006

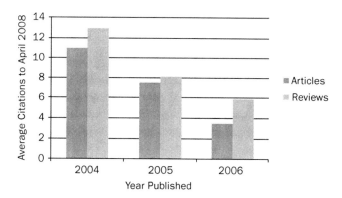

mini-review, to a perspective or a tutorial. This heterogenicity is likely to lead to local differences in expected citation counts. For example, since 1985, *New Phytologist* has published its Tansley Reviews, reviews written by specialists but aimed at a readership beyond that which could be expected from a specialist review journal. This prestige may elevate them further above research articles than might otherwise be expected.

Because of the powerful effect they can have, many journal editors are keen to publish review articles. This is not simply to increase the Impact Factor, however. The data in Figure 9.4 suggest that as well as having

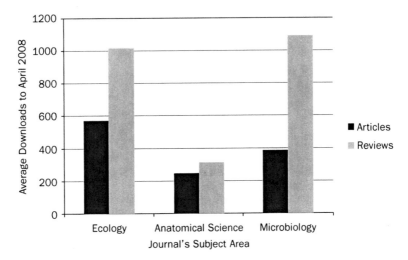

Figure 9.4 Average article downloads (to end April 2008) for journal articles published in 2007 in three areas of science

a positive effect on the Impact Factor, review articles are typically downloaded significantly more often than primary research articles and can broaden readership.

It is interesting to note the gross differences in download ratios for the three journals in the different subject areas. Broadly speaking, the ratio for the anatomical science journal more closely mirrors the citation ratios of the medical journals (Figure 9.3b and 9.3c), while the ecology and microbiology journals reflect the citation ratios of the plant science journal (Figure 9.3a).

Writing a high-quality, comprehensive, review article takes a significant amount of effort on the part of an author; most are more driven to publish primary papers because it is these that earn them tenure or continue to advance their reputations. Journal editorial teams also invest a significant amount of energy into devising strategies for acquiring review articles.

The question of whether the proliferation of review articles is desirable and whether this effort is warranted has been investigated in the pathology literature (Ketcham and Crawford, 2007). Ketcham and Crawford identified a sixfold increase in review articles between 1991 and 2006, compared with a twofold increase in primary research articles. Similarly, examining papers using hepatitis as a title or keyword, the authors identified a 13-fold increase in review articles over a 20-year period, compared with a sixfold increase in primary research articles. In both cases, the growth of the review literature was largely outside review journals. Most importantly, from the perspective of a journal editor who may be seeking to improve an Impact Factor, the authors demonstrate that only a small proportion of review articles achieve a high number of citations. Thus, the energy put into acquiring review articles by journal editorial teams may, in many cases, be misdirected.

Increasing the focus on areas more likely to attract citations

Within all journals, some subject areas will be cited more frequently than others or will fit the two-year Impact Factor window better. It is not inconceivable that editors might devote more space in a journal to areas more likely to attract citations, though many editors oppose this practice as it would result in their journals not representing full and balanced coverage of their disciplines. Philip Campbell of the Nature Publishing Group, for example, has rejected the suggestion that *Nature* focuses on areas likely to attract more citations as the journal continues to publish papers in such areas as geology and palaeontology, rather than focusing on more highly cited subjects such as molecular biology (see Monastersky, 2005).

Picking up papers from higher-impact journals

In many cases, an author will prefer to submit to a high-impact, broad-based journal rather than a journal of lower impact which is perhaps more suited to the subject matter of the manuscript in question. An unofficial hierarchy of broad to niche, and high to low quality emerges. If a generalist journal rejects the paper as of insufficient broad interest, but methodologically sound, some high-level, subject-specific journals now informally encourage authors to submit referees' comments along with their manuscript – this frequently negates the need for further peer review as a decision can be made on the suitability of the paper using the reviews from the first journal. This has the dual effect of increasing the speed of review and publication while lessening the peer-review load on the community.

A more organized attempt at transferring reviewed papers between journals has been established in neuroscience. On 1 January 2008, the

Neuroscience Peer Review Consortium (*http://nrpc.incf.org*) began operating for an initial 12-month period with the intention of reducing the load on reviewers. At the time of writing, more than 30 journals are participating in the trial, with others in the process of joining. On receiving a rejection, authors are given the option of having the reviews of their article automatically forwarded to another journal of their choice in the consortium.

Decreasing the denominator

ISI does not include all document types in the denominator of its calculations of the Impact Factor, whereas all citations to any document type are counted on the numerator. This can lead to situations where some citations are not offset by the presence of a publication on the denominator, effectively meaning these citations are 'free' citations. What ISI does include it terms as 'citeable items', which are commonly referred to as source items. Source items typically include research articles, review articles, case reports and articles published in any supplements. Items frequently excluded from the denominator of the calculation include letters (unless they function as articles, e.g. in *Nature* or *Ecology Letters*), commentaries, meeting abstracts, book reviews and editorials. Although the document type designation of a journal's papers can be readily determined once they have been indexed in Web of Science, it is not always clear how that decision has been reached, and this can be a source of some frustration for editors and publishers (PLoS Medicine Editors, 2006). Editors and publishers are able to contact ISI to request that they treat certain article types as non-source items, but this channel is informal, and it is entirely at ISI's discretion as to whether requests are granted.

Self-citation

Self-citation, and specifically a journal editor suggesting during the peer-review process that authors may wish to consider citing more work from that journal (either suggesting particular papers or suggesting the authors identify some themselves), is regarded as the least acceptable way for a journal to improve its Impact Factor.

Editorials focusing on the journal's own recent content can also be used to increase the number of citations. This approach was observed *in extremis* in an editorial by Potter et al. (2004), which cited 100 of its own articles from previous years; furthermore, the editorial was published in not one, but five different journals. In reality, however, only one of these editorials was indexed by ISI, and these self-citations were actually only a small proportion of the citations received, and did not unduly disturb the journal's Impact Factor.

While obvious effects such as this can be readily identified (Reedijk and Moed, 2008), more subtle effects prove harder to quantify, although with the widespread availability of citation data it is unlikely that these practices could go undetected indefinitely.

The JCR now identifies the proportion of self-cites for individual journals and even recalculates an Impact Factor once the effect of self-citing has been removed. In JCR 2007, published summer 2008, eight journals were ejected from the JCR due to excessive self-citation. The following statement was posted on the JCR website:

> Due to the significant effect of Self Citations on their Impact Factors, metrics for a number of titles were not published in the 2007 JCR. Suppressed titles were found to have exceptionally high self citation rates, some over 90%. This level of self citation has a profound effect on the rank of the journal in its category and does not reflect accurately the journal's true participation, by way of citation, in the scholarly literature of its subject. (Thomson-Reuters, 2008)

McVeigh (year unknown) states that 82 per cent of journals in JCR 2002 had a self-citation rate no higher than 20 per cent, with a population mean of 12 per cent and median of 9 per cent. Finally, it is readily acknowledged that there is often a good reason for a journal having a high self-citation rate. Journals that are very specialized or are the dominant publication for a particular subset of a subject are more likely to show high rates of self-citation than those where research is spread among a number of journals with similar aims and scope.

Download statistics

Although librarians have been monitoring use of print copies using a number of elaborate processes for some considerable time (Butkovich, 1996), comprehensive statistics based on actual user activities have until recently not been possible. With the transition from print to online delivery of journal content, a new method for evaluating journals was born based on the actual activities that the user undertook while at the journal website, namely measuring the number of full-text articles downloaded.

A terminology question arises when describing usage statistics. What does a full-text download actually represent? One cannot be certain that the user read the item they downloaded, or even that they truly intended to download the item in the first place. Further, while specific filters have been developed to eliminate double-counting of multiple versions of the same article (i.e. toggling between HTML and PDF formats), users may choose to re-download an item every time they wish to view it, or they may download the PDF and store it locally for subsequent use.

It is clear that download figures need to be addressed cautiously. While the activities that can lead to under or over-counting of actual use can be assumed to take place in comparable ratios between different journals, there is no simple way of retrospectively examining any anomalous data, other than sifting through the server logs while questioning the user as to their motivation for each and every activity. Citation-based measurements are by no means without their flaws, but they do at least provide a permanence of record, and an ability to adjust data to account for factors such as self-citation; this is not possible through the use of usage data.

As online journals proliferated from the late 1990s, and data on page impressions (views), numbers of sessions, and crucially the numbers of articles downloaded could be easily collected, it became clear that a common standard was required in reporting usage information, in order to make valid comparisons between journals supplied by different publishers. In 2002, the Counting Online Usage of Networked Electronic Resources (COUNTER) project was launched. The aim of COUNTER was to provide a code of practice for the reporting of online usage data, in order to facilitate inter-journal and inter-publisher comparisons. As of August 2008, the current code of practice is release 3. Any COUNTER 2 compliant publisher wishing to remain classed as COUNTER compliant has until August 2009 to implement all the standardized reporting criteria as described in release 3.

While it is technically possible to measure every mouse-click on a website, a technique known as deep-log analysis (Nicholas et al., 2006), a discussion of such analysis is beyond the scope of this chapter. Suffice to say, the headline usage figure that is most commonly reported is the number of full-text downloads per journal per time period, which is referred to as Journal Report 1.

COUNTER Journal Report 1 and cost per access

From Journal Report 1, library administrators can compare the level of full-text downloads of their journal collection over monthly reporting periods. A common measure that is then derived is the cost per access (cost per use), which enables a comparison of the cost-effectiveness of different parts of a collection. Although superficially a simple process (just divide the cost of the journal by the number of full-text downloads in a specified period), the range of mechanisms by which journals are sold to institutions has a large bearing on the relevance and validity of this figure.

In the print era, journals were typically sold as single entities. Subscription agents made the process of subscribing to different journals from the same publisher a much simpler proposition, but in essence, the cover price of a journal was what was paid, and a publisher's revenues could be estimated by multiplying the cover price (minus the agent's commission) by the number of subscriptions. In today's online era, journals are sold as a mixture of single sales and larger bundles, and to a combination of individuals, institutes and vast library consortia occasionally spanning an entire nation, where the terms and conditions of the deal are collectively brokered. A consequence of this is that access to the journal literature has never been greater, with many institutions subscribing to a publisher's entire collection of titles.

A by-product of this bundling process is that the actual cost to the library of an individual title is typically significantly less than the cover price. Precisely how much less will vary depending on the particular subscription model the publisher operates. Now factor in the changes in the operational cost structure of the library as a result of print to online migration (Schonfeld et al., 2004), and a simple cost per access calculation suddenly becomes a far more intricate undertaking (Price, 2007).

Usage Factor

As with counting citations, the number of downloads is determined by the number of articles online and accessible. All things being equal, a larger journal will experience more downloads than a smaller journal. This size effect can be mitigated by calculating an average number of downloads per article, in the same manner as the Impact Factor is an average of citations per article. This so-called Usage Factor, as proposed by COUNTER and the UK Serials Group (UKSG) (UKSG, year unknown), has the potential to make meaningful comparisons between journals based on their usage, although a number of problems need to be overcome before such a measure can be universally accepted.

The main challenge is in creating a measurement which is resilient to deliberate and systematic abuse. This is of particular relevance when considering a usage-based pricing model, or where reward of individuals is based (even partly) upon the usage of their journal articles by others.

Peer-review panel judgments

As discussed in the section on subject-specific citation differences, certain subject areas do not lend themselves to citation analysis. It can be no coincidence that while ISI produces three citation indexes, for Science, Social Science, and Arts and Humanities, it only produces a Science and Social Science Journal Citation Report (the product which contains metrics such as the Impact Factor). Evidently, the validity of an Impact Factor based on journals which only appear in the Arts and Humanities citation index is too low to be meaningful.

In the absence of a simple quantitative metric for the large numbers of journals without Impact Factors, particularly, but not exclusively, in the arts and humanities, the most common form of ranking is that which originates from peer opinion.

European Reference Index for the Humanities

An example of peer opinion being used to rank journals is the European Reference Index for the Humanities (ERIH), a project run by the European Science Foundation (*http://www.esf.org*). The ERIH project intends to provide a categorized list of journals in 15 areas of the humanities. Expert panels will split the journals into three categories (A, B and C), based on peer review. The stated motivation for creating the ERIH is as follows:

> ...in the view of funding bodies such as the ERC, it is becoming increasingly important to identify and compare Humanities excellence at a supra-national European level.
>
> ERIH intends to contribute to the creation of appropriate tools to achieve this and operates as a process led by academics for academics. At present, it is a reference index of the top journals in

15 areas of the Humanities, across the continent and beyond. (ERIH, 'Context and Background', year unknown)

According to the ERIH Summary Guidelines (year unknown), the categories are defined as follows:

- *Category A* (expected to be 10–25 per cent of all titles):
  - high-ranking, international-level publication;
  - very strong reputation among researchers of the field;
  - regularly cited all over the world.
- *Category B*:
  - standard, international-level publication;
  - good reputation among researchers of the field in different countries.
- *Category C*:
  - important local/regional level publication;
  - mainly local/regional readership, but occasionally cited outside the publishing country;
  - Only European publications to be considered (member organizations of the European Science Foundation).

While such broad categorization of journals is a step away from the over-precision that is implied when journals are ranked according to Impact Factors quoted to three decimal places, there are likely to be heated debates on the margins between the different categories and of the overall wisdom of applying any such ranking to the humanities. In a joint editorial entitled 'Journals under threat: a joint response from *History of Science, Technology and Medicine* editors', which has been archived in numerous online discussion lists and fora, editors from over 40 journals raised concerns regarding the process:

> This Journal has concluded that we want no part of this dangerous and misguided exercise. This joint Editorial is being published in journals across the fields of history of science and science studies as an expression of our collective dissent and our refusal to allow our field to be managed and appraised in this fashion. We have asked the compilers of the ERIH to remove our journals' titles from their lists. (*History of Science, Technology and Medicine* Editors, 2008)

It remains to be seen what the long-term future of the ERIH will be. The recognition that bibliometric methods, as typically applied in the physical, life or medical sciences, should not be applied in the humanities is unquestionably a sound decision. Inelegant and subjective though the A, B, C lists may be, they do at least form an outer barrier to the metricization of the humanities.

Combination peer review and quantitative evaluation

In an effort to provide a balance between peer review and purely quantitative evaluation, a ranking combining elements of both systems can be created. Such evaluations are gaining popularity in the evaluation of not only journals, but also research groups, departments, institutes and universities. However, the success of such a mixed model will depend on the distribution of the weighting factors. With a multivariate approach, it is possible to come up with any number of different overall rankings simply by varying these factors.

The UK Research Assessment Exercise and forthcoming Research Excellence Framework

The Research Assessment Exercise (RAE), managed by the Higher Education Funding Council for England (HEFCE) was conducted in the UK in 1992, 1996, 2001 and 2008. The broad intention of the RAE is to collect and evaluate publications from each of the UK's higher education institutes, and from those evaluations to provide an overall ranking of the research being undertaken in that institute. Subject areas are divided into units of assessment (UOAs), with each UOA reporting into a broader panel which covers related UOAs. The evaluation of publications is wholly based on peer review, and metrics such as Impact Factors or article-level citations in theory have no bearing on the outcome. In practice, however, it may be difficult for evaluators to disregard these factors.

It is planned that the RAE will be replaced by the Research Excellence Framework (REF) after RAE 2008. A November 2007 HEFCE consultation document (Research Excellence Framework, 2007) noted that quantitative indicators, and particularly bibliometrics, will be a key element of the judgment of research quality. One of the major criticisms of the RAE, notably that it compels authors and institutions to chase high Impact Factor journals, is explicitly dealt with in the consultation paper. The rate of citations to an individual piece of research output will be one of the measures applied. HEFCE stresses in the consultation document that this principle will not involve the use or recording of journal Impact Factors.

As described in the consultation document, for science-based disciplines the REF intends to combine this bibliometric data with data about research income coming from bodies other than the Research Councils. (The same document indicates social sciences, arts and humanities will instead be subjected to light peer review.) However, before the implementation of a countrywide assessment, HEFCE (2008) have announced their intention to run a pilot exercise covering 22 institutions.

The intention of this pilot exercise is to investigate and develop bibliometric measures of research quality, including such fundamental tasks as establishing in which subject areas bibliometric indicators can be considered robust; establishing which sources of citation data are most appropriate and what data cleaning is required; and developing methods for analysing citations alongside international benchmarks. The results of this pilot exercise are expected in spring 2009, at which point further consultation regarding future steps will be undertaken.

An interesting question that arises both from the RAE and the REF is to what extent researchers modify their behaviour in response to the evaluation process itself. In an assessment of UK science spanning the period 1985–2003, Moed (2008) concluded that the observed behaviour of UK scientists varied depending on the assessment criteria in the prevailing RAE. For instance in RAE 1992 when total publication counts were requested (rather than the current situation of submitting a subset of 'best' work), UK researchers dramatically increased their article output. Furthermore, in RAE 1996 when the emphasis shifted from quantity to quality of output, the proportion of papers from UK researchers in high-impact journals increased. When a system of evaluation is created, generally those who are being evaluated will rapidly work out the practices to adopt in order to allow them to exploit the evaluation criteria. This 'gaming the system' is an inevitable consequence, and is an important factor to consider when developing any evaluation framework.

Excellence in Research for Australia

Another example of journals ranking can be found within the Excellence in Research for Australia (ERA) initiative (Australian Research Council,

2008), announced in February 2008. ERA aims to assess the research quality of the Australian higher education sector, and although still in the consultation phase, aims to use a combination of indicators and expert review.

Indicators have been subdivided into three categories:

- research activity and intensity;
- research quality;
- applied research and translation of research outcomes.

Each will contain a number of sub-indicators which build together to a composite measure. One of these sub-indicators is an analysis of publication outlet, i.e. where the research has been published. To this end, the Australian Research Council has created a journal ranking index where they will place more than 17,000 journals into four tiers on the basis of their overall quality: Tier A* (top 5 per cent); Tier A (next 15 per cent); Tier B (next 30 per cent); and Tier C (bottom 50 per cent).

While this tiered approach of ranking journals is very similar to that of the European Reference Index for the Humanities, ERA goes beyond this by also bringing in citation analysis of the individual articles themselves.

Alternative measurements

In the years since the Impact Factor was created, numerous alternative journal ranking metrics have been proposed. Many of these have been minor modifications of the Impact Factor itself, with an aim of addressing some of the most commonly voiced concerns, while keeping the fundamental simplicity of the measure. There have also been some complete departures, including a recent focus on eigenvector-based measurements. Whether any of these measurements provide a more accurate ranking picture of the journal hierarchy is debatable:

> For decades, scholars have complained about the misuses of the impact factor, and there is an extensive literature of such complaints and admonitions. But in a world gone mad with an obsession to evaluate everything 'objectively', it is not surprising that desperate and sometimes incompetent evaluators use a poorly understood, but easily calculated, number to comfort them. (Ewing, 2006)

What is clear is that the tools with which to build alternative ranking systems are readily available. The raw data that form the foundation for any new ranking system are becoming increasingly available from a variety of different sources, and the field of scientometrics has moved into the mainstream scientific consciousness. This has been accelerated by the influence of citation-based performance measurements, such as those being piloted for the UK REF which will affect increasingly large numbers of individuals.

The h-index and its descendants

Before describing some of the new methods for ranking journals, it is worth mentioning in passing the emerging methods for ranking individuals based not on the aggregate performance of the journals they have published in, but the actual citation performance of their individual articles. Beginning with Hirsh's h-index (Hirsch, 2005), and quickly followed by a number of related indexes including the H^2 index (Kosmulski, 2006), the G-index (Egghe, 2006), and the R and AR Indexes (Jin et al., 2007), there has been a growing realization that the journal as the unit of measurement is not the most appropriate measure.

Hirsch's original h-index, as applied to the individual, is calculated as the natural number 'h' such that the individual has published 'h' articles which have each been cited 'h' or more times. An h-index of 3, therefore, means three papers have been cited at least three times each, while an h-index of 10 means ten papers have been cited at least ten times each, and so on.

Criticisms have been levelled against the h-index since its inception (Costas and Bordons, 2007; Schubert and Glänzel, 2007) and the subsequent indexes attempt to address these criticisms, while retaining the simplicity of the original index. Some of these prove better suited to the task than others (Bornmann et al., 2008).

Impact Factor modifications

Numerous alternative Impact Factor measurements have been proposed over the years. Examples of these include the 'Per document type Impact Factor' (Moed and Van Leeuwen, 1995), where the differences in the inherent citeability of different document types published within the same journal, such as original research articles, review articles and letters, are mitigated; the 'Rank-normalized Impact Factor' (Pudovkin and Garfield, 2004), where a percentile ranking based on the Impact

Factor of all the journals in a particular subject category is calculated; and the 'Cited Half-life Impact Factor' (Sombatsompop et al., 2004), where the age of the cited references is factored into the calculation.

The fact that none of these has gained widespread acceptance may be interpreted in a number of ways. It may simply be a consequence of a 'better the devil you know' attitude among the community. While the Impact Factor is imperfect, who is to say that any new measurement will be more equitable? Alternatively, it may simply represent a deeper-seated dissatisfaction with the whole process of ranking by citations. Another explanation is related to the fact that all these modifications rely upon the underlying citation data as provided by ISI. They may have little incentive to change a formula which works perfectly well within the defined limitations that they have set out.

Eigenvector analysis

In traditional journal ranking measurements such as the Impact Factor, a citation from a high Impact Factor journal is treated exactly the same as a citation from a low Impact Factor journal, i.e. no account is taken of the citing source, only that a citation linkage exists. In an eigenvector-based journal measurement, such as the EigenFactor (*http://eigenfactor.org*) or the SCImago Journal Rank (SJR) indicator (*http://www.scimagojr.com*), the computation takes into account a quality 'characteristic' of the citing journal.

It should be noted that the eigenvector style analysis applied to the ranking of scholarly journals is not a new phenomenon; indeed the process was described and applied to a selection of physics journals in the mid-1970s (Pinski and Narin, 1976). The re-emergence of this type of measurement has been driven by the success of the Google PageRank algorithm, which is itself based on eigenvector analysis. Google defines PageRank as follows:

> PageRank reflects our view of the importance of web pages by considering more than 500 million variables and 2 billion terms. Pages that we believe are important pages receive a higher PageRank and are more likely to appear at the top of the search results.
>
> PageRank also considers the importance of each page that casts a vote, as votes from some pages are considered to have greater value, thus giving the linked page greater value. We have always taken a pragmatic approach to help improve search quality and

create useful products, and our technology uses the collective intelligence of the web to determine a page's importance. (Google, year unknown)

The most significant of the eigenvector-style measurements is the SCImago Journal Rank Indicator, which was released in November 2007. Its significance is not related to the mathematics of the calculation, but to the underlying source of the citation data, in this case, Scopus data.

Comparing different ranking systems

The differences between the journal rankings as produced by three different ranking systems (JCR, EigenFactor and SJR) can be examined, and relative performance in each scheme determined. Tables 9.2 to 9.4 and Figure 9.5 examine the rankings of journals in dentistry and associated subject areas. JCR data from the year 2005 were retrieved from *http://isiknowledge.com/jcr* for the subject category of Dentistry, Oral Surgery and Medicine; EigenFactor data from the year 2005 were retrieved from *http://eigenfactor.org* via the Advanced Search, using the subject category of Dentistry, Oral Surgery and Medicine; and SJR data from the year 2005 were retrieved from *http://www.scimagojr.com* for the SJR subject area of Dentistry, focusing on the subject categories of

Table 9.2   Top ten journals ranked by Impact Factor

Journal	JCR IF	EigenFactor	SJR
*Critical Reviews in Oral Biology and Medicine**	1	29	
Journal of Dental Research	2	1	4
Periodontology 2000	3	24	7
Oral Oncology	4	13	
Journal of Clinical Periodontology	5	3	12
Dental Materials Journal	6	48	45
Journal of Adhesive Dentistry	7	37	13
Oral Microbiology and Immunology	8	23	3
Dental Materials	9	6	22
Journal of Periodontal Research	10	27	8

Critical Reviews in Oral Biology and Medicine merged with *Journal of Dental Research* at the start of 2005, hence its absence from the SJR in Table 9.4.

Table 9.3 Top ten journals ranked by EigenFactor

Journal	JCR IF	EigenFactor	SJR
Journal of Dental Research	2	1	4
Journal of Periodontology	14	2	16
Journal of Clinical Periodontology	5	3	12
Oral Surgery, Oral Medicine, Oral Pathology, Oral Radiology, and Endodontology	27	4	24
Journal of Oral and Maxillofacial Surgery	26	5	31
Dental Materials	9	6	22
Clinical Oral Implants Research	13	7	11
Journal of Prosthetic Dentistry	38	8	45
International Journal of Oral and Maxillofacial Implants	23	9	22
Journal of Endodontics	11	10	14

Table 9.4 Top ten journals ranked by SJR

Journal	JCR IF	EigenFactor	SJR
Sleep Medicine Reviews			1
Sleep Medicine			2
Oral Microbiology and Immunology	8	23	3
Journal of Dental Research	2	1	4
Journal of Oral Pathology and Medicine	18	25	5
Oral Diseases	22	33	6
Periodontology 2000	3	24	7
Journal of Periodontal Research	10	27	8
Archives of Oral Biology	25	14	9
European Journal of Oral Sciences	14	20	10

All Oral Surgery and Medicine. Note that it is currently not very simple to perform a like-for-like comparison, or even to establish what the most appropriate comparison would be.

Although the EigenFactor, being based on ISI data, allows the user to restrict the search to the standardized ISI categories, it is noticeable that the number of journals is actually greater than that included in the actual JCR itself, 51 versus 49, presumably as a result of recent additions to the underlying ISI data and/or name changes of existing titles. By contrast,

Figure 9.5 Schematic illustrating constituent journal overlap between three ranking systems

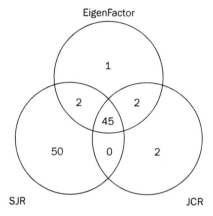

the SJR data include 97 titles. Of the 97 unique titles covered in these systems, 45 are common to all three systems. The overlap in terms of journal titles is provided in Figure 9.5.

Tables 9.2 to 9.4 describe the top ten ranked titles in terms of their Impact Factor, EigenFactor and SCImago Journal Ranking respectively. A superficial comparison of this small sample of data suggests that there are differences between the three systems. Many journals highly ranked by Impact Factor have relatively low rankings by EigenFactor and vice versa. Similarly, when looking at the SCImago Journal Rankings (Table 9.4), and discounting the top two journals *Sleep Medicine* and *Sleep Medicine Reviews* which are clearly out of scope, there are few journals which do well in all three systems. The one journal which consistently scores highly is *Journal of Dental Research*. However, it is universally acknowledged that this journal is one of the pre-eminent journals in this field, and could be said to be the one journal that would not need to market its rankings as a means to encourage submissions or attract readership. Whatever it is that each metric is measuring, it appears not to be the same thing, and even using a number of metrics in parallel will struggle to separate all but the top tier of journals.

Combining usage and citation statistics

It is often argued that for a librarian managing their collection, local rankings are more appropriate than global ones, and many advocate the counting of local citations (i.e. citations from and to articles authored by local authors) rather than all citations as a more valid measure of the usefulness of that particular journal to the local authors.

Currently, the reporting of full-text downloads takes place at the level of the subscribing institution, and allows administrators to observe usage of their content at the local level. In terms of ranking journals, however, this will produce a localized ranking based on the specific characteristics of the subscribing institution in question. These characteristics, such as whether the institute has a large undergraduate programme or is purely research focused, or whether the institute has a broad or niche subject base, play an enormous role in determining the download figures, and hence the ranking.

In early 2006, ISI announced a product which would allow the combination of COUNTER compliant usage data and institution-specific publication and citation data. The Journal Use Report promised to 'provide users with a 360° view of how journals are being used at their institution' (Newman, 2005). With emerging standards such as SUSHI (National Information Standards Organization, year unknown) enabling the aggregation of usage data from different publishers, the activity of evaluating journals from a local standpoint becomes a far simpler proposition than previously.

Building on the small-scale local comparisons of usage and citation data, the Metrics from Scholarly Usage of Resources (MESUR) project being undertaken by the Digital Library Research and Prototyping Team of the Los Alamos National Laboratory Research Library, aims to create a large-scale semantic network consisting of 50 million articles, 500 million citations and 1 billion usage-related events (*http://www.mesur.org*). The creation of a semantic network will enable the context of the citation to be quantified, rather than simply assuming that the citation is positive. This could significantly add to the richness of the metrics one could imagine, with the finished network serving as a platform for the definition and validation of new metrics for the evaluation of the scholarly communication landscape. Early results have been posted to arXiv (Bollen et al., 2008), with a fuller report expected in 2009.

Conclusion

In the not too distant future, new metrics will emerge to complement or even replace existing ones. For some of us, this future is almost within our grasp (Harnad, 2007). What will ultimately determine which of this new battery of measurements succeed and which fail, either individually or as composite measures, is likely to be how strongly they resonate with the communities they serve. The best ideas do not always make the best products, but instead simplicity and transparency can be the difference between success and obscurity.

Acknowledgments

The authors thank Professor Tim Cowan, previously Editor-in-Chief of *Aging Cell*, for sharing the data used in Figure 9.2. The authors also wish to thank Siew Huay Chong and Robert Campbell, both at Wiley-Blackwell, for providing the analysis in the 'Review articles' section, and for a critical reading of the draft.

Bibliography

Australian Research Council (2008) 'Excellence in research for Australia', available at: *http://www.arc.gov.au/era* (accessed 29 October 2008).

Bensman, S. (2007) 'Garfield and the impact factor', *Annual Review of Information Science and Technology* 41(1): 93–155.

Bollen, J., Van de Sompel, H. and Rodriguez, M. A. (2008) 'Towards usage-based impact metrics: first results from the MESUR Project', arXiv:0804.3791v1.

Bornmann, L., Mutz, R. and Daniel, H.-D. (2008) 'Are there better indices for evaluation purposes than the h index? A comparison of nine different variants of the h index using data from biomedicine', *Journal of the American Society for Information Science and Technology* 59(5): 830–7.

Butkovich, N. J. (1996) 'Use studies: a selective review', *Library Resources and Technical Services* 40: 359–68.

Case, D. and Higgins, G. (2000) 'How can we investigate citation behavior? A study of reasons for citing literature in communication', *Journal of the American Society for Information Science* 51(7): 635–45.

Costas, R. and Bordons, M. (2007) 'The h-index: advantages, limitations and its relation with other bibliometric indicators at the micro level', *Journal of Informetrics* 1(3): 193–203.

Egghe, L. (2006) 'An improvement of the h-index: the G-index', *ISSI Newsletter* 2(1): 8–9.

ERIH (year unknown) 'Context and background of ERIH', available at: *http://www.esf.org/research-areas/humanities/research-infrastructures-including-erih/context-and-background-of-erih.html* (accessed 29 October 2008).

ERIH (year unknown) 'Summary guidelines', available at: *http://www.esf .org/index.php?eID=tx_nawsecuredl&u=0&file=fileadmin/be_user/ research_areas/HUM/Documents/ERIH/ERIH%20summary_ guidelines_ Sept_07.pdf&t=1225363424&hash=f03aa02475321ef4e5a438b7f5 922515* (accessed 29 October 2008).

Ewing, J. (2006) 'Measuring journals', *Notices of the American Mathematical Society* 53: 1049–53.

Garfield, E. (1955) 'Citation indexes to science: a new dimension in documentation through association of ideas', *Science* 122(3159): 108–11.

Google (year unknown) 'Corporate information: technology overview', available at: *http://www.google.com/corporate/tech.html* (accessed 29 October 2008).

Harnad, S. (2007) 'Open access scientometrics and the UK Research Assessment Exercise', In D. TorresSalinas and H. Moed (eds) *Proceedings of ISSI 2007: 11th International Conference of the International Society for Scientometrics and Informetrics, Madrid, 25–7 June*, Vol. I, pp. 27–33.

HEFCE (2008) 'Bibliometrics pilot exercise', available at: *http://www.hefce .ac.uk/research/ref/pilot* (accessed 29 October 2008).

Hirsch, J. E. (2005) 'An index to quantify an individual's scientific research output', *Proceedings of the National Academy of Sciences USA* 102(46): 16569–72.

History of Science, Technology and Medicine Editors (2008) 'Journals under threat: a joint response from *History of Science, Technology and Medicine* editors', available at: *http://listserv.liv.ac.uk/cgi-bin/wa? A2=ind0810&L=classicists&T=0&P=5072* (accessed 29 October 2008).

Jin, B. H., Liang, L., Rousseau, R. and Egghe, L. (2007) 'The R- and AR-indices: complementing the h-index', *Chinese Science Bulletin* 52(6): 855–63.

Kessler, M. M. (1963) 'Bibliographic coupling between scientific papers', *American Documentation* 14: 10–25.

Ketcham, C. M. and Crawford, J. M. (2007) 'The impact of review articles', *Laboratory Investigation* 87(12): 1174–85.

Kosmulski, M. (2006) 'A new Hirsch-type index saves time and works equally well as the original h-index', *ISSI Newsletter* 2(3): 4–6.

Lehmann, S. J. (2006) 'Measures for measures', *Nature* 44: 1003–4.

Marshakova, I. (1973) 'System of documentation connections based on references (SCI)', *Nauchno-Tekhnicheskaya Informatsiya Seriya* 2(6): 3–8.

McVeigh, M. E. (year unknown) 'Journal self-citation in the Journal Citation Reports – Science Edition (2002)', available at: *http://thomsonreuters.com/business_units/scientific/free/essays/selfcitation 2002* (accessed 29 October 2008).

Moed, H. F. (2005) *Citation Analysis in Research Evaluation*, Dordrecht: Springer.

Moed, H. F. (2008) 'UK Research Assessment Exercises: informed judgments on research quality or quantity?', *Scientometrics* 74(1): 153–61.

Moed, H. F. and Van Leeuwen, T. N. (1995) 'Improving the accuracy of institute for scientific information's journal impact factors', *Journal of the American Society for Information Science* 46(6): 461–7.

Moed, H. F., Van Leeuwen, T. N. and Reedijk, J. (1996) 'A critical analysis of the journal impact factors of Angewandte Chemie and the Journal of the American Chemical Society: inaccuracies in published impact factors based on overall citations only', *Scientometrics* 37(1): 105–16.

Monastersky, R. (2005) 'The number that's devouring science', *The Chronicle of Higher Education* 52(8): A12[19].

Morris, S. (2007) 'Mapping the journal publishing landscape: how much do we know?', *Learned Publishing* 20(4): 299–310.

National Information Standards Organization (year unknown) 'Standardized Usage Statistics Harvesting Initiative (SUSHI)', available at: *http://www.niso.org/workrooms/sushi* (accessed 29 October 2008).

Newman, D. (2005) 'Journal use reports: easier collection development', available at: *http://scientific.thomsonreuters.com/news/2006-01/8310175* (accessed 29 October 2008).

Nicholas, D., Huntington, P., Jamali, H. R. and Tenopir, C. (2006) 'What deep log analysis tells us about the impact of big deals: case study OhioLINK', *Journal of Documentation* 62(4): 482–508.

Peters, H. P. F. and Van Raan, A. F. J. (1994) 'On determinants of citation scores: a case study in chemical engineering', *Journal of the American Society for Information Science* 45(1): 39–49.

Pinski, G. and Narin, F. (1976) 'Citation influence for journal aggregates of scientific publications: theory with application to literature of physics', *Information Processing and Management* 12(5): 297–312.

PLoS Medicine Editors (2006) 'The impact factor game', *PLoS Medicine* 3(6): e291.

Potter, C.V., Dean, J. L., Kybett, A. P., Kidd, R., James, M. and Canning, M. (2004) 'Comment: 2004's fastest organic and biomolecular chemistry!', *Organic and Biomolecular Chemistry* 2(24): 3535–40.

Price, J. (2007) 'Are they any use? Hazards of price-per-use comparisons in e-journal management', paper presented at *30th UKSG Annual Conference, Warwick, 17 April,* available at: *http://www.uksg.org/sites/uksg.org/files/jprice_plenary_presentation_2007.pps* (accessed 4 January 2008).

Pudovkin, A. I. and Garfield, E. (2004) 'Rank-normalized impact factor: A way to compare journal performance across subject categories', *Proceedings of the American Society for Information Science and Technology* 41(1): 507–51.

Reedijk, J. and Moed, H. F. (2008) 'Is the impact of impact factor decreasing?' *Journal of Documentation* 64(2): 183–92.

Research Excellence Framework (2007) 'Consultation on the assessment and funding of higher education research post-2008', available at: *http://www.hefce.ac.uk/pubs/hefce/2007/07_34/* (accessed 29 October 2008).

Rowlands, I. and Nicholas, D. (2005) 'New journal publishing models: the 2005 CIBER survey of journal author behaviour and attitudes', available at: *http://www.publishing.ucl.ac.uk/papers/2005aRowlands_Nicholas.pdf* (accessed 29 October 2008).

Schonfeld, R., King, D., Okerson, A. and Fenton, E. (2004) *The Nonsubscription Side of Periodicals: Changes in Library Operations and Cost between Print and Electronic Formats,* Washington, DC: Council of Library and Information Resources.

Schubert, A. and Glänzel, W. (2007) 'A systematic analysis of Hirsch-type indices for journals', *Journal of Informetrics* 1(3): 179–84.

Seglen, P. O. (1992) 'The skewness of science', *Journal of the American Society for Information Science and Technology* 43(9): 628–38.

Seglen, P. O. (1997) 'Why the impact factor of journals should not be used for evaluating research', *BMJ* 314(7079): 498–502.

Small, H. (1973) 'Co-citation in the scientific literature: A new measurement of the relationship between two documents', *Journal of the American Society of Information Science* 24(4): 265–9.

Sombatsompop, N., Markpin, T. and Premkamolnetr, N. (2004) 'A modified method for calculating the impact factors of journals in ISI Journal Citation Reports: polymer science category in 1997–2001', *Scientometrics* 60(2): 217–35.

Testa, J. (year unknown) 'The Thomson Scientific journal selection process', available at: *http://thomsonreuters.com/business_units/scientific/free/essays/journalselection* (accessed 29 October 2008).

Thomson-Reuters (2008) 'Journal Citation Report notices', available at: *http://admin-apps.isiknowledge.com/JCR/static_html/notices/notices.htm* (accessed 29 October 2008).

UKSG (year unknown) 'Usage factors study', available at: *http://www.uksg.org/usagefactors/final* (accessed 29 October 2008).

Part III
Academic practices

10

'Cannot predict now': the role of repositories in the future of the journal

Sarah L. Shreeves

Repositories, whether institutional or subject-based (disciplinary), typically provide open access to preprints and final manuscripts of accepted journal articles, among other material. While repositories generally do not perform all of the traditional activities of formal publication such as peer review, editing and formatting, and, except for a few exceptions, have struggled to attract researchers to deposit articles, it is fair to ask what impact such repositories have or might evolve to have on the academic journal. A handful of disciplinary repositories have become loci for scholarly dissemination and interaction. Academic libraries and other institutional-based hosts of repositories are slowly gaining experience in building and maintaining the infrastructure necessary for participation in the scholarly publishing sphere. While a few libraries have begun to use this experience to offer support for publishing, others have developed programmes to raise awareness of 'author rights' and to encourage faculty advocacy within the scholarly publishing arena. This chapter provides an overview of the repository landscape and outlines some of the ways in which repositories may have an impact on the future of the academic journal. The title of this chapter refers to one of the responses given by Mattel's Magic Eight Ball when asked to answer a yes or no question. With two rather momentous events in early 2008 – the mandate that research funded through the National Institutes of Health be deposited into PubMed Central and the unexpected mandate from Harvard's Faculty of Arts and Sciences that published articles be deposited into the institutional repository – it is clear that this rapidly changing landscape is subject to upheavals, reversals, and sudden surges forward.

I should also make the disclaimer that I manage an institutional repository and thus have certain prejudices and hopes. I have tried to minimize these in the presentation of this discussion.

The current repository landscape

What is a repository? For the purposes of this discussion, a repository is a digital assets management system of some kind or a network of systems that allows for the deposit and subsequent distribution of digital files over the internet. The type of content contained in repositories can vary widely: published articles, conference papers and book chapters, as well as unpublished papers, technical reports, working papers, presentations, data sets, scholarly websites, dissertations and theses, digitized material from library holdings, audio, video, and other materials. Most of the discussion in this chapter will focus on repositories that contain preprints (papers not yet accepted for publication in a peer-reviewed journal) and postprints (papers accepted for publication in a peer-reviewed journal). These are sometimes collectively called e-prints (Bailey, 2006). Postprints may be the author's final manuscript version (post peer review but before final formatting and editing) or the published version (with the formatting, pagination, and headers and footers of the journal).

In most cases, the content of these repositories is available freely to anyone with access to the internet. Repositories typically collect content and some descriptive information either through direct deposit by researchers or through deposit by another on behalf of the researcher. Repositories thus fit into the 'self-archiving' model of open access, which is sometimes referred to as the 'green' road to open access (as opposed to the 'gold' road which is publishing in an open access journal) (Harnad et al., 2004). (Another form of self-archiving is to make the content openly available via a personal or departmental website; this form of self-archiving is not discussed in this chapter.) It is important to note here that repositories typically do not have any formal peer review or editorial process for deposited items; the researcher's institutional or organizational affiliation is usually the authentication needed for deposit. Notably, however, arXiv, the well-established disciplinary repository for physics, now requires the endorsement of a would-be depositor by a current contributor (Ginsparg, 2006: 9607).

Repositories expect that researchers have the right or have secured the right to deposit content. This expectation is most problematic for postprints or other content that has been published. If a publisher requires the transfer of copyright from the author(s) and does not have a policy that allows the deposit of the article (in either the final manuscript form or the published form) into a repository, or if the author has not explicitly secured the right to do so, the author does not have the right to deposit. However, many publishers *do* allow some form of an article to be self-archived. As of February 2009, the SHERPA/ RoMEO database of publisher copyright policies and self-archiving policies indicates that of the 539 publishers surveyed, 63 per cent allow some form of self-archiving (i.e. either the preprint or postprint or both) and that 51 per cent allow the postprint to be deposited (see *http:// www.sherpa.ac.uk/romeo.php?stats=yes*). While this nominally would allow a large percentage of articles published each year to be deposited, the publisher's conditions on these policies are often quite confusing. For example, Elsevier allows authors to deposit a preprint into a disciplinary repository, but a postprint may only be made available on the author's personal or institutional website or server (note that Elsevier does not specifically rule out institutional repositories). The published PDF version of the article may never be made available publicly. In addition, authors must ensure that they include the complete citation with a link to the digital object identifier. (These conditions are set out on Elsevier's website, see: *http://www.elsevier.com/wps/find/authorsview.authors/ copyright*). Negotiating the confusing and often conflicting publisher policies on self-archiving is a barrier to deposit not only for authors but for repository managers as well (Salo, 2008).

Repositories are generally optimized for crawling by search engine web spiders, and most make their metadata (i.e. the descriptive information describing the contents) harvestable via the Open Archives Initiative Protocol for Metadata Harvesting in order to help services such as OAIster (*http://www.oaister.org/*) perform integrated searches with content from other repositories. Both efforts serve the purpose of maximizing the distribution of the content contained in the repository. In addition, many, but not all, repositories make some level of commitment to the long-term preservation and persistent access to the material contained within them.

Two useful resources for exploring the range of repositories are the Directory of Open Access Repositories (OpenDOAR; see *http://www .opendoar.org/*) and the Registry of Open Access Registries (ROAR; see *http://roar.eprints.org/*).

Repositories can be organized according to any number of principles; this discussion will focus on two: subject or disciplinary repositories and institutional repositories. According to the OpenDOAR service, these two types of repositories represent 93.5 per cent of all repositories as of February 2009.

A *subject-based* or *disciplinary repository* collects, manages and disseminates scholarship in a broad or specific area of research. This means, of course, that the research represented comes from individuals based in a wide variety of institutions and organizations. These repositories are sometimes called e-print servers or e-print archives. The type of content tends to be preprints and postprints. In both cases, the emphasis of disciplinary repositories is on the rapid, open dissemination of research; in the case of a preprint, the role may also be to offer the author an opportunity to get feedback on an article before it is submitted for publication (Harnad, 2003). Disciplinary repositories can be supported by a specific institution or scholarly society or by a network of institutions. As of February 2009, the OpenDOAR service reports 179 disciplinary repositories around the world. The most prominent examples of a disciplinary repository is arXiv (*http://arXiv.org/*) for preprints and postprints in physics, mathematics, computer science, quantitative biology and statistics. arXiv was established by Paul Ginsparg in 1991 at the Los Alamos National Library. It is now supported by the Cornell University Library, and contains over 526,000 papers deposited by researchers as of February 2009.

An *institutional repository* collects, manages and disseminates materials produced at an institution. Most institutional repositories are based at colleges and universities, although they also exist in governmental agencies, museums, corporations and other organizations, and began to become prevalent in the early part of this decade. Lynch (2003) describes institutional repositories as: 'essentially an organizational commitment to the stewardship of ... digital materials, including long-term preservation where appropriate, as well as organization and access or distribution'. An institutional repository can contain a range of materials, but tends to focus on the research and scholarship of faculty, students and staff, as well as other materials that reflect the intellectual environment of a campus. Examples of institutional repositories include Ohio State University's KnowledgeBank (*http://kb.osu.edu/*), the Queensland University of Technology QUT Eprints (*http://www.qut.edu.au/*), and the University of California's eScholarship Repository (*http://repositories.cdlib.org/escholarship/*).

Departmental repositories are also worth mentioning here. These are similar to institutional repositories except that they are organized around a specific academic department or research centre. Departmental repositories tend to focus on the rapid dissemination of content produced by their researchers as well as promotion of the department itself. An example of a departmental repository is the University of Southampton's School of Electronics and Computer Science ECS EPrints Repository (*http://eprints.ecs.soton.ac.uk/*). As of February 2009, OpenDOAR lists 1,082 institutional or departmental repositories from around the world.

The current impact of repositories on academic journals

Crow (2002) describes scholarly communication as having four specific parts: 'registration' of new ideas and research, 'certification' of the quality and validity of the research, 'awareness' of the research through dissemination and access, and 'archiving' research and scholarship for future access and use. The academic journal inherently performs three of these roles; archiving or preservation has traditionally been dependent on the libraries collecting the journal in paper form, but is now performed by services like Portico (*http://www.portico.org/*). Repositories also inherently perform three of these roles to greater or lesser degrees; the certification or peer-review process, however, has generally been left to journals. Open access advocates like Stevan Harnad generally stress that the most important role that repositories, especially institutional repositories, can play is to provide immediate open access to the published research and that peer review should rightly live with journals (for a typical example of Harnad's argument, see Harnad, 2008). Only a handful of researchers suggest that the review function should live within or perhaps overlay the repository sphere (see Ginsparg, 2007; Guédon, 2004).

The other relevant piece of the environment is, of course, the business of journals. The serials crisis – the tension between the ever-increasing price of journals, particularly in the science, technology and medical (STM) fields, large scholarly societies' reliance on journal subscriptions to underwrite their activities, and the ever-tightening budgets of academic libraries – has been written about extensively (for a good overview, see Panitch and Michalak, 2005). The 2008 *Library Journal*

Periodicals Price Survey reports that in 2006, the top ten STM publishers took in 53 per cent of the revenue in the $16.1 billion periodicals market (Van Orsdel and Born, 2008). From 2004 to 2008, the average price of US journals included in the Institute of Scientific Information's (ISI) Science Citation Index has increased 40 per cent; non-US journals in the same database have increased 34.3 per cent. The social sciences and arts and humanities have not fared much better (though the actual costs of the journals are lower). US social science journals have increased 37.8 per cent over those same four years and non-US journals have increased 40.9 per cent. US arts and humanities journals have increased 29.7 per cent while the non-US journals have increased 36.9 per cent (Van Orsdel and Born, 2008). In contrast, the serials budgets of members of the Association of Research Libraries only increased 11.5 per cent from 2004 to 2006 (Krillidou and Young, 2008: 12). It is no wonder that libraries have been actively looking for alternative models, and certainly the early rhetoric around institutional repositories in particular suggested that they could perhaps be an active part of a shift (for examples, see Crow, 2002; Prosser, 2003).

So could repositories supplant or change the journal as we know it? Could repositories help change the economics of the current environment? Yes and no – and the answer is even more muddied depending on who one talks to and whether one is talking about institutional or disciplinary repositories. The biggest reason why one might answer no is simply that researchers are not depositing their published peer-reviewed articles into repositories except for a few disciplinary repositories (to be discussed below). In her study to evaluate the deployment of institutional repositories, McDowell (2007) found that from 2005 to 2006, the median annual increase was 366 items, or essentially one new deposit a day. She writes, 'At a median growth rate of one item a day, IRs [institutional repositories] in America will likely not achieve the critical mass to significantly impact open access or change modes of scholarly communication for some time to come'.

The single deposit a day average is depressingly low, though not a surprise for any repository manager. Reasons for this slow deposit rate are diverse and include lack of awareness; uncertainty about open access and a desire not to disrupt relationships with publishers; a lack of time; the effort required to deposit; or that faculty are already self-archiving on their own or departmental website and do not see the advantage in depositing into a repository (Markey et al., 2007: 73). Fundamentally, institutional repositories have not been designed with services that faculty want and with benefits that they can easily see (Foster and Gibbons,

2005; Salo, 2008). Interest is also highly dependent on discipline; in my own experience as a repository manager, faculty in disciplines that do not have an active preprint or working paper culture are suspicious of sharing the non-authoritative version of an article (i.e. their final manuscript version post peer review).

Institutional repositories also include a mass of non-peer reviewed, published material. McDowell (2007) estimates that only 13 per cent of the material in institutional repositories is peer reviewed. Institutional repositories often contain presentations, historical research conducted at the university that has been converted into digital form, working papers, technical reports, electronic theses and dissertations, and data sets.[1] For most institutional repositories, these materials fit well into their collection policy and are entirely appropriate, but this has brought them under attack by some open access advocates for diverting the focus from the goals of the open access movement (Poynder, 2006). Salo (2008) does an admirable job analysing the dilemma of institutional repository managers and getting beyond the rhetoric of some open access advocates. The point to make for this argument is that the very low rate of author self-archiving makes it difficult to imagine that institutional repositories – unless a large number of institutions follow the Harvard mandate (discussed further below) – will themselves be much of a threat to either the role that journals play in certifying research and scholarship or to the business model itself.

There are exceptions to the low deposit rate, but these are in the disciplinary arena, rather than institutional. arXiv is probably the most cited example of how a community can actively engage with a repository and come to rely on it to register and date-stamp an idea or concept, to solicit feedback and review from the community, and to raise awareness of the community's own work. arXiv has its roots in the paper preprint physics community; preprints of papers were sent to colleagues as an expected part of the scholarly communication process. Moving this community into the online environment accelerated the process and made a more explicit date-stamp of when a new concept was first discussed (Pinfield, 2001). These roles should sound familiar, so the question of whether arXiv has affected the journals in its area has been raised. By all accounts, it has not. Sally Morris, writing when she was the Chief Executive of the Association of Learned and Professional Society Publishers (ALPSP), says that 'In the realm of physics, where the arXiv preprint repository has been in operation since 1991, publishers do not report any unusual drop either in submissions or in subscriptions' (Morris, 2004: 305). In listserv discussions, Morris has also stated that arXiv has had an effect on the usage of articles on publishers' websites (e.g. see *http://www.library.yale.edu/~llicense/ListArchives/0703/msg00189 .html*), though there does not seem to be evidence of journal cancellations. A recent study of the interplay between astrophysics journals and the e-prints in arXiv shows that use of the e-print in arXiv falls dramatically once the journal article is published. The authors speculate that the astrophysics community still values the peer review and the authority that journal publication confers on an article (Henneken et al., 2007). However, the future does not rule out a role for arXiv; According to arXiv's founder, 'The arXiv repository functions are flexible enough either to coexist with the preexisting publication system or to help it evolve into something better optimized for researcher needs' (Ginsparg, 2006: 9606).

arXiv already has some cursory review in place; a network of volunteers quickly scans deposits to ensure they fit the scope of the subject area where they have been deposited. It is not too hard to imagine a more formalized review process being put in place. The question is not whether or not this could be done with the infrastructure arXiv has in place, but whether the review process would have buy-in from the participating researchers and the committees responsible for the promotion and tenure process.

The economics domain is another in which there exists a culture of sharing papers prior to publication. These have traditionally been shared through working paper or discussion paper series that are distributed by economic departments or research centres. For example, the Harvard Institute of Economic Research distributes a working paper series with the goal 'to make this early research available to fellow economists, scholars and institutions all over the world' (*http://www.economics.harvard .edu/journals/hier*). Economic preprints, whether or not in working paper series, tend to be distributed through the Social Science Research Network (SSRN) or through the Research Papers in Economics (RePEc) network of distributed repositories. But, again, there is little evidence that these practices have had a significant impact on the primacy of journals for validating and certifying work. Ellison (2007) studied the publication patterns of economists in top departments and found that few publish papers in the so-called field journals (journals that represent the subfields of economics), and that Harvard's economics faculty are publishing fewer papers overall in peer-reviewed journals. He posits that:

> The 'decline of peer review' theory ... is that the necessity of going through the peer-review process has lessened for high status

authors: in the old days peer-reviewed journals were by far the most effective means of reaching readers, whereas with the growth of the internet high-status authors can now post papers online and exploit their reputation to attract readers. (Ellison, 2007: 1)

He points to the extraordinarily slow publication process in economics as a deterrent (see also Ellison, 2002) and notes that technology has made it possible to make research instantly accessible. He ends the paper:

One could imagine that new institutions may arise and perform many of the same functions as the current peer-review system more efficiently. Given how central peer-review has been to academic research over the past century, however, the thought that the current system might collapse before any successor is clearly established is troubling. (Ellison, 2007: 36)

Ellison does not explicitly mention repositories as one of these new institutions, but clearly this is a potential role for discipline-based repositories. But caution should be taken in assuming that these models (which both have roots in a print tradition) will hold true for other disciplines. While these are not the only examples of disciplines with strong e-print practices, there are relatively few.

Emerging trends

Based on the analysis of the current landscape, it is pretty clear that most repositories will probably not change the role of journals or the business of journals in the near to mid-term future. However, institutional and disciplinary repositories have prompted or played an important part in some emerging trends that may in the long term affect the future of the journal. Three are highlighted below.

Education and advocacy around scholarly communication issues and author rights

While libraries have long tried to educate their faculty about the serials crisis (often when informing faculty of impending journal cancellations), education and advocacy around broader issues of scholarly communication are relatively new. Issues covered vary by library but usually include retaining rights when publishing (usually referred to as author rights), open access through self-archiving, publishing in open access journals, reuse of materials and associated copyright issues, and the future of scholarly societies, among other topics. There is strong support among national library associations for this new role for librarians. The Association of Research Libraries (ARL) and the Association of College and Research Libraries of the American Library Association jointly sponsor a workshop on scholarly communication education. The Scholarly Publishing and Academic Resources Consortium (SPARC) has developed a large number of resources to support education and advocacy around author rights, open access, and other issues (see *http://www.arl.org/sparc/advocacy/index .shtml*). In a recent survey of members of ARL, 75 per cent of respondents have conducted scholarly communication education; and 32 per cent have a librarian with explicit responsibility for education and outreach around scholarly communication issues (Newman et al., 2007).

Education and advocacy around author rights have been especially visible in the last two years, partly because of the low deposit rate in institutional repositories. The adoption by institutions such as MIT and the members of the Consortium for Institutional Cooperation of addenda for authors to attach to copyright transfer agreement forms in order to retain certain rights has meant that librarians have needed to talk to faculty about actually *reading* copyright transfer agreements.[2] Libraries are also engaging with graduate students – the future faculty – regarding these issues. All of these efforts have in turn forced publishers to be more explicit about the copyright transfer process and to specify what rights may be retained by authors. Long term, as the current undergraduate generation and their juniors – who are so used to open, free access and the ability to reuse and remix material – move into academe, publishers will need to adopt different models for copyright transfer and the licensing of articles.

Development of infrastructure and services

As libraries build out repositories and digital library services, they are building a robust and stable technical infrastructure, expertise in a range of scholarly communication and publishing topics, and connections with their faculty regarding a new set of issues. For some libraries this has meant a readiness to participate directly in the scholarly publishing sphere through providing the technical infrastructure for their faculty to publish and edit journals. Hahn writes:

> expectations are rising that research libraries will take responsibility for current scholarship as well as legacy scholarship, especially for a wide range of locally produced works of scholarship. Evolving repository services, which house and disseminate institutional records, theses and dissertations, preprints, postprints, learning objects, and research data, can inspire a range of inquiries about potential publishing services. It could be a short step to managing publication of works like journals and monographs, and faculty are approaching research libraries seeking publishing services. (Hahn, 2008: 10)

Jean-Gabriel Bankier, the president of the Berkeley Electronic Press, and Irene Perciali, the Director of Journals for BePress, ask 'What if, in addition to an archive, an institutional repository were a place for authors to create and publish scholarly content in the first place?' (Bankier and Perciali, 2008: 22). Accordingly, the Berkeley Electronic Press now provides a software suite that includes both repository and journal publishing software. At a presentation at the Digital Library Federation 2008 Spring Forum, Randall Floyd described Indiana University Library's effort to move from a repository-centric viewpoint to a services-centric viewpoint; one of the key pieces of this was supporting a faculty member in publishing an open access journal (Floyd, 2008). Libraries, realizing the initial investment in institutional repositories has not produced the desired changes (particularly if one of the reasons for the repository was to prompt change in the scholarly publishing arena), may find that leveraging investment in the technical infrastructure through the support of journal publishing makes financial sense and meets their service missions to support faculty research.

Mandates for open access

In October 2005 the Wellcome Trust, the largest private funder of medical research in the UK, made it a condition of funding that published research be made publicly available through deposit into UK PubMed Central. In 2006, several other UK and European funders followed suit by requiring that funded research be made publicly available through deposit into an open access repository and/or publishing in an open access journal. In

January 2008, the European Research Council announced that grant recipients must make funded research openly available within six months of publication. And in December 2007, an appropriations bill was signed into law that required grantees of the US National Institutes of Health (NIH) to make published articles available in PubMed Central a year after publication.

PubMed Central is a repository for biomedical and life sciences journal literature and is supported by the NIH and managed by the National Center for Biotechnology Information in the National Library of Medicine. Strictly speaking, PubMed Central does not share many of the characteristics of repositories as described in the first part of this discussion; the majority of its content has been contributed directly by publishers rather than by authors. In the three years prior to the 2008 mandate, there had been a strong recommendation that researchers deposit their work into PubMed Central; this resulted in the deposit of about 5 per cent of funded research.

The argument for open access mandates by funders is closely tied to increasing the impact of funded research through open access and, in the case of government-sponsored research, giving taxpayers access to the research they have funded. In 2006, the Federal Research Public Access Act was introduced to the US Senate. This legislation would have mandated all federal agencies expending funds above a certain threshold to require their grantees to make their research publicly available. This was vigorously opposed by many publishers; the Association of American Publishers issued a strong statement denouncing the legislation and made many of the same arguments that would be made in response to the NIH mandate.[3]

There have also been a few departmental and institutional mandates, but none made the noise that was heard in February 2008 when Harvard University's Faculty of Arts and Sciences voted unanimously to grant the university permission to deposit their published articles (in the form of a final manuscript postprint) into Harvard's institutional repository (for the text of the resolution, see *http://www.fas.harvard.edu/~secfas/February_2008_Agenda.pdf*). This mandate will require faculty to publish in journals whose publishers allow self-archiving, although faculty can get a waiver to opt out on a case-by-case basis. Among other reasons, this development is remarkable because it originated with the faculty and not with the library or the administration. This development is so new that, as of February 2009, Harvard had yet to make public its institutional repository (although a preliminary version is available to the Harvard community); it is hard to say how this mandate will play out in the long term. Certainly it is too soon to say how the Harvard faculty and publishers will respond as the mandate is implemented. Nevertheless, libraries and some faculty have certainly taken notice. SPARC and Science Commons have recently published guidelines for faculty who are interested in pursuing an open access mandate at their institution (Nguyen, 2008).

So what role will repositories play in the future of the journal? If more funders and institutions mandate that research be made available through open access repositories, then the business model of journals will be affected even if the research is embargoed for a period of 6–12 months (for an up-to-date list of funders that mandate some form of open access, see *http://www.sherpa.ac.uk/juliet/index.php*). If disciplinary repositories begin to experiment with peer-review structures, particularly in communities with a strong preprint culture, journals will face another entity that provides registration, certification, awareness and archiving.

This chapter has attempted to lay out the current environment and interactions between repositories and journals as well as guess at a handful of emerging trends. While this is a complicated landscape with many interdependencies, it is clear that both institutional and disciplinary repositories will likely play some kind of role in the long-term evolution of the journal.

Notes

1. As a side note, data sets are themselves an interesting case to consider, as most journals articles do not include an entire data set but an analysed subset of the data. In some cases, the data set is deposited into a disciplinary data repository and the journal article links to the data set. In other cases, the data set is never made accessible or curated. This is perhaps a role that institutional repositories could play, particularly for small to mid-size data sets.
2. For the MIT author addendum, see *http://info-libraries.mit.edu/scholarly/mit-copyright-amendment-form/*.
3. For the AAP press release and a response by an open access advocate, see *http://www.earlham.edu/~peters/fos/2006_05_07_fosblogarchive.html#1147 26726169346460*.

Bibliography

Bailey, Jr., C. W. (2006) 'What is open access?' in: N. Jacobs (ed.) *Open Access: Key Strategies, Technical and Economic Aspects*, Oxford: Chandos Publishing, pp. 13–26.

Bankier, J.-G. and Perciali, I. (2008) 'The institutional repository rediscovered: What can a university do for open access publishing?' *Serials Review* 34(1): 21–6.

Crow, R. (2002) 'The case for institutional repositories: a SPARC position paper', available at: *http://www.arl.org/sparc/bm%7Edoc/ir_final_release_102.pdf* (accessed 28 April 2008).

Ellison, G. (2002) 'The slowdown of the economics publishing process', *Journal of Political Economy* 110(5): 947–93.

Ellison, G. (2007) *Is Peer Review in Decline?* Cambridge, MA: National Bureau of Economic Research.

Floyd, R. (2008) 'The NEW IUScholarWorks at Indiana University: Repositories, journals and scholarly publishing', paper presented at the Digital Library Federation Spring Forum, 28–30 April, Minneapolis, MN.

Foster, N. F. and Gibbons, S. (2005) 'Understanding faculty to improve content recruitment for institutional repositories', *D-Lib Magazine* 11(1), available at: *http://www.dlib.org/dlib/january05/foster/01foster.html* (accessed 7 May 2008).

Ginsparg, P. (2007) 'As we may read', *Journal of Neuroscience* 26(38): 9606–8.

Guédon, J.-C. (2004) 'The 'green' and 'gold' roads to open access: the case for mixing and matching', *Serials Review* 30(4): 315–28.

Hahn, K. (2008) *Research Library Publishing Services: New Options for University Publishing*, Washington, DC: Association of Research Libraries, available at *http://www.arl.org/bm~doc/research-library-publishing-services.pdf* (accessed 8 March 2009).

Harnad, S. (2003) 'E-prints: electronic preprints and postprints', in: M. J. Bates, M. N. Maack and M. Drake (eds) *Encyclopedia of Library and Information Science*, New York: Marcel Dekker, pp. 990–2.

Harnad, S. (2008) 'OA needs open evidence, not anonymous innuendo', available at: *http://openaccess.eprints.org/index.php?/categories/3-Peer-Review* (accessed 16 February 2009).

Harnad, S., Brody, T., Vallieres, F., Carr, L., Hitchcock, S., Gingras, Y, Oppenheim, C., Stamerjohanns, H., and Hilf, E. (2004) 'The access/impact problem and the green and gold roads to open access', *Serials Review* 30(4): 310–14.

Henneken, E. A., Kurtz, M. J., Warner, S., Ginsparg, P., Eichhorn, G., Accomazzi, A., Grant, C. S., Thompson, D., Bohlen, E. and Murray, S.S. (2007) 'E-prints and journal articles in astronomy: a productive co-existence', *Learned Publishing* 20(1): 16–22.

Krillidou, M. and Young, M. (2008) 'ARL statistics 2005–06: A compilation of statistics from the one hundred and twenty-three members of the association of research libraries', available at: *http:// www.arl.org/bm~doc/arlstats06.pdf* (accessed 7 May 2008).

Lynch, C. A. (2003) 'Institutional repositories: essential infrastructure for scholarship in the digital age', *ARL: A Bimonthly Report*, No. 226, available at: *http://www.arl.org/resources/pubs/br/br226/br226ir.shtml* (accessed 28 April 2008).

Markey, K., Rieh, S.Y., St. Jean, B., Kim, J. and Yakel, E. (2007) *Census of Institutional Repositories in the United States: MIRACLE Project Research Findings*, Washington, DC: Council on Library and Information Resources.

McDowell, C. S. (2007) 'Evaluating institutional repository deployment in American academe since early 2005: repositories by the numbers, part 2', *D-Lib Magazine* 13(9/10), available at: *http://www.dlib.org/dlib/ september07/mcdowell/09mcdowell.html* (accessed 28 April 2008).

Morris, S. (2004) 'Open access: how are publishers reacting?', *Serials Review* 30(4): 304–07.

Newman, K. A., Blecic, D. D. and Armstrong, K. L. (2007) *Scholarly Communication Education Initiatives: SPEC Kit 299*, Washington, DC: Association of Research Libraries.

Nguyen, T. (2008) *Open Doors and Open Minds: What Faculty Authors Can Do to Ensure Open Access to Their Work through Their Institution*, Washington, DC and Cambridge, MA: SPARC and Science Commons.

Panitch, J. M. and Michalak, S. (2005) 'The serials crisis: a white paper for the UNC-Chapel Hill Scholarly Communications Convocation', available at: *http://www.unc.edu/scholcomdig/whitepapers/panitch-michalak.html* (accessed 7 May 2008).

Pinfield, S. (2001) 'How do physicists use an e-print archive? Implications for institutional e-print services', *D-Lib Magazine* 7(12), available at: *http://www.dlib.org/dlib/december01/pinfield/12pinfield .html* (accessed 7 May 2008).

Poynder, R. (2006) 'Clear blue water', available at: *http://ia310134.us .archive.org/1/items/The_Basement_Interviews/BlueWaterMain.pdf* (accessed 7 May 2008)

Prosser, D. C. (2003) 'Scholarly communication in the 21st century – the impact of new technologies and models', *Serials* 16(2): 163–7.

Salo, D. (2008) 'The innkeeper at the roach motel', *Library Trends* 57(2): 98–123.

Van Orsdel, L. C. and Born, K. (2008) 'Periodical price survey 2008: embracing openness', *Library Journal*, available at: *http://www .libraryjournal.com/article/CA6547086.html* (accessed 28 April 2008).

11

Libraries and the future of the journal: dodging the crossfire in the e-revolution, or leading the charge?

J. Eric Davies

For the library manager providing access to materials and information in general, and to journal literature in particular, these are turbulent times. At the heart of this situation is the perennial quest by a range of stakeholders, including librarians, to make better use of limited resources and to enhance what is on offer, by exploiting the possibilities offered by technology in response to an ever-more demanding user community. Thus, the library manager finds himself, or herself, operating in a context that is always dynamic, frequently challenging and at times unstable.

Library budgets have encountered stormy waters and demonstrated their limitations as costs and demands have risen and funding has failed to keep pace. Modes of information delivery have evolved through the liberating capacity of information and communications technology. New business models in journal publishing have emerged to take advantage of the technology and as a response to market forces. The expectations of library users, conditioned by the immediacy and range of electronic systems, have escalated. The robustness and sophistication of systems have increased with an attendant demand on the skills and imagination that are necessary to exploit their full potential. Scholars now exercise a new power to apply a range of options to communicate ideas, facts and discoveries, both formally and informally. A constant that remains for the librarian is the need to maximize value, and to be seen to be maximizing value, through a perennial emphasis on improved accountability with limited resources.

Attitudes, practices and business models that threaten to undermine the traditional view of the library as a storehouse and intermediary demand a rethink about what the library is for. The picture that emerges is one with a little less emphasis on the library as place and more on the library as a channel for a wide range of information and a source of support in finding and using it. However, paper remains a staple in many areas of publishing. So the hybrid library emerges where workstations and networks coexist with rows of bound volumes and reams of documents. Thus, new challenges emerge, but old ones do not readily recede. In this universe, however, the library's overall objective remains, as it always has been, namely facilitating access to the right material, at the right time, to the right person, in the right format (and at the right price). It is basically a system for connecting creators and users of information, past and present, with as little fuss as possible.

Funding – a perpetual balancing act

When scholarly communication moved out of the realm of exchanges of personal correspondence between specialists such as Newton and Liebniz into a more formal structure that emerged as the *Philosophical Transactions of the Royal Society* and the *Journal des Sçavans*, the library as a formal archive of the scholarly record took up its role. The growth of the scholarly journal over the following three and a half centuries or so has led to libraries playing an even more important role in ensuring access to, and the preservation of, a comprehensive collection of scholarly output. From the 100 or so titles being published in the early nineteenth century, scholarly journals have now reached a reported 300,000 titles or more, available in some form or another in the early twenty-first century (see *http://www.ulrichsweb.com/ulrichsweb/*). Gradually, however, libraries have lost ground in this endeavour, navigating as they have, against the tide of ever-increasing journal subscription costs compounded by significant increases in the number of titles that match scholarly research output. Recent data on journal prices trends reveal a picture signalling inevitable strains on library budgets (Creaser and White, 2008; White and Creaser, 2007).

Faced with a finite budget and escalating costs, libraries have had to trim acquisitions. It is not only journal subscriptions that have suffered; spending on books and other media has also been curtailed. Indeed, given the lead time to cancel subscriptions, book purchasing has, in many cases, offered a much readier option to reduce spending, and it can be claimed that the bibliographic bedrock of scholarly research has significantly suffered. These exercises in economy have not served to endear libraries to their users either.

Data on budgeting in UK higher education institutions' libraries indicate that, in real terms, resources being channelled towards meeting users' information needs hardly keep pace with the growth in the user population (LISU, 2008). More detailed data reveal that, in the academic year 2004/05, an average of £30 was spent on books per full-time-equivalent student, £57 on journals (including e-journals), £16 on other electronic sources and £3 each on binding and inter-library loans (LISU, 2007).

The situation regarding access to scientific publishing has come under the scrutiny of the UK House of Commons Science and Technology Committee. Its wide-ranging report has explored the scholarly journal from various perspectives, identifying the strains brought about by diminished library purchasing power. According to the report, 'Pressure on library journal acquisitions budgets has resulted in cancelled subscriptions and has contributed to a decline in book purchasing. This compromises the library's ability to provide the full range of services required by its user community' (House of Commons Science and Technology Committee, 2004).

The discussion about journal prices and their affordability has, to some extent, polarized attitudes across a broad spectrum of interests that include scholars, librarians, publishers and even governments. At its extremes, on the one hand, the producers of journals are viewed as profiteering unfairly on a captive market in a commodity that does not readily lend itself to competitive forces. On the other, both authors and readers, and with them libraries and their parent institutions, are regarded as unwilling to pay a fair price for the added value and quality assurance that is represented in the scholarly journal. Sometimes caught in the middle is the librarian, as the agent who selects and pays for material that others demand, and within a budget that yet others determine. The librarian's predicament is to be exposed from all sides.

In this situation, library managers seeking to maintain the semblance of a reasonable service in journals provision, while retaining some financial stability, have limited options. Clearly the most obvious, but least likely, is to find some way of increasing funding for materials. In some institutions, those seeking research funding have been encouraged to include a sum for information seeking and materials in their budgeting which may be directly channelled to the library. The introduction of the concept of full cost-recovery for research grants from the UK government also offers scope to improve matters.

As noted earlier, managers may reduce the number of titles to which the library subscribes, but this may have severe effects on the quality of the collection and is almost always unpopular with users. Libraries may seek price reductions or discounts but the scope for these regarding individual titles or publishers is limited. Competition, in the conventional sense, does not play a part in balancing demand and prices where each journal is a unique assemblage of intellectual property, so the economics of the marketplace are somewhat fugitive.

Perhaps a more fruitful strategy centres on seeking economies of scale through cooperative purchasing and bulk buying as exemplified by the NESLI deals featuring 'bundled' aggregations of titles (see *http://www.nesli2.ac.uk/*). However, such approaches may not suit every institution, especially the smaller ones, as research into NESLI deals has demonstrated (Davies and White, 2005; White and Davies, 2001).

Another aspect of resource-sharing would involve cooperative acquisitions of expensive titles that could be used jointly within a city or region. Such approaches have rarely met with success, however. Scholars are often reluctant to travel very far to view titles and, in the digital context, copyright and licensing considerations rightly preclude electronic transfer of material on such a scale. An early exploration of library cooperation in the East Midlands region of the UK has illustrated the potential and the limitations of such an approach (MacDougall and Wheelhouse, 1989).

Yet another option sees a shift from acquiring journals on a title-by-title subscription basis to fulfilling individual article demand through document delivery, effectively moving from a 'just in case' to a 'just in time' approach. In this way, it may be argued that only material that is really needed is acquired, but critics respond that not all requested articles are useful (or even read) and the facility for browsing and serendipity is lost. Moreover, as demand for articles may be fairly elastic, this approach does not, of itself, ensure savings unless a cap is placed on the budget for document delivery. Other reservations on the concept of individual article delivery persist; many extol the virtues of a coherent journal which has an identity, branding and a reputation, the latter of which is significant for scholars who require the status of the journal to support reputations.

Inter-library lending and document supply from the British Library have also featured for some time as options for satisfying demand for material, particularly that which is outside the core remit of the library.

It has its attendant costs in administration and charges, however, and should not be viewed as a panacea for the shortcomings in funding.

Information and communications technology interventions

The phenomenal development of information and communications technology has radically altered the general landscape regarding scholarly communication. Suddenly, the Newton-Leibniz opportunity for dialogue has been reinvented as electronic mail renders the global 'invisible college' of scholars a living reality. The difference, this time, is that the exchanges are almost instantaneous and the participants do not have to wait weeks to share each others' ideas.

Technology has changed the nature of scholarly publishing and, in particular, the journal, not only in its physical format, but also in the way it has expanded its scope. Journals have gained a capacity to accommodate new forms of content and, through hyper-linking, to permit the reader to go beyond the linear constraints of the format and access supplementary data. Technology has also overturned the business models for distributing the scholarly article and provided a range of flexible options for delivery. According to the Ulrich's Periodicals Directory website:

> As of June 2007, there are 59,549 active online serials in the Ulrich's knowledgebase. Many of these e-serials represent electronic editions of publications that have been around for years in a print format, or which have become available at the same time as a new print launch. Yet a significant number of e-resources are produced solely in electronic format. The number of online-only publications approaches 7,089 and their frequencies of publication vary widely. (*Ulrich's Periodicals Directory Online*, 2008)

The library has had to respond to, and accommodate, these changes in the way it operates (and pays for) its acquisitions model and, not least, to ensure that the appropriate infrastructure and support is in place to exploit e-journals properly. The library has also capitalized on these developments in terms of access options, as well as retrieval and dissemination models, which will be discussed later.

Electronic journals have extended the concept of the library without walls. 'Wired' university campuses and networked research organizations bring the electronic information content negotiated by the library to the scholar's workstation, wherever it is located. Thus, we see visits to academic libraries gradually diminishing, but use of resources increasing significantly. (Interestingly, book loans from university libraries appear to have held up.) The technology has enabled the library to deliver a better, more focused service, and a different service that is not trammelled by a user's capacity, or inclination to visit the library.

In terms of funding, however, it must be recognized that far from reducing costs, in the short term, e-journals have entailed added investment in workstations, networks and access licences. Corresponding economies in physical storage that would follow dispensing with paper copies have yet to be fully realized until back-run information is adequately digitized and archived. Some progress in this direction is evident for both mainstream and specialized sources. In addition, there are the resource implications of retraining and reorienting staff to manage the additional challenges of a digital environment – a challenge which has, incidentally, been enthusiastically accepted.

Technology has enabled librarians, as almost never before, to assess the use and usefulness of the electronic collection through far more refined metrics of access and activity (Davies, 2002). At a basic level, the number of online searches and downloads can be measured to reveal patterns of demand. The Counting Online Usage of NeTworked Electronic Resources (COUNTER) initiative represents a fruitful partnership between publishers and librarians in developing a coherent and consistent approach to measuring the use and value of journals (see *http://www.projectcounter.org/*). Measurement and research at a more sophisticated level, such as deep log analysis, enables one to derive a fuller picture of what scholarly journal users do, and why (Jamali et al., 2005; Nicholas et al., 2005). Library managers are thus enabled to design a more relevant and directed approach to provision and to target acquisitions funds more effectively to obtain a better return on investment.

However, the application of technology to deliver journal content in this way is still in its relative infancy and there remain important issues to be resolved in terms of the management of electronic subscriptions. These include the relationships between vendors and purchasers, continuity of service when titles are sold from one vendor to another, the question of access to journal archives when subscriptions cease, and the scope of licensing agreements where libraries provide services to remote users and casual visitors. These issues signal the need for an even stronger working relationship between journal publishers and library managers if this aspect of the scholarly communications chain is to flourish properly in the digital age.

Another development opened up by technology, and already noted above, relates to electronic document delivery of individual articles on demand as an alternative to the subscription-based electronic journal. This 'just-in-time' approach only really became a serious option when digitized content distributed over networks, coupled with real-time accounting, enabled material to be delivered on demand.

The library as scholarly e-communication centre – a new service paradigm

Just as the candle-maker who realized that he was in the illumination business adjusted to manufacturing electric lighting and now low-energy lamps, so library managers are in the vanguard of adjusting to a new environment of information dissemination.

They have been quick to adopt and adapt to the potential for content delivery offered by technology. They have also been forthcoming in forming a coalition with creators and users of information by encouraging open access journals and institutional repositories. In many cases, the library has taken the lead in assembling the infrastructure, including creating appropriate metadata, and managing the institutional repository. There are also examples where libraries are prominent in promoting and facilitating funding to support scholars to meet processing charges in the 'author-pays' model of open access journals (Cockerill, 2008).

Libraries, with their tradition of user support and embedded expertise in facilitating access to a range of material, are also instrumental in creating mechanisms to assist scholars to navigate through this modern maze of scholarly information. The development of 'seamless' electronic interfaces to real and virtual collections through library information portals has simplified and streamlined resource discovery and exploitation by providing, in many cases, a single point of entry to a range of databases and associated primary sources in a 'one-stop shop' concept. Moreover, the introduction of portals has offered attendant and demonstrable advantages to the publishers of information products. By making such material easier to access and use, their value and utility has increased (Hamblin, 2005; LISU, 2004). Thus, it may be argued that library portals have supported the marketing and exploitation of information products, including electronic journals, and at the same time added value. In another example, the Tic Tocs project (*http://www.tictocs .ac.uk/*), which provides a conduit for a range of tables of contents, exemplifies what can be achieved when libraries and publishers collaborate in facilitating access to material.

As well providing the technical solutions to the complexities of information access, librarians also offer direct support to information users. This they perform by offering, at the point of use, help and advice in using the range of sophisticated systems and sources that are available, including journals, books, databases and datasets of all kind. This help extends to providing advice, not only on finding, but also evaluating material. In this way the library frequently offers a personalized service in a context of mass provision. In an academic institution, for example, the library may be one of the few remaining areas where face-to-face, one-to-one interaction is the norm. This kind of interaction may also be conducted at a distance through an e-mail dialogue with individuals.

There is, moreover, a strong tradition of providing more formal instruction in information seeking and use in academic libraries. Timetabled skills development programmes and 'drop-in' sessions that include access to the journal literature may be encountered. As an example, the Pilkington Library at Loughborough University offers weekly Lunch-time in the Library sessions and monthly Database of the Month workshops during the university semester (see *http://www.lboro .ac.uk/library/skills/informationLiteracy.html*). An online tutorial is also provided. More generally, there is a growing movement towards developing information literacy skills in library programmes throughout the UK.

In addition, libraries are often the centre for support in copyright matters as their personnel are frequently well-versed in the practicalities of the matter. This they achieve through, on the one hand, interpreting the limits of fair dealing and ensuring that users do not infringe copyright and, on the other, advising authors on the most favourable use of their copyright material. They contribute, for example, advice on licensing issues relating to open access.

The library has thus become a conduit not only for information content, but also for matters pertaining to scholarly communication generally. It is well placed to develop this role further as the emphasis on improving the efficiency, economy and effectiveness of scholarly activity continues.

The imperative to innovate and develop imaginative new ways of facilitating scholarly communication clearly has a momentum. According to the most recent review of trends conducted by ACRL (2008), the challenges facing academic librarians in particular, and the scholarly communications universe in general, will continue unabated. These will be driven by further developments in technology as well as the economic and social pressures to deliver effective solutions within an ever-more complex and demanding academic regime. The report's findings identify several strands, including, among other things, an increased emphasis on digitization; the continuing evolution of librarians' skill sets; demand from students and faculty for increasing access to resources and technology; a new outlook on intellectual property issues, with calls for freer access to the output of publicly sponsored research; a greater business orientation for higher education, with students behaving as customers; and also as the growth of e-learning, especially to a far more distributed learning community.

What next: what do libraries want?

It is pertinent to ponder exactly what libraries want from the scenario that is unfolding regarding the future of the journal. The fundamentals of library service and the objectives embedded within them, as rehearsed in the introduction to this chapter, have not altered. Therefore, what libraries want and need are solutions that achieve those objectives. First, librarians need solutions that accommodate the constraints, financial, logistical and physical within which they operate. Second, we need solutions that offer a degree of stability, reliability and transparency in terms of delivery configurations and business models. Finally, we need solutions that incorporate libraries' important role as agencies with a wealth of expertise in information organization, retrieval and management. This chapter has addressed some of the ways in which libraries are responding to the situation and has indicated the opportunities that remain to be exploited.

Libraries do not operate in isolation. They are held accountable by their paymasters and users through performance indicators. Some 15 years ago, the Follett review of libraries isolated performance criteria that remain appropriate (Joint Funding Councils' Libraries Review Group, 1993). These criteria relate to the individual library's effectiveness in providing relevant services and resources as economically and efficiently as possible, in a context that identifies and integrates with the objectives of the wider organization, and which recognizes the imperative of achieving and sustaining user satisfaction. These will inevitably remain the drivers for future development for journal provision as for anything else. They will need to be coupled with the imagination and enterprise of library managers ready and willing to innovate. Although somewhat beyond the scope of library managers acting alone, making the scholarly dissemination process more efficient and creating new sourcing models offer distinctly longer-term benefits for all involved.

The future success of the journal relies heavily on a working coalition of a range of stakeholders. The library offers the potential for becoming the neutral territory for the exchange of ideas and the development of plans for scholarly communications that involve all who are involved in the endeavour: authors, publishers, technologists, fund providers and readers.

Bibliography

Association of College and Research Libraries (ACRL) (2008) 'Environmental scan 2007', available at: *http://www.acrl.org/ala/acrl/acrlpubs/whitepapers/Environmental_Scan_2.pdf.* (accessed 31 July 2008).

Cockerill, M. (2008) 'Why have a central open access fund?', *CILIP Library + Information Update* 7(3): 30.

Creaser, C. and White, S. (2008) 'Trends in journal prices: an analysis of selected journals, 2000–2006', *Learned Publishing* 21(3): 214–24.

Davies, J. E. and White, S. (2005) 'Simplifying serials sourcing: a case study in decision support for managing electronic journals access', *The Bottom Line* 18(1): 7–13.

Davies, J. E. (2002) 'Counting on serials: management and serials metrics', *Serials* 15(1): 35–9.

Hamblin, Y. (2005) 'Library portals case studies', *Assignation* 22(3): 26–9.

House of Commons Science and Technology Committee (2004) *Scientific Publications: Free for all? Volume 1: Report*, London, Stationery Office.

Jamali, H. R., Nicholas, D. and Huntington, P. (2005) 'The use and users of scholarly e-journals: a review of log analysis studies', *Aslib Proceedings* 57(6): 554–72.

Joint Funding Councils' Libraries Review Group (1993) *Follett Report*, Bristol: HEFCE.

LISU (2004) *LibPortal Project: Access to Library Provided Resources. A Survey and Review of Library-orientated Portals in Higher and Further Education*, Loughborough: LISU, Loughborough University.

LISU (2007) 'LISU annual library statistics 2006 featuring trend analysis of UK public & academic libraries 1995–2005', available at: *http://www.lboro.ac.uk/departments/dis/lisu/downloads/als06.pdf* (accessed 31 July 2008).

LISU (2008) 'Libraries Archives Museums Publishing Online Statistics [LAMPOST]', available at: *http://www.lboro.ac.uk/departments/dis/lisu/lampost.html* (accessed 31 July 2008).

MacDougall, A. F. and Wheelhouse, H. (1989) *A Study of Various Aspects of Cooperation between the East Midlands University and Polytechnic Libraries: Final Report*, Loughborough: Pilkington Library, Loughborough University.

MacDougall, A. F., Wheelhouse, H. and Wilson, J. M. (1989) 'Academic library cooperation and document supply: possibilities and considerations of cost effectiveness', *Journal of Librarianship* 21(3): 186–99.

Nicholas, D., Huntington, P. and Watkinson, A. (2005) 'Scholarly journal usage: the results of deep log analysis', *Journal of Documentation* 61(2): 248–80.

Ulrich's Periodicals Directory Online (2008) available at: *http://www.ulrichsweb.com/ulrichsweb/* (accessed 31 July 2008).

White, S and Creaser, C. (2007) 'Trends in scholarly journal prices 2000–2006', LISU Occasional Paper No. 37, available at: *http://www.lboro.ac.uk/departments/dis/lisu/downloads/op37.pdf* (accessed 31 July 2008).

White, S and Davies, J. E. (2001) 'Economic evaluation model of National Electronic Site Licence Initiative (NESLI) "Deals"', LISU Occasional Paper No. 28, available at: *http://www.lboro.ac.uk/departments/ls/lisu/downloads/NESLI%20deals.pdf* (accessed 31 July 2008).

12

Academic publishing and the political economy of education journals
Michael A. Peters

The history of scientific communication, even in the postwar period, is a mammoth undertaking where technological developments and the new paradigm of open knowledge production seem to outstrip our capacity to give an adequate theoretical account of them. There is so much experimentation by way of new electronic journals launched and new projects being established that it is near impossible to document even the range in its diversity let alone theorize its main characteristics and implications for the digitization of scientific communication. One source, perhaps the most comprehensive, provides a bibliography on scholarly electronic publishing that runs to 1,400 references in English under such categories as economic issues, electronic books and texts, electronic serials, general works, legal issues, library issues, new publishing models, publisher issues, repositories, e-prints and America Online (Bailey, 2006; see also 2001).

The history of electronic scientific communication itself is now nearly 20 years old if we date the process from the appearance of the first electronic journals. The electronic revolution of those first utopian years in the early 1990s with predictions of the collapse of the traditional print-based system, the demise of academic publishers, and the replacement by electronic journals has not yet happened. As Valauskas argues:

> electronic scholarly journals differentiate themselves from printed scholarly journals by accelerated peer review, combined with mercurial production schemes ... The sheer interactive nature of digital journals ... and the ability to access the complete archives of a given title on a server make that sort of publishing a significant

departure from the long established traditions of print. (Valauskas, 1997)

He concludes:

> Electronic scholarly journals are indeed different from traditional print scholarly journals, but not as radically different as some would argue. They are different in terms of process, but not in terms of the ancient traditions of peer review and verification. (Valauskas, 1997)

At the same time, while slower than originally thought, there are certainly massive and revolutionary changes taking place that I will refer generically to as 'open knowledge production', a term that might be said to embrace open source, open access, open 'science' (referring to systematic knowledge) and open courseware.

The history of scientific communication demonstrates that the typical form of the scientific article presented in print-based journals in essay form is a result of development over two centuries, beginning in the seventeenth century with the emergence of learned societies and cooperation among scientists. *Journal des Sçavans*, the first journal, was published in Paris in 1665 as a 12-page quarto pamphlet, appearing only a few months before the *Philosophical Transactions of the Royal Society*, the oldest journal in continuous production (Fjällbrant, 1997; Guedon, 2001).[1] The development of the journal and scientific norms of cooperation, forms of academic writing and the norm of peer review were part of the institutionalization of science. The model of the Royal Society that was emulated elsewhere in Europe and the USA, and subsequently institutionalized, received a strong impetus from the emergence of the modern research university, beginning with the establishment of the University of Berlin in 1810 in the reforms of Humboldt. This institutionalization of science was also a part of the juridical-legal system of writing that grew up around the notion of a professional scientist and academic, the notion of the academic author, the idea of public science or research, the ownership of ideas, and academic recognition for the author who claimed originality for a discovery, set of results or piece of scholarship (Kaufer and Carley, 1993).

Over 180 years later, the form, style and economics of the socio-technical ecology and infrastructure of scientific communication were to undergo another set of changes. The prehistory of the emergence of electronic forms of scientific communication can be traced back at least to Ted Nelson's notion of 'hypertext', which he coined in 1963 and went on to develop as a hypertext system. The prehistory reveals the development of networking and network publishing in the Advanced Research Projects Agency Network (ARPANET) launched by the US Department of Defense in 1969 and in the Education Resources Information Center (ERIC) launched by the US Department of Education's Office of Educational Research and Improvement and the National Library of Education.[2]

In this context, it is important to recognize that the concept of 'information' emerged from the combination of the development of modern military intelligence (breaking codes, deciphering messages, encoding information, resolving conflict of sources, etc.) and the development of new communication technologies. Information theory is strongly related to the military context and the cooperation between the military and business sector. Some obvious examples include the US Advanced Research Projects Agency (ARPA) which, in response to Sputnik, developed the RAND's contribution to packet-switching through its research on the control of missiles, as well as the ARPANET, which was constructed in 1969, linking the University of California at Los Angeles, SRI at Stanford, University of California at Santa Barbara, and the University of Utah.

Some account of the impact of computers on writing is required to understand the shift from literacy to orality and the way that computers reintroduce oral characteristics into writing along with a range of other characteristics including linearity to connectivity, fixity to fluidity, and passivity to interactivity (Ferris, 2002). Jay David Bolter's (1991) *Writing Space: The Computer, Hypertext and the History of Writing* is the seminal text that explores the computer's place in the history of symbolic (textual) media. The consequences of the networking of science and culture have yet to be worked through fully; yet as Bolter points out, the new definition of literacy is synonymous with computer literacy. Thus, while it is the case that the computer signifies the end of traditional print literacy, it does not signify the end of literacy (Cope and Kalantzis, 2008). The web has now spawned a whole set of new media genres and forms, and the internet has been enthusiastically accepted into education and in a way that previous technologies like television were not. We have not begun to systematically identify the way these new media forms and the development of visual literacy have affected and will continue to affect scientific communication, but already there have been some telling signs (see Nentwich, 2003; Woolgar, 2000).

In 1987, *New Horizons in Adult Education*, perhaps the earliest electronic journal, was established by the Syracuse University Kellogg Project.[3] In 1989, this was followed by *Psycoloquy* (*http://psycprints.ecs .soton.ac.uk/*), established by Stevan Harnad, and the *Newsletter on Serials Pricing*. The next year saw the launch of another three electronic journals,[4] and there was serious talk of a crisis in scholarly communication which has grown ever-more insistent. The origins of the crisis are the increasing volume and high cost for print journals and books together with loss of control in the marketplace and through copyright.[5]

This chapter begins by providing a brief account of the political economy of academic publishing before focusing on education journals in the English-speaking world. The chapter then outlines the distribution and specialization of education journals, before going on to provide an analysis of education journals in the Social Science Citation Index followed by an analysis of open access education journals. Finally, the chapter concludes with some reflections on the political economy of education journals.

The political economy of academic publishing

In 2004, the world of academic publishing in the Western world was dominated by 12 publishing corporations with combined annual sales of approximately $65 billion and somewhere in the order of 250,000 employees.[6] These corporations, largely European (five British, three German, one Dutch) and North American (two US, one Canadian), were established first as booksellers in the nineteenth century, although a few go back even earlier with close historical links to the beginning of the publishing and printing industries. As Munroe notes:

> They are not new companies. The oldest company in the group is Taylor & Francis, founded in 1797, and only Thomson was founded after 1900. Most started as booksellers or printers, but there was a hat maker, a building contractor, and a radio station owner among them. (Munroe, 2007)

Munroe documents the fact that the 'founders were all single owners or partners, and most of the firms were, until recently, owned and managed by family members. Almost all of them still have family members on the board or in the hierarchy of the company.' She goes on to indicate that most of the companies now have professional CEOs and, since the Second World War, have undertaken serious redevelopment to secure a steady and profitable niche market for their products, as can be seen by the series of mergers and acquisitions. Table 12.1 lists the 12 largest publishing corporations as at 2004.

Since Munroe's original investigation, there has been further concentration of ownership in academic publishing, and Munroe's site now lists all the mergers and acquisitions in the industry instead of the 2004 sales and employment data. In May 2003, Cinven and Candover, leading European buyout specialists, acquired BertelsmannSpringer, one of the world's leading academic publishers, for a consideration of €1.05 billion, from parent company Bertelsmann AG. Candover and Cinven also merged BertelsmannSpringer with Kluwer Academic Publishers, another leading international publisher acquired for €600 million from Wolters Kluwer in January 2003, to create the second largest science, technology and medicine (STM) publisher in the world, with total combined revenues of about €880 million and earnings before interest,

Table 12.1 The 12 largest academic publishing companies, 2004

Company	Sales volume	No. employees
Blackwell	$4.5bn	18,393
Bertelsmann	$23.2bn	76,226
Candover & Cinven	€8.4bn	n.d.
John Wiley & Sons	$974m	3,300
McGraw-Hill	$5.25bn	17,000
Pearson	$7.5m	33,389
Reed Elsevier	$9.3bn	35,100
Springer	$16m	90
Taylor & Francis	$971m	4,000
Thomson	$8.1bn	39,550
Wolters Kluwer	$4.5bn	607
Verlagsgruppe Georg von Holtzbrinck GmbH	DM423m	12,500

All figures based on 2004 data.
Source: Munroe, M. H. (2007) 'The academic publishing industry: a story of merger and acquisition', available at: *http://www.niulib.niu.edu/publishers/* (accessed 30 August, 2007).

taxes, depreciation and amortization of €155 million in the period ended 31 December 2002. This effectively reduced the number of academic publishing companies to ten. In 2006, John Wiley acquired Blackwell for a price of £572 million (US$1.08 billion), continuing the trend toward consolidation in the publishing industry. The newly merged organization publishes approximately 1,250 scholarly peer-reviewed journals (over 1 million pages) and an extensive collection of books with global appeal across the range of sciences, technology, medicine and health, social sciences and humanities. The largest five players (Reed Elsevier, Thomson, Wolters Kluwer, Springer and Wiley-Blackwell) now account for over half (52.3 per cent) of total market revenues.

There has clearly been increasing rationalization in the academic publishing industry since Munroe's original analysis, and in 2008 there were only nine companies with accordingly greater economies of scale. It is also worth noting, as Munroe states, that up until very recently most companies had strong historical roots in bookselling and/or publishing going back at least to the nineteenth century and some even earlier. Given the recent Cinven and Candover acquisitions, trend appears to have been broken. In the 2007 site update Munroe indicates that 'Together the companies [Springer and Kluwer] will publish 1,350 journals and more than 5,000 book titles with revenues of about €880 million'.

A media industry overview conducted by Morgan Stanley (2002) revealed a US$7 billion market for global STM publishing broadly divided into scientific publishing (with libraries as major markets) and medical publishing (with hospitals and practitioners as major markets), with Reed as the market leader (Table 12.2). The report indicated that scientific publishing is the fastest-growing media subsector of the past 15 years and that since 1986, 'the average price of a journal has risen by 215% while the number of journals purchased has fallen by only 5.1%' (Morgan Stanley, 2002: 2).

The report concludes that the nature of the industry is unlikely to change, although it will experience a cyclical slowdown due to budget cuts. It also suggests that large publishers will enjoy economies of scale through 'bundling', and margins will expand for those publishers with successful online platforms.

The Wellcome Trust's report, 'Economic analysis of scientific research publishing', largely concurs with the report from Morgan Stanley and provides a useful overall picture that forms the context for understanding journal publishing in the field of education. The report suggests that 'The current market structure does not operate in the long-term interests of the research community' and that while 'Commercial

Table 12.2	Global scientific publishing market players, 2001	
	Revenue (US$m)	Market share (%)
Reed Elsevier (Elsevier Science)	1,055.3	23.3
American Chemical Society	357.3	7.9
Thomson	259.0	5.7
John Wiley & Sons	243.6	5.4
Institute of Electrical & Electronics Engineers	200.3	4.4
Wolters Kluwer	169.3	3.7
McGraw-Hill	146.2	3.2
Taylor & Francis	144.6	3.2
Springer-Verlag	44.0	1.0
Others	1,916.9	42.3
Total scientific market	4,536.4	100.0

Source: Morgan Stanley (2002: 2).

publishers are dominant ... many top journals are published by not-for-profit organizations'. The major conclusion seems to strongly indicate a role for governments, stating 'The "public good" element of scientific work means market solutions are inefficient' (Wellcome Trust, 2003: iv).

The report provides both a demand and supply-side analysis of why commercial publishers are so dominant. On the demand side, demand is price-inelastic because 'price is unimportant at point of use for the research community' and 'journals are not easily substitutable for each other'. In addition, 'Libraries operate in the commercial market and purchase up to their budget limits' and 'Other sources of demand, such as private companies and health services, are uncoordinated' (Wellcome Trust, 2003: iv). On the supply side:

> Authors face a limited number of journals, through which their work is 'purchased'. The primary concerns of authors are the reputation and reach of the journal. In general, authors are not concerned with price and cost characteristics. There is also a limited amount of substitutability between journals for authors when offering their work for publication.
>
> Journals are published by not-for-profit publishers and commercial publishers – institutions with different objectives and modes of working.

> All publishers, including commercial publishers, provide authors and editorial boards with the services and outputs they need. (Wellcome Trust, 2003: iv)

The Wellcome Trust's report also indicates that the market has two interlinked parts – an academic market and a commercial market – that 'operate according to different rules and priorities'. The report maintains that where 'The academic market operates with little recognition of the existence of the commercial market. The commercial market attempts to manage the academic market' (Wellcome Trust, 2003: iv). The report argues:

> Commercial publishers are currently more active than other institutions in operating in both markets. They attempt to control supply in the commercial market through mergers/takeovers and to manage demand through price and service to libraries. The commercial publishers have set up price-service packages which enhance their position and undermine the position of the not-for-profit sector. A major example of this – the 'big deal' – in effect requires libraries to take more journals than they might otherwise choose from the commercial publishers. The limits on the libraries' abilities to change the package in the 'big deal' result in cuts in subscriptions to journals from other publishers whenever the libraries face financial constraints. A further implication of these arrangements is that citations to the commercial publishers' journals are likely to increase, at the expense of the not-for-profit sector, thus increasing the apparent value of those journals. (Wellcome Trust, 2003: iv)

Finally, the report notes that 'commercial publishers offer good service and speed to the academic market and many academics are currently largely unaware and unconcerned about the state of scientific publishing' (Wellcome Trust, 2003: iv). It might also be said in line with Munroe's analysis that most commercial publishers have historically grown up with the academic market and have close links with universities and ongoing intimate and trusting relationships with faculty and university administrators that go back many generations. Furthermore, commercial publishers have an ethos of innovation and experimentation that has led to improvements and efficiencies in all phases of the production cycle, including most recently publishing-on-demand and just-in-time printing, the introduction of fully electronic editorial journal offices, online delivery of journals, complete digitization of collections and archives, the creation of searchable databases, digitization of book and series collections, development of webometrics, bibliometrics and citation analyses, as well as advances in web design and portal development. It is an interesting question why academics and academic knowledge cultures have not supported this kind of innovation even though universities have led cutting-edge developments in informatics, computer science and innovations with web technologies.

The European Commission's 'Study on the economic and technical evolution of scientific publication markets in Europe' corroborates and updates the Morgan Stanley and the Wellcome Trust reports, confirming that:

> The core STM (science, technology and medicine) publishing market is estimated between USD 7 billion and USD 11 billion, while in 2001 OECD countries allocated USD 638 billion to R&D. In the last 30 years, the prices of scientific journals have been steadily increasing. Between 1975 and 1995, they increased 200–300% beyond inflation. (European Commission, 2006: 5)

The report goes on to record that as of 1995, publishers started to adopt digital delivery modes and to provide online access to their journals, but while the new technologies and the internet have dramatically improved the accessibility of scientific publications for researchers the actual access to the literature still relies on their library's ability to pay subscriptions.

The report outlines the broad market trends from 1995, which is taken as the approximate start of the 'electronic revolution', including the following main features that have remained constant since about 1975:

> (i) the increasing reliance on journals as the main channel for dissemination of scientific knowledge, with a growth that parallels the growth of research produced;
>
> (ii) the dominance of the 'reader-pay' or 'library pay', as opposed to the 'author-pay' model of journal dissemination;
>
> (iii) the existence of many publishers in the market, with two big groups of publishers: For-profits (FP) and Not-for-profits (NFP), the latter group including learned societies and university presses;
>
> (iv) the very fast growth of some big FP publishers, through new journal introduction, through the running of journals from learned societies, and through mergers (European Commission, 2006: 7).

Most recently, Brown et al. (2007) have commented on how information has transformed the landscape of scholarly publishing, increasing the importance of 'grey literature' and blurring the boundaries between formal and informal forms of publication and scholarship. It has also changed consumption patterns away from individual books to electronic resources and platforms, creating new digital formats that enable 'real-time dissemination, collaboration, dynamically-updated content, and usage of new media' (Brown et al., 2007: 4). Changes in content creation and publication have been accompanied by the establishment of alternative distribution models (institutional repositories, preprint servers, open access journals) that have the capacity 'to broaden access, reduce costs, and enable open sharing of content' (Brown et al., 2007: 4). A range of different economic models have become available that depend on different content and different audiences. The report remarks:

> It seems critical to us that there continues to be a diverse marketplace for publishing a range of content, from fee-based to open access, from peer reviewed to self-published, from single author to collaboratively created, from simple text to rich media. This marketplace should involve commercial and not-for-profit entities, and should include collaborations among libraries, presses, and academic computing centers. (Brown et al., 2007: 4)

In light of these changes, the authors of the report were interested 'to gauge the community's interest in a possible collective investment in a technology platform to support innovation in university-based, mission-driven publishing' – 'an infrastructure that could serve as the foundation for new forms of university-centred academic publishing in the digital age'.

The distribution and specialization of education journals

The concentration of education journals is even more limited given that a number of the big ten do not publish journals. The Thomson Corporation, with $8.40 billion revenues in 2005 and some 40,500 employees worldwide, is organized into four global markets of which learning is one (together with legal and regulatory, financial, and scientific and healthcare). Thomson Learning generated about $2.18 billion in 2005, with some 9,480 employees in 39 countries. It specializes in providing tailored education, training, reference, courseware, assessment solutions and web-based learning to organizations and education institutions. Pearson Education, with combined sales for 2005 of nearly $5 billion, specializes in US school pre K-12 curriculum, testing and software, 'achievement solutions' and higher-education textbooks, learning tools and technologies. Harcourt Education (part of Reed Elsevier until 2007) focuses on the provision of learning and testing materials to teachers. Neither John Wiley & Sons nor McGraw-Hill publishes journals in this area. In the English-speaking world, the largest concentration of education journals is represented by just four companies, with Taylor & Francis dwarfing the others. In 2006, some 400 journals were published by the main four companies as follows:

- Springer (C&C): 38 journals;
- Blackwell: 49 journals;
- Sage: 49 journals;
- Taylor & Francis: 264 journals.

Tables 12.3 to 12.6 present the different distribution of education journals published by these companies. This brief analysis reveals that

Table 12.3 Education journals by category (Springer)

Category	No. journals
Health	1
Children, early childhood	2
Curriculum	2
Science, maths	9
Information technology	6
Learning, psychology	4
Educational policy	1
Higher education	1
Chinese education	1
Philosophy, theory	4
Reading, writing	1
Research	1
Vocational, personal evaluation	2
International, development	3
Total	38

Table 12.4 Education journals by category (Blackwell)

Category	No. journals
History/philosophy of education	4
General/educational theory	4
Educational research	6
Child development	5
Health, medical, pastoral	6
Special, disabilities education	6
Curriculum (& specialist)	5
Higher education	1
Measurement & stats	3
Policy, social science	2
Reading, literacy, language	4
Teacher-related	2
Technology	1
Total	49

Table 12.5 Education journals by category (Sage)

Category	No. journals
Administration, management & leadership	8
Curriculum & content	10
Early childhood education	4
Education studies	3
Higher/adult education	4
Inclusive education & exceptional students	3
International education	3
Research design, skills & methods	2
Staff development/professional development	1
Student assessment	3
Student behaviour, motivation & discipline	3
Teaching & learning	3
Urban education	2
Total	49

Table 12.6   Education journals by category (Taylor & Francis)

Category	No. journals
Biomedical education	9
Comparative and international education	6
Education policy	36
Education research	54
Educational media, technology & science	15
Further & higher education	27
Health, sex and medical education	13
History of education	4
Leadership and management education	9
Moral and religious education	9
Multicultural education	8
Performing arts and English	7
Quality and assessment	5
Sociology of education	21
Special needs	17
Teacher education	24
Total	264

there is a high degree of functional specialization with a small degree of overlap. The different specializations of the publishers can be summarized as follows:

- Springer
  - science and maths;
  - information technology;
  - learning theory.
- Blackwell
  - educational research;
  - health and medicine;
  - special education;
  - curriculum;
  - philosophy and history.

- Sage
  - curriculum and content;
  - admin., management and leadership.
- Taylor & Francis
  - educational research;
  - educational policy;
  - further and higher education;
  - teacher education;
  - sociology of education.

Education journals and the Social Science Citation Index

The Social Sciences Citation Index (SSCI) is part of a wider science citation index covering the sciences, the social sciences and the humanities. It is owned by Thomson Scientific, which according to its homepage, provides 'information based solutions [which] keep academic, government, corporate and pharma R&D professionals at the forefront of their markets by providing must-have authoritative content with innovative technologies that assist with discovery, analysis, product development and distribution' (*http://scientific.thomson.com/*).

Thomson Scientific is part of the Thomson Corporation, which advertises itself as 'a leading global provider of integrated information-based solutions to business and professional customers' (*http://www.thomson.com/about/*). In 2006, its revenues amounted to $6.6 billion (an 8 per cent increase over 2005) and it employs 32,000 workers in 37 countries. Thomson Scientific is one of five segments comprising the company, contributing $0.6 billion in revenues and employing some 2,400 workers. The other segments include Thomson Financial, Thomson Healthcare, Thomson Legal and Thomson Tax & Accounting. On 26 October 2006, Thomson announced that it was divesting itself of Thomson Learning Business with annual revenues of over $6 billion per year, current assets of over $3 billion and total assets of over $20 billion.[7] Apax Partners (Apax) and OMERS Capital Partners (OMERS) acquired the higher education, careers and library reference assets of

Thomson Learning, and a consortium of funds advised by OMERS and Apax acquired Nelson Canada, for a combined total value of approximately $7.75 billion in cash (in May 2007 prices). Thomson Scientific provides multidisciplinary information from scientific literature and the web, advertising itself in these terms:

> Thomson resources give you the tools you need to access high quality information from international research literature covering 250 disciplines in the sciences, social sciences, and arts and humanities. Through a variety of multidisciplinary products, you can discover current and retrospective information from approximately 8,500 of the globe's leading, peer-reviewed journals. These publications represent about 1.3 million articles and 30–35 million citations a year. (*http://scientific.thomson.com/aboutus/*)

The Thomson website provides the following information on the SSCI.

> The Social Sciences Citation Index® (SSCI®) and Social SciSearch® provide access to current and retrospective bibliographic information, author abstracts, and cited references found in over 1,700 of the world's leading scholarly social sciences journals covering more than 50 disciplines. They also cover individually selected, relevant items from approximately 3,300 of the world's leading science and technology journals. (*http://scientific .thomson.com/products/ssci/*)

The ISI database covers about 8,700 international journals on an annual basis and in accordance with Bradford's Law (which holds that 'a relatively small number of journals publish the bulk of significant scientific results'[8]), the website indicates that the primary criterion of the evaluation process is timeliness of publication, meaning the ability to publish on time. Other criteria mentioned are: standard international editorial conventions, including abstract and full bibliographical information, author address etc.; preference for English language titles, abstract and keywords; application of peer review; and international diversity among authors of both source articles and cited articles.

As of 2007, there were listed 113 journals in the category 'education and educational research' with another 28 in the category 'education, special' (see Tables 12.7 and 12.8).

Table 12.7   Social Sciences Citation Index – education and educational research journal list, 2007

Journal	Country of publisher
Academic Psychiatry	USA
Academy of Management Learning & Education	USA
Adult Education Quarterly	USA
Advances in Health Sciences Education	Netherlands
Aids Education and Prevention	USA
American Educational Research Journal	USA
American Journal of Education	USA
Anthropology & Education Quarterly	USA
Applied Measurement in Education	USA
Asia Pacific Education Review	South Korea
Australian Educational Researcher	Australia
Australian Journal of Education	Australia
British Educational Research Journal	UK
British Journal of Educational Studies	UK
British Journal of Educational Technology	UK
British Journal of Sociology of Education	UK
Chinese Education and Society	USA
Comparative Education	USA
Comparative Education Review	USA
Computers & Education	UK
Curriculum Inquiry	UK
Early Childhood Research Quarterly	USA
Economics of Education Review	UK
Education and Urban Society	USA
Educational Administration Quarterly	USA
Educational Evaluation and Policy Analysis	USA
Educational Gerontology	USA
Educational Leadership	USA
Educational Policy	USA
Educational Research	UK
Educational Review	UK

Table 12.7 Social Sciences Citation Index – education and educational research journal list, 2007 (*Cont'd*)

Journal	Country of publisher
Educational Studies	UK
Educational Technology & Society	New Zealand
Elementary School Journal	USA
Educational Technology Research & Development	USA
European Physical Education Review	USA
Foreign Language Annals	USA
Gender and Education	UK
Harvard Educational Review	USA
Health Education Research	UK
Higher Education	Netherlands
Innovations in Education & Teaching International	UK
Instructional Science	Netherlands
Interactive Learning Environments	UK
International Journal of Art & Design Education	UK
International Journal of Education Development	UK
International Journal of Science Education	UK
Journal for Research in Mathematics Education	USA
Journal of Adolescent & Adult Literacy	USA
Journal of American College Health	USA
Journal of College Student Development	USA
Journal of Computer Assisted Learning	UK
Journal of Curriculum Studies	UK
Journal of Economic Education	USA
Journal of Education Policy	UK
Journal of Educational & Behavioral Statistics	USA
Journal of Educational Research	USA
Journal of Engineering Education	USA
Journal of Experimental Education	USA
Journal of Geography in Higher Education	UK
Journal of Higher Education	USA
Journal of Legal Education	USA

Table 12.7 Social Sciences Citation Index – education and educational research journal list, 2007 (*Cont'd*)

Journal	Country of publisher
Journal of Literacy Research	USA
Journal of Moral Education	UK
Journal of Philosophy of Education	UK
Journal of Research in Reading	UK
Journal of Research in Science Teaching	USA
Journal of School Health	UK
Journal of Social Work Education	USA
Journal of Teacher Education	USA
Journal of Teaching in Physical Education	UK
Journal of the Learning Sciences	USA
Language Learning	USA
Language Learning & Technology	USA
Language Teaching Research	USA
Learning and Instruction	UK
Minerva	Netherlands
Oxford Review of Education	UK
Paedagogica Historica	UK
Perspectives in Education	South Africa
Phi Delta Kappan	USA
Quest	USA
Reading and Writing	Netherlands
Reading Research Quarterly	USA
Reading Teacher	USA
Research in Higher Education	USA
Research in Science Education	Netherlands
Research in the Teaching of English	USA
Review of Educational Research	USA
Review of Higher Education	USA
Review of Research in Education	USA
Revista Espanola De Pedagogia	Spain

Table 12.7 Social Sciences Citation Index – education and educational research journal list, 2007 (*Cont'd*)

Journal	Country of publisher
Russian Education and Society	USA
School Effectiveness & School Improvement	UK
Science Education	USA
Scientific Studies of Reading	USA
Second Language Research	UK
Sociology of Education	USA
South African Journal of Education	South Africa
Sport Education and Society	UK
Studies in Higher Education	UK
Teachers College Record	UK
Teaching and Teacher Education	UK
Teaching in Higher Education	UK
Teaching of Psychology	USA
Teaching Sociology	USA
Tesol Quarterly	USA
Theory into Practice	USA
Urban Education	USA
Young Children	USA
Zeitscrift fur Erziehungwissenschaft	Germany
Zeitschrift Fur Padagogik	Germany
Zeitschrift Fur Soziologie der Erziehung und Sozialisation	Germany

In terms of country of origin, the journals are not widely distributed. For example, in the category 'education and educational research', the 113 journals are distributed as follows:

- USA: 61 journals;
- UK: 37 journals;
- Netherlands: five journals;
- Germany: three journals;
- Australia: two journals;

Table 12.8 Social Sciences Citation Index – education, special journal list, 2007

Journal	Country of publisher
American Annals of the Deaf	USA
American Journal on Mental Retardation	USA
Annals of Dyslexia	USA
British Journal of Developmental Disabilities	Austria
Dyslexia	UK
Education and Training in Developmental Disabilities	USA
Exceptional Children	USA
Focus on Exceptional Children	USA
Gifted Child Quarterly	USA
High Ability Studies	UK
Infants and Young Children	USA
International Review of Research in Mental Retardation	USA
Intervention in School and Clinic	USA
Journal of Deaf Studies and Deaf Education	UK
Journal of Early Intervention	USA
Journal of Fluency Disorders	USA
Journal of Intellectual & Developmental Disability	UK
Journal of Intellectual Disability Research	UK
Journal of Learning Disabilities	USA
Journal of Positive Behavior Interventions	USA
Journal of Special Education	USA
Learning Disability Quarterly	USA
Mental Retardation	USA
Remedial and Special Education	USA
Research and Practice for Persons with Severe Disabilities	USA
Research in Developmental Disabilities	UK
Topics in Early Childhood Special Education	USA
Volta Review	USA

- South Africa: two journals;
- New Zealand: one journal;
- Spain: one journal;
- South Korea: one journal.

As can be seen, the overwhelming majority of these journals are located in the USA or UK – 98 journals out of the total of 113. Only six other countries are represented, only one of which is a 'developing' country, namely South Africa. Such predominance is also evident in the 'education, special' field, which has 21 US-based journals and six UK, with only one other country represented.

Table 12.9 ISI 'education and educational research' journals by publisher

Publisher	No. journals
Commercial publishers	
Routledge (Taylor & Francis)	21
Sage	14
Blackwell (& Wiley)	11
Springer	8
Pergamon-Elsevier	4
Lawrence Erlbaum	5
Heldref	4
M.E. Sharpe	2
Human Kinetics	2
Guilford Publications	1
Juventa	1
Julius Beltz	1
Subtotal	74
University presses	
University of Chicago	2
Ohio State University Press	2
Johns Hopkins	2
Small specialist presses	3
Oxford University Press	1
Subtotal	10
Associations, councils, learned societies, institutes etc	29
Total	113

Breaking down the 113 'education and educational research' journals to the publisher level (Table 12.9) shows not only the high concentration of ownership by the big US and UK-based publishers, but also that independent publishers, small presses, university presses and journals published by associations, learned societies or councils account for a significant proportion of the educational journals published in the USA.

Open access and education journals

Open access publishing provides an innovative format with the possibility of using multimedia including images and sound as well as datasets and embedded software. It also offers new navigational tools that allow search function and hyperlinks. One of the most fundamental advantages of open access e-journals is that they have the capacity to increase user involvement and to encourage audience interactivity along with new distribution formats such as the continuous addition of articles rather than serialization (Owen, 2007).

Many of these new formats, tools and distribution forms apply directly to electronic journals. Open access journals have the extra advantage of providing free content. Generally speaking, there are two modes of e-journals that represent the existing patterns of ownership, with large publishers developing e-journal formats for existing journals in print format and fully digitized back copies. Many of the journals mentioned above have e-journal formats as well as print copies. There is no doubt that electronic journals provide scholarly 'data warehouse' functions enabling computationally-enabled representation of knowledge that in the future will develop expansively in new interactive formats rather than existing as mere passive archives.

The Budapest Open Access Initiative (BOAI) defines 'open access' as:

> free availability on the public internet, permitting any users to read, download, copy, distribute, print, search, or link to the full texts of these articles, crawl them for indexing, pass them as data to software, or use them for any other lawful purpose, without financial, legal, or technical barriers other than those inseparable from gaining access to the internet itself. The only constraint on reproduction and distribution, and the only role for copyright in this domain, should be to give authors control over the integrity of their work and the right to be properly acknowledged and cited. (BOAI, 2002)

According to the BOAI public statement, this category primarily encompasses 'peer-reviewed journal articles, but it also includes any unreviewed preprints that [scholars] might wish to put online for comment or to alert colleagues to important research findings' (BOAI, 2002).

Typically, such statements and declarations also make reference to the serials crisis, the economics of academic publishing and to an emerging global intellectual property (IP) regime that expands and looks after the interests of IP owners without the same or sufficient regard for the rights of users, especially in the third world. More activist associations provide histories of the open access movement and develop alliances across a variety of organizations involved with scientific communication including libraries and their associations, research institutions, universities and university consortia, learned societies, open access journals, small university presses, government and state agencies, and publishers. There is general concern about the extent of new IP regulations, increased duration of copyright, and the extension of IP to new areas of activity including databases and software. There is also strong concern for questions involving the governance of the internet, the protection of its intellectual commons, and the way that private interests are being allowed to muscle in and enclose some areas of the public domain (Höök, 1999; Jacobs, 2006; Open Society Institute, year unknown).

Most of the formal statements in support of open access also place their faith in the promise of open access and the architecture of the internet to distribute and disseminate public knowledge. Thus, the Statement of the Libraries & Publishers Working Group (2003) declares a belief that 'open access will be an essential component of scientific publishing in the future and that works reporting the results of current scientific research should be as openly accessible and freely useable as possible' (see *http://www.earlham.edu/~peters/fos/bethesda.htm*). The statement then itemizes a set of proposals for libraries and journal publishers aimed at encouraging the open access model.

The Statement of Scientists and Scientific Societies Working Group from the same source reads:

> Scientific research is an interdependent process whereby each experiment is informed by the results of others. The scientists who perform research and the professional societies that represent them have a great interest in ensuring that research results are disseminated as immediately, broadly and effectively as possible. Electronic publication of research results offers the opportunity

and the obligation to share research results, ideas and discoveries freely with the scientific community and the public. (see *http://www.earlham.edu/~peters/fos/bethesda.htm*)

In the preface to the Berlin Declaration on Open Access to Knowledge in the Sciences and Humanities (2003) there is a recognition of the way the internet has changed scientific practice, focusing on how the internet has emerged as a 'functional medium for distributing knowledge' that will also significantly 'modify the nature of scientific publishing as well as the existing system of quality assurance':

> The internet has fundamentally changed the practical and economic realities of distributing scientific knowledge and cultural heritage. For the first time ever, the internet now offers the chance to constitute a global and interactive representation of human knowledge, including cultural heritage and the guarantee of worldwide access. (Berlin Declaration on Open Access to Knowledge in the Sciences and Humanities, 2003)

In its 'Principles and strategies for the reform of scholarly communication', the Association of College & Research Libraries (ACRL) defines scholarly communication as:

> the system through which research and other scholarly writings are created, evaluated for quality, disseminated to the scholarly community, and preserved for future use. The system includes both formal means of communication, such as publication in peer-reviewed journals, and informal channels, such as electronic listservs. (ACRL, 2003)

The ACRL document then goes on to examine the system in crisis, citing, in particular, increasing prices, commercialization and economic pressures facing university presses and the humanities, creeping licensing agreements and the expansion of copyright, long-term preservation and access to electronic information, and the way that powerful commercial interests have been successful at the national level in limiting the public domain and reducing principles of fair use. It goes on to stipulate a set of principles and strategies.

Both the UN World Summit on the Information Society (2003) and the Organization for Economic Cooperation and Development (2004) have emphasized the importance of shared knowledge and the significance of the international exchange of data, information and knowledge for the advancement of scientific research and innovation, and for meeting the development goals of the Millennium Declaration. In addition, open access is recognized as having the potential to maximize the value derived from public investments in science, help with training researchers, increase the scale and scope of research and enhance the participation of developing countries in the global science system. The World Summit goes further by politically linking open access and open knowledge production to the principles of democracy and to the fundamental human rights of freedom of expression and opinion under the United Nations. Furthermore, it emphasizes the role of governments in the promotion of ICT for development, and the importance of the information and communication infrastructure as an essential foundation for an inclusive information society. There are a broader set of arguments that predate open access, open knowledge production systems and open education that argue for the necessity of open information to democracy more broadly (see Peters, 2007).

The Directory of Open Access Journals

At the First Nordic Conference on Scholarly Communication in Lund/Copenhagen (*http://www.lub.lu.se/ncsc2002*), the idea of creating a comprehensive directory of open access journals was discussed. The conclusion was that it would be a valuable service for the global research and education community. The aim of the Directory of Open Access Journals is to increase the visibility and ease of use of open access scientific and scholarly journals, thereby promoting their increased usage and impact. The directory defines open access journals as journals that use a funding model that does not charge readers or their institutions for access. The Directory of Open Access Journals adopts the BOAI definition of 'open access' that emphasizes the right of users to 'read, download, copy, distribute, print, search, or link to the full texts of these articles' as mandatory for a journal to be included in the directory (see *http://www.doaj.org/doaj?func=loadTempl&templ=about*).

The Directory of Open Access Journals holds 3,308 journals, of which 1,088 are searchable at article level and, as of early April 2008, 176,739 articles were available. In March 2007 (at the time of this original investigation) the journal listed education under social sciences. Table 12.10, based on the latest revised figures, shows how the greatest number of open access journals belongs to the category of education, the

Table 12.10 Social sciences listed by subject in the Directory of
Open Access Journals, 2007 and 2008

Subject	2007	2008
Anthropology	43	53
Education	181	249
Ethnology	11	11
Gender studies	22	24
Library & information science	74	89
Media & communication	38	56
Psychology	69	96
Social sciences	112	166
Sociology	59	69
Sports science	6	13
Total	615	834

Source: http://www.doaj.org/doaj?func=subject&cpid=127 (accessed 18 April 2007 and
17 October 2008).

largest single category, even more than the category social sciences.
Education journals make up over 30 per cent of the total, by far the
largest proportion contributed by any single discipline grouping.

By early April 2008, education had increased to a total of 232 journals,
as compared with 152 in the social sciences. This is a significant number
compared with the 'big 400' (the dominant 400) and SSCI journals. The
analysis of open access journals in education by country of origin reveals
a heavy preponderance of journals located in the USA, but with a greater
geographical spread than education journals from the large publishers,
with a surprisingly high number of journals coming from Spain, Brazil
and Mexico, and a high number from both Canada and Australia. Over
a period of 19 months (from 18 April 2007 to 17 October 2008), the
number of open access journals in the directory grew by 219, with the
increase in education journals (68) outstripping all other categories; social
science also grew rapidly by some 54 journals in the same period.
Table 12.11 lists open access journals in education by country of origin.

Most of these journal haves emerged in the late 1990s and early
2000s, with approximately 50 new e-journals established in the year
April 2007 to April 2008. This is massive growth in a discipline that was
one of the first to experiment with new electronic forms and continues
to demonstrate a keenness to innovate often driven by intellectual and

Table 12.11 Open access journals in education by country of origin, Directory of Open Access Journals classification, 2007

Country	No. journals
USA	64
Spain	18
Canada	13
Australia	13
UK	12
Brazil	10
Germany	9
Mexico	8
Turkey	6
Venezuela	4
France	3
Costa Rica	2
Italy	2
NZ	2
Countries with only one journal*	13
Total	179

*Austria, Chile, Cuba, Georgia, Hong Kong, Hungary, India, Malta, Norway, Poland, Portugal, South Africa and West Indies.
Source: http://www.doaj.org/doaj?func=subject&cpid=127 (accessed 18 April 2007).

political motives. There is no doubt that the suite of e-journals in education will continue to grow, although it will probably not be able to sustain such growth. Despite a number of differences between the data from the Directory of Open Access Journals and from the American Educational Research Association (AERA), there are also clear overlaps.

The American Educational Research Association

The AERA established its Communication of Research special interest group to 'facilitate research on the nature of communication of educational research' and to 'expand the understanding and promote the effective use of information technology and library-based resources in educational research'. On its website it provides a list of 247 open access journals in the field of education (as of 4 April 2008). The country of origin for these journals provides an interesting geographical distribution (see Table 12.12).

Clearly, open source and open access do have the potential to undermine the existing privilege of the big academic journal publishers even though there are many legal protection measures including IP rights, restrictive licences and copylefting. The fact is that there has been a huge growth in open access journals since the early 1990s as well as spectacular growth in the 2000s, with 50 new e-journals in education over the year from April 2007 to April 2008. Comparing the two different datasets, without detailed comparison of the actual journals in both sets, it is clear that there is spectacular growth to judge by these independent sources – averaging 3–4 new education journals per month,

Table 12.12 Open access journals in education by country of origin, AERA classification, 2007

Country	No. journals
USA	123
Australia	27
Canada	11
UK	9
Brazil	7
Spain	7
Turkey	6
Venezuela	4
New Zealand	3
Germany	2
Mexico	2
Countries with only one journal*	1
International	2
Australia/USA	1
Canada/USA	1
Total	222

*Austria, Bulgaria, Chile, China, Costa Rica, Cuba, France, Greece, Hong Kong, India, Italy, Malta, Norway, Portugal, South Africa, Sweden and United Arab Emirates.
Source: http://aera-cr.asu.edu/ejournals/ (constructed 10 May 2000 and last updated 23 February 2007; accessed 19 March 2007).

judging by additions to the Directory. This rapid growth leads to qualms about long-term sustainability and quality.

There is great variation in quality among these e-journals, with top e-journals in education like *First Monday* and *Education Policy Archives* as good if not better than the best print-based journals. At the other end of the scale there are many where quality is an issue, and in the list provided by AERA there are some journals where links do not work and others where journals have been suspended. Sustainability is clearly an issue, as is quality. Given the huge growth of e-journals, there needs to be an increase in the quality and perhaps number of specialist subject directories in education that provide a guide to journal quality. E-journals lend themselves easily to the development of webometric evaluation and measurement. Many new e-journals have a very specialized focus and presumably also a very small group of readers. This is the long tail of academic publishing, and the e-journal, especially with open journal, conference, archives and monograph systems (e.g. see the Public Knowledge Project at *http://pkp.sfu.ca/*), seems the ideal vehicle for the specialized academic community.

There is no doubt that the new format of the electronic and open access journal in education has led to a better geographical distribution of knowledge creation and dissemination and, perhaps, also greater internationalization among journals, with a growing number of genuine international e-journals that have articles in more than one language and also in translation.

It is early days yet in the open access movement, but with further growth, innovation and experimentation, the open access journal in education will develop into an open knowledge system. In this regard, I should mention the open education agenda, which is diverse in terms of ideology and experimentation but makes use of open access to promote open educational resources (see Iiyoshi amd Kumar, 2008; Peters and Britez, 2008). As Peters and Britez explain in their introduction:

> Open education involves a commitment to openness and is therefore inevitably a political and social project. The concept of openness in regard to education predates the openness movement that begins with free software and open source in the mid-1980s with roots going back to the Enlightenment that are bound up with the philosophical foundations of modern education with its commitments to freedom, citizenship, knowledge for all, social progress and individual transformation. (Peters and Britez, 2008)

Peters and Britez argue that the early origins of openness and also the basis for open education in a variety of forms – from the 'open classroom' to the 'open university' – have taken place in parallel with the history of a movement that has heightened the effects of certain political and epistemological features and technological-enabled affordances. These developments together have emphasized questions of access to knowledge, the co-production and co-design of educational programmes and of knowledge, the sharing, use, reuse and modification of resources, while enhancing the ethics of participation and collaboration. Open education as a movement, they argue, sits within the broader framework of the history of openness that brings together a number of disciplines, fields and developments that have had a direct impact on the value of knowledge and learning, their geographic distribution and ownership, and their organization. Open education and increasingly 'open science' have contributed to new knowledge ecologies that will become not only indispensable, but will change the political economy of academic publishing in education, including patterns of ownership of scientific knowledge, even if open knowledge systems and traditional publishing systems become more integrated or develop better mutually-supportive strategies.

Notes

1. The journal's website records that 'The Royal Society was founded in 1660 to promote the new or experimental philosophy of that time, embodying the principles envisaged by Sir Francis Bacon. Henry Oldenburg was appointed as the first (joint) secretary to the Society and he was also the first editor of the Society's journal *Philosophical Transactions*' (*http://www.pubs.royalsoc.ac .uk/index.cfm?page=1085*). The first issue appeared in 1665 and included Oldenburg's correspondence with some of Europe's scientists, as well an account by Robert Boyle of a Very Odd Monstrous Calf. Subsequent early issues include 'articles' by Robert Hooke, Isaac Newton and Benjamin Franklin. The entire archive is available online.
2. ARPANET was discontinued in 1990. ERIC advertises itself as 'the world's largest digital library of educational literature' with free access to more than 1.2 million bibliographic records of journal articles (see *http://www.eric .ed.gov/*).
3. The journal is now titled *New Horizons in Adult Education & Human Resource Development* and run from the College of Education at Florida International University (*http://education.fiu.edu/newhorizons/*).
4. The three 1990 online journals launched in 1990 were: *Electronic Journal of Communication* (*http://www.cios.org/www/ejcmain.htm*), *Postmodern Culture* (*http://www3.iath.virginia.edu/pmc/contents.all.html*) and *Bryn Mawr Classical Review* (*http://ccat.sas.upenn.edu/bmcr/*).

5. See, for instance, the statements of the Universities of Connecticut (*http://www.lib.uconn.edu/about/publications/scholarlycommunication.html*) and Iowa State (*http://www.lib.iastate.edu/libinfo/reptempl/origins.html*) respectively.

6. Mary H. Munroe, Associate Dean for Collections and Technical Services and Associate Professor at Northern Illinois University Libraries, provides a brief introduction to this situation, complete with bibliography, profiles, timelines and the list of imprints for each corporation on her website, 'The academic publishing industry: a story of merger and acquisition' (*http://www.ulib.niu.edu/publishers/*). Her website was prepared for the Association of Research Universities and the Information Access Alliance and was last updated on 13 March 2007.

7. The full financial details including consolidated statement of earnings, balance sheet and cash flow can be found at *http://www.thomson.com/pdf/corporate/financial_tables/Q4_2006_Financial_Tables.pdf*.

8. 'Recent citation analyses have shown that as few as 150 journals account for half of what is cited and one quarter of what is published. It has also been shown that a core of approximately 2,000 journals now accounts for about 85% of published articles and 95% of cited articles (*http://scientific.thomson.com/free/essays/selectionofmaterial/journalselection/*).

Bibliography

Association of College & Research Libraries (ACRL) (2003) 'Principles and strategies for the reform of scholarly communication', available at: *http://www.ala.org* (accessed 2 March 2009).

Bailey, C. W., Jr (2001) 'Evolution of an electronic book: The Scholarly Electronic Publishing Bibliography', *The Journal of Electronic Publishing* 7(2), available at: *http://www.press.umich.edu/jep/07-02/bailey.html* (accessed 2 March 2009).

Bailey, C. W., Jr. (2006) 'Scholarly electronic publishing bibliography', available at: *http://www.digital-scholarship.org/sepb/sepb.html* (accessed 2 March 2009).

Berlin Declaration on Open Access to Knowledge in the Sciences and Humanities (2003) 'The Berlin Declaration on Open Access to Knowledge in the Sciences and Humanities', available at: *http://oa.mpg.de/openaccess-berlin/berlindeclaration.html* (accessed 13 February 2009).

Bethesda Statement on Open Access Publishing (2003) available at: *http://www.earlham.edu/~peters/fos/bethesda.htm* (accessed 2 March 2009).

Bolter, J. D. (1991) *Writing Space: The Computer, Hypertext, and the History of Writing*, Hillsdale, NJ: Erlbaum.

Brown, L., Griffiths, R., and Rascoff, M. (2007) 'The Ithaka Report: University publishing in a digital age', available at *http://www .ithaka.org/strategic-services/Ithaka%20University%20Publishing% 20Report.pdf* (accessed 2 March 2009).

Budapest Open Access Initiative (BOAI) (2002) 'Budapest Open Access Initiative', available at: *http://www.soros.org/openaccess/read.shtml* (accessed 13 February 2009).

Cope, W. and Kalantzis, M. (2008) (eds) *Ubiquitous Learning*, Campaign-Urbana, IL: University of Illinois Press.

European Commission (2006) 'Study on the economic and technical evolution of scientific publication markets in Europe', available at: *http://ec.europa.eu/research/science-society/pdf/scientific-publication-study_ en.pdf* (accessed 2 March 2009).

Ferris, S. P. (2002) 'Writing electronically: the effects of computers on traditional writing', *The Journal of Electronic Publishing* 8(1), available at: *http://www.press.umich.edu/jep/08-01/ferris.html* (accessed 2 March 2009).

Fjällbrant, N. (1997) 'Scholarly communication – historical development and new possibilities', available at: *http://www.iatul.org/conference/ proceedings/vol07/papers/full/nfpaper.html* (accessed 2 March 2009).

Guédon, J. C. (2001) 'In Oldenburg's long shadow: librarians, research scientists, publishers, and the control of scientific publishing', available at: *http://www.arl.org/resources/pubs/mmproceedings/ 138guedon.shtml* (accessed 2 March 2009).

Höök, O. (1999) 'Scientific communications: history, electronic journals and impact factors', *Scandinavian Journal of Rehabilitation Medicine* 31(18): 3–7.

Iiyoshi, T. and Kumar, M. S. V. (2008) *Opening up Education: The Collective Advancement of Education through Open Technology, Open Content, and Open Knowledge*, New Haven, CT: MIT Press.

Jacobs, N. (ed.) (2006) *Open Access: Key Strategic, Technical and Economic Aspects*, Oxford: Chandos Publishing.

Kaufer, D. S. and Carley, K. M. (1993) *The Influence of Print on Sociocultural Organization and Change*, Hillsdale, NJ: LEA.

Morgan Stanley (2002) 'Scientific publishing: knowledge is power', available at: *http://www.econ.ucsb.edu/~tedb/Journals/morganstanley.pd* (accessed 2 March 2009).

Munroe, M. H. (2007) 'The academic publishing industry: a story of merger and acquisition', available at: *http://www.ulib.niu.edu/publishers/* (accessed 17 October 2008).

Nentwich, M. (2003) *Cyberscience: Research in the Age of the Internet*, Vienna: Austrian Academy of Sciences Press.

Open Society Institute (year unknown) 'Intellectual property reform and open knowledge', available at: *http://www.soros.org/initiatives/information/focus/access/grants/reform* (accessed 13 February 2009).

Organization for Economic Cooperation and Development (2004) 'Declaration on access to research data from public funding', available at: *http://www.oecd.org* (accessed 2 March 2009).

Owen, J. M. (2007) *The Scientific Article in the Age of Digitzation*, Dordrecht: Springer.

Peters, M. A. (2007) 'The political economy of informational democracy', in C. Kapitzke and M. A. Peters, *Global Knowledge Futures*, Rotterdam: Sense, pp. 209–22.

Peters, M. A. and Britez, R. (2008) *Open Education and Education for Openness*, Rotterdam and Oxford: Sense Publications.

UK House of Commons Science and Technology Select Committee (2004) 'Tenth Report of the House of Commons Science and Technology Select Committee', available at: *http://www.publications.parliament.uk/pa/cm200304/cmselect/cmsctech/399/39903.htm* (accessed 2 March 2009).

UN World Summit on the Information Society (2003) 'Declaration of principles and plan of action', 12 December.

Valauskas, E. (1997) 'Waiting for Thomas Kuhn: *First Monday* and the evolution of electronic journals', *The Journal of Electronic Publishing* 3(1), available at: *http://www.press.umich.edu/jep/03-01/FirstMonday.html* (accessed 2 March 2009).

Wellcome Trust (2003) 'Economic analysis of scientific research publishing', available at: *http://www.wellcome.ac.uk/doc_WTD003181.html* (accessed 2 March 2009).

Woolgar, S. (ed.) (2000) *Virtual Society? Technology, Cyberbole, Reality*, Oxford: Oxford University Press.

13

Doing medical journals differently:
Open Medicine, open access and academic freedom

John Willinsky, Sally Murray, Claire Kendall and Anita Palepu

The movement of academic journals to the internet has led to a proliferation of new approaches to publishing. It is a new medium, after all, and in economic terms, the subscription model is no longer the only game in town. Among the emerging alternatives, 'open access' has become a key phrase, describing the ability of readers to find and read research articles on the web without having to be a member of a subscribing library (Chan et al., 2002). Authors and readers have begun to discover the advantages of open access, with the early evidence pointing to increased readership and citations for work that has been given open access (Hitchcock, 2007). If the major corporate players in academic publishing such as Elsevier and Springer are introducing million-dollar, thousand-title journal bundles to university libraries, they are at the same time permitting authors to archive copies of published work on the authors' own websites or in open access archives. More recently, these same publishers are also enabling authors to purchase open access for their articles in online editions of journals (to which libraries are otherwise subscribing). And this is only the beginning of the new complexities of access.

Biomedical publishing upstarts, such as BioMed Central and the Public Library of Science, are offering complete and immediate open access to their journals, largely financed by the fees charged to authors. In fields where such author fees would not fly – think of meagrely funded sociologists or grant-less philosophers – groups of scholars are creating open access journals, free of print editions and fuelled by little more than editorial commitment. Funding agencies are further complicating this many-headed market with new mandates that compel authors to deposit a copy of their work, wherever it was published, in open access archives some months after it is published. While the publishers may permit self-archiving by authors, they are also actively lobbying against such mandated archiving, warning it 'risks destabilizing subscription revenues', and threatens to 'destroy the peer review system upon which researchers and society depend' (International Association of Scientific, Technical and Medical Publishers, 2007).

In this complex scramble for the new best economic model for internet publishing, it is easy to lose sight of scholarly publishing's other basic principles; beyond the editors' commitment to disseminating knowledge and increasing access to that knowledge, they are typically dedicated to protecting and furthering scholarly innovation, intellectual integrity and academic freedom.

The coming together of new access principles with more traditional scholarly values is nowhere more apparent, we would argue, than with the launch of *Open Medicine* on 18 April 2007. The decision of the editorial team at *Open Medicine*, of which we are part, to introduce a new general medical research journal in an already crowded and highly competitive field was not taken lightly.[1] It was inspired by first-hand experience, through our work with the *Canadian Medical Association Journal (CMAJ)*, of how current models in biomedical publishing, operating at the intersection of revenue-driven and professional interests, can all too readily violate editorial independence in scholarly publishing.[2]

In this chapter, we treat the circumstances leading to the formation of *Open Medicine* as a critical incident in biomedical publishing. The authors of this chapter are each participant-observers in the incident, given our prior association with the *CMAJ* and now with *Open Medicine*, though we do not strictly follow the research traditions of 'critical incident technique', in which the researcher records observations and conducts interviews around such incidents with a goal of 'solving practical problems' (Flanagan, 1954: 327). We have sought to document the incident that led to the formation of this new journal, drawing largely on the public record, and to place that incident within both the recent history of editorial interference in medical publishing and the emergence of new open access publishing models enabled by new technologies. In starting a journal as editors and publisher in response to this critical incident, we were certainly party to an exercise in practical problem-solving, yet this chapter is just as much about how this critical incident leading to the launch of *Open Medicine* reflects a new convergence between increased access and academic freedom that has not figured previously in discussions of either of these two important concepts for scholarly work.

We see this convergence as advancing the traditional goals and principles of scholarly publishing, even as *Open Medicine* is one of a new generation of journals setting new standards for the integrity of biomedical publishing. Not only does the open access that this journal provides to its content redress inequitable access to scientific knowledge, but its independence from medical advertising and professional-association support also challenges standards in medical publishing that have proven, on occasion, susceptible to undue political, professional and commercial influence.

The openness in scholarly communication that *Open Medicine* exemplifies is part of both a longstanding scientific tradition and a very recent development. This openness represents a long history of efforts to extend and increase the circulation of ideas, to open those ideas to evaluation and critique, and to build on and augment those ideas, which dates back, most directly in the case of *Open Medicine*, to the Early Modern period of experimental science and the founding of scholarly journals (David, 2004). Yet there is also a particularly twenty-first-century aspect to creating open access to research and scholarship through online archiving and publishing, which has greatly extended and accelerated the degree and quality of access on a global scale well beyond that achieved by print (Willinsky, 2006). The possibility of greatly extending the openness of scholarly work through new technologies, much as the introduction of the press did centuries ago, is not only about increasing the number of people who have access to this work, but can, as we argue here, affect other qualities that determine the scholarly contribution of research and scholarship. But first, let us set out the critical incident in question.

The violation of editorial independence at the *CMAJ*

Several of the *Open Medicine* team members were involved in editing the *CMAJ* in the period leading up to the highly publicized firing of its editor-in-chief John Hoey and senior deputy editor Anne Marie Todkill on 20 February 2007. The dismissal of the two editors, who had been working with the journal since 1994 and 1996 respectively, was the culmination of the growing tension between the journal's editors and its publisher, CMA Holdings, which is the business arm of the Canadian Medical Association (CMA), representing more than 60,000 physicians in Canada.

Under John Hoey's editorship, the *CMAJ* had developed into the fifth most-cited journal among general medical titles. The journal was receiving 100 submissions a month, with close to 70,000 subscribers (including the membership of the CMA). At the same time, the *CMAJ* had on more than one occasion published papers and editorials that had noticeably upset the CMA. As an example, a *CMAJ* editorial that was critical of new Québec legislation on hospital emergency-department staffing (*CMAJ* Editors, 2002) pointed a finger at the doctors in a Québec community who had failed to keep an emergency department open, resulting in the death of a patient and this legislative intervention. In response to this editorial, Dana W. Hanson, president of the CMA, published a letter in the *CMAJ* calling for a retraction of the editorial's judgment that the tragic incident at that Québec hospital represented a breakdown in the trust so important to the patient–doctor relationship (Hanson, 2002).

As a result of this and other instances in which the CMA took exception to what was published in the *CMAJ*, as John Hoey and Anne Marie Todkill explained in a *CMAJ* commentary, 'in September 2002 the Canadian Medical Association's board of directors agreed to put in place a Journal Oversight Committee as a mechanism for resolving the association's rare but sometimes strong disagreements with the editors of its wholly-owned journal *CMAJ*' (Hoey and Todkill, 2003: 287). Hoey and Todkill envisioned the committee's duties to include, among other things, 'protecting the journal from undue influence by its publisher and owner' (Hoey and Todkill, 2003: 287). The oversight committee was not to prove very effective in this capacity.

Three years later, on 12 December 2005, the *CMAJ* posted online an editorial entitled 'The editorial autonomy of *CMAJ*', in which the editors flatly stated that they had 'a transgression to report' (see *CMAJ* Editors, 2006: 9). They went on to describe how the publisher had interfered in the publication of an investigative journalism piece (Eggertson and Sibbald, 2005), at the behest of the Canadian Pharmacists Association. The paper described how Canadian pharmacists were engaging in invasive questioning (dealing with sexual histories) of women who were seeking to purchase the emergency contraception drug known as Plan B, an over-the-counter drug in Canada. The paper was based on the experience of 13 women who had been recruited by a reporter for the *CMAJ* to approach pharmacists across the country. In order to run the piece in the *CMAJ*, the editors had been forced by the publisher to remove any references to women's experiences with the pharmacists, ostensibly on the grounds that the reporter's procedures did not constitute a proper research method for a medical journal. In response to this interference, the editors stated in the journal's editorial on this incident that they had established 'an advisory group' made up of medical editors and a health reporter 'to examine *CMAJ*'s editorial autonomy and governance structure' (*CMAJ* Editors, 2006: 9).

On 7 February 2006, the *CMAJ* posted a news story on its website with the headline 'Two-tier Tony Clement appointed new minister of health' (*CMAJ*, 2006). The press had previously nicknamed the minister 'two-tier Tony' because of Mr Clement's stated interest in permitting private health plans, which was widely seen to undermine support for the country's public health system. Once more, the editors of the *CMAJ* were pressured by the publisher to revise one of their papers, reducing its critical aspects and replacing the original title with 'Tony Clement appointed as Canada's new health minister', while retaining the CMA president Ruth Collins-Nakai's endorsement of Tony Clement's appointment (Kondro and Sibbald, 2006).

It was later that month, on 20 February 2006, that John Hoey and Anne Marie Todkill were dismissed by Graham Morris, president of CMA Holdings and *CMAJ* publisher, who told the press that he 'just felt that it was time for a fresh approach' (Webster, 2006: 720). By way of further explanation, Ruth Collins-Nakai, president of the CMA, commented later and somewhat more candidly in a letter to the journal that it was 'a case of irreconcilable differences' (Collins-Nakai, 2006). While denying that the firings had to do with any particular paper, she points more than once in her letter to the tension between 'on the one hand, the rights of the editor for independence and, on the other, the responsibility of the publisher to protect the organization's legal, financial and liability interests' (Collins-Nakai, 2006). Collins-Nakai's letter was in response to *CMAJ*'s publication of the report on editorial autonomy that Hoey commissioned (Kassirer et al., 2006; more on this below). For their part, Hoey and Todkill were contractually constrained from talking about the incident.

The firing of the two editors was covered by *The Globe and Mail* (Curry, 2006) and *The New York Times* (Austen, 2006) among other newspapers, as well as by medical journals *The Lancet* (Webster, 2006) and *The New England Journal of Medicine* (Shuchman and Redelmeier, 2006). In each case, it was made clear that editorial autonomy was the probable cause of dismissal; as *The Globe and Mail*'s Helen Branswell put it, 'The firings are believed to be the culmination of an ongoing struggle between Dr. Hoey's team and the journal's owners over the editorial independence of the publication' (Branswell, 2006: A7). In a 'perspective' piece on the incident for *The New England Journal of Medicine*, Shuchman and Redelmeier concluded that the political nature of the medical profession should not be minimized:

> Organized medicine is a political and social entity, and Canada has emphasized its political functions by doing such things as giving provincial medical associations the authority to negotiate all fees for physicians' services under universal health care. It shouldn't be surprising that Canada is now the epicenter of the ongoing struggle over the scope and limits of editorial freedom at association-owned journals. (Shuchman and Redelmeier, 2006: 1339)

A week after Hoey and Todkill were dismissed, acting editor Stephen Choi resigned from the journal, after the CMA refused to accept his proposed 'Editorial governance plan for *CMAJ*', which sought to ensure the 'absolute' independence of the editor (see Kassirer et al., 2006).

Not long after this, the committee that Hoey and Todkill had announced on 12 December 2005, which had been struck to examine editorial independence at the *CMAJ*, issued a highly critical report, first released by the *CMAJ* on 28 February 2006. The brief, 'Editorial autonomy of *CMAJ*', stated that 'despite claims by the CMA ... the editorial autonomy [of the *CMAJ*] is to an important degree illusory' (Kassirer et al., 2006: 950). The report did fault the journal editors, including Hoey, for their willingness 'to respond to pressure from the CMA by modifying a report slated for publication in the journal', while saving their major criticism for the CMA 'for blatant interference with the publication of a legitimate report' (Kassirer et al., 2006: 947).

Meanwhile, the resignations continued at the *CMAJ*, with 15 members of the 19-member editorial board stepping down on 13 March 2006, reflecting an overall loss of trust in the CMA's ability and willingness to preserve the autonomy and intellectual integrity of the journal (Ubelacker, 2006). This loss of trust was not to be restored by the CMA's striking of an outside governance review panel, whose 25 recommendations for ensuring editorial independence at the *CMAJ* were accepted by the CMA when the report was published on 14 July 2006

(Gandhi, 2006). The governance review panel, headed by Dick Pound, recommended in its report that, for example, the *CMAJ* Mission Statement 'enshrine, as a specific goal and objective of the *CMAJ*, the principle of editorial integrity, independent of any special interests' (Pound, 2006: 36).

By that point, however, the dismissed and deserting alumni of the *CMAJ* had become convinced that what was needed, on the part of the CMA, was something more than the acceptance of a series of well-intentioned recommendations. There needed to be recognition on the CMA's part that something had gone terribly wrong in the mix of professional-association politics and medical research publishing. Failing this recognition on the part of the CMA, the former editors and editorial board members pursued the possibility of establishing an entirely independent journal in the field of general medicine – a journal that did not have to depend on a careful set of checks and balances to minimize the inevitable conflict of interests. This was not, after all, the first time that a publisher had interfered in the editorial content of a medical journal. And before considering the role that open access can play in the formation of independent journals, it is worth considering the larger pattern of undue influence and interference that has beset medical journal publishing in recent times, as it will make apparent the reasons why this concept of editorial independence is particularly critical in medical publishing.

A brief history of editorial interference in medical journal publishing

In 1992, the *Annals of Internal Medicine* published a paper on pharmaceutical advertising that concluded that 'many advertisements contained deficiencies in areas in which the FDA has established explicit standards of quality [for medical advertising]' (Wilkes et al., 1991). As a result of publishing this study, several large pharmaceutical companies withdrew an estimated US $1.5 million in advertising from the journal. Ensuing tensions between the journal's co-editors, Robert and Suzanne Fletcher, and its publisher, the American College of Physicians, led to the editors' resignations in 1993. A subsequent survey of North American journal editors found that 12 per cent observed conflicts between editorial decisions and advertisers' wishes and almost one-quarter had no control over the advertising that ran in their journal (Wilkes and

Kravitz, 1995). As Robert Fletcher later put it, 'The pharmaceutical industry showed us that the advertising dollar could be a two-edged sword, a carrot or a stick. If you ever wondered whether they play hardball, that was a pretty good demonstration that they do' (cited by Tsai, 2003: 759).

The political side of biomedical publishing came into the glaring light of press coverage on 15 January 1999, when George Lundberg, editor-in-chief of the *Journal of the American Medical Association*, was dismissed after he published a paper by Stephanie Sanders and June Reinisch (1999) examining college students' perception of what constituted 'having sex', based on Kinsey Institute data, which included the results that nearly two-thirds of the students did not count oral sex in their definition. The paper was published just as President Clinton was publicly asserting that he did not have sex with Monica Lewinsky. The AMA executive vice-president, Dr E. Ratcliffe Anderson Jr, claimed that Lundberg's publishing of the paper 'threatened the historic tradition and integrity of [the journal] by inappropriately and inexcusably interjecting *JAMA* into a major political debate that has nothing to do with science or medicine' (cited by Hoey et al., 1999: 508).[3]

Later that same year, Jerry Kassirer, editor-in-chief of the *New England Journal of Medicine* (*NEJM*), was forced to resign in a conflict over how the *NEJM* 'brand' was being used to start new publications for doctors and the general public by the journal's publisher, the Massachusetts Medical Society (Altman, 1999). Kassirer felt that such use of the 'brand' was inappropriate, given that these materials would not go through the same level of scrutiny and review; he had asked in an earlier annual report, 'Does the society want to become a business?'). It might be said that any journal that generates $15 million in profits on $75 million in revenue (estimates for 2005), even if it is for the non-profit Massachusetts Medical Society, is very much a business already (Smith, 2006). That Kassirer's resignation as editor-in-chief was followed by the appointment of Jeffrey Drazen, who had a history of strong ties to the pharmaceutical industry, only served to further affirm the financial orientation of the journal.

Pharmaceutical companies placed $448 million worth of advertisements in medical journals in 2003, making it possible for the American Medical Association to reap a $40.7 million profit from its journals in 2004 (Fugh-Berman et al., 2006).[4] In addition, pharmaceutical companies purchase millions of reprints to distribute to physicians whenever a paper reflects well on their medications, just as they are known to provide physicians with sponsored subscriptions to

The Lancet, the *NEJM* and other journals. Finally, studies have shown that authors conducting clinical trials have far too often held consulting contracts with the participating pharmaceutical companies (Perlis et al., 2005).[5]

Clearly, medical journals are in a financial class of their own, compared with journals in any other field within scholarly publishing. By the same token, medical journal editors have taken special steps to protect the integrity of their journals. It is now standard practice, for example, to ask authors for a statement of competing interests (financial and otherwise; see note 2 for a statement from the authors of this paper), with many journals requiring the same for reviewers and editors (Lee and Bero, 2006). In addition, the International Committee of Medical Journal Editors adopted a policy in 2004 that called for all clinical trials to be registered before the results would be published, in a move that would prevent drug companies from burying unfavourable studies (De Angelis et al., 2004).

Open Medicine as an independent medical research journal

In light of this history, the editors of *Open Medicine* are not only committed to adhering to the safeguards that are now becoming common practice for medical journals, but have also made it a policy neither to seek nor accept sponsorship from professional associations nor to accept drug or medical device advertising. They were inspired, in part, by the example of the editors of *PLoS Medicine*, who had announced a few years earlier that they would not accept medical advertising, as they were determined not to become 'part of the cycle of dependency ... between journals and the pharmaceutical industry' (Barbour et al., 2004).

The editors at *Open Medicine* also decided that once the journal was underway, papers would be published as soon as they were ready, and that the journal would not engage in the common practice of sending out 'advance articles' to the press with an embargo ensuring that any press coverage is withheld until the journal publishes the paper, a practice that Vincent Kiernan argues does more to direct and control press coverage of medical research issues than to serve public interests (Kiernan, 2006).

The editors of *Open Medicine* were also committed to establishing a journal with open access in ways that went beyond John Hoey's original initiative with the *CMAJ*, which had made the online edition free to readers while restricting reprints and other use of the content. With *Open Medicine*, authors are not asked to turn over the copyright for their work to the publisher. The published paper is placed under a Creative Commons licence that enables its reuse and further distribution, as long as it includes proper attribution to the author and journal, and on the grounds that access will continue to be open. The Creative Commons licence enables others not only to freely access papers, but to utilize the work in new productive ways through such bio-informatic innovations as data mashups and information mining (Good et al., 2006; Hodgkinson, 2007). The rise of open access in scholarly publishing is proving critical to the formation of independent and innovative journals, and this new approach to the circulation of knowledge needs to be considered in more detail.

The open access model

Open access represents, above all, the use of the internet to extend the circulation and sharing of knowledge. In light of the considerable and persistent digital divide, that extension is certainly not to everyone everywhere, but open access does represent an extension that goes well beyond what was proving possible with print journals. As should be clear by this point, open access is not taking any one form, either in terms of economic models or conditions of access to a journal's content. Open access is part of an important new chapter in the long historical process of opening science and scholarship to a wider world. That chapter includes open data initiatives (Uhlir, 2005), open source biology (Maurer, 2003), open encyclopaedias, and a variety of 'open science' projects (David, 2004).

Among open access journals, there are those that have been born digital and free, which have risen to the very top of their fields in a relatively short time, such as the Public Library of Science's *PLoS Biology*, and there are highly ranked *éminences grises*, such as *The New England Journal of Medicine*, which makes each issue free to readers six months after initial publication. In addition, most publishers in the biomedical field also support the World Health Organization's HINARI project and other initiatives that provide free online journal access to research libraries in low-income countries, although the implementation of this support by commercial publishers has been questioned (Villafuerte-Gálvez et al., 2007).

Scholarly societies are also finding ways to contribute to this greater openness without jeopardizing the subscription revenues on which they depend. For example, among medical societies using Highwire Press, a division of Stanford University Libraries, for their online editions, one finds titles whose contents are freely available (*CMAJ*) or delayed by a matter of months (*NEJM*), adding up to the free availability of 1.7 million papers drawn from Highwire's collection of more than 1,000 journals. Among the funders of biomedical research, the Wellcome Trust insists that all grant recipients deposit copies of their published work in the open access PubMed Central six months after publication, while the US National Institutes of Health request a similar form of deposit. This sort of open access mandate for grant-funded research has been taken up or is under consideration by a number of funding bodies.[6]

Yet up to this point, the argument for open access among libraries, journal editors and researchers has been about increasing access to research for researchers, professionals (such as physicians) and the public (Willinsky, 2006). At issue has been the human right to know what is known, and all the more so, surely, when that knowledge has been funded by public and philanthropic sources. There is yet another side to the access question, however, which has to do with who is able to participate in the circulation of knowledge and on what terms. This is the point at which, as we have learned through our work with *Open Medicine*, open access provides a means of defending and furthering academic freedom.

Academic freedom and open access

The concept of 'academic freedom' took shape during the twentieth century as a way to protect the right of faculty members to pursue independent lines of research and scholarship, with this work judged solely on its scholarly quality and contribution. A critical incident in the formation of this concept, for example, came when Edward Ross was dismissed by Stanford University in 1901 because his ideas about economic reform met with the disapprobation of Jane Stanford, wife to Leland Stanford, an act followed by the resignation of seven professors in protest. When John Dewey became the first president of the American Association of University Professors in 1915, he struck a committee to examine the state of academic freedom and tenure; the committee included Arthur O. Lovejoy, one of the professors who had resigned at

Stanford (Pollitt and Kurland, 1998). The standard statement in the field of academic freedom from the American Association of University Professors, known as the 1940 Statement of Principles on Academic Freedom and Tenure, states as its first principle that 'Teachers are entitled to full freedom in research and in the publication of the results' (American Association of University Professors, 1940).

While the concept of academic freedom has typically involved undue interference in a faculty member's ability to pursue research and teaching that otherwise meets common academic standards, we take the editorial independence of scholarly journals to be a natural extension of this concept. We see this editorial independence as no less necessary for the realization of faculty members' academic freedom, given that this freedom depends on their work receiving a fair hearing and opportunity for wider circulation. The journal editor, in this sense, is the handmaid of academic freedom. The editor creates opportunities and guidance for the publication of innovative work, nurtures authors' work, and mediates differences between reviewers and authors to ensure that the work receives a fair and critical reading (at least in principle).

Certainly, in the humanities, journal papers are where trial balloons are floated and new ideas given their first run, with authors going on, not infrequently, to fully develop their papers into book-length manuscripts. The journal is also where new and old ideas are most readily and immediately contested. Books and papers are subject to extensive public review in journals, in addition to the closed peer review. This closed and open review process is particularly important to academic freedom, as it is not simply an instance of free speech or a civil liberty (Slaughter, 1980). Furthermore, the peer-reviewed journal is the best available device – though by no means perfect (cf. Horrobin, 1990) – for providing the level of review and scrutiny needed to ensure that academic freedom can continue to make its contribution to the generation of knowledge.

Journals are also where disciplines define themselves – where the old guard, as editors and reviewers, carefully maintains traditional definitions of the field and its boundaries. By the same token, new journals are often about the formation of new disciplines. Consider how the emerging field of women's studies was marked by the launch of *Women's Studies Quarterly* in 1972, with *Signs* following in 1975 and *Feminist Review* in 1979 (preceded in biomedical publishing by the *Journal of the American Medical Women's Association*, founded in 1947). It seems fair to say that these journals made a significant contribution to the academic freedom of scholars working in what was then a new area. The journals, with their interdisciplinary titles, provided a vehicle for work that challenged entrenched disciplinary approaches and boundaries. They created a sense of possibility for going with one's work where others had not gone before.

If the journal can serve as one of the great defenders of academic freedom, then the ability to start a journal that is able to establish its intellectual, as well as financial, independence from forces and traditions that might otherwise compromise that freedom becomes all the more important. Among the factors today inhibiting the initiation of new titles is the corporate publishers' practice of licensing to research libraries bundles of hundreds, if not thousands, of titles at a single price, which locks down a growing proportion of those libraries' serial budgets with multiple-year and no-cancellation contracts. Prior to 2003, when Cornell University cancelled its bundle of 900 Elsevier titles (Elsevier now has 2,000 titles), it had been paying 20 per cent of the library's serial budget for 2 per cent of its titles through this bundling process (*Cornell Chronicle*, 2003). With the journal market squeezed by the major publishers – the six leading publishers now control 60 per cent of peer-reviewed titles and a much larger portion of libraries' serials allocations given the much higher pricing of commercially published journals (Bergstrom, 2002; Crow, 2006) – it has become that much harder for a new journal or a journal that is not part of a major organization to secure library subscriptions.

This is where the many forms of open access in scholarly publishing come into their own. Open access enables a new journal to become part of the larger academic community immediately, without first having to convince a major corporation or organization to sponsor it or having to assemble sufficient resources to sell initial subscriptions through some combination of advertising and agents. (Page et al., 1997, estimate the price of securing 500 subscribers in the first three years to be roughly $50,000).

Open access enables journals to establish a global online presence to reach readers worldwide. In addition, open access versions of scholarly indexing, such as Google Scholar, PubMed and Citeseer, enable readers to find this work and in some cases to track who has cited the work and in what context. This improves the ability to appreciate how new developments in research are taking root long before the ideas become sufficiently well established to be picked up by citation indexes such as the ISI Web of Science. Finding a way into libraries and, even more challenging, being picked up by the major indexes – once necessary for a journal to begin to offer its authors a fair and widespread reading – no longer stand as major barriers to a new journal's ability to serve the cause of academic freedom.

The newfound support for academic freedom afforded by open access is also being realized by universities in low-income countries. It has long been a challenge for new journals in such settings to gain recognition and circulation for local research initiatives. Yet work that is made open access can turn up in the same search results as work from the leading journals. In addition, open access is serving the emergence of regional initiatives, with journal hosting programmes such as African Journals Online (*http://www.ajol.info*) and Bioline International (*http://www.bioline.org.br/*), indexes like SciELO (*http://www.scielo.org/*) and LatinIndex (*http://www.latindex.unam.mx/*), and individual open access titles, whether or not they are the born-digital, such as the *African Journal of Biotechnology* (*http://www.academicjournals.org/AJB*) or the 85-year-old *East African Medical Journal* (*http://www.eamj.com/*).

The opening ahead

Open access may enable immediate presence, but it still leaves in question the longer-term sustainable economic model for publishing the journal. In the case of *Open Medicine*, the editors who had been working with the *CMAJ* had come off a multi-million-dollar annual budget devoted to publishing a biweekly, highly-ranked journal with a full-time professional production and management staff. They are now engaged in an all-volunteer professional editorial effort, which has resulted in a high-quality first issue as well as editorial processes and a flow of manuscripts that will enable it to publish papers on a continuing basis, with an output initially equivalent to a quarterly. Open access made it possible to establish a journal with an immediate presence, visited by tens of thousands of readers in its first month, while attracting press coverage from across Canada. It enabled *Scientific American* (Mims, 2007), as well as a number of bloggers, to pick up one of its initial papers, which compared healthcare expenditures and outcomes in the USA and Canada (Guyatt et al., 2007).

At this point, the *Open Medicine* team is considering a variety of economic models aimed at sustaining and expanding this open access journal. A number of donations have already been made to the journal, and it will be soliciting non-medical advertising. The team is also considering nominal author fees, a library cooperative, and other ideas, but at each point it remains committed to realizing and reasserting the basic principles of scholarly publishing in the medical field. It does not pretend to be unique in taking this principled stand, as *PLoS Medicine*, which was first issued in 2004, remains very much an inspiration in its open access policies and independence in terms of professional associations and medical advertising. But *Open Medicine* has been able to demonstrate how this reassertion of scholarly principles can happen on a far more modest and immediate scale, born of an urgent national need for an alternative model in general medicine.

Open Medicine was able to mount a peer-reviewed journal from scratch with a first issue of ten papers in less than a year, through the dedicated commitment and experienced professionalism of its editors. But these tireless efforts were also facilitated by parallel developments in the field of software and publishing systems. What enabled the editors and board members to collaborate across Canada (and with Sally Murray in Australia), was another open development, this time in the form of open source software for journal publishing. The journal uses the freely downloadable Open Journal Systems (Willinsky, 2005) to manage and publish the journal (just as the open access archives in many libraries use the open source EPrints and DSpace systems to enable authors to archive their published work).[7] In addition, Tarek Lubani, a recent medical school graduate and part of a new generation of physicians with technical savvy, has used the open source Drupal to establish the journal's OM Blog, which Dean Giustini uses to bring almost daily currency and immediacy to the journal, and a wiki to help organize editorial meetings. It is thus such a combination of open access to research and open source software that has become the new enabler of academic freedom in an age in which access to knowledge can otherwise operate like just another commodity market.

It may be fair to say that *Open Medicine* has yet to arrive at a long-term financial model (although, for that matter, *The New York Times* is also still searching for a stable model for online publishing, judging by the array of initiatives with which it continues to experiment). But given the commitment of everyone involved in *Open Medicine*, it is very unlikely that it will back away from its open access principles. While we cannot predict which economic model will prevail with this journal, or with the field of online journal publishing generally, what is clear is that people are finding innovative ways of increasing access to this body of knowledge.

Yet it is also fair to claim that *Open Medicine* has raised the stakes for open access by demonstrating how this combination of open access and open source can be used today to reassert editorial independence, intellectual integrity and academic freedom. These principles of scholarly communication, as this critical incident in the development of scholarly publishing also demonstrates, are never entirely secure from the competing interests of a knowledge-based economy in biomedical journal publishing. Constant and critical vigilance are needed to protect research principles from undue influences, and only innovation and experimentation will provide corrective measures and a way forward. Fortunately, such critical and innovative work is the stock in trade for the academic community, even if this critical sensibility is seldom applied to the communication practices at work in our own particular corner of the knowledge economy. It takes a critical incident to help us realize what principles underwrite this form of communication and to test our commitment to them.

Acknowledgments

This work has been supported in part by the Pacific Press Endowment in the Faculty of Education, University of British Columbia. This chapter was originally published in the *Canadian Journal of Communication* (Vol. 32, No. 3, 2007).

Notes

1. At the launch of the journal, the *Open Medicine* editorial team consisted of editors Stephen Choi and Anita Palepu; deputy editor Claire Kendall; associate editors James Brophy, William A. Ghali, Dean Giustini, John Hoey, James Maskalyk, Sally Murray and Anne Marie Todkill; contributing editor David Moher; technical advisor Tarek Lubani; publisher John Willinsky; marketing consultant Joanne Currie; and media liaison Lindsay Borthwick.
2. Prior to resigning from the *Canadian Medical Association Journal* in 2006, Palepu and Kendall were associate editors with the journal, Murray was an editorial fellow, and Willinsky was an editorial board member; their current positions with *Open Medicine* are listed in note 1.
3. In their editorial on the Lundberg firing, Hoey et al. (1999: 508) point out that the AMA is a political organization – 'Since 1989 the AMA Political Action Committee has given more than US$14 million to US Senate and House candidates; these donations have favored Republicans over Democrats by a ratio of 2 to 1' – and they note how the paper in question lent support to Clinton's claim. The editorial concludes with a note on the firing, some seven years before it would happen to at least two of the editors of the *CMAJ*: 'Editors can of course be fired, like anyone else. But firing a respected editor in the absence of any frank misconduct on his part, without debate or witnesses, does not meet anyone's criteria for fairness' (Hoey et al., 1999: 508).
4. Fugh-Berman, Alladin and Chow (2006) report that the *JAMA*, the *NEJM*, *The Lancet* and *British Medical Journal* (*BMJ*), all weeklies, had advertising rates in 2006 that ranged from $7,000 to $15,000 a page and circulations

ranging from 34,000 to 344,000. Also see Kassirer (2007) on pharmaceutical advertising in biomedical journals.

5. Richard Smith (2006) points to a particularly troubling instance in which Merck purchased 900,000 reprints of a study from the *NEJM*, with the *NEJM* later publishing a cautionary note on the accuracy of the study and Merck withdrawing the drug featured in the study. In an earlier, boldly titled paper, 'Medical journals are an extension of the marketing arm of pharmaceutical companies', Smith (2005) pointed to the power of the reprint: 'For a drug company, a favourable trial is worth thousands of pages of advertising, which is why a company will sometimes spend upwards of a million dollars on reprints of the trial for worldwide distribution. The doctors receiving the reprints may not read them, but they will be impressed by the name of the journal from which they come. The quality of the journal will bless the quality of the drug'.

6. See Peter Suber's Open Access Newsletter for reviews of the current state of open access mandates: *http://www.earlham.edu/~peters/fos/newsletter/archive.htm*.

7. Open Journal Systems (OJS) was developed by the Public Knowledge Project, in a partnership between the Faculty of Education at the University of British Columbia, Simon Fraser University Library and the Canadian Centre for Studies in Publishing. Open Journal Systems is being used by more than 1,000 journals, 20 per cent of which are new titles and all of which offer some form of open access, with somewhat more than half being published in low-income countries.

Bibliography

Altman, L. K. (1999) 'Editor forced to resign in dispute over marketing of medical journal's name', *The New York Times*, available at: *http://query.nytimes.com/gst/fullpage.html?sec=health&res=9C04E1 DA1E3EF934A15754C0A96F958260* (accessed 25 May 2007).

American Association of University Professors (1940) '1940 statement of principles on academic freedom and tenure', available at: *http://www.aaup.org/AAUP/pubsres/policydocs/1940statement.htm* (accessed 24 May 2007).

Austen, I. (2006) 'Canadian medical group fires top editors of journal', *The New York Times*, available at: *http://www.nytimes.com/2006/02/22/business/media/22journal.html?_r=2&oref=slogin&oref=slogin* (accessed 25 May 2007).

Barbour, V., Butcher, J., Cohen, B. and Yamey, G. (2004) 'Prescription for a healthy journal', *PLoS Medicine* 1(1), available at: *http://www.pubmedcentral.nih.gov/articlerender.fcgi?artid=523840* (accessed 24 May 2007).

Bergstrom, T. (2002) 'Journal pricing across disciplines', *The Economics of Journal Publishing*, available at: *http://octavia.zoology.washington.edu/publishing/pageprice_table.html* (accessed 24 May 2007).

Branswell, H. (2006) 'Beleaguered medical journal loses fourth editor in a month', *The Globe and Mail*, 16 March, p. A7.

Chan, L., Cuplinskas, D., Eisen, M., Friend, F., Genova, Y., Guédon, J.-C., Hagemann, M., Harnad, S., Johnson, R., Kupryte, R., La Manna, M., Rév, I., Segbert, M., de Souza, S., Suber, P. and Velterop, J. (2002) 'Budapest Open Access Initiative', available at: *http://www.soros.org/openaccess/read.shtml* (accessed 25 May 2007).

CMAJ (2006) 'Two-tier Tony Clement appointed new minister of health', originally published on *Canadian Medical Association Journal* website, 22 February and subsequently removed, now available at: *http://www.healthcoalition.ca/twotier.pdf* (accessed 24 May 2007).

CMAJ Editors (2002) 'Quebec's Bill 114', *Canadian Medical Association Journal (CMAJ)* 167(6): 617.

CMAJ Editors (2006) 'The editorial autonomy of *CMAJ*', *Canadian Medical Association Journal (CMAJ)* 174(1): 9, available at: *http://www.cmaj.ca/cgi/content/full/174/1/9* (accessed 24 May 2007).

Collins-Nakai, R. (2006) '*CMAJ*: Moving forward', *Canadian Medical Association Journal (CMAJ)* 174(7), available at: *http://www.cmaj.ca/cgi/eletters/174/7/945#3961* (accessed 24 May 2007).

Cornell Chronicle (2003) 'After failed negotiations, CU Library cancels Elsevier journal package', *Cornell Chronicle* 35(17), available at: *http://www.news.cornell.edu/Chronicle/03/12.11.03/CUL_Elsevier.html* (accessed 24 May 2007).

Crow, R. (2006) 'Publishing cooperatives: An alternative for non-profit publishers', *First Monday* 11(9), available at: *http://firstmonday.org/issues/issue11_9/crow/index.html* (accessed 24 May 2007).

Curry, B. (2006) 'Interference alleged at medical journal', *The Globe and Mail*, 22 February, p. A14.

David, P. A. (2004) 'Understanding the emergence of "open science" institutions: functionalist economics in historical context', *Industrial and Corporate Change* 13(4): 571–89.

De Angelis, C., Drazen, J. M., Frizelle, F. A., Haug, C., Hoey, J., Horton, R., Kotzin, S., Laine, C., Marusic, A., Overbeke, A., John, P.M., Schroeder, T. V., Sox, H. C. and Van Der Weyden, M. B. (2004) 'Clinical trial registration: a statement from the International Committee of Medical Journal Editors', *New England Journal of Medicine* 351(12): 1250–1.

Eggertson, L. and Sibbald, B. (2005) 'Privacy issues raised over Plan B: Women asked for names, addresses, sexual history', *Canadian Medical Association Journal (CMAJ)* 173(12): 1435–6.

Flanagan, J. C. (1954) 'The critical incident technique', *Psychological Bulletin* 51(4): 327–59.

Fugh-Berman, A., Alladin, K. and Chow, J. (2006) 'Advertising in medical journals: Should current practices change?' *PLoS Medicine* 3(6): e130, available at: *http://dx.doi.org/10.1371/journal.pmed .0030130* (accessed 24 May 2007).

Gandhi, U. (2006) 'Panel urges autonomy for CMA Journal editors', *Globe and Mail,* 15 July.

Good, B., Kawas, E., Kuo, B. and Wilkinson, M. (2006) 'iHOPerator: User-scripting a personalized bioinformatics web, starting with the iHOP website', *BMC Bioinformatics* 7(1): 535.

Guyatt, G., Devereaux, P.,J. Lexchin, J., Stone, S., Yalnizyan, A., Himmelstein, D., Woolhandler, S., Zhou, Q., Goldsmith, L. J., Cook, D. J., Haines, T., Lacchetti, C., Lavis, J. N., Sullivan, T., Mills, E. Kraus, S. and Bhatnagar, N. (2007) 'A systematic review of studies comparing health outcomes in Canada and the United States', *Open Medicine* 1(1), available at: *http://www.openmedicine.ca/article/view/8/1* (accessed 24 May 2007).

Hanson, D. W. (2002) 'Questions of trust', *Canadian Medical Association Journal (CMAJ)* 167(9): 986.

Hitchcock, S. (2007) 'The effect of open access and downloads ("hits") on citation impact: A bibliography of studies', available at: *http://opcit .eprints.org/oacitation-biblio.html* (accessed 24 May 2007).

Hodgkinson, M. (2007) 'Mashups, mirrors, mining and open access', available at: *http://journalology.blogspot.com/2007/01/mashups-mirrors-mining-and-open-access.html* (accessed 24 May 2007).

Hoey, J. and Todkill, A. M. (2003) 'Why a journal oversight committee?' *Canadian Medical Association Journal (CMAJ)* 168(3): 287–88.

Hoey, J., Caplan, C. E., Elmslie, T., Flegel, K. M., Joseph, K. S., Palepu, A. and Todkill, A. M. (1999) 'Science, sex and semantics: The firing of George Lundberg', *Canadian Medical Association Journal (CMAJ)* 160(4): 507–8.

Horrobin, D. F. (1990) 'The philosophical basis of peer review and the suppression of innovation', *Journal of the American Medical Association* 263(10): 1438–41.

International Association of Scientific, Technical and Medical Publishers (2007) 'Brussels declaration on STM publishing', available at:

http://www.publishers.org.uk/paweb/PAweb.nsf/0/45C9AD2A0D583 BB6802572810048BDCB!opendocument (accessed 24 May 2007).

Kassirer, J. (2007) 'Pharmaceutical ethics?' *Open Medicine* 1(1), available at: *http://www.openmedicine.ca/article/view/16/2* (accessed 24 May 2007).

Kassiser, J. P., Davidoff, F., O'Hara, K. and Redelmeier, D. A. (2006) 'Editorial autonomy of *CMAJ*', *Canadian Medical Association Journal (CMAJ)* 174(7): 945–50.

Kiernan, V. (2006) 'Embargo no more', *American Physical Society News* 16(3), available at: *http://www.aps.org/publications/apsnews/200703/ backpage.cfm* (accessed 24 May 2007).

Kondro, W. and Sibbald, B. (2006) 'Tony Clement appointed as Canada's new health minister', *Canadian Medical Association Journal* 174(6): 754.

Lee, K. and Bero, L. (2006) 'What authors, editors and reviewers should do to improve peer review', *Nature*, available at: *http://dx.doi.org/10 .1038/nature05007* (accessed 24 May 2007).

Maurer, S. M. (2003, 19 November) '*New institutions for doing science: From databases to open source biology*', paper presented at the European Policy for Intellectual Property Conference, University of Maastricht, The Netherlands, 24–5 November, available at: *http://www.merit.unimaas.nl/epip/papers/maurer_paper.pdf* (accessed 24 May 2007).

Mims, C. (2007) 'We're number two: Canada has as good or better health care than the US', *Scientific American*, available at: *http:// www.sciam.com/article.cfm?chanID=sa004&articleID=53B61670- E7F2-99DF-3E9FD5664899BF24* (accessed 24 May 2007).

Page, G., Campbell, R. and Meadows, J. (1997) *Journal Publishing*, Cambridge: Cambridge University Press.

Perlis, R. H., Perlis, C. S., Wu, Y., Hwang, C., Joseph, M. and Nierenberg, A. A. (2005) 'Industry sponsorship and financial conflict of interest in the reporting of clinical trials in psychiatry', *American Journal of Psychiatry* 162(10): 1957–60.

Pollitt, D. H. and Kurland, J. (1998) 'Entering the academic freedom arena running: The AAUP's first year', *Academe: Bulletin of the American Association of University Professors* 84(4): 45–52.

Pound, D. (2006) '*CMAJ* governance review panel: Final report', available at: *http://www.cmaj.ca/pdfs/GovernanceReviewPanel.pdf* (accessed 24 May 2007).

Sanders, S. and Reinisch, J. (1999) 'Would you say you "had sex" if...?' *Journal of the American Medical Association* 281(3): 275–7.

Shuchman, M. and Redelmeier, D. A. (2006) 'Politics and independence – The collapse of the *Canadian Medical Association Journal*', *New England Journal of Medicine* 354(13): 1337–9.

Slaughter, S. (1980) 'The danger zone: academic freedom and civil liberties', *The Annals of the American Academy of Political and Social Science* 448(1): 46–61.

Smith, R. (2005) 'Medical journals are an extension of the marketing arm of pharmaceutical companies', *PLoS Medicine* 2(5): e138, available at: *http://dx.doi.org/10.1371/journal.pmed.0020138* (accessed 24 May 2007).

Smith, R. (2006) 'Lapses at the *New England Journal of Medicine*', *Journal of the Royal Society of Medicine* 99: 380–2.

Tsai, A. C. (2003) 'Conflicts between commercial and scientific interests in pharmaceutical advertising for medical journals', *International Journal of Health Services* 33(4): 751–68.

Ubelacker, S. (2006) 'Three-quarters of medical journal board quit in dispute', *The Globe and Mail*, 17 March, p. A8.

Uhlir, P. (2005) 'World Summit on the Information Society science and development tool kit', available at: *http://www.interacademies.net/Object .File/Master/5/076/WSIS%20Tool%20Kit_Access%20to%20Sc%20Info .pdf* (accessed 24 May 2007).

Villafuerte-Gálvez, J., Curioso, W. H. and Gayoso, O. (2007) 'Biomedical journals and global poverty: is HINARI a step backwards?' *PLoS Medicine* 4(6): e220, available at: *http://dx.doi .org/10.1371/journal.pmed.0040220* (accessed 25 May 2007).

Webster, P. (2006) '*CMAJ* editors dismissed amid calls for more editorial freedom', *The Lancet* 367(9512): 720. *http://dx.doi.org/10.1016/ S0140-6736(06)68286-X* (accessed 24 May 2007).

Wilkes, M. S. and Kravitz, R. L. (1995) 'Policies, practices and attitudes of North American medical journal editors', *Journal of General Internal Medicine* 10(8): 443–50.

Wilkes, M. S., Doblin, B. H. and Shapiro, M. F. (1991) 'Pharmaceutical advertisements in leading medical journals: experts' assessments', *Annals of Internal Medicine* 166(12): 912–19.

Willinsky, J. (2005) 'Open Journal Systems: An example of open source software for journal management and publishing', *Library Hi-Tech* 23(4): 504–19.

Willinsky, J. (2006). *The Access Principle: The Case for Open Access to Research and Scholarship*, Cambridge, MA: MIT Press.

Part IV
The journal internationally

14

The status and future of the African journal

Pippa Smart

Journals published within the African continent strive to achieve the same as their counterparts within the developed world: to disseminate research findings and advance scientific knowledge. Due to economic and social factors that disable their operations, however, the majority of them struggle to exist and their future is far from certain.

History

The first African journals were launched in the late nineteenth century with the *South African Medical Journal* and the *South African Law Journal*, both in 1884. However, as within Europe, the majority of journals started publishing in the 1960s and 1970s at a time when the newly independent African countries were optimistically increasing their foothold on the world with increased funding of tertiary education and economic growth. Journals represented a means of promoting their intellectual development, and provided a vehicle whereby their academia could implement the 'publish or perish' accreditation used in the industrial countries. Many university faculty and associations launched their own titles as a means of capturing their research and providing recognition for their institution.

Journal statistics

There are no comprehensive facts about the journal publishing market in Africa as a whole although some countries maintain records. In

Table 14.1 African titles indexed in international directories

	Ulrich's*	ISI Web of Science	Medline	AJOL
Ghana	30	0	0	16
Kenya	73	2	2	18
Nigeria	216	4	8	129
South Africa	500	56	10	57[†]
Tanzania	39	0	2	11
Uganda	15	0	1	8
Other sub-Saharan Africa	284	1	13	70
Total	1,157	26	36	309

AJOL, African Journals OnLine
*Academic/scholarly publications with active publication status as of 25 August 2008.
Used with permission from Ulrichsweb.com™, Copyright 2008 ProQuest LLC. All rights reserved.
†Many South African journals chose to use the sales service, Sabinet, to host their titles exclusively, which led to about 80 titles leaving AJOL in 2005.

South Africa, the National Science Foundation (NSF) and the Academy of Science of South Africa (ASSAf) recognize about 450 titles, of which they accredit 230. From the numbers indexed in African Journals OnLine (*www.ajol.info*), and other information from around the continent, I estimate that in sub-Saharan Africa there are probably about 2,000 titles in total, of which Nigeria and South Africa hold the largest number – about 450 each (See Table 14.1). The majority are published in English, with French and Afrikaans the next most predominant languages.

South Africa is the most productive country within the African continent, and analysis of the SA Knowledgebase at the University of Stellenbosch shows that about 7,000 articles are published with one or more South African author each year. Of these, about 3,500 are published within journals indexed by the ISI Thomson Journal Citation Reports, leaving a further 3,500 published within non-indexed titles (ASSAf, 2006).

The current publishing environment within Africa

One important difference between the history of journal publishing in Africa compared with that within Europe and America is the involvement of commercial publishers. Unlike the developed countries, there were (and continue to be) few links between journals and professional publishers, and this has had tremendous impact on the growth and success of the African journal industry.

There are relatively few publishers within Africa as books are an expensive luxury, and the market is small (UNESCO, 2004). Although Africa has around 15 per cent of the world's population, it only produces around 2 per cent of the world's books. Part of the reason for this is that there is a greater oral than literary tradition within the continent and literacy in most African countries is low, ranging from 23.9 per cent (Burkina Faso) to 88.7 per cent (Zimbabwe) – compared with 79.9 per cent average for the world. Enrolment in tertiary education ranges from 0.4 per cent (Guinea-Bissau) to 15.2 per cent (South Africa) compared with 22.9 per cent as the world average, which further impacts on the market for textbooks and related higher-level information literature.

As textbooks represent the main market for publications in Africa, this is where African publishers tend to focus their output (approximately 95 per cent of their total output, according to Stringer, 2002). Throughout the continent, the book industry is dominated by multinational publishers, such as Macmillan and Longman (Pearson), who are the dominant publishers in certain countries such as Namibia and Botswana. Their impact is both positive and negative as their profits are not retained within the countries, but they are able to take more economic risks than a smaller local publisher, and therefore supply a greater choice of publications (Chakava, 2007). Perhaps the most detrimental international influences are the well-intentioned donation programmes which provide free books. For example, CTA (*www.cta.int*), an EU-funded organization based in the Netherlands, runs a book service whereby individuals and organizations can apply for vouchers to 'purchase' books from them. During 2007 they distributed over 75,000 books to countries within Africa, the Caribbean and Pacific. Although this is a wonderful service, it undermines local publishers, making it increasingly difficult to build a business when the consumers expect books for free.

Exacerbating these external influences, there are problems in making sales between countries within the continent. There are some 'common market' agreements in East and West Africa, but these do not resolve all the problems of transferring money from one country to another, which limits distribution. Publishers frequently have European bank accounts as it is easier to transfer to these than to an account in another African country. This economic limitation results in publishers unable to develop into areas where the local market is too small to sustain a publication.

Research-level publications (including journals) have a small and poorly-funded audience, and therefore do not represent a viable business for the majority of publishers. However, there are of course exceptions, such as Nisc in South Africa which publishes ten journals on behalf of associations, and Hindawi in Egypt, which publishes 141 open access titles.

University presses

In an attempt to improve the availability of locally-produced publications for the university and research market, efforts have been made to develop university presses to serve this need. Unfortunately, they have in most cases been unsuccessful; this is due to a variety of reasons, the main one being a lack of funding. It was assumed that they would operate on the commercial model, whereby they would make a profit for their institution and not require funding. Unfortunately, as many university presses have found, it is not possible for the majority of them to be self-sustaining, and funding is required – which is not forthcoming in many African situations. In Kenya, Nairobi University Press was established in 1984, but by 2000 had only published 40 titles due to poor funding; similarly, in Uganda, Makerere University Press was established in 1979, but by 2000 had only published 12 titles (Chakava, 2007).

In Ethiopia, Addis Ababa University Press is run with only one administrative member of staff, assisted by volunteers from the university and managed by a member of faculty seconded for a three-year term (Wole and Habte, 2007). Although they have formed some useful publishing partnerships in the past, they, in common with other university and academic publishers, focus their attention on the content quality of publications, rather than the publishing function. This means that they have not been able to distribute their publications widely, and lack a sustainable economic model for most of their books. Many authors subsidize the publication of their titles – a situation not uncommon in many African university presses.

The poor funding (and poor working practices) of many university presses have made them unsuitable to support the journals published within their institutions, and they rarely become involved in providing publishing services for them. Some journals use their printing facilities as they would an external supplier – although this is often more expensive than other local presses, and sometimes poorer quality. Although there may be potential to develop university presses as centres of publishing skill for the benefit of their institution, the problems of funding and operational structure make them a difficult resource to develop.

Journals, publishers and money

Without the support of a professional publisher – or the university press – many journals are effectively 'self-published' and rely on the editor, with perhaps an assistant, to operate all functions required to produce the journal. In addition, they are frequently unable to introduce any innovative changes, as strategic decisions need to be approved by a (frequently large) committee of the parent association or faculty. Not surprisingly, the result of this is a conservative approach to publishing and a focus on the editorial content of the journal, rather than the publishing activities. In addition, poor funding means that once the effectively 'free' work has been done (e.g. the editorial review and selection), many issues have to wait until cash becomes available for typesetting, printing and distribution. This is often a lower priority than the editorial work, and so publication of an issue can take months (and in some cases years).

Many journals do not publish regularly – a result of funding and copy-flow problems. There is often a lack of understanding of how detrimental this can be to the journal and a lack of impetus to avoid delays. This intermittency has led to the failure of several support initiatives, one of the most notable being incorporation of selected journals within Project Muse. Supported by both the University of Michigan African e-journals project and the International Network for the Availability of Scientific Publications (INASP), several journals were accepted to join Project Muse (a sales collection of online journals). Unfortunately, with the exception of one title, the journals were all removed from this initiative due to irregular publication, which made it impossible for Muse to fulfil its obligations to subscribers.

Sadly, online publishing does not appear to have improved problems with timeliness. For example, the monthly *East African Medical Journal*, one of the most prestigious (and oldest) journals within the continent, appears to be publishing eight months behind schedule, which must cause authors and subscribers to doubt its health. However, given that print publication is accorded higher priority than online publication, it is also quite possible that the journal has simply not yet put its recently published content online (at the time of writing, the journal was only five months behind schedule according to the African Journals OnLine site).

This not only has an impact on the perception of the journal, but also on the likelihood of obtaining subscription revenue in the future.

Online publishing is certainly an opportunity from which many journals are benefiting – particularly from initiatives to freely host or index journals. There is a huge amount of interest in publishing online from African journals, but also several concerns. Primarily, funding is an issue, both in implementing online publishing, and also ensuring that it does not reduce their precious revenues. Lack of knowledge about online publishing is preventing many journals from going online, and others have extremely poorly constructed websites, often embedded within their institution site and not discoverable through the major search engines. Inevitably, this means that full advantage of what online publishing can offer is not yet realized. Online editions are frequently published after the print – even when the print has been halted due to lack of funds.

Without professional publishing input into the operation, journals suffer from a lack of development – into online systems, through sales (and income) development, in indexing and technological improvements to their operation (e.g. online submission systems). Equally, the journals operate in isolation, without the benefit of experience from other journals and publishers. Of course there are sophisticated, well-established titles that operate in an extremely professional and successful manner, but these are – unfortunately – in the minority.

Distribution

Many journals do not distribute to a subscriber list. Some are distributed locally, to members of the association or university; many others are distributed to other institutions on a 'swap' system – as part of a barter system to obtain other journals for their libraries. This can be a lifeline for some institutions, as several libraries in sub-Saharan Africa have not subscribed to any journal for years (Arunachalam, 2003) and rely on international programmes of donor support to provide access to research publications for their faculty.

Distribution between African countries is very poor, and increasingly libraries are finding it easier to obtain international publications through initiatives such as HINARI, AGORA, OARE and PERI than African-published ones. This further disadvantages African-published journals as the librarians make less effort to find and subscribe to them when they can obtain international journals for free. There is a perception that the journals from developed countries are superior for international science, but there remains a need to capture information that is only available within the African titles – as proven by the amount of use made of the African journal support initiative, African Journals OnLine (AJOL) (see below).

Few journals make substantial sales through subscriptions – although the income received from just a few international sales may provide sufficient funding to print the next issue, making them crucially important to the journal's continued existence. Fluctuations in currency can be a major problem, and some journals have found that the high bank charges associated with processing international payments may be higher than the sale itself (for example in Zimbabwe; Cumming, 2007, personal communication).

Journals, authors and editors

Many journals have poor author services, and this encourages poor author practices. It can take months (or years) to review papers, and communication with authors is poor, with many journal editors neither informing authors of acceptance nor publication: one result of this is that authors frequently submit to more than one journal at a time to gain the fastest possible publication. The combined problems of lack of timeliness and halts on publishing due to resource issues often result in a lengthy 'in press' stage that leaves authors in limbo for an extensive period of time.

The situation is – of course – two-way, and journals themselves also suffer at the hands of authors. Several editors report that after they have spent extensive time reviewing and suggesting improvements to an article, the author will then submit it to another title on the basis that it is now more likely to be accepted by the better journal. Equally, few authors follow guidelines as there is a general perception that it is the editor's responsibility to put the paper in the journal style.

Online submission technology could greatly assist the communication issues between journals and their authors, and it is slowly being introduced. Unfortunately, it is hampered by the cost of implementing such systems, as they take financial and human resources which many journals do not have (even when the software may be free – as in the case of the Open Journals System from the Canadian-based Public Knowledge Project). The Africa Health Journals Partnership initiative has negotiated free use of the ScholarOne submission system for some members of the Forum for Medical Editors as part of their support for this organization. At the time of writing, it has been implemented by one title, and is under investigation by two others. The medical journal arena is an ideal test-bed for this type of software, as its authors will have more ready access to the internet than some other disciplines, where such systems may currently be difficult to introduce – although as access to the internet is growing fast, this situation will change rapidly.

There is a huge need to train future authors, and several initiatives are trying to address this, such as AuthorAid (*www.authoraid.info*), a new initiative to support research authors. AuthorAid is providing some workshop-based training for authors and hopes to establish a mechanism of mentoring – linking new authors with experienced ones who can help them to develop their research results into publishable articles. Many of the agencies that support research also run training programmes for their researchers (e.g. the International Foundation for Science) but these are commonly aimed at writing funding proposals rather than writing up the results of research for publication.

Editorially, the majority of journals have developed similar systems to their Western counterparts. Most operate with an editor-in-chief plus an editorial board, and manage a system of peer review. There are problems of reviewing a paper within a small research community where the referees probably know the author, and bias arising out of respect or disdain is likely to colour the review. Many journal editors will only use referees that they know, and are loath to search indexes to identify specialists in other regions, as many articles require understanding of local systems and knowledge to correctly identify whether the article is important and novel. In addition, within some African countries, and some disciplines, there is an expectation of payment by referees, and this cost may be crippling to a journal and lead to minimal reviewing. Paying referees is uncommon within Europe and America, and its existence within certain regions of Africa must be ultimately detrimental to the research community, although it does acknowledge the work required to ensure high-quality content.

Why are journals published?

Given these regional problems it is worth asking the question of why African journals continue to be published – and new ones are launched. The reasons are the same as for the rest of the world: that journals confer prestige on an association or university faculty, and to be published is an important activity on which many academics and researchers build their careers and disseminate the findings of their research (Adomi and Mordi, 2003).

To be published in an international, well-established journal is, of course more prestigious than to be published in a local, struggling title. However, researchers from Africa face many difficulties in achieving publication in international titles. In the first place, the quality of their research may not be good enough; it may be parochial and, although important within their region, of limited interest to academics and researchers elsewhere. Many academics in African countries feel that western journals are biased against them, and are less likely to publish their articles than those coming out of Europe and America. While many Western editors protest that they do not discriminate in this way, they are likely to decide against papers written by authors who are unable to describe their research for an international audience – perhaps because their first language is not English, or they have not been trained in writing to a standard demanded by international journals. The reasons for rejection tend to be pragmatic rather than discriminatory, but the result is the same.

This causes a problem for the authors (unable to find a journal in which to publish), and also for other researchers (unable to find relevant research for their locality). The journal *African Health Science* was launched specifically to address this problem because the editor could find no published research on a prevalent disease in Uganda, called 'nodding disease'. He realized that although there was some research on this disease, it was not published in international journals as it was of little interest, and there was no vehicle in which authors could publish their findings (Yamey, 2003).

Although international journals may not publish African research, there is certainly interest in what is being published within African journals. African Journals OnLine, the largest site of African-published journals, hosts over 300 titles, and records visitors from around the world. During 2008, only 32 per cent of the total visitors came from Africa, with almost 300,000 unique visitors from the rest of the world; these overseas visitors also requested 29 per cent of the 6,700 document deliveries that the service fulfilled in the same period (Murray, 2009, personal communication). However, there is, of course, great interest from within the continent, and AJOL fulfilled 4,850 document deliveries in 2008 for researchers and librarians within Africa. As mentioned above, inter-country distribution is difficult, and services such as AJOL play a vital role in making researchers aware of African papers from elsewhere in the continent, and making them available.

The South African government has recently endorsed the continuance and development of its indigenous journal publishing industry, and established a programme to support it (ASSAf, 2006). Their rationale is a belief that a healthy, high-quality journal publishing system is beneficial to the country, both in academic and economic terms. They have especially highlighted the benefits of participation in journal editing as a means of developing the skills to critically analyse published research and to communicate one's own research effectively. They consider a strong journal publishing industry essential if South Africa is to contribute to the general body of research, and at the same time ensure a local focus and application to its own country needs.

African research

Compared with the westernized countries, the level of research within Africa is low, and the sustainability of all journals depends on sufficient research being undertaken to result in enough papers to publish.

Although there is increasing investment in universities, and a World Bank recommendation that increased numbers of the population should attend further education, research and development (R&D) spending remains low in both absolute and relative terms. In 2005, the total GDP of the sub-Saharan region was $375 billion – just over half the US expenditure on R&D in the same year. Sub-Saharan African countries spend less than 1 per cent of their GDP on R&D, and the majority of this goes into salaries rather than into core research (Oyelaran-Oyeyinka, 2006). The result of this is that there is both a small community of researchers and relatively little research being undertaken that can result in publications. However, the increasing numbers attending universities, and the activity within them indicate that this is changing.

An indicator of the level of international-quality research can be derived from articles indexed by the Thompson Web of Science and the Journal Citation Indexes. Although the number of indexed articles with an African-based author increased approximately 3 per cent from 1995 to 2005, the overall representation of African authors within the indexes reduced from 0.72 per cent of all articles to 0.59 per cent during the same period (National Science Foundation, 2008). This downward trend shows that although there is a slow increase in the amount of research undertaken on the continent, it is not increasing at the same rate as in the rest of the world.

From bibliographic research it appears that in some countries whole areas of expertise have vanished – however, this may not indicate a lack of research but rather that the type of research undertaken does not lend itself to publication. For instance, research into agricultural science seems to have disappeared within Kenya and Côte d'Ivoire in the past decade. However, there is evidence to suggest that this research is moving out of the public universities and institutions and into the hands of private (and international) consultants, whose work is not subsequently published (Waast, 2002).

There is also evidence that greater numbers of African researchers are co-authoring articles with international colleagues (outside Africa). This increase (from approximately 34 per cent to 50 per cent of articles between 1990 and 2004) is encouraging as it indicates increased participation in international science (Tijssen, 2007). Unsurprisingly, the ability to produce international quality science is closely linked to the country's technological development. However, there are some disciplines that are more international in nature (such as medical sciences), and therefore more likely to obtain funding, international collaboration and greater publication. One outcome of this is that if a country decides to develop into an area that is more locally relevant (e.g. agriculture), then their international publication record will suffer, resulting in a reduced international influence and recognition – and a greater need for local journals to capture the research findings.

The future

Donor support for African journals

There is some support for African journals provided by international development agencies, although the majority of this support is provided as hosting for online journals, without publishing skills and knowledge development.

Bioline (*www.bioline.org.br*) provides a free service for journals to publish full-text online open access. It is managed from Toronto University, with the hosting in Brazil. It freely hosts 58 open access journals from developing countries (21 from Africa). As part of its support it provides some training in producing files for online hosting, although it does not provide support for other publishing skills.

African Journals OnLine was originally started as a project to index African journals, but rapidly introduced hosting of abstracts and provided a document delivery service around the world. Based in South Africa, today it hosts more than 300 journals published throughout the continent, and fulfils over 6,000 document delivery requests annually.

Open Journals System is an open source software project developed by the Public Knowledge Project (*http://pkp.sfu.ca*) with the aim of providing a full publishing solution (from online author submission through to publishing) to assist journals from developing countries. The organization is also undertaking research into strengthening scholarly publishing in Africa, led by Samuel Smith Esseh and Professor John Willinsky, to investigate how online and university systems can support the journals within their faculty. The organization also provides some training and assistance for journals to use its software to develop an online presence.

Several initiatives twin African journals with successful Western ones in the same discipline, with the idea that they can share experiences and benefit each other. The success of these models has been patchy as the experiences of each journal are so different. One of the most successful projects is the African Journal Partnership Project initiated in 2004 by the US National Library of Medicine, the John Fogarty International Center for Advanced Study in the Health Sciences, and the US National Institute of Environmental Health Sciences. The project has twinned four of the most prestigious African-published journals with leading Western journals. The project has provided financial and practical support for improving journal systems, and has also provided training support for journal staff (Goehl and Flanagin, 2008).

Publishing training workshops are not well established within Africa, and are run by few organizations. INASP (*www.inasp.info*) provides some publishing workshops covering subjects such as marketing, production, design, online development, business management, etc.

Most support that is provided focuses on editorial skills. For example, the HINARI Access to Research Initiative (the initiative to enable access to biomedical and health journals) supports members of the Forum for African Medical Editors through the provision of some workshops and the establishment of guidelines for good editorial practice (*http://www.who.int/tdr/svc/resources/partnerships-networks/fame-guidelines*).

Development of journal business models

The majority of journals operate with extremely limited budgets, and rely on 'free' labour to produce the journals. Journals are often not published on time, and many appear to have stopped publishing when they have temporarily stopped printing or distributing due to a lack of cash. Perhaps the worst case of this is the *East African Forestry Journal*, which ceased regular publishing in 1998. Since then, the journal has continued to accept papers and assign them to an issue, and it occasionally publishes special, funded, issues – out of sequence. However, the enormous backlog of articles and issues means that it would take a huge amount of funding to bring the journal back to regular publishing. Alternatives, such as publishing online only, cannot be developed due to disagreement about the ownership of the journal, and the inability for anyone to make a decision about how to move the journal forward.

Political instability also causes problems. In Zimbabwe, for example, many good journals have temporarily ceased publishing as the editors have left the country.

Few international initiatives support any kind of business model to enable the journals to grow. The only one to do so is AJOL, which provides the journals with small amounts of revenue from document delivery, and is investigating a model to sell its collection of full-text journals. The reason for this lack of financial development is that development agencies feel uncomfortable with commercial models in the area of research communication where primary attention is on making research readily available worldwide. They promote open access as the way forward for journal publishing and research dissemination.

Open access is a methodology for publishing that has gained a lot of popularity within many Asian and South American countries, where there is a desire to make research readily available and existing support models allow for conversion to open access online publishing. Unfortunately, within Africa there has not been such a groundswell of change in attitudes, and many journals have a resistance to making their content freely available. The reasons for this are not readily apparent, as the journals do not already have a successful commercial model and would greatly benefit from the increased visibility that free online publication would give them. There is however a fear of losing the small but valuable revenues that the journals obtain from international sales, and a concern about the additional cost of publishing online without somehow gaining additional income. Finally, there remains the problem that most journals need to continue to provide print as this is what their readership requires (due to lack of internet access). Therefore any online development would be of most benefit to users outside Africa and those in the better-funded African institutions.

Some journals, of course, are publishing online, open access – many because it is too technically difficult to publish in a subscription environment. Some have developed innovative models for their online publication. For example, *South African Family Practice* publishes full-text research articles online, open access, but within the print journal (which is distributed to members of the association) only the abstracts are printed, along with general news and views. In this way they have divided the journal into a research communication vehicle (open access online) and a general medical journal (in print). This has solved their problem of trying to produce a hybrid that brings research information to general practitioners and also provides other types of content such as opinions, news and case studies. In this case, the online development is funded through the membership income which supports the journal publication.

In another development, a group of Nigerian researchers have developed a series of 20 journals under the publishing name 'Academic Journals' which are born-digital titles that publish open access, online only (*www.academicjournals.org*). Their model is financed through author submission fees – set at approximately $550 to $750 per article. Author submission fees are not unusual in Nigerian journals, although they are usually about $50 per article.

In South Africa, the Department of Science and Technology provides funding to authors working at its institutions who publish in one of approximately 230 recognized South African journals, or any other ISI-indexed title. The objective of this financial reward is to support the author's department or faculty, and hence the money for each published article is paid to the institution directly. Although this system is being investigated as part of the overall programme for supporting South African research publication (ASSAf, 2006), it is likely to stay in some form, as a means of rewarding publication and ensuring local publication. One option under discussion is to subsidize the recognized journals for each article that they publish authored by a South African researcher, and in this way fund them to publish open access.

Journals or repositories

Given the journal environment worldwide, it is unlikely that most African journals will be able to substantially change their financial situation, or gain additional funding to support their publication. Equally, grants from parent institutions or development agencies are short term and quick to be cut, so cannot be relied upon. Unfortunately, some journal editors believe that there are untapped funds within Western libraries and development agencies, and that there are sales revenues to pursue. This prevents the development of other, more sustainable, business models and there is a pressing need to find cheaper and more professional methods of making research communication more effective within Africa (Smart, 2007).

Repositories may be a partial solution, if a way can be found to match publication in a repository with academic and research accreditation. There is considerable discussion of repositories within sub-Saharan Africa, although they are slow to develop and (as elsewhere) concentrating on capturing theses and dissertations. At the time of writing there are 14 within South Africa, one each in Ethiopia, Ghana, Kenya, Uganda and Zimbabwe, and two in Namibia. Unfortunately, development of repositories within Africa has been set back by the pan-African Database of African Theses and Dissertations (*www.aau.org/datad/database/login.php*). This large and extremely expensive development managed by the Association of African Universities established a database of content from 11 universities across ten countries. The database is freely available to the participating institutions, but otherwise requires a paid subscription. Unfortunately, the project did not initially capture the full text of the theses and thus found few subscribers. Although the project has now matured and full text is being added, it has never achieved its original aim – to become financially self-sustaining. With the benefit of hindsight, this was unlikely to happen, but it showed the thinking within African academia, and the problems with developing systems for commercial sale within the academic environment.

Collaboration, however, is a strength within sub-Saharan Africa, and something that is culturally very attractive. If a way could be found to share resources and use technology to develop repositories to capture research articles (such as the PubMed Central model), then it would be possible to provide an invaluable resource within the continent, and provide a means to replace the traditional journal model.

Conclusion

It is hard to envisage any substantial change to the way in which the majority of African journals operate, as the lack of professional, collective management leads to a fragmented and inherently conservative approach to journal publishing. Journals anywhere in the world are expensive to produce, both in terms of the time required from the academic research community, and in the funding required to meet technological challenges and benefit from opportunities. Africa has attempted to work with a journal model based on the commercial Western one, but within an environment where the required financial support is simply not available. It is hard to see where additional funding for the continuance of this model can come from. Ultimately, I suspect that the only way research information within Africa will increase its reach and impact is if more efficient and cost-effective ways of publishing and disseminating research are discovered.

Several authors support a collaborative model for the future for journals and research communication within Africa (Nwagwu, 2005; Ondari-Okemwa, 2007; Tijssen, 2007; Waast, 2002). The increasing use of ICT for communication of research may also provide a solution if such technologies are developed for the African requirement rather than mimicking Western models. However, if journals are to be replaced by more effective means of communication, this will require a substantial change to the accreditation system for both individuals and institutions: this will take visionary and persuasive intervention from within the continent.

Bibliography

Adomi, E. E. and Mordi, C. (2003) 'Publication in foreign journals and promotion of academics in Nigeria', *Learned Publishing* 16: 259–63.

Arunachalam, S. (2003) 'Information for research in developing countries – information technology, a friend or foe?' *International Information & Library Review* 35: 133–47.

Academy of Science of South Africa (ASSAf) (2006) *Report on a Strategic Approach to Research Publishing in South Africa*, Pretoria: Academy of Science of South Africa.

Chakava, H. (2007) 'Scholarly publishing in Africa: the perspectives of an East African commercial and textbook publisher', in A. Mlambo (ed.) *African Scholarly Publishing*, Oxford: African Books Collective, pp. 91–7.

Goehl, T. J. and Flanagin, A. (2008) 'Enhancing the quality and visibility of African medical and health journals', *Environmental Health Perspectives* 116: A514–A515.

National Science Foundation (2008) 'Science and Engineering Indicators: Appendix Table 5-34', available at: *http://www.nsf.gov/statistics/seind08/start.htm* (accessed 22 April 2008).

Nwagwu, W. (2005) 'Deficits in the visibility of African scientists: implications for developing information and communication technology (ICT) capacity', *World Review of Science, Technology and Sustainable Development* 2(3–4): 244–60.

Ondari-Okemwa, E. (2007) 'Scholarly publishing in sub-Saharan Africa in the twenty-first century: challenges', paper presented at the PKP Scholarly Publishing Conference, Simon Fraser University, Vancouver, 11–13 July.

Oyelaran-Oyeyinka, B. (2006) 'Don't make a fetish out of R&D spending', available at: *www.scidev.net/en/opinions/dont-make-a-fetish-out-of-rd-spending.html* (accessed 22 April 2008).

Smart, P. (2007) 'Journals – the wrong model for Africa?' *Learned Publishing* 20: 311–13.

Stringer, R. (ed.) (2002) *The Book Chain in Africa*, Oxford: INASP.

Tijssen, R. J. (2007) 'Africa's contribution to the worldwide research literature; new analytical perspectives, trends, and performance indicators', *Scientometrics* 71(2): 303–27.

UNESCO (2004) 'Gender and education for all, 2003/4 report', available at: *www.unesco.org/education/efa_report/zoom_regions_pdf/ssafrica.pdf* (accessed 22 April 2008).

Waast, R. (2002) *The State of Science in Africa: An Overview*, Paris: IRD.

Wole, D. and Habte, M. (2007) 'The Addis Ababa University Press: Experiences and reflections', in A. Mlambo (ed.) *African Scholarly Publishing*, Oxford: African Books Collective, pp. 91–7.

Yamey, G. (2003) 'Africa's visionary editor', *BMJ* 327(7419): 832.

15

The future of the journal in Asia: an information ethnographer's notes

David Hakken

In 1976, sitting in a reading room in the library at Sheffield University in England, I became perplexed. The previous summer, I had arrived from the USA to commence my anthropology dissertation fieldwork on class, culture and the industrial day-release form of adult education pioneered by the university's Extramural Department. Finding my way around the university's journal collections, I noticed that there were some gaps. A PhD student panic ensued: away from some of my 'home' sources, I might miss something important and return hopelessly out of touch with what others had to say, or my research might be 'scooped' or even ruined...

By this time I had encountered the collectivist working-class culture pervading the city that considered itself 'Labour's home'. This culture's tone stressed 'really useful' social education, as in the slogan 'To rise with, not out of, my class'. I was able to channel my panic toward a different perspective on writing, toward scholarship less about what *I* thought *as an individual*, but more on what my Sheffield contacts, academic interlocutors, and I thought *together* (Hakken, 1978).

On returning to the USA, my writing was changed again, by my new teaching job in a technology-oriented state university. As someone who had learned to type (quickly but not accurately) in high school, I still depended upon the departmental secretary for final copy. Whenever I gave her my corrected manuscript, I tensed for her question, 'Are you *sure* there are no more corrections?' I dreaded unpleasantness were I to have to ask, in spite of my assurances, for retyping a page or two. Yet I knew this was likely to happen: what I would think tomorrow, or at least the way I would express it, was likely to be different from what I had written today. A typed text was too rigid for the way my brain worked.

Such experiences primed my writing imaginary. My appetite for alternative ways to represent and facilitate talk among the international networkers with whom I shared interests – whether academic, social or political – was whetted by the emerging forms of computing that I was teaching. For example, early floppy disks suggested a kind of flexible writing that could be more collective. One person would write and save a text and mail the floppy to another. They would read, comment on, and alter the text as they saw fit, then send it on to somebody else, etc.

At some later point, impossible to predict, a more-or-less-agreed-upon-by-all text would be printed, along with other, similar pieces, in a new type of journal. While publishing would indicate the network's sense that its thinking had become stable enough for a public hearing, its chief aim would be to stimulate another, broader round of commenting on, changing, and re-circulating texts, again afforded by flexible media. In such journaling, the important thing would be to be a participant in the chain of writing, to be 'in the read' along with one's close colleagues (in my case, at that time, largely people attempting a rapprochement between anthropology and Marxism). Using the technology over time, we would get better at warding off the individualistic tendencies fostered by academic competitiveness and develop more collective (and therefore, I believed, more effective) knowledge, and do it more rapidly. A new kind of academic journal would be a prime tool.

As my academic career as an information ethnographer developed, I have periodically joined in similar efforts to pursue alternative forms of scholarly communication. As indicated elsewhere in this volume, academic journals have changed since my days as an assistant professor. While they did not become what I then hoped, automated information/communication technologies (AICTs)[1] are now associated with certain more flexible forms of journaling, such as preprints, the Public Library of Science, and diverse forms of open access publishing (Smart, 2006). Moreover, the internet itself, the world wide web, Wikipedia, free/libre and open source software, even MySpace, all manifest more liquid, social and interactive ways for scholars to communicate. They parallel AICTed activities in real life, like meet-ups, unconferences, and hacker festivals (and even technology, knowledge, and society conferences). Retaining some disciplined forms of expression, these ways of talking and gathering are more spontaneous and participatory, arguably at least in part because of their virtual complements. Even in formal computing education, prior preoccupations with abstract formalism now compete with attending to computer-supported collaborative work, participatory design and community computing, indicative of movement from computing in the abstract to computing *in use.*

The authors of this volume were asked to consider a number of questions. Will the journals business continue to grow? Open access initiatives still form a relatively small part of journals publishing, but will they become the norm? How do I as an academic see the future for journals? Will other forms of access to knowledge become more important? How will this part of publishing be affected by public policy, changes in copyright law, and the views of learned societies and research bodies?

My particular brief was the future of the journal in Asian contexts. Based on the personal motivations and perspectives outlined above, I rephrased these mammoth questions somewhat: How much do AICTed interventions matter communicatively among Asian scholars? How significant are more general open cultural imaginaries to Asian patterns of scholarly communication? What of the future?

What follows is best understood as being in the genre of anthropological field notes. That is, this chapter is my effort to articulate my best responses to these questions based on the relevant personal and field experiences that I have had, expressed in the understanding that they will be considered in the light of the arguments of other writers in this volume.

These experiences are varied. Like other North American activists of my generation, I have learned and thought quite a bit about Vietnam, China, and the peoples and nations of Western Asia. While the locus of my previous scholarship was the North Atlantic, I have recently been doing fieldwork in Asia, focusing in particular on Asian forms of free/libre and open source software (FLOSSing) and US/Asian university links. I have structured the following comments on Asia, AICTs and alternative visions of academic knowledge networking around three topics – an initial case from Malaysia, some academic dynamics of higher education institutions in China with journaling implications, and some 'global' initiatives in techno-science, all of which suggest something about the future of the journal.

A Malaysian example

To frame what follows, I begin with the publishing activities of ATMA (Institut Alam & Tamadun Melayu, or the Institute on the Malay World and Civilization) of the Universiti Kebangsaan Malaysia (UKM), the National University of Malaysia. At ATMA, scholarly techno-communicative imaginaries like mine outlined above are alive and well. Consider, for example, the following webpage comment on plans for the special holdings in the ATMA library and research centre:

> Running a research institute in today's information age without an open access collection is not advisable. The days of closed collections that belonged to a time when the readership was relatively small, restricted and trustworthy are gone. Our goal now is make it possible for … highly specialized material to travel globally, along the information highway. In other words, we want to open up [materials like] N. A. Halim's collection and make all the items accessible worldwide. With every item digitalized, intelligently filed, classified and integrated, we can ensure an effective retrieval of them on one hand, and maximum preservation and security on the other hand. We foresee that the content of information will change rapidly, and in this way, the collection will have high research value. This will influence the kind of users and the information industry at large, and will enhance ATMA's reputation as a premier research and documentation centre. (ATMA, 2008)

This statement articulates several perspectives on academic knowledge networking that in my experience are common in Asia. One matter of note is the website's use of English; use of the colonial language has been a common issue of contention at UKM, the first university founded after Malaysian independence. Second is the global framing of the contemporary, and its framing as the information age. Third is performance of an open cultural imaginary, as through use of the term 'open access'. Fourth, the goal of making available all materials – including some valuable historic manuscripts that play a key role in nationalist discourses – is to be achieved primarily through advanced use of AICTs: digitization, accompanied by *intelligent* filing, classification and integration. Moreover, the collection is to be added to regularly, which is presumed to increase its research value. This in turn should lead to new kinds of users, which is expected to give ATMA an important place in the information *industry*. (Like many contemporary universities, UKM is now committed to leveraging its 'intellectual property' (sic) to create substantial revenue streams. Malaysian universities have been assigned a key role in creating the knowledge society, something central to the programme, first articulated by ex-prime minister Mohammed Mahathir, to make Malaysia a 'fully developed society by 2020'.)

In short, AICT mediation, expected to achieve a great deal, could be understood as the strategic communicative priority at ATMA. This is strongly implied via invocation of familiar techno-utopian registers of enthusiasm:

> Users can now expect convenience they never dreamed of in the past. They are no longer required to remove or open an envelope or box or wallet to inspect the contents. There will no longer be any unnecessary physical handling of the material. In other words, digitalization *has made possible what was once impossible*: maximized safety and maximized accessibility at one and the same time. Retrieval with staff help will be limited to special cases, and guidance in how the system works will require a minimal number of staff. No updating and cataloguing personnel will be needed. (ATMA, 2008)

In my view, because it tends to present the most difficult problems as having already been solved, overly utopian 'computer revolution' talk like this is perhaps the main impediment to transforming scholarly communication via AICTs. It certainly gets in the way of understanding what is actually going on among researchers. While there have been many correlates of the integration of AICTs into libraries, staff elimination is not one of them. Indeed, during fieldwork at ATMA, I learned of an entire series of problems regarding electronic filing, classifying and integrating (not to mention digitizing) of both existing and new materials. Many of these problems had to do with a key aspect of the proprietary database tools that the staff were attempting to use. The problems could be traced, I came to believe, to some basic ontological 'lacks of fit' between notions about the kinds of things that existed in past Malay worlds and the kinds of things imaginable in Redmond, Washington, USA. These in turn led to important epistemological issues that complicated filing, etc.

In any case, I helped set up a meeting with a start-up Malaysian open source firm claiming to develop knowledge-base products more reflective of indigenous Malay knowledge networking categories and practices than the available off-the-shelf proprietary products. I was unfortunately unable to follow up on this initiative. That my analysis was at least of theoretical interest was no doubt related to ATMA's creation of the Institute Kajian Oksidental (IKON) – the Institute of Occidental Studies (*http://www.ikon.ukm.my/*) – at the same time as my fieldwork (early 2005). This new organization was to be an Eastern outpost for the study of the West, albeit, of course, one not intended to implement the obverse of the 'Orientalism' (the tendency to see the East through Western eyes) critiqued by Edward Said (2003).

Basic to IKON was the presumption that geography was correlated with intellectual (and therefore scholarly) diversity. Perhaps blinded by techno-utopianism, such IKONic differences disappear in ATMA talk about technology. Any complications derive not from the technology itself, nor from technologies' interactions with social factors, but from social networking contexts alone:

> We believe that IT will bring about a better world in information management and accessing information. The backbone of this project is N. A. Halim's collection. But, this project of Malaycivilization.com would not be a success without the cooperation and contribution, in one way or the other, from [other]... bodies and the people... (ATMA, 2008)

In Malaysia, as in this statement, social context never seems far away from consciousness. In the USA, when I tried to explain my interest in the relevance to FLOSSing of where it was done, I often got quizzical looks in response. Coding is generally taken to be relatively free of culture. In Malaysia, FLOSSers understood immediately why this question was important; they often responded by outlining their own thinking on the subject. National, racial and political contexts are common topics on relevant listservs and blogs.

Still, it is only rarely that technology, too, is placed deeply in context, as opposed to being treated *sui generis*. In Malaysia, academic publishing in public higher education strongly reflects more general developments within the state sector. The neo-liberal encouragements to turn university units into direct profit centres, as alluded to above, mean that journaling is approached from a 'branding' perspective. (Publishing in the frankly more proprietary private sector, now roughly equal in student numbers to the state sector, is even more entrepreneurial.) However, public universities like UKM are also prime arenas for performance of government policies of positive action for *bumiputras* or 'people of the soil' – that is, those *not* Chinese, South Asians or *bumiputeh* (whites). Central to the political domination of the United Malay National Organization, such positive action policies are at the centre of the national election being conducted at the time of writing. I believe that, in the long run, such policies will not be compatible with the neo-liberal trade regimes of the World Trade Organization or the bilateral trade deal currently being mooted between Malaysia and the USA. Moreover, such policies are in practice antithetical to another favourite national policy, that of promoting Malaysia as the logical higher-education 'hub' of Asia. Leveraging Malaysian assets in higher education makes sense because of its multilingualism, there being large Bahasa, Chinese (including Hokien and Hakka as well as Mandarin), Tamil and English-speaking communities. Further, if China is your primary future economic partner, educational policies that discriminate against and alienate the large Chinese population are not a good idea. This is particularly true given the high visibility of Chinese Malaysians among the 'overseas' Chinese who have played a disproportionate role in launching 'mainland' China's economic resurgence.

These are a few of the several contexts exerting contradictory influences on academic journaling in Malaysia. The ATMA/Malaysia case illustrates several such influences. In addition to the manifestly vigorous AICT-connected technological imaginary, attention should also be given to the attribution of a central role in national development to educational institutions and activities (and thus, by extension, to academic publishing), as well as the promotion of higher education reforms along what are described as Western (especially American) institutional models.

As I've pointed out (Hakken, 2003) in relation to many other places, the sublime tones of techno-determinism allow avoidance of extremely delicate questions like, 'whose knowledge, for what purpose?' In the absence of clear answers to these questions, the correlates of AICT mediation are less likely to be transformative, and more likely to reflect existing patterns of social formation reproduction. In light of broad contradictory pressures, connected to powerful national development dynamics, the prospects for truly alternative forms of academic communication are not bright.

Relevant scholarly dynamics in China

Before stating in more detail my anticipatory anthropology of Asian academic journaling, I want to express some of what I understand about academic developments in China. Here, older forms of journal publishing, as central components of reputation building, appear to be being actively reinforced.

My knowledge of academic communication in China derives from two roles. One is administrative; I am currently the Director of International

Activities for the School of Informatics at Indiana University. The school itself is a new professional school, one of many diverse academic attempts to broaden and reorganize educational and research efforts relevant to AICTs. While we Indiana academics have diverse perspectives on what is constituted by 'informatics', we seem to agree that, as a profession, it is/will be practised internationally. Therefore, informatics education should have a substantial international component. My task has been to try to figure out what this should be, which has among other things meant talking at length with representatives of universities, many from Asia, who wish to link with us or to whom we might wish to link.

The other prod to my learning about the context of journaling in China is research. The East Asian Studies Center and the Department of East Asian Languages and Cultures at Indiana University are examples of what in the USA are called 'area studies' programmes, which are federally funded. The 2006 reallocation for these units, in conjunction with their organizational counterparts at the University of Illinois Urbana/Champaign, included support for a project known as the Science and Technology in the Pacific Century (STIP) initiative. Interpreting STIP as an effort to direct humanistic scholarship to the broader social correlates of techno-scientific development in Asia, I agreed to co-direct it. Out of the project has grown a specific research interest in US/Asian university links, on which I am currently conducting field research in a specific project we call 'Partnerships across the Pacific' (PxP). PxP aims to understand what such links mean to the scientists and technologists actively involved in them. We feel that such an understanding will provide a window on to the potentially global transformations that are STIP concerns. By understanding in particular what counts as a successful partnership for participants on both sides, and the extent to which these views overlap, PxP hopes to make a practical contribution to both the creation of such links and thus to techno-scientific creativity and innovation in general.

Although my work on this programme and this project is far from complete, I have developed some ideas about what is happening in Asian universities that are relevant to the future of journaling there. Particularly in China, academic institutions are going through major transitions, including:

- a massive increase in scale (aimed at increasing student numbers at least fourfold in a short time) which includes the building of entire new universities and/or campuses;

- considerable reorganization (e.g. the merger of many formerly independent units into larger ones) to enable previously marginal academic units to compete more effectively for prestige as well as centrally-funded research grants;

- expansion and reorganization, notably in the research function, which means a shift away from the former, Soviet-style 'academy' toward a more US-style system, in which research is carried out increasingly by academics who also teach;

- increased decentralization, including fiscal autonomy, combined with closer links to local and regional states and economic ventures (e.g. large 'science parks' charged with moving academic creativity into innovative products quickly);

- increasing (over already high) levels of concern with international and national quality rankings;

- massive increases in support for foreign study, particularly in the USA, both for students and younger faculty; and

- the rapid advance of scholars, especially those who have studied in the USA, up academic hierarchies.

In conjunction with economic development, these factors mean universities are less centrally and more regionally and locally controlled (Lan, 2008). Consequently, for example, while the central government generally promotes links with US universities, it apparently does not have the mechanisms in place (or at least is not making the effort) to carry out a census of academic partnerships. Informed observers suggest that even specific university offices of international exchange and cooperation do not have accurate lists of the partnerships involving their own campuses.

The problem of environmental pollution offers an interesting example of how current academic dynamics are playing out more broadly in Chinese society. It seems clear that the national Communist Party leadership recognizes pollution as a major problem, but recentralizing control to solve it might put the economic expansion attendant to decentralization at risk. Jennifer Turner (2008) of the Woodrow Wilson Center's Environmental Change and Security Project describes technically sophisticated water treatment plants, for example, built to new national standards but never turned on by local authorities. The central government's approach instead seems to depend upon the development of a civil society of non-governmental organizations (NGOs) to pressure regional and local governments to solve such problems. Many of the new, tolerated NGOs turn out to be led by academics (see also Turner, 2008).

Such developments fit with another justification for expansion of higher education often articulated: a desire for more independent, not just more, thinking (e.g. Hurlbert, 2007). (This pattern also makes sense given the Confucian tradition in China.) At the same time, it would appear that increased autonomy at a time of expansion has fostered some negative developments. These include falsification of scientific data, as well as 'back door', non-competitive admission to desired academic programmes. Another problem is that much of the labour in the science parks is student labour, which adds to already high levels of concern about the quality of education due to its rapid expansion. A recent study team of US computer scientists organized by the US National Science Foundation, for example, expressed concern that a substantial part of the work given high academic credit in Chinese universities was too product-oriented to count in the USA (US NSF Senior Scholars, 2007).

Perhaps out of concern for problems like these, the Chinese academic units with which I have had direct contact are at pains to demonstrate how their techno-scientific work qualifies as being of quality and significant in relation to standard academic measures. Featured in presentations to visiting academic delegations/potential partners is attention to the same measures of scholarly productivity urged on the School of Information at Indiana by my colleagues trained in nature science. These include the h-index, a measure of the relationship between the number of references to a scholar's publications in 'high-level' journals and the total number of their referenced publications. These scores are taken as an index of impact on the field, and so having a large number of scholars with high h-indexes is taken as indicating high general standing for an academic unit (Cronin and Meho, 2006).

While the relative dearth of property law might currently be supportive of innovation, it is likely that legal institutions being borrowed from the West will reinforce rather than undermine such academic mimicry. In short, to publish in academic journals, especially international ones held in high regard, is presented as being extremely important. It seems that a main motivation for creating links with US scholars is the idea that this increases chances of co-authoring papers published in prestigious journals. These practices, in the context of the developments cited above, suggest that Chinese academic journaling, at least in the short run, will be highly conservative. That is, factors like the rapid expansion of the number of scholars, the increased likelihood of their being from an academic organization with a new name and organizational structure, and the increased value placed on international links, all fit with the high priority placed verbally on demonstrated success in the existing journal world.

This is not to suggest that the Chinese are in general unaware of the new forms of academic knowledge networking provided by AICTs. I do not have extensive knowledge of the extent to which individual Chinese students and faculty are innovative social thinkers, but the ones I have met are generally young (because of the rapid expansion) and technologically hip. Avid adoption of blogging and broadband by large numbers of Chinese are only a few of the developments that indicate skill with AICTs.

It is possible that such factors will eventually lead to a more experimental approach to publishing. Yet things like the 'great firewall' used by the national state to control political speech on the internet – perhaps of even greater importance is the self-censorship that ambiguity in the structures of content control induces – discourage unofficial talk. In this context, and at a moment of great expansion, especially in education and its resources – for example, a proposed 45 per cent one-year increase in national spending on education (Dickie, 2008) – writers are likely to choose publications outlets that are conservative in form.

Consider the following experience. While staying at an upscale Hangzhou hotel, I thought I would experience the 'great firewall' myself. I used a public hotel PC to do a Google search on 'Tiananmen Square'. The search results included several items with tags that suggested they were highly critical of the actions of the Chinese government, very similar in content and ranking to the results I just got while writing this piece in Indiana. However, in China, when I clicked on critical links, I got only a 'page failed to load' message, while tourist sites loaded easily. Thus, a Chinese surfer performing this search would be likely to know that such critical perspectives existed, but also that there was something preventing them from being viewed. The high visibility of 'great firewall' avatars on the web would suggest that the state may even want people to know that such perspectives exist, but that its concern is about a Rumsfeldian 'known unknown', the *act* of reading them.

Last summer, a group of undergraduates from Zhejiang University visited Indiana University, taking advantage of a (presumably parent-financed) two-week opportunity to experience a bit of what graduate education in the USA would be like. These students came from very diverse academic backgrounds. During an orientation session on informatics, I asked them first to carry out a complicated task involving the downloading of a utility to collect websites visited. I then asked them to explore the image of China on the web in Indiana. Not only did they all handle the download, but their search histories often indicated imaginative strategies, including visits to both official and very unofficial sites. This was echoed in the vigorous discussion they had of similarities and differences between the internal and external views of their nation.

These are my journaling-relevant impressions of Chinese students and young scholars. While generally quite polite, they do manifest aspects of the 'prince' and 'princess' characteristics often alluded to in newspaper stories, especially in their degree of self-confidence. They are able to act like beneficiaries of the 'one child' policy, with parents and grandparents spending much of their large savings on them. These students and scholars are IT-savvy, seem to have good search skills, and are presumably adept at avoiding conflict with officially-sanctioned performances of reality, knowing 'what ropes to skip and what to jump'. There is much to suggest that they are quite nationalistic. Given the expansion of the academic system, there is considerable opportunity for them to win prestige and leverage this into an improved quality of life. As long as there is much room to succeed in 'normal' scholarly discourse, they are less likely to innovate in academic communication. I would expect, for example, that Chinese Wikipedia-style initiatives will attain only semi-independence, perhaps even becoming semi-official, but they are unlikely to become standard points of reference for some time.

Asian journaling: a regional and global perspective

Academic and science policy remain largely national, but China, like Japan, Korea and several other Asian countries are using national institutions to raise the international profile of their techno-sciences. These include, for example, prizes, funding and institutional supports to increase the number of Asian Nobel Prize winners. In an important sense, such institutions reinforce Kuhnian 'normal' science, in that they involve the latest, most internationally respected laboratory technology and promote international publishing and prestige conferencing. Yet at the same time, these institutions are often informed by a sense that Asian scholarship has not fared as well as it should have because it is discriminated against (Bartholemew, 2007). This sense seems especially strong in Japan, which now seems much more selective in the international links that it promotes. It is also manifest in Korea, as in the national responses to 'Hwang-gate' (the scandal surrounding premature and probably illegitimate claims about stem-cell science), which tended to combine expressions of shame at Dr Hwang's over-zealousness with strong commitments to continued state funding of his research.

For some time, the correlates of these institutions may be contradictory, both honouring Asians doing 'mainstream' science (that is, techno-science as acknowledged in the West) *and* promoting distinctly Asian approaches to science. Perhaps the current dynamic, in which traditional patterns of academic journaling are reinforced, may eventually be transformed. Patterns of scholarship may 'decouple' from the West in a manner not unlike current economic patterns (e.g. the projected but ultimately unfulfilled hope that Asian economies would avoid the ongoing credit squeeze in the West). That is, these nations have substantial techno-scientific traditions of their own. Further, by being oriented at least to some extent toward national priorities for research topics, efforts to accelerate techno-science creativity and innovation within a national or regional (adjacent nations) frame may foster concentration on forms of research in which the particular nation or region has an advantage, whether industrial, historical, or even biographical (i.e. the preoccupations of particular leading techno-scientists). Success at promoting national science heroes in open competition could feed national techno-scientific differentiation as much as global convergence. As trajectories of national techno-science diverge from the 'standard' Western programme, the benefits of innovation (e.g. using more interactive forms of AICTed communication) may start to outweigh the costs of deviating from 'approved' forms.

This possibility can be seen as compatible with presumptions present in current scholarship in science, technology and innovation policy. Here, an earlier consensus, that the best way to promote national techno-science progress was to try to create a US-style national science policy and set of institutions, has passed from favour (e.g. Wagner, 2007). Instead, nations are urged to, on the one hand, cultivate existing national advantages and, on the other, link strongly and appropriately to what has been reconceptualized as an international, even global, techno-science innovation system. Of course, AICTs are often seen as key to the latter move, as at the World Summit on the Information Society and in social movements like 'Access to Knowledge'.

What will be the long-term result – distinct (even competitive) national or regional patterns of scientific communication, or a single international scientific public sphere and associated pattern of techno-scientific 'discursive redemption' (to use the Habermasian term)? Techno-scientists tend to assume the latter, as they are prone to presume that their way of talking is the prototype of cosmopolitan, universalistic discourse. For example, North Atlantic FLOSS projects project themselves as spaces 'where geography is not relevant'. If there is some sort of structural imperative toward universalism in science, the heightened presence of Asian techno-scientists, including via their involvement in traditional academic journals, should accelerate a single shared set of practices. Yet the continued relevance of culture and location are argued for by considerable literatures in social science and the humanities.

Two sets of informatics practices cast some light on the convergence/divergence issue. Considerable resources have recently gone into the creation of means to share techno-scientific materials across scientific cultures. An example from the recent past is the creation of 'global grids' (GGs), like those that my IU Informatics colleagues Geoffrey Fox, Dennis Gannon and Beth Plale have been advocating. While the creation of GGs requires the overcoming of technical issues following from diversity in national as well as hardware and software standards, getting people to use them, especially in diverse nations, is at least as challenging. In comparing the relatively slow uptake of GGs versus the rapid global growth in social networking (e.g. MySpace), Fox (2007) points out how GGs have been preoccupied with issues of security, issues which have been largely ignored by social networking sites. In his view, global gridding must be able to learn from this experience, while still attending to, for example, national security concerns.

As a social informist, it seems to me that GG uptake problems may also be related to those associated with initiatives manifesting what look like 'if we build it, they will come' presumptions. Such problems are hard for techno-scientists to focus on. General problems regarding AICTed techno-science were recently addressed in an IU colloquium by Malcolm Atkinson (2008), professor of e-science in the School of Informatics at Edinburgh University in Scotland. For Atkinson, e-science includes any scientific activity in which computing is involved. Even though he heads the (British) National e-Science Centre, the thrust of his talk was in support of an international strategy for pursuit of e-science. Among the reasons he cited for such a strategy are:

- the growing data glut;
- the growth of transnational research; and
- the changes in the cultures of science that will be required for e-science to progress, especially an increase in cross-cultural trust so that data are truly shared.

While Atkinson acknowledged the contribution that social sciences and humanities can make to dealing with this last issue, the central place in his strategy is assigned to developing shared approaches to data, especially those that make it persistent. This is to be accomplished by creating shared standards, well engineered from their foundation. If this were not done in a worldwide manner, the resulting tools would not be used, data would not be manageable, and the e-science programme would collapse.

If Atkinson's plea is taken in a 'weak' form, a call for international discourse on standards as part of a broader conversation of the role of computing in science, it is unexceptional. However, it could be taken as a 'stronger' argument, for a standards-first approach to creating truly global science. As such, it is vulnerable to the critique that arriving at truly shared standards presupposes the existence of much more robust means of techno-scientific communication than those that currently exist. To cast this as a purely 'technical' discourse means that one must ignore the issues of culture and trust that he himself raises.

Conclusion

I have come to believe that that achieving the international discourse necessary for truly global science depends upon having first solved the culture of science/trust issues identified by Atkinson (2008). Such considerations bring me back to my original point, about the need for more collective, egalitarian means of scholarly communication. Since my earliest hopes for computer-enabled scientific communication when I was in Sheffield, AICTs have clearly become a central (arguably *the* central) repository of relevant imaginaries. While new computerized forms of journaling hold out the promise of democratizing scholarly communication, I see in the short term little reason to expect Asia to be the first place for this to become modal. Rather than transformative, AICTed forms replacing current academic journaling, I expect hyper-traditional patterns to be the norm for some time.

However, as models of techno-science that are indigenous to Asia become better developed and understood locally, they *may* nationalize/regionalize (glocalize/lobalize) rather than globalize techno-scientific practices. Conversely, through participation in the efforts described by Fox and Atkinson, Asian techno-scientists may contribute more to the creation of truly global techno-science. How much Asian techno-science is 'placed', and how much it is likely to remain so, is one of the things my colleagues and I hope to be able to illuminate through our current research on US/Asian university links (Gieryn et al., 2007).

I suspect that the kinds of Asian academic institutions which I have described here will have to mature before one can assess their prospects for contributing substantially to the engineering approaches to global gridding/e-science policy proffered by Fox and Atkinson. In the meantime, those of us concerned about the future of scholarly communication (indeed, like scholars of many forms) would do well to pay attention to what is happening in Asia, especially to the practices techno-science promotes there. In this regard, Japan, with the most mature techno-science practices, may be the most instructive place, and hence the place in which alternative, more participatory approaches to publishing open up most quickly.

Note

1. It is common to use 'ITs', 'ICTs', or 'new technology' to refer to what I insist on calling 'AICTs'. There is, I think, general agreement on the need to draw attention to the 'communicative' as well as 'informational' aspects of these technologies; hence 'ICTs' is preferable to 'ITs'. However, as an anthropologist, I insist on the idea that all human cultures have information and communication technologies. Hence, it is not the mere existence of ICTs, but what about new forms of them that is distinctively different, for which we need a term. ('New' itself is too vague.) I submit that it is their being 'automated' that makes computer-based ICTs so distinctive (or at least, that this word points usefully in the direction of the complex of distinctivenesses). That is, their ability to manipulate data 'behind our backs' is what gives them both the speed and opacity to be socially transformative (as well as making it harder for us to understand what is going on; Hakken 1999).

Bibliography

Atkinson, M. (2008) 'A global strategy for e-science', paper presented at the Colloquium for the School of Informatics, Indiana University, Bloomington, IN, April.

Institute on the Malay World and Civilization (ATMA) (2008) Homepage, available at: *http://www.atma.ukm.my/* (accessed 4 May 2008)

Bartholomew, J. (2007) 'East Asian scientists and the challenge of professional marginality', paper presented at the Science and

Technology in the Pacific Century Project, Indiana University, Bloomington, IN, November.

Cronin, B., and Meho, L. (2006) 'Using the 'h'-index to rank influential information scientists', *Journal of the American Society for Information Science and Technology* 57(9): 1275–8.

Dickie, M. (2008) 'China says curbing inflation is priority', *Financial Times*, 6 March, p. 4.

Fox, G. (2007) 'Cyberinfrastructure and scientific collaboration', paper presented at the School of Informatics colloquium, Indiana University, Bloomington, IN.

Gieryn, T., Hakken, D. and Ross, H. (2007) 'Cross-cultural challenges in thinking about innovation and creativity: the case of Asian/US university partnerships in science and technology', in *Proceedings, Georgia Institute of Technology Conference on 'Challenges and Opportunities for Innovation in the Changing Global Economy*, October.

Hakken D. (1978) 'Workers' education: the reproduction of working class culture in Sheffield, England and "Really Useful Knowledge"', unpublished dissertation at American University, Washington, DC, available from, Ann Arbor: University Microfilms.

Hakken D. (1999) *Cyborgs@Cyberspace?: An Ethnographer Looks to the Future*, New York: Routledge.

Hakken D. (2003) *The Knowledge Landscapes of Cyberspace*, New York: Routledge.

Hurlbert, A. (2007) 'Re-education', *The New York Times Magazine*, 1 April, pp. 36–43, 56, 59–61.

Lan, X. (2008) 'Reform and expansion: challenges and opportunities for China's higher education system', paper presented at the Science and Technology in the Pacific Century Seminar, Indiana University, Bloomington, IN, April.

Said, E. (2003) *Orientalism*, New York: Penguin.

Smart, P. (2006) 'Online publishing – strategies and issues', available at: *http://www.inasp.info/file/55/homepage.html* (accessed 4 May 2008).

Turner, J. (2008) 'The growing role of Chinese green NGOs and environmental journalists in China', Woodrow Wilson Center's Environmental Change and Security Project, available at: *http://www.cecc.gov/pages/roundtables/012703/turnerHandout.php* (accessed 3 May 2008).

US NSF Senior Computer Scientists Delegation (2007) 'Communication, understanding, friendship, innovation: insightful understanding of China's higher education and research in computer science and information technology', available at: *http://dimacs.rutgers.edu/Workshops/China/* (accessed 3 May 2008).

Wagner, C. (2007) 'The myth of the national innovation system', paper presented at Atlanta Conference on Science, Technology, and Innovation Policy, Georgia Institute of Technology, Atlanta, GA, October.

16

The future of the academic journal in China

Kang Tchou

How do I begin a chapter that treats the future of the academic journal in China, especially when this chapter is to appear in a book that mainly focuses on the future of journals in the Western world? As the majority of my readers will be from Western cultures (I am assuming this because of the location of the press that is publishing this book), I will begin by establishing common ground within the world of information management to find bridges between the situation in China and the situation in the West.

In the West, 'publishing' in the modern sense begins with Gutenberg. The history of publishing in China also begins with a name, but while no press is named after Ts'ai Lun, he is traditionally believed to have invented something of such crucial importance that even Gutenberg owes him thanks: paper (Twitchett, 1983: 11). Then, Bi Sheng is credited with the invention of moveable type in 1041, some four hundred years before Gutenberg.

Before we delve into the heady waters of information management in China, let me first introduce the thematic and temporal arrangement of this chapter. Following the theme of this collection of papers and the title of this chapter, our goal is to understand the future of academic journals in China. The path to this goal will be organized through the metaphor of an antique wagon wheel that is a metal ring supported by six spokes. This chapter positions its readers at the centre of the six spokes, and makes them the linchpin of this narrative. After all, the understanding that this chapter offers to its reader is dependent on their interpretation.

Following this analogy, our discourse will travel along the circumference of the wheel, and will be supported by each of the spokes.

The future, being the first term of substance in the title of this chapter will also be the beginning of our discourse. Our conversation will begin and also end with the theme 'future'. This term represents a temporal element; in order to understand what lies in the future for China's information management industry, we must first explore the past and the present. While ordinarily we might proceed chronologically, the history of publishing in China is so vast that it behoves us to start with the present and then attempt to understand it through the veil of history. When dealing with any subject related to a country with 5,000 years of continuous history, the past is always a part of the present and will also influence the future. So 'present', 'past' and 'future' will form the three temporal spokes in our wheel of conversation and shape the order of our discourse. As we proceed on this temporal path, we will inevitably ask what the terms 'academic', 'journal' and 'publishing' mean in regard to China. These three terms will become the focal point of the three thematic spokes of our discussion. Ultimately, when we have explored all six spokes of our wheel, our conversation will have come full circle.

The beginning of a chapter seldom survives a reader's scrutiny. Too often academicians, being short on time, will read only the beginning and the end of an essay. I hope a set of statistics (the most recent and reliable that are available) will emphasize the importance of some understanding of information management in China. I stress the need for 'some understanding' because no one chapter will cover the breadth of our topic to any satisfying depth, and so this chapter serves only as a vehicle that moves across this vast topic in the hope that it will lead the reader of this volume to further sources for a more in-depth investigation.[1] While much of the information presented here is the result of others' research, this chapter is unique in uniting their separate discourses under the six temporal and thematic themes related to information management in China.

When exploring the publishing industry in the most populous nation in the world, numbers are worth a thousand words. There are presently between 566 and 573 registered publishing houses in China (Z.Q. Zhang, personal communication, 2008) and, with the exception of university presses, they are all administered by one government entity, the General Administration of Press and Publication (GAPP) of the People's Republic of China (PRC). This one office is also responsible for issuing all International Standard Book Numbers (ISBNs) and all International Standard Serial Numbers (ISSNs) in China. GAPP's central office in Beijing directly administers the 221 publishing houses in the city, and its regional offices in major cities are responsible for the remaining 345 publishing entities (Baensch, 2003: 13). The majority of these publishing houses were established after 1949 and some of them, such as the China Agriculture Publishing House, China Science and Technology Publishing House, China Taxation Press, and The Electric Power Publishing House have very close relationships with their respective government ministries (Baensch, 2003: 13). Local publishing houses that focus on a variety of disciplines and categories are present in every province (Baensch, 2003: 13). Functioning outside of the direct control of the GAPP are the university presses that publish academic research and reference books, journals and textbooks (Baensch, 2003: 13). As of 2001, the combined yearly production of information in book form is upwards of 154,000 titles, with 40 per cent of the publications being reprints (McGowan, 2003, 53). Not included in this figure are the serials publishers, which produce over 8,000 periodicals, including academic journals (Buckwalter, 2003: 44). The sum of these figures also does not include what has now become the most popular medium for the exchange of information – the internet.[2] While there are Chinese counterparts for most types of Western media for information exchange over the internet, what is popular in China is not always the same as what is popular in the West. For example, in the USA, AOL Instant Messenger (AIM) chat is the most popular online chat provider. In China, the general public in urban areas prefer MSN and Yahoo Chat. While YouTube is known in China, much more popular is its Chinese equivalent Tudou (*www.tudou.com*). With respect to search engines, Baidu (*www.baidu.com*) is the most popular Chinese text-based search engine and its efficiency rivals that of Google in English. Recently, wikis have also become popular as Wikipedia has developed a Chinese language version. Finally weblogs or blogs are as plentiful in China as in any other country. While these are still not recognized as established media for the publication of peer-reviewed information, their popularity hints at this possibility in the future.

Numbers relating specifically to academic journals[3] are no less staggering. The publication of academic journals in the PRC has increased dramatically following Deng Xiaoping's reforms that began in 1978. According to Wang:

> From 1981 to 1987, the average increasing rate [for the number of new academic journals] was 11 per cent. There were 2,951 different STM [scientific, technical, medical and professional] journal titles available in 1988 and the number increased to 4,420 titles by the end of 2001. (Wang, 2003: 77)

Between 1978 and 2001, the total circulation for these journals also nearly doubled to approximately 401 million copies (Wang, 2003: 77). The increase in both the number of titles and circulation is coupled with an improvement in quality, with some 64 journals becoming recognized by international scientific communities (Wang, 2003: 77). With the general popularity of the internet as a medium for the exchange of information, the Chinese Academy has since 2003 begun to develop databases for the electronic publication of academic journals. The National Science and Technology Library[4] is a prime example of China's national effort to make Chinese academic journals available to both Chinese scholars and their global audience. Due to the ease of accessibility and the format's relatively low cost of production, the trend is for new Chinese journals to be created in electronic format. Around 2005, the availability of e-journals began to surpass hardcopy journals in both public libraries and university libraries. While both Chinese language and foreign language e-journals are more popular than their hardcopy versions, foreign language e-journals are still less readily available at public libraries (Bin and Miao, 2005: 183).

For most of the twentieth century, China (and the state of its information management industry) remained a part of the mysterious and distant Orient. 'In the wake of Orientalism',[5] however, the information management industry in twenty-first-century China will become more familiar to its global audience and vice versa. If numbers alone do not convince one of the significance of the information management industry in China and its desire to connect with its global audience, then perhaps a succinct image in multimedia format will illustrate both the role that China plays within this field on the global stage and the desire of the Chinese academy and society at large to interact with the global academic community by increasing the managed flow of information both into and out of China.

The opening ceremony of the 29th Olympiad in Beijing provides an iconic image that emphasizes the importance of print culture in the Chinese psyche. The ceremony began with a 60-second countdown that was announced by the synchronized beating of 2,008 drums constructed according to designs over a thousand years old. Marching to the beat of these ancient drums, giant footprints formed by fireworks in the night sky marched towards the Bird's Nest stadium (10 minutes). The display of fireworks symbolized China's invention of gunpowder and represented the first of its four great contributions to human civilization. After the singing of the Chinese national anthem by the representatives of the 56 ethnic identities of modern China, the second of the four great

Chinese inventions – paper – made its appearance in the form of a giant paper scroll illuminated by LED technology, which displayed images of paintings from China's cultural history while serving as the canvas for a modern interpretative dance performance (18 minutes). The movements of the four dancers in black traced their footprints on the paper canvas, forming the strokes of an abstract contemporary landscape painting on paper (20 minutes). Immediately following the appearance of ink on paper, Confucian scholars, representing the importance of the role of the academy in Chinese civilization, entered the stadium carrying bamboo scrolls of their sacred texts repeating in unison two phrases attributed to Confucius. The opening utterance, recited from the *Analects of Confucius* [论语], translates as 'Fraternity across the four seas' [四海之内皆兄弟], while the second phrase, from the *Great Learning* [大学], translates as 'Isn't it a joy that friends have come from afar' [有朋自远方来不亦乐乎]. These two phrases are cultural, social and historical echoes of the official welcome uttered by President Hu Jingtao to all visitors to a modern China that is now opening its doors to the rest of the world (24 minutes).

Continuing with the themes of paper, writing and the academy, 28 minutes into the performance 2,008 young Chinese males (mostly volunteers from the People's Liberation Army) hid themselves within the individual blocks that formed a fully-operational, football-pitch sized, replica of an ancient set of Chinese movable type. Each individual block was carved with a distinct Chinese character, exemplifying Chinese characters as standardized by the first emperor of China. This human-powered movable type comprised of undulating blocks danced upon the enormous scroll and became a giant living printing press, showing the various forms (from archaic to modern) of the word for Harmony [和] in Chinese. These men animated the movable printing blocks and, in conjunction with the lighting on the paper scroll, formed an enormous cybernetic organism that (at least from a Western perspective) was reminiscent of the writing machine in Kafka's 'The Penal Colony', the calligraphy in Peter Greenaway's film *The Pillow Book*, and the title to Jeanette Winterson's love story *Written on the Body*. At the end of the performance, the 2,008 young Chinese men (as representatives of the future of a patriarchal China) revealed themselves by popping out of each of the movable blocks with their arms waving as additional gestures of welcome (30 minutes). Thirty-five minutes into the opening ceremony, signifying the commitment of Chinese civilization once again to engage with the world at large, the voyages of the great Chinese navy admiral Zheng He and the treasure boats under his command were re-enacted before the international and domestic audience. At the 40-minute mark, a single dancer holding a large model of a Chinese magnetic compass (the last of China's four great inventions) walked to the centre of the paper stage, forming a narrative transition between two great dynasties in Chinese history.

This moment of a modern Chinese person, dressed in ancient robes echoing an imperial design, holding an antique Chinese compass over his head, creating ink-like footsteps upon a piece of paper composed of both traditional wood fibre and modern LED technology provided the worldwide audience with a sign full of significance. The components of this signifier are easily identifiable. The ink traced on both traditional and LED paper represented the communication of information. The modern Chinese person dressed in traditional robes signified the creator of information both ancient and modern, and the compass, as a universal symbol for direction, completed the signifier by gesturing toward China's global present and future. The combination of the symbolic creator of information standing upon both the traditional and modern means for the dissemination of information, and a hand-held compass pointing toward the international audience, clearly showed China's intention of communicating through media both ancient and modern to the world at large. From a certain perspective, the dance of the 2,008 Chinese men in costumes that resembled movable type and the signifier composed of creator, medium and compass together represented a synecdoche that united the present, past and future of information management in China into a single statement. From a Chinese perspective, this image represented China taking control of the management of information, past, present and future so that it no longer will be veiled behind that 'great wall of discourse'[6] known as Orientalism. Having the 29th Olympics in China also signified both the world's willingness to be the receiver of the information that China produces as well as the global community's agreement to participate in a reciprocal exchange of information. At the 40-minute mark, the seemingly oppositional binary between the Chinese signifier (the person holding the compass) and the international audience that symbolized the West, was no longer there; indeed, the tension was resolved as each became vectors marking the harmonious confluence of a multidirectional flow of information that now also includes knowledge and wisdom between China and the rest of the world.

As stated at the beginning of this chapter, the present condition of China's information management industry and, more importantly, the state of its academic journals must be understood in the context of the long history of printing in China. Of course, printing not only means the production process but also the management and exchange of information through the printed page. Large-scale printing in forms that might be recognizable to a Western contemporary of Gutenberg did not occur in China until the tenth century (Twitchett, 1983: 30). Between AD 925 and AD 952, during a turbulent period in Chinese history known as the Five Dynasties, one of the legitimate heirs to the late Tang dynasty seized control of the modern-day province of Sichuan [四川] (Twitchett, 1983: 31). Impressed by the *Wén Xüǎn* [文选] *Anthology of Literature* produced from wood-block printing by a rival faction, the ministers Feng Tao and Li Yu decided to standardize and monopolize the wood-block printing of the entire Confucian canon (Twitchett, 1983: 31). As the canonical Confucian texts[7] formed the core body of knowledge for an academic education system that prepared students for the state examination system [科举制度] that was the primary process of selecting administratively inclined scholarly candidates for governmental office, these texts, beside being the fundamental works of the Chinese literary corpus, were also 'the source for all official ideology and point of reference for intellectual discourse' (Twitchett, 1983: 31).

Standardized and officially approved versions of the Confucian canon were first engraved in stone around AD 837 and then printed with wood-block printing after the middle of the tenth century (Twitchett, 1983: 32). As with the advent of the Gutenberg press in Europe, the Chinese state immediately realized that wood-block printing provided the dual benefit of making official state ideology widely available and of ensuring conformity. Printing, as a form of information management, became such a critical governmental industry that after the tenth century it remained largely in the control of the Chinese state (Twitchett, 1983: 32). In China, block printing as a technique for the management of information that equated to the Gutenberg press came into vogue as early as AD 770 with the distribution of block-printed Buddhist charms on paper (Twitchett, 1983; 14). From then on till the rise of the commercial press in the mid-fifteenth century, the state monopoly regarding the control and dissemination of information remained strong and the respective bureaucratic entities of each of the subsequent dynasties responsible for the management of information inherited the state monopoly on the dissemination of information (Twitchett, 1983: 45). With the gradual relaxation of the state monopoly during the Ming dynasty (AD 1368–1644), official permission to print information through governmental imprimatur gradually evolved into a concept of authors' and publishers' rights. The earliest known book to claim copyright under government protection was printed around AD 1190 in the area that is now modern-day Sichuan (Twitchett, 1983: 62). While copyright, as a concept, came into existence during the Ming dynasty, it was rarely enforceable, which encouraged unauthorized reprints, and allowed for alterations to the text without the approval of the initial author or the authorized publisher (Twitchett, 1983: 62). The patterns established in twelfth-century China may even explain the current lack of cultural affinity for concepts such as intellectual property rights that has led China to be open to the production and distribution of pirated software and the distribution of plagiarized information through publication. This phenomenon has only increased with the mass adoption of the electronic distribution of information through the various interfaces of the internet.

While scholars both inside and outside of China suggest different sets of dates as the starting point of the current system of information management in China (ranging from 1911 to 1949), they are in agreement on the persistent domination of the information management system by state bureaucracies. From a diachronic perspective, the GAPP of today is the direct descendant of the bureaucratic entities that were set up by Chinese ministers of state nearly a millennium past.

While similarities in the development of printing technology (such as wood-block printing) abound between the history of print culture in China and in the West, the relationship between the academy and the state and their mutual role in information management reveals a stark contrast that requires our attention. Arguably, from the beginning of the Platonic ideal of the academy in Greece to the establishment of the monastic orders of what might be roughly glossed as the medieval period, to the modern-day colleges and universities, the Western academy has always maintained an identity that is mostly independent from state control. In contrast, from the earliest form of the Chinese academy, students (often heirs of royalty that had fallen from power) following the wandering sage Confucius, to the state-sponsored imperial examination system, to the present-day colleges and universities in China, the education system referred to nominally as the academy has been more or less a system of training the best and the brightest intellectuals to become members of an elite ruling bureaucracy.

The Chinese academy (with sporadic dissident individuals and movements such as the Taiping rebellion or even the May Fourth Movement) has largely remained integral to the state apparatus. Even more significant, in China, throughout much of the existence of a system of information management through publishing, the state and the academy together decided the direction and content of information exchange. A succinct fact from history will demonstrate the veracity of this claim. Throughout Chinese history, the top three candidates of the imperial examination system ([进市], those who earned the right by examination to enter the Forbidden City) became the most trusted advisors to the imperial family. The most senior members holding this status were integrated into the Hanlin Academy [翰林院] (established in the eighth century) so that they might become official tutors and secretaries for the imperial court with the additional duty of overseeing the official examination system. Differing from Western cultures, where the greatest minds tend to become critics of the established order (examples from history include Socrates, Copernicus and Martin Luther) the top intellectuals in China almost always became the top managers of information for the state. While arguable, even the objectivity of modern dissidents of renown, such as Lu Xun [鲁迅] and Deng Tuo [邓拓], who attacked the state through veiled and unveiled criticism, remains under suspicion. After Lu Xun's death and subsequent deification by the Chinese Communist Party, his brother Zhou Zuoren [周作人] criticized the resulting mythical figure who became 'the father of Chinese literature' as an empty construction manufactured by official party propaganda. Deng Tuo, whose protest against Maoist doctrine resulted in his suicide, also served for ten years as the editor-in-chief of the *People's Daily* newspaper [人民日报] (1948–1958).[8] Set against these rare examples of elite intellectual dissidents are the numerous luminary alumni of Tsing-Hua, Peking and Fudan Universities that fill the ranks of the current leadership of the Chinese government. While history may not be cyclical, at least within the scope of the information management industry, our glimpse of Chinese history reveals certain dominant patterns. While the term 'academic' refers to similar concepts in the Chinese and Western psyche (roughly meaning 'pertaining to a body of scholars in pursuit of the advancement of knowledge'), its relationship to the ruling power is starkly different. This assessment is not to make any moral or ethical judgment based on this difference but merely to emphasize the contrasting role of the Chinese academy and thereby the Chinese academic information management industry with those in the West. An overly risky critical assessment may be that while in the West the academy enjoys a certain degree of freedom, Chinese society from ancient to modern benefits from an equal degree of academic filial-piety to the state.

The filial-pious nature of the academy to the state became destabilized only when (under pressure from foreign powers to modernize) the

Manchu court sponsored the opening of China's first institution for training in Western languages and learning. The establishment of the College of Foreign Languages (同文馆) in 1862 was strongly opposed by the entire Hanlin Academy, led by Woren, the Mongol Neo-Confucian moralist, and tutor to the emperor. The Hanlin academicians thought Western 'barbarian' subjects were unfit for teaching in Court-sanctioned institutions (Yeh, 1990: 7). Despite their opposition, the New Culture Movement (新文化运动) led by Western and Japanese trained scholars such as Hu Shi (胡适) and Lu Xun became dominant in the Chinese academy. The majority of the pre-eminent universities in China were established during the 1920s and 1930s under the influence of this movement. Toward the end of the 1930s, universities established by missionaries arose in commercial centres outside of Beijing and Nanjing. Ironically, these universities of Western origin, such as St. John's in Shanghai, emphasized traditional Chinese scholarly practice and became refuges for old-school Confucian scholars who were displaced by members of the New Culture Moment (Yeh, 1990: 28–9). The impact of this shift from the traditional mode of Confucian scholarship can still be seen in today's academia in both Taiwan (that supported Hu Shi) and China (that supported Lu Xun).[9]

Even in our digital age, it is hard to come by sufficient up-to-the-minute data concerning the information management industry in China. As a statistically significant study proves unfeasible, I must once more rely on anecdotal evidence to support my 'overly risky critical assessment'. In the introduction to her monograph *The Origins of the Modern Chinese Press: The Influence of the Protestant Missionary Press in Late Qing China*, Zhang concludes with the following lengthy but poignant caveat. Commenting on her own previous experience as an investigative reporter in China, she writes:

> I soon learned not be too fussy about this routine censorship. All the media, no matter whether newspapers, radio or broadcasting, are 'state-owned' in contemporary China. Despite the rapid development in media marketization, the state can intervene in any media organization and pull the plug without much difficulty. So intuitively avoiding overstepping the political line has become the common sense of media practitioners.
>
> To put it in simple words, in market-socialist China, the state enjoys control of the media and the idea of 'press freedom' is not accepted. The journalist is, of course, constantly encountering the

consequences of this and, as a result, journalism can be a deeply frustrating profession ... This is the moral and political issue – so close to the core of contemporary Chinese society – that prompts this book. However, what follows is neither a documentation nor a critique of the state-controlled media in China today. Rather, it is an attempt to give some sort of answer to the question of why the modern press in China has been so *consistently* dominated by the state. And why journalists – sophisticated in their practice in all other ways – still struggle for (or else pragmatically acquiesce in the denial of) basic political professional rights taken for granted in most parts of the world.

To blame the Communist Party for everything can offer a simple, convenient and immediate explanation. But this would be to confuse the particular regime with the more general and historically persistent trend. To develop a proper understanding of the issue requires, I believe, a broader socio-historical analysis. (X. T. Zhang, 2007: 1–2)

Long as the above quotation is, it provides a powerful intellectual analysis of the current state of information management in China. J. T. Ma [马大任] [10] reports that the state control of publishing also extends to the dissemination of academic information. He writes that 'all publishing houses in China today are state-owned and there is no private commercial publisher. And almost all Chinese publishing houses can publish academic books, especially books on the subject of learning or studying the English language' (Ma, personal communication, 2008). The lack of a clear separation between academic and commercial publishing leads to the lack of freedom in academic publishing that parallels the aforementioned lack of press freedom in China.

In my own personal experience, the campus walls surrounding Chinese universities pay homage to the Great Wall and serve the dual purpose of keeping the intruders out and the intellectuals within confines controlled by the state. Even today, pre-eminent Chinese universities such as the ones I have mentioned are strictly controlled through the Ministry of Education. As recently as October 2008 and despite the official Chinese rhetoric of espousing an openness to the world, any and all conferences attended by more than 150–200 individuals that seek Chinese university sponsorship must apply for permission through the national Ministry of Education two years in advance of the conference date. While no specific regulation can be cited by my contacts in China, it is an unwritten rule of educational joint ventures in contemporary China – *caveat emptor*.

There are bright spots in the future of the Chinese academy. Since the 1970s, the Chinese Communist Party has continued its policy of a managed decentralization of Chinese higher-education institutions. This policy has led to two dominant trends in the higher education in China. As Mok has stated:

> the Chinese Communist Party (CCP) called for resolute steps to streamline administration, devolve powers to units at lower levels so as to allow them more flexibility to run education. Central to the reform, strategies are closely related to the policy of decentralization, whereby higher education institutions have been given mopre autonomy to run their own businesses. (Mok, 2006: 103)

This trend of decentralization has led to a surge in Min-Ban universities (民班, literally 'Classes for the People Universities') and the development of transnational institutions of higher education in China (F. T. Huang, 2005: 170–2; Mok, 2006: 104–6). The popularity of Min-Ban universities and institutes of learning is so overwhelming that even the *New Yorker* has reported on the phenomenon of the Li Yang Crazy English and Culture Training Centers [李阳疯狂英语文化培训中心]. In his intense English and culture training camps, the founder Li Yang [李阳] has used the motto 'Conquer English to Make China Stronger!' to motivate his students to be prepared for the influx of foreign visitors to China (Osnos, 2008: 44). In addition to Min-Ban institutions, transnational institutes such as the Hopkins-Nanjing Center, Associated Colleges in China, and the IES programmes in Beijing and Shanghai are market leaders in the Chinese transnational education market. These trends are likely to continue in the near future.

We have at last come full circle along the rim of our wheel of discourse concerning the future of the academic journal in China. I hope this chapter has made a first step towards the socio-historical analysis encouraged by Zhang. While the dominant patterns of history and contemporary conditions in China remain undecided, inside every cloud there is always a silver lining. My hope for the future of information management in China lies in a firm belief in the people of China and the overseas Chinese. This hope, however, depends on the role that the academic journal will play in the future of China's information management industry. Z. Q. Zhang[11] reports:

[Today] within the Chinese Academy, [the academic journal] is the most crucial medium for the evaluation of scholarly contribution. Within universities and research institutions, the publication of articles in academic journals and other academic works is essential for promotion. Some major universities will only recognize articles published in major academic journals. For example, in the Natural Sciences, academics must be published in journals that are recognized by the international Science Citation Index (SCI);[12] scholars in the Humanities and the Social Sciences must have articles in journals that are a part of the international Social Science Citation Index (SSCI)[13] or the national Chinese Social Science Citation Index (CSSCI).[14] Some graduate programs at research institutions stipulate the publication of articles in an academic journal related to their respective disciplines as a part of the requirements for masters' and PhD degrees. In summation, academic journals play a crucial role in the Chinese Academy. (Z. Q. Zhang, personal communication, 2008)

Despite the contemporary significance of the academic journal in China, journals as a form of publication are less than 200 years old. As a form of periodical, the journal belongs to a format for the dissemination of new ideas that only began when Robert Morrison established the first Chinese periodical, the *China Monthly Magazine* [查世俗每月统计传], in 1815 (Fang, 1997; Ge, 1935; H. Huang, 2001; Zhang, 2007: 3). In light of the relatively recent appearance of the journal format as a medium for information exchange, there is hope that scholars within the Chinese academy will choose to define the academic journal as the refuge for the relatively free exchange of worthy ideas. Chinese scholars and other members of the academic community believe that 'digitization' (which facilitates the exchange of information through its ease of access and its low cost of production) and 'internationalization' (which brings Chinese academic journals up to a global standard of publication) should be the primary focus in the future development of the academic journal in China (Z. Q. Zhang, personal communication, 2008). In patient sympathy, I continue to watch from afar with full hope that one day in the not so distant future, the publication of Chinese academic journals might indeed allow 'the blossoming of hundreds of flowers as numerous schools of thought enjoy the light of day' [百花齐放百家争鸣] (a paraphrase of a Confucian idiom made both famous and infamous by China's great helmsman Mao).

Notes

1. As this chapter comprises approximately 5,000 words, each word of this chapter will represent the passage of one year of the history of information management in China.
2. By internet, I mean to include search engines, webpages, blogs, MySpace, Skype, MSN chat, and the like, which are now the medium for the exchange of new information.
3. Chinese scholars and researchers prefer the acronym STM for scientific, technical, medical and professional journals. For the sake of clarity and in keeping with the title of this volume, I have chosen to use the more usual term 'academic journals' throughout this chapter.
4. The National Science and Technology Library [国家科技图书文献中心] is available in Chinese at *http://www.nstl.gov.cn/index.html*.
5. See Rice (2000) for an article with this very title.
6. Here I am referring to the title of Saussy (2002), the second chapter of which provides a wealth of information on Jesuits and print culture in China.
7. According to tradition, the Confucian canon is composed of the four books and five classics [四书五经]. The four books are the *Great Learning* [大学], the *Doctrine of the Mean* [中庸], the *Analects of Confucius* [论语] and the *Mencius* [孟子]. The five classics are texts compiled or edited by Confucius. These are *The Book of Changes* [易经], *The Book of Poetry* [诗经], *The Book of Rites* [礼记], *The Book of History* [书经] and the *Spring and Autumn Annals* [春秋].
8. For the general Chinese reading public, the *People's Daily* remains the definitive source for the public dissemination of official Chinese government policy on a wide variety of issues. Those who are interested in the very complex role that Deng Tuo played during the political upheavals in Maoist era China should look forward to a forthcoming monograph on this topic by the Lu Xun and Deng Tuo expert James R. Pusey.
9. Here the separate mentioning of Taiwan and China is not an attempt to make any political statement but merely distinguishes two entities that have their own individual academic systems.
10. Mr Ma is a consultant for the Asia and Middle East Division of the New York Public Library and can be contacted via e-mail: *johntajenma@att.net*.
11. Professor Zhang Zhiqiang is currently the Director of the Institute of Publishing Science at Nanjing University and also the Harvard-Yenching Postdoctoral Fellow in Book Culture and Librarianship. He may be contacted via e-mail: *njuzzq@gmail.com*.
12. The SCI can be accessed at *http://thomsonreuters.com/products_services/scientific/Web_of_Science*.
13. The SSCI can be accessed at *http://www.thomsonreuters.com/products_services/scientific/Social_Sciences_Citation_Index*. In the USA, Thomson-Reuters is currently integrating access to both the SCI and the SSCI as a product known as Web of Knowledge.
14. The CSSCI can be accessed at *http://cssci.nju.edu.cn/index.htm*. Thomson-Reuters has announced plans to introduce a product line that will allow international users to access the CSSCI.

Bibliography

Baensch, R. E. (2003) 'Introduction', in: R. E. Baensch (ed.) *The Publishing Industry in China* [中国出版], New Brunswick, NJ: Transaction Publishers, pp. 25–50.

Bin, F. and Miao, Q. H. (2005) 'Electronic publications for Chinese public libraries: challenges and opportunities', *The Electronic Library* 23(2): 181–8.

Brokaw, C. J. and Chow, K. W. (eds) (2005) *Printing and Book Culture in Late Imperial China*, Berkeley, CA: University of California Press.

Buckwalter, C. (2003) 'Guidelines for magazine publishing in China', in: R. E. Baensch (ed.) *The Publishing Industry in China* [中国出版], New Brunswick, NJ: Transaction Publishers, pp. 1–17.

De Burgh, H. (2003) *The Chinese Journalist: Mediating Information in the World's Most Populous Country*, London and New York: Routledge.

Fang, H. Q. [方汉奇] (1997) *A History of Modern Chinese Journalism* [中国近代报刊史], Beijing: Renmin University Press [人民大学出版社].

Ge, G. Z. [戈公振] (1935) *Chinese Journalism History* [中国报业史], Shanghai: The Commercial Press [商务印书馆].

Huang, F. T. (2005) 'The growth and development of transnational higher education in China', in: K. H. Mok and R. James (eds) *Globalization and Higher Education in East Asia*, Singapore: Marshall Cavendish Academic, pp. 170–84.

Huang, H. [黄瑚] (2001) *A History of Chinese Journalism* [中国新闻史], Shanghai: Fudan University Press [复旦大学出版社].

Kong, S. Y. (2005) *Consuming Literature: Best Sellers and the Commercialization of Literary Production in Contemporary China*. Stanford: Stanford University Press.

McGowan, I. (2003) 'Book publishing in China', in: R. E. Baensch (ed.) *The Publishing Industry in China* [中国出版], New Brunswick, NJ: Transaction Publishers, pp. 51–66.

Mok, K. H. (2006) *Education Reform and Education Policy in East Asia*, Oxon: Routledge.

Osnos, E. (2008) 'Crazy English', *The New Yorker*, 28 April, pp. 44–51.

Rice, J. P. (2000) 'In the wake of Orientalism', *Comparative Literature Studies* 37(2): 223–38.

Saussy, H. (2002) *Great Walls of Discourse and Other Adventures in Cultural China*, Cambridge: Harvard Asia Center.

Sleeboom, M. (2004) *Academic Nations in China and Japan*, London and New York: Routledge.

Tsien, T. H. (1985) 'Chemistry and chemical technology', in: J. Needham (ed.) *Science and Civilization in China* [李约瑟] (Vol. 5), Cambridge: Cambridge University Press.

Twitchett, D. C. (1983) *Printing and Publishing in Medieval China*, New York: Frederic C. Beil Publishing.

Wang, J. X. (2003) 'Scientific, technical, medical, and professional publishing', in: R. E. Baensch (ed.) *The Publishing Industry in China* [中国出版], New Brunswick, NJ: Transaction Publishers, pp. 67–84.

Yao, F. S. [姚福申] (2005) *A History of Editing in China.* [中国编辑史], Shanghai: Fudan University Press [复旦大学出版社] .

Yeh, W. H. (1990) *The Alienated Academy*, Cambridge, MA: Council on East Asian Studies, Harvard University.

Zhang, X. T. (2007) *The Origins of the Modern Chinese Press: The Influence of the Protestant Missionary Press in Late Qing China*, London and New York: Routledge.

Zhang, Y. M. (2008) *Opening Ceremony of the 29th Olympics*, Beijing and New York: National Broadcast Company.

Part V
Digital transformations

17

Effects of the internet lifecycle on product development

Michiel van der Heyden and Ale de Vries

If we are to write about the future of the academic journal, we need to look at its historic role first. What is it that it does, and why? What are the forces that shaped its existence, and how are these forces changing to affect its future?

At its core, scholarly communication is about the exchange of ideas. This goes back to the days of René Descartes, whose work was published by the Elzevir brothers in seventeenth-century Holland. Descartes exchanged letters with his peers in other academic centres in Europe, writing about his work and discoveries. Those peers commented on his letters, and also sent the letters and their comments on to others. This laid the groundwork for today's principle of scholarly knowledge exchange – specifically, sharing one's ideas to allow others to comment on and validate those ideas, and to let them build upon those ideas for their own work.

As this concept evolved over the centuries, and exploded into large-scale adoption in Western society following the Second World War, it was influenced by, and influenced the way research was conducted and organized. Formal publication became the standard for getting credited for breakthrough discoveries, which in turn has an effect on research funding; furthermore, capitalization on discoveries became more dependent on published work, as, for example, patents are granted dependent on when and by whom a certain discovery was published.

In a nutshell, this basic set of forces has shaped scientific publishing as it exists today, and has created a symbiotic relationship between publishers and the academic community that is strongly tied to the fundamental characteristics of how research is done and evaluated.

The current state of journal publishing

More than any form of information exchange, scholarly communication is dependent on two major factors for its success:

- the will of contributors to share their work;
- the will of contributors to review each other's work.

For these contributors, this concept is ingrained into their everyday work – it is the essential facilitating process for their own core business: doing fundamental research to create new insights, to improve products and services, and to improve quality of life.

Elsevier sees itself as an organizer of this facilitating process. Traditionally, this has taken the shape of centralizing the review and exchange of scientific papers, and Elsevier – as many other publishers – has built a substantial operation around this. To the academic community, this has proven to be of great value: the economies of scale associated with centralizing a complex process like peer-review publishing has facilitated the widespread exchange of scholarly information, while continuously improving the quality control embedded in the process, and lowering the total cost.

These days, Elsevier's contribution to the global research community focuses on four areas, reflecting both the company's traditional role, as well as its focus on innovation and progress. They are defined as follows:

- *World-class information*: Elsevier publishes trusted, leading-edge scientific, technical and medical (STM) information – pushing the frontiers and fuelling a continuous cycle of exploration, discovery and application.

- *Global dissemination and preservation*: Elsevier disseminates and preserves STM literature to meet the information needs of the world's present and future scientists and clinicians.

- *Innovative tools*: Elsevier develops electronic tools that demonstrably improve the productivity of those it serves.

- *A commitment to working together*: Elsevier works in partnership with the communities it serves to advance scholarship and improve lives. This interrelationship is expressed the company's motto, *Non Solus* – 'not alone'.

Changing forces

With the emergence of internet technology, economies of scale in the information industry still exist, but in different ways, thus changing the parameters under which the classic peer-review model has evolved.

Until about two decades ago, no real global and high-capacity infrastructure for communication and information exchange existed, and if it did to any extent, it was the sole domain of multinational companies and organizations. This is no longer the case. The internet is open, owned by no one and everyone, and although it provides companies like Elsevier with the opportunity to lift their traditional role to a higher level, it also allows smaller organizations – and even individuals – to benefit from the economies of scale that were previously not available to them.

Since the emergence of the internet, web technologies have continuously evolved, and have spawned new applications or have made existing applications easier to build. Over the past few years the pace of evolution has increased significantly, and the sophistication of technology and tools nowadays is reaching a level that allows large numbers of people – including laymen – to create content for and communicate through the web in a way that publishers could only dream of a decade ago. This development, sometimes characterized as 'Web 2.0', is unfolding at our feet, and publishers like Elsevier need to assess how this affects the forces this shape their business, and rethink the role they play in their communities.

Web 2.0

Tim O'Reilly is credited with popularizing the term 'Web 2.0', and he elaborates extensively on its meaning in his seminal article, 'What is Web 2.0' (O'Reilly, 2005). It is not our intention to scrutinize his definition, or to come up with an authoritative one of our own. Instead, we would like to point out how relatively new developments in web technology and applications are gradually changing the way people interact with online information, and how this relates to the world of academic publishing.

At the time that the world wide web started to get adopted by mainstream users, the level of expertise needed for generating online content was still considerable – only people with sufficient knowledge of coding and markup languages and with access to web servers, were able to generate and publish online content to any significant extent. Consequently, the one-way nature of traditional publishing was maintained, and arguably even amplified – it was far easier for everyone to access large bodies of content on a large scale than it ever was before, but not necessarily equally easier for everyone to publish content.

As the web has evolved, so technologies have become sophisticated. User-friendly layers have been added on top of complex design applications; computer code has become increasingly modulated; and architectures have become more standard and open, allowing applications to interface in a common way. This has greatly lowered the barrier for layman internet users to start putting their 'stuff' online – their own webpages, their pictures, their written work, their music and their videos – and to leave their mark on other people's stuff: to link to it, to comment on it and to discuss it.

If anything, this is what Web 2.0 is all about – a gradual evolution of internet technology that has made it functionally easier to put things online, and that, in combination with the ever-growing penetration of high-speed internet connections and cheap computers, has led to an accelerated growth of end-user participation in online communications and generating online content.

Examples of this movement are abundant. Established services like Amazon and IMDB have been incorporating user feedback on their sites for ages, allowing users to write reviews of products and movies, respectively, and thus creating a review system that derives authority from the sheer number of reviews, instead of relying on the individual opinions of a few (alleged) experts (see, for example, Figure 17.1).

Technologies like CSS (*http://www.w3.org/Style/CSS/*) allow people to write pieces of text and put them online, without the need to know

Figure 17.1 Example of user feedback on Amazon

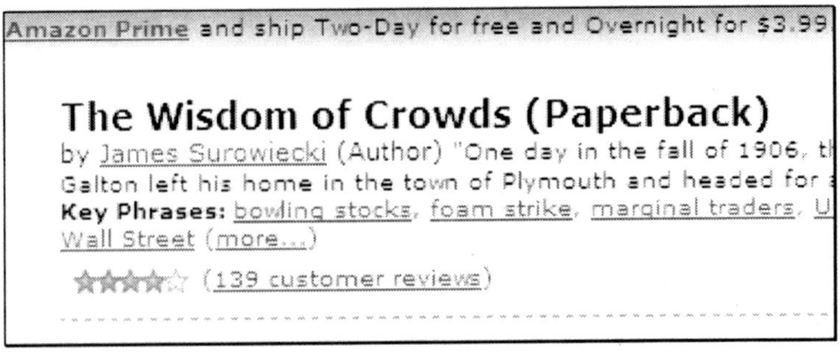

Amazon Prime and ship Two-Day for free and Overnight for $3.99

The Wisdom of Crowds (Paperback)

by James Surowiecki (Author) "One day in the fall of 1906, t| Galton left his home in the town of Plymouth and headed for | **Key Phrases:** bowling stocks, foam strike, marginal traders, U| Wall Street (more...)

★★★★☆ (139 customer reviews)

HTML markup to format the text correctly for display on a webpage – CSS does it all for them. The growth of the number of web logs is directly attributed to this, as it has allowed more people to write online content, and with more efficiency. Another good example is the wiki movement, of which Wikipedia is the most notable exponent: an online encyclopaedia, containing articles written and edited by end users like you and me (Figure 17.2). Preliminary research shows that, seemingly, Wikipedia is on average as factually correct as renowned works like the *Encyclopaedia Britannica* (Giles, 2005).

The standardization of data formats has made it easier for content to be distributed over the internet. RSS (*http://cyber.law.harvard.edu/rss/rss.html*) – based on the XML (*http://www.w3.org/XML/*) group of computer languages – is a standard for structuring data logically and consistently in a way that makes it universally readable by a myriad of applications. This allows online content pages to be 'syndicated' – in other words, a webpage or a blog to be 'read' by something other than a human being using a web browser – and thus be reused in many other applications.

Figures 17.3 and 17.4 show one of these applications. The screenshot of Figure 17.3 is of a blog post – basically, an entry in an online diary.

Figure 17.2 Example of a Wikipedia article being edited

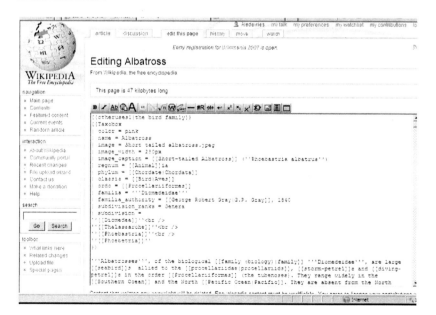

Figure 17.3 A blog in 'standard' view

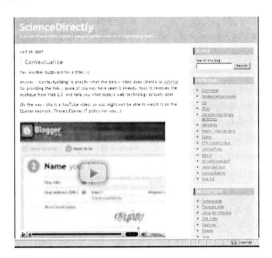

Figure 17.4 A blog in RSS format

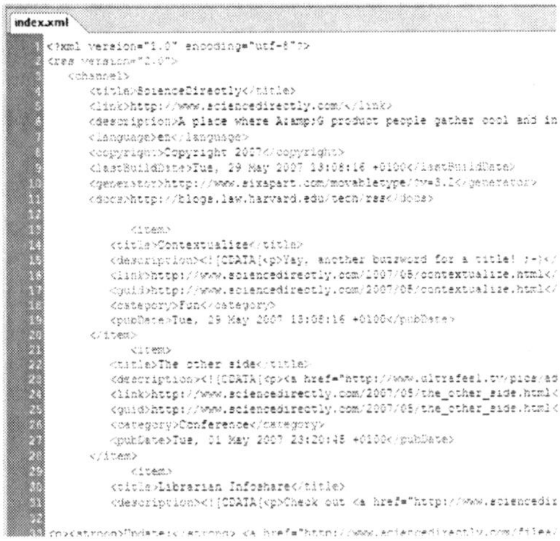

It is formatted to be read online, so anyone bumping into that page can read it quite easily. The screenshot in Figure 17.4 is of exactly the same page – but displayed in the RSS format. It is not easy for an actual human being to read, but it is not meant to be – it is meant to be read by another piece of software, which can then process it further into something else.

The standardization of data formats allows information to be put together by computer, where earlier manual, human intelligence was needed. A common application of this is the use of structured location names and an online map service to display certain themed information in its relative geographical context. Such an example is shown in Figure 17.5, where *Nature* has used Google Maps to create a map of avian flu locations.

Higher internet bandwidth, on top of these flexible technologies, allows services like YouTube (*http://www.youtube.com*) and Flickr (*http://www.flickr.com*) to flourish – high-volume media files, like video and photography, are now posted online by everyday users who want to share their experiences with their friends, families and other people who might be interested (Figure 17.6).

Figure 17.5 *Nature's* avian flu map

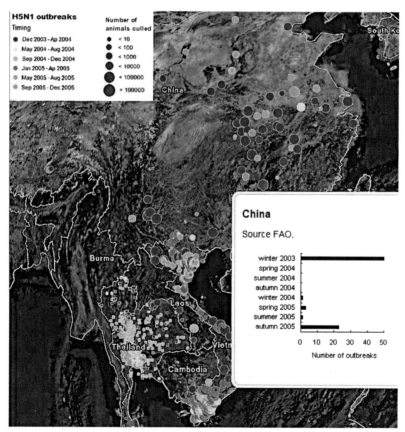

Source: http://www.nature.com/nature/googleearth/avianflu1.kml.

Figure 17.6 Photo sharing on Flickr

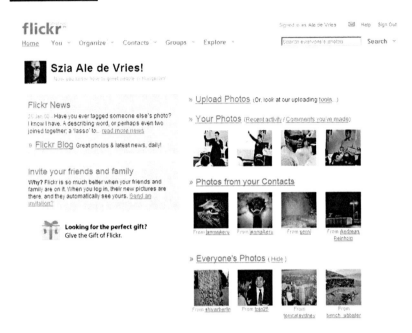

Building on all this, many sites are dedicated to managing one's social network online, and sharing one's life. The enormous number of youngsters on MySpace (*http://www.myspace.com*) is a good example. Similarly, LinkedIn (*http://www.linkedin.com*) is a site that brings this concept to the professional world, allowing professionals all over the globe to create their own profile (Figure 17.7) and link to one another, thus creating an extended network that can be used for job referrals, business propositions, etc.

Web 2.0 and the academic environment

The trends in consumer-oriented online services prompt one to think about what the effect of changing online behaviour will be – or could be – on scholarly communication. This is truly a mind leap – consumers are very different from academic researchers, yet both groups consist of people interacting with computers and online services. The challenge, therefore, lies in identifying what the core differentiators are – what makes an online service specifically useful for an academic researcher? These are the characteristics that Elsevier looks for, as this is where it can

Figure 17.7 A user profile on LinkedIn

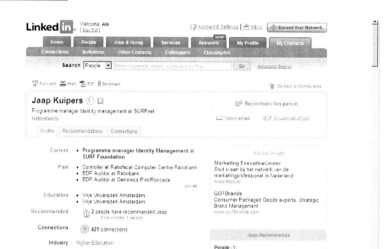

create value amidst the big-gun players going for the general public's mindshare and eyeballs.

User behaviour

It is Elsevier's aim to provide information and workflow solutions that help institutional decision-makers and researchers to create significant value by building insights, enabling advancement in research, and improving research-driven returns-on-investment.

If we want to develop solutions that really make a difference, we need to know how and where to improve the life of the customer, and for that, we need insight into some fundamental elements of ourselves and the environment. A good understanding of our internal competences is a starting point, and with a publishing history of many years – as outlined earlier – knowledge about primary scientific information is secured within the company. Furthermore, we need to develop a deep understanding, as discussed earlier in this chapter, of the way the internet as a working space is evolving. And last but not least, we need to understand, in detail, the way our end users behave.

For this, and mainly in the context of product development, we have analysed the huge amount of information Elsevier has generated for the development of products like ScienceDirect and Scopus – user tests, field studies, literature, market research, etc. The result of this is a framework that helps to get insight into an academic researcher's workflow, which Elsevier has found to aid in identifying opportunities for new tools (Frans Heeman, Joy van Baren and Stephan Stipdonk, personal communication). To make these insights more active and less abstract we often use personas: a detailed fictional character that encompasses everything what we know about a certain type of user.

A day in the life

John has been a professor of molecular biology at a well recognized US university for six years. He supervises three PhD students and teaches and advises a class of MSc students. At the same time, he collectively has up to ten research projects running. John is an experienced Mac user. He has one PC for writing papers and another for running experiments in his office; however he is not a great surfer of the internet. His main work is to research and develop new molecules in software. He does benchworking with a research assistant.

His secondary work includes editorial work and some faculty teaching and administrative work. The research groups of which John is a member generate a lot of e-mail. Of all the e-mails John receives, only a few are relevant to him, and filtering out the important ones is time-consuming. Like any scientist, John does want to stay informed about what his groups are doing, but he feels this process should be less intrusive than a constant flow of e-mails. He wants to be able to tap into discussions at a time of his choosing and in a manner that suits him. Discussions over e-mail tend to result in a lot of duplicate messages being sent to him from different people.

John has collaborators all around the world. He mainly uses e-mail for communication. He prefers going to conferences. He says, 'I see colleagues at conferences and meetings (two or three times a year) and I use these as opportunities to keep in touch and collaborate'. He rarely uses the telephone for collaboration purposes. He also asks advice from professional consultants regarding his work.

Data management

The storage and archiving of documents is for a large part done on an individual level. There is a lack of a shared data store. The effort put into organizing documents and data is being replicated by all individuals in the group. It is hard enough for John to keep track of the data in his own groups, never mind tap into other groups' data. Being able to see the data from key articles and related researchers could be of great value. As a scientist you want control over who you share your data with. Not all data are suitable for the public domain.

John has scattered his data over different computers and applications. He uses e-mail, FTP, CD-ROMs or a memory-stick to move information between computers and applications. Access to full-text articles can be problematic outside of the university network, so he downloads full-text articles and prints them out to ensure he has permanent access to them. John uses EndNote as the tool to organize his personal collection of articles. Files he receives via e-mail are stored in local folders on his computers to avoid exceeding his e-mail storage quota. He has developed a personal skill to organize his data but his 'system' cannot be readily used by others.

Framework

Figure 17.8 presents a workflow framework for an academic researcher. An incremental bottom-up approach was used to create this framework. Rather than fitting the data into preconceived categories, we started grouping similar data elements into higher-level categories, which were later grouped into activities, tasks and roles.

The main rationale behind this framework is that user roles, consisting of main tasks, are the main guiding angle, and within these roles and tasks we can identify common activities:

- *Roles*: A top level is formed by user roles that are to a large extent mutually exclusive. Depending on users' workflow, one or more of these roles will be applicable. The most important selection criterion in determining this level was to be as specific about our users as possible, rather than being more generally applicable to any knowledge worker. At the same time, we wanted this level to be largely independent of other factors, such as subject area, organization type, position in organization, seniority or technology. We look mainly at academia and government, and less so at the corporate sector. However, when we come across corporate-specific information, we will include it (e.g. patents are critical for corporate organizations, same as articles in academia). We include students, as

Figure 17.8 Workflow framework for an academic researcher

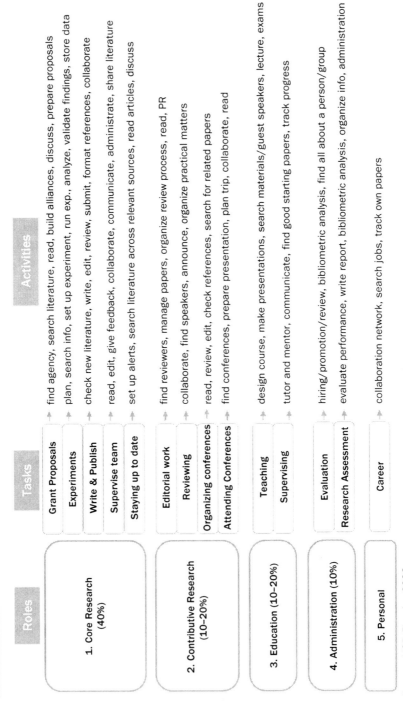

Roles	Tasks	Activities
1. Core Research (40%)	Grant Proposals	find agency, search literature, read, build alliances, discuss, prepare proposals
	Experiments	plan, search info, set up experiment, run exp., analyze, validate findings, store data
	Write & Publish	check new literature, write, edit, review, submit, format references, collaborate
	Supervise team	read, edit, give feedback, collaborate, communicate, administrate, share literature
	Staying up to date	set up alerts, search literature across relevant sources, read articles, discuss
2. Contributive Research (10–20%)	Editorial work	find reviewers, manage papers, organize review process, read, PR
	Reviewing	collaborate, find speakers, announce, organize practical matters
	Organizing conferences	read, review, edit, check references, search for related papers
	Attending Conferences	find conferences, prepare presentation, plan trip, collaborate, read
3. Education (10–20%)	Teaching	design course, make presentations, search materials/guest speakers, lecture, exams
	Supervising	tutor and mentor, communicate, find good starting papers, track progress
4. Administration (10%)	Evaluation	hiring/promotion/review, bibliometric analysis, find all about a person/group
	Research Assessment	evaluate performance, write report, bibliometric analysis, organize info, administration
5. Personal	Career	collaboration network, search jobs, track own papers

Source: UCD Elsevier, 2006.

well as librarians in as far as related to the general research workflow. We have identified the following roles, based on our data:

- core research;
- contributive research;
- education;
- management/administration;
- personal.

■ *Tasks*: The second level contains specific tasks within roles. These tasks are still independent of other factors, similar to the roles.

■ *Activities*: The third level contains common activities that are carried out across roles and tasks. Explicit care should be taken to check how these elements may span multiple roles and tasks. Common activities include:

- searching information;
- reading literature;
- organizing information;
- analysis;
- collaboration;
- sharing information;
- preparing presentations;
- administration tasks.

Within the descriptions of roles, tasks and activities, we highlight recurring themes such as:

- any subject-specific information;
- differences related to position;
- tools;
- problems;
- trends;
- user wishes – suggestions and 'dreams' expressed by users;
- user needs – observed, actual user needs.

Core research

Around 40 per cent of time is spent on core research. This also includes such information organization as searching, reading and writing, and any work to do with grant proposals. Senior staff spend less time than this and more time on administration. Within this role the main needs and problems are:

- Balancing research-related work with bureaucratic work. Grant applications divert scientists from spending time doing science. A funded chemist in the USA can easily spend 300 hours per year writing proposals. While some of this effort undoubtedly generates knowledge, much of it is bureaucratic 'bean counting' and adds little of social value.

- Balancing risk and innovation with chance of acceptance.

- Knowing whether all the relevant literature has been found.

- The need to keep coming up with original research.

- The need to keep a log/archive/backup of gathered data.

- Is research time-sensitive? Does it require upfront planning of method and timing; appropriate equipments, substances, etc.? Depending on the experiment there may also be the need to get approval (e.g. animal testing).

- Sometimes it is not possible to break during experiments.

- Factors outside researcher's control may cause delay (availability of lab/room, equipment, enlisting participants).

- Research also may involve spin-off projects, patents or licensing.

- Type of research and analysis differs per subject area (e.g. experiment with participants, lab experiment, simulation, literature review).

Contributive research

Approximately 10–20 per cent of time is spent on contributive research. This can be much higher for specific user groups such as editors. Within this role the main needs and problems are:

- Editorial work, such as finding good reviewers with the right knowledge. In addition, authors want quick feedback, while reviewers want as much time as possible.

- General correspondence with authors, reviewers, associative editors, administrative staff and publishing staff. This is the single-most time-consuming part of job – it never ends, new tasks arrive constantly, and there is always more to do.

- Reviewing – manually checking references.

- Organizing conferences, seminars – this is very time-intensive and often has to be done in own time.
- Attending conferences, seminars – there is little or no administrative support, so researchers have to plan their own travels and accommodation, which takes time.

Education

Approximately 10–20 per cent of time is spent on education. Some people don't teach at all (e.g. researchers on special grants), while others teach most of their time (e.g. lecturers). Within this role the main needs and problems are:

- Teaching often increases the time pressure of researchers because it is so time-intensive and there is a large administrative component.
- Finding good examples is tough.
- Depending on position or main interest, research can be seen as taking time away from teaching, or the other way around.

Management/administration

Around 10 per cent of time is spent on management/administration. This is higher for senior staff, and can even be close to 100 per cent. Within this role the main needs and problems are:

- Evaluating people – different name variants can make it difficult to track an author in a system.
- The difficulty finding all publications in one database.
- Finding all publications and citations for one author.
- Objective measures for evaluation – on the one hand there is a need for objective measures to evaluate a person, while on the other there is much criticism of the existing measures (mainly impact factor).
- Differences between institutes and departments in how people are evaluated.
- Research assessment is time-intensive.

Personal

Academic researchers have insufficient time to devote to personal matters. PhD students nearing the end of their contract will spend some more time here. Senior researchers make sure they publish in journals with more status, partly to increase their success rate when applying for grants. The main needs and problems are:

- There is a need to come up with original research.
- More ties with industry are also needed, leading to more applied research, development of technologies and publishing patents.

Concepts

We have seen that the web has undergone a dramatic change in the last few years with a shift towards increasing user interaction with content. As well as using the insights from the user behaviour framework, several concepts were shaped from a set of themes created by the ScienceDirect team. ScienceDirect, Elsevier's online full-text platform, has a programme to translate these changes to solutions for the scientific communities.

Collaboration tools

New forms of media have resulted in the democratization of information. Nowadays everyone is able to add information to the internet. Globalization is in theory a good thing. Transparency, freedom, democracy and accessibility are what we want. However, this also results in an overload of information. Which information can be trusted? In reality this results in confusion and uncertainty as to whether the information is complete: 'Have I missed anything?' In addition, there remains the fact that information can be manipulated, as we see happening in the news every day. The predicted democratization of information turns into chaos and disinformation.

There is therefore an urgent need to bring transparency back to the information. In a way this is already happening through sharing and collective intelligence. 'Nowadays, a product or a brand becomes a platform where knowledge, resources and people come together in what can be called the economy of collaboration' (Artmiks and André Platteel, personal communication).

Researchers, students, authors, librarians, and teachers are always looking for the most relevant and up-to-date scientific literature. The number of electronic sources has increased enormously. Users would like to have tools that allow them to store and organize scientific articles and understand this kind of (scientific) information. User tests have suggested that the combination of organizing, sharing and discussing is seen as useful and has added value over traditional reference managers, such as EndNote. Furthermore, users would like to share and discuss interesting papers and webpages with others as well. This could be with their research group, their class or their colleagues, but also with people who share the same interest, but may be working at the other side of the globe.

Knowing all this makes it easy to understand the need to start exploring the opportunities of mixing the qualified Elsevier information with user-generated content. The collaboration tool, 2collab.com (Figure 17.9), will be first step into this direction. This tool should offer functionality where end users can store, share and discuss bookmarks to scientific information. It aims to fill in a 'missing piece' in the user's workflow.

From a business perspective, we would like to increase the visibility of our current products and content like ScienceDirect and Scopus. As it will be a free product, stickiness, how to keep and bring end users to the primary products, and usage, i.e. the increase of full-text downloads on ScienceDirect and more usage of Scopus, are key factors.

Social bookmarking is becoming an accepted and highly used web tool. Del.icio.us and Nature's Connotea.org have paved this road. Where

Figure 17.9 Screenshot of a collaboration tool

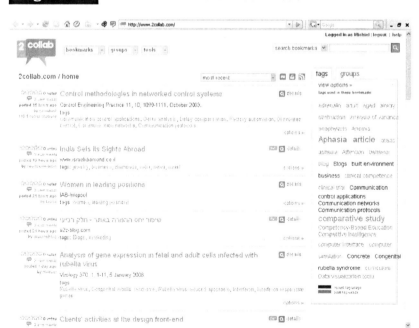

these tools focus on the individual use, with 2Collab there is a focus on the collaboration, going beyond existing bookmarking tools by allowing users to share information within defined groups, such as classes or research teams.

According to a user trial organized by the Library of the University of Amsterdam, the main functionality options of social bookmarking tools are:

1. Quick and easy bookmarking and storing of literature references

2. Organizing a personal reference collection

3. Discovering new literature references through group functionality

Indeed, in the group discussion and from the questionnaire at the start of the user trial, a large majority of the participants indicated the need for these functionalities. Especially a clear need existed for (1) organizing literature references and adding personal comments 'to keep the value of what I have read'; and (2) to use comments and qualifications of colleagues to select literature for reading. In addition, it became apparent that a majority of the participants did not have a systematic method for finding and managing literature references. In other words, academic social referencing tools solve a problem that really appears to exist. (Heesakkers et al., 2007)

According to the study respondents, the two most important potential improvements offered by academic social referencing tools are the better management of literature references and improved collaboration with colleagues regarding literature (Heesakkers et al., 2007). These points are at the foundation of Elsevier's strategy to build a professional tool that focuses on collaboration.

This first step in the sphere of user-generated content will be a starting-point for future development. In combination with author and institutional information, it creates a social network. From the publishing point of view it will give an insight into scientific trends and the general opinion of individual research.

Dynamic usage information

Usage can be used as an indicator of value in much the same manner as citations. The current usage reporting system is geared to internal users and librarians, and accumulates information about all aspects of usage of ScienceDirect, allowing analysis across multiple demographic dimensions. The focus here, however, is on giving customers information about the usage of this online platform with a focus on full-text downloads. Two directions can be distinguished: (1) integrating usage information in existing products, giving users new ways to select and assess information, and (2) creating an autonomous service that allows users to measure the performance of academic output.

Integration of usage information

This concept is best explained by some examples:

- *Most read articles*: Presentation of the top x downloaded articles per subject area and/or journal (e.g. see Figure 17.10). This will provide the end user with a quick insight into a specific field. This would be especially appreciated by undergraduates.

- *Presenting the actual download numbers*: This will provide users with another indicator of the relative value of articles, and will provide authors and editors with usage data (see Figures 17.11 to 17.12).

Figure 17.10 *New York Times* 'most popular articles'

Figure 17.11 Mock-up of filter option for most downloaded articles on ScienceDirect's search result page

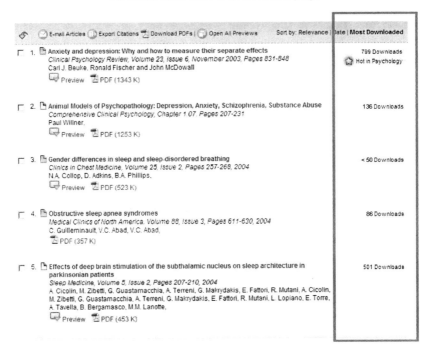

- *Search queries*: For many undergraduates, especially for non-native speakers of English, it can be difficult to select or even come up with the best or correct search terms. Like Google we could present search terms suggestions based on the queries used by others (Figure 17.13).

- *Usage data service*: Another option will be to provide web services for article usage information for integration with other products/systems. This will make it possible to present usage information on external systems (Figure 17.14). In this example the profile information on a social networking tool is connected to an article by the author.

- *The measurement of academic output*: Research performance measurement allows universities, corporations, funding agencies and governments to make investment decisions by means of information that allows them to benchmark their own performance and spot trends, talent and new science based on the usage of the largest single full-text database mapped to authors and institutions. Using usage information gives customers a two-year head-start over existing

Figure 17.12 Mock-up of a graphical representation of the article usage over time on ScienceDirect

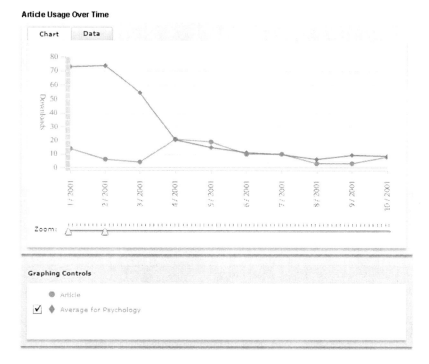

Figure 17.13 Mock-up of search query suggestion

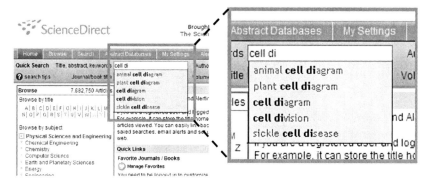

citation-based research performance measurement tools, because usage figures are two years ahead of citation figures. Figure 17.15 provides a mock-up of a research performance measurement tool based on usage information.

Figure 17.14 Mock-up of LinkedIn with article information

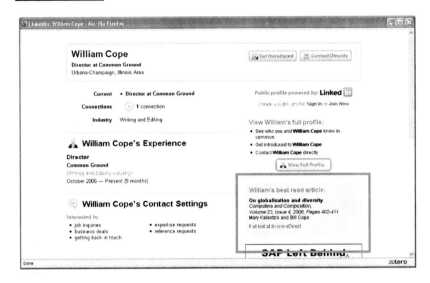

Figure 17.15 Mock-up of research performance measurement tool based on usage information

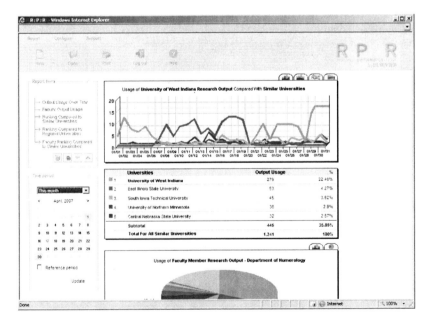

Conclusion

Academic publishers have traditionally played a key role in the dissemination of scholarly information. The forces that shaped that role are changing more rapidly than before, mostly due to the rise of the world wide web, and the development of technologies that upset the economies of scale traditionally associated with information distribution. As a result, publishing companies like Elsevier are rethinking major aspects of their businesses.

By looking at trends in the consumer information industry, it is possible to chart the background against which core user constituencies are using products and services. Combined with in-depth research into users' behaviours, likes and dislikes, it is possible to identify new applications that bring together traditional forms of scholarly information with user-generated content and analytics. This opens up new insights in ways that did not exist before, allowing researchers to both deepen their knowledge in their chosen fields, but also enabling them to branch out into new areas.

It is our challenge to guide the development of these new applications into a meaningful direction. This requires breaking with a paradigm in which the journal and its article are the sole pivotal point of scholarly information, and creating and executing a vision of a world in which the academic journal is one element, albeit a key one, in an ecosystem of applications that are rich in both content and functionality, and deeply embedded in the daily lives of our users.

Bibliography

Giles, J. (2005) 'Internet encyclopaedias go head to head', *Nature* 438: 900–1.

Heesakkers, H. J., Hoekstra, M. and van der Graaf, M. (2007) *Academic social referencing tools: a user trial with BibSonomy and Cite-U-Like organized by the Library of the University of Amsterdam*, Version 2007-03-07, Amsterdam: University of Amsterdam.

O'Reilly, T. (2005) 'What is Web 2.0?', available at: *http://www .oreillynet.com/pub/a/oreilly/tim/news/2005/09/30/what-is-web-20.html* (accessed 2 March 2009).

18

Beyond the static text: multimedia interactivity in academic journal publishing in the humanities and social sciences (not)

Andrew Jakubowicz

Four postulates of inertia

Despite the discourses that herald the innovation associated with Web 2.0 (Sharp and Salomon, 2008; Slane, 2008) and the opportunities created by open source and open access computing (Miller and Berners-Lee, 2008), there is a simple truth. The web has not delivered an interactive environment for ongoing engagement with scholarly research publishing that uses and is enlivened by multimedia data. There are four major reasons for this failure to bridge the two dominant silos – on the one hand multimedia data (video, audio, animation, real-time mapping etc.) with its possibilities for interactivity (as revealed for instance by, but not limited to, social networking on the web); and academic journal-based publishing, with its linear and traditionally constrained presentation of knowledge in 'finished' blocks, albeit illustrated and hyperlinked.

These four elements can be summarized as follows:

- a political economy of web publishing in which large multinational corporates aim to optimize returns by seeking ownership and control of intellectual property (IP) in discrete objects called 'papers' assignable to the authorship of single individuals or groups, while they minimize expenditure on infrastructure within an increasingly Fordian production-line environment (Smith, 1999, 2005) (complex and interactive multimedia publishing is perceived to have a low return-to-investment ratio, and has dangers to IP regimes associated with its continuing and 'unfinished' nature);

- a system of hierarchies of journals (based on esteem), the value of which to publisher, editor and author is a function of their difficulty to enter, while the demand by author communities to be published in high-impact titles assumes an efficiency factor in which papers represent the 'least-time-cost' form of publishing research outcomes;

- the control of access to journals acts as a rationing system ostensibly determined by peer esteem, but in fact controlled by well-established and usually traditionalist disciplinary elites who for the most part have neither the skills, motivation nor the experience to referee or manage the publication of interactive multimedia projects;

- younger scholars who might otherwise be innovators in the use of interactive digital media for publishing face disincentives both from the criteria used to assess for tenure and promotion (traditional journals, academic monographs) and the fact that older mentors have no experience in innovatory multimedia research and publishing and are unable to provide role models.

In this chapter I want to explore the case for each of these assertions, and then suggest a model for resolving this combination of factors that have hitherto been woven into a 'shark-net' of resistance to innovation.

The political economy of web publishing

In their analysis of the opportunities for publishing humanities and social sciences research in open source online journals in the UK, Heath et al. (2008) argue that the humanities and social sciences have been slow (compared with the physical and life sciences) to take up the opportunities offered by the new technologies. In preparing their case they explore the structure of journal publishing and in particular the development of open source and open access publishing. The expansion of the commercial publishing of journals has transformed the knowledge landscape, and has only been possible because of the knowledge management technologies underpinning the industry. However, the involvement of multinational corporations in the industry has had problematic consequences; high-status journals have enormous masthead value – value that depends on the competition for entry among prospective authors. With the ever-greater institutionalization of quality and impact metrics within national university funding models (Weale, 2007), driven by governments working with neo-liberal economic models dependent on 'objective' criteria, the intellectual property bound up in high-valued discipline-leading journals has become a source of serious struggle.

The complex economic base from which the intellectual property is generated includes many different forms of value creation. While the brain-work of the researchers/authors supplies the essential commodity, the value embedded in that commodity and the costs of realizing that value reveal the nub of the drive towards open access journals. Most research published in journals in the humanities and social sciences is produced by scholars employed either as full-time researchers or as combined teachers/researchers. Their salaries are paid by research grants or funds, and core funding to universities that is then allocated to 'research time'. The labour value of the research is thus already covered by the state or by other corporate funds, and is not an item with which most publishers need to concern themselves. The editorial role taken on by academic editors and the labour carried out by referees of submitted articles are also not covered by the journal publisher.

At this point, the process of realizing the value of the research in the marketplace begins – journals have to be sold to university libraries and research institutions. That is, for the research to be available, a cash exchange is necessary, and it is an exchange in which the purchasing parties have until recently had very little real leverage. Moreover, the IP produced by academic labour and paid for by the state (i.e. the public), is not freely available but rather has to be purchased at considerable cost (Brown et al. 2007).

Publishers argue that they play a crucial role in managing the process and realizing the value embedded in the research. Only they have the capacity to program and support the production process and utilize economies of scale to create the underlying knowledge management structures that allow effective database searching and delivery of high-quality products to users in a timely way. Some publishers recognize that they add value to something that already has value and accept the grey publishing preprint environment where drafts are circulated; usually they seek to control the IP at the point at which they start to introduce 'their' intellectual input via the editors and the reviewers. Moreover, and more importantly for our purposes, the Fordian production line approach that reduces all online journals produced by a publisher to basically the same format makes breakouts in creativity very unlikely and also costly.

Most innovation focuses on the bibliographical and search functions, rather than interactive or creative functions.

The open source movement of course confronts these issues from outset to final presentation – and has received strong government support in countries like Australia, where the Australian Research Council now mandates the free availability of government-funded research through open repositories. In the USA, Congress mandated in 2007 that any research funded through the National Institutes of Health had to be made publicly and freely available within a year of publication through the National Library of Medicine's PubMed Central online repository. In early 2008, Harvard University declared its own right to make available the work of its scholars published in other journals to the scholarly community without charge.

The Heath et al. (2008) survey of open access journals in the UK notes that the humanities and social sciences (HSS) still remain more dependent on print journals, and far less comfortable with journals that only appear in an online form. They ascribe this phenomenon to a number of important factors, one being the long half-life of research (especially in the humanities where the intellectual trajectory under review may stretch back decades), another being the low general level of funding for HSS research and thus the long development time in the writing of journal papers. Even here they note the rapid take-up of the JSTOR archive by HSS researchers, despite their reluctance to publish in electronic forms.

So the political economy of current journal publishing means that large publishers are unlikely to innovate, while individual researchers are less equipped with economic resources to do so easily. Even in the open access community such innovation is not widespread, as the craft-based design-driven innovation that is often thought necessary for HSS interactivity in publishing is not easily supported by most open-source systems.

Journal hierarchies, the publishing race and creative scholarship

Given the broader contextual constraints, how do the barriers between innovatory research and traditional publishing work in practice? Innovation in the use of interactive digital technologies in the gathering of data and the presentation of material is widespread. The UK humanities computing schemes over the last decade have generated substantial databases of materials from ancient history through to sociology and political science. In their joint attempt to find a shared common ground between the various stakeholders in the process of academic publishing, the Research Information Network (2007) argues that one of the key policy principles should be that 'researchers, publishers and others are innovative in exploiting new technologies, new publication and dissemination models and a variety of media to communicate the results of research as widely, rapidly and effectively as possible'. Yet we have seen that the boundary forces that exist seem to militate against such an outcome.

A British Academy report on peer review, metrics and quality (Weale, 2007) was unimpressed by most 'metric' based approaches, criticizing validity, reliability and the distorting effects such an approach might have on the quality of research and in particular, its direction. On my reading, at least, the Academy seemed to fear that more exploratory, challenging and quirky research would be underplayed, and publishers seeking high metric gradings would be drawn inevitably towards blander and more centre-ground research. Moreover, in their discussion of innovation in particular, they were aware of innovative projects that had failed in mainstream journals, only to be picked up by 'lesser' journals, and then becoming classics. However, the Academy was mainly concerned with the role of peer review in traditional publishing environments, and did not address alternative and innovatory forms of research publishing.

Innovatory forms of research may include, for instance, the use of extensive ethnographic video recording (a traditional practice in anthropology, which has produced the filmography and the bibliography as parallel but distinct forms of publishing) (see Kennedy, 2003), the application of animation and programming to the manipulation of images and their interpretation, and the development of interactive projects where the audience engagement changes the data and transforms the output through time (Dicks et al., 2005).

Yet even where this research is very interactive and seeks to produce interactivity as an outcome, it is reported in a fairly flat and traditional way (Khut, 2007). The Arden project at Indiana University is a valuable example of this issue. The team draws on Edward Castranova's 'Synthetic Worlds Initiative' to build a Shakespearean space 'that he could use as a platform for social-science experimentation while providing interesting and arguably useful content for players' (Castranova et al., 2008). It is an exciting and highly-proficient project, and yet even though the article about it is produced as a PDF file by the

IEEE MultiMedia journal, it contains no sense of interactivity, such as an embedded video file that presents some of the action and gives readers a feel of the experience. That said, in 2006 *IEEE MultiMedia* began to include a videoblog, where scholars can present and debate their perspectives. The first contributions are perhaps scholarly rather than creative, but there are undoubtedly possibilities for exploration, even if new additions to the blog tended to dry up in early 2007, within months of the initiative being launched (*IEEE MultiMedia* Editors, 2006).

Another project that works well online is Norie Neumark and Maria Miranda's 'Talking about the Weather' (Neumark and Miranda, 2006). It comes in many forms – including a series of installation and performance pieces. However, its online version works as a mixture of blog, photographic display, exhibitions, YouTube videos and essays, mostly backed by radiophonic pieces. It has both an artistic design problem that it seeks to solve, and a research question – what happens when you go into different societies seeking to have people simply breathe into the microphone while being videoed, in the name of combating global warming? The project is published through SCANZ, a New Zealand artists site (Solar Circuit) based on a creative residency camp in 2006. Yet publishing an article in a refereed journal that managed to capture the experience of the site – other than by linking to it – would be very difficult.

It is clear though that with a metric-driven government mindset, and competition for prestigious positions in prestigious institutions, early and mid-career researchers have to be very tough about how they allocate their time (Jaschik, 2008). One journal that has recognized this problem, *Vectors*, published out of the University of Southern California, has decided to 'wrap' the interactive project within a series of texts, thus bridging the divide between creative project and journal article (*http://www.vectorsjournal.org/*). These texts include the editors' comments, the author and creative director's statements, and a commentary field for audience engagement. Each issue is produced as a set of connected projects linked to a theme. *Vectors* seeks to bridge the humanities and social sciences, drawing in projects as diverse as interactive programmed onscreen games, photo/audio documentaries, political philosophy simulations and historical sociology.

The editors are closely connected with the Humanities, Arts, Science, and Technology Advanced Collaboratory (HASTAC – pronounced haystack) project (*http://hastac.org*), which also gives access to blogs such as those of MIT Humanities Professor Henry Jenkins. Jenkins uses his blog to publish multimedia interviews he does with scholars using the web for innovatory explorations – including one about a YouTube course at a California college, run by Alex Juhasz, in which YouTube becomes a publishing medium (*http://www.henryjenkins.org/2008/02/ learning_from_youtube_an_inter.html*).

These are extremely interesting and transformational publishing exercises, yet none can be encompassed by traditional journals. For the most part, the innovation is being carried by scholars in fairly secure situations who use their resources and influence to lever up the work of early-career researchers. An attempt to advance these innovations has been instituted through the Digital Arts and Humanities site created by the Centre for eResearch at Kings College London (*http://www.arts-humanities.net*), and by the US National Endowment for the Humanities Office for Digital Humanities, which opened in March 2008 (*http://www.neh.gov/ODH/ODHHome/tabid/36/Default.aspx*).

Commenting on the development of these resources and the emergence of e-publishing, HASTAC associate Cathy Davidson asks:

> Why use a new technology to address (badly, incompletely, and even falsely) one problem? Why not use a new technology to explore new possibilities? … And it should make us think about those things in terms of credentialing and the values we give to how we credential young scholars in a profession … Perhaps making a new kind of data base available in searchable form is even more valuable then yet another historical monograph that makes use of that data base? Maybe universities need to think about the kind of intellectual labor that goes into making such a data base available and usable. If we believe all Foucault has to tell us about what an archive is, then creating an archive is itself a form of argumentation and, indisputably, a major contribution to knowledge. That should constitute an argument for tenure at those institutions that collectively decide it should constitute tenure. (Davidson, 2008)

Power and control in academic publishing

During a research interview on innovation in multimedia publishing a senior MIT computing academic asked me what I saw as the problem. I spoke about gatekeepers and their reluctance to shift paradigms that had served them well. He said that the solution was clear – either go around them or wait till they die. It was an in-your-face comment that was designed to address the issues of institutional power and willingness to change. In many ways the 'going around' has occurred – new journals, particularly those with an interdisciplinary bent, are opening regularly, both through established and new commercial publishers, and in independent exercises online by university departments and centres (e.g. *Transforming Cultures eJournal* (*http://epress.lib.uts.edu.au/ojs/index .php/TfC*) or professional associations. Many of the latter use open source programs – such as DSpace (*http://dspace.org*) based at MIT, for both journal and repository development. Others use development environments and content management systems such as Joomla (*http://www.joomla.org*) and even the blog-focused Drupal (*http:// drupal.org*). As numerous reports have documented, the value of scholarly articles is in part derived from their validation by peers; yet with innovatory research and publishing pressing at the doors of the old established journals, there may not be sufficient or even any ranked peers capable of reviewing the new approaches.

Senior academics are not necessarily all that skilled at adapting their world views to constantly changing circumstances; while a minority will be anxious to grasp new opportunities, the majority will rely on the corpus of practice built up in a discipline over generations. Even where the ambition to innovate exists there may be barriers that simply cannot be overcome. A classic example of this problem can be found in the leading journal *American Historical Review* (*AHR*). The *AHR* has an electronic projects section (*http://www.indiana.edu/%7Eahr/elec- projects.html*), with the majority of projects associated with the advocacy of the late Roy Rosenzweig of George Mason University. Rosenzweig had established the Center for History and New Media (*http://chnm.gmu.edu*) as a focal point for innovation in the presentation of historical analysis (Rosenzweig, 2007). The pivotal test for the journal would be how it handled the challenge of a project on the American Civil War by Thomas and Ayers (2003), from the University of Virginia Center for Digital History. In introducing their project, they note:

> scholars have only begun to craft scholarship designed specifically for the electronic environment. In this article, we attempt to translate the fundamental components of professional scholarship – evidence, engagement with prior scholarship, and a scholarly argument – into forms that take advantage of the possibilities of electronic media. (Thomas and Ayres, 2003)

The original concept, according to Rosenzweig (interviewed in November 2004), was to incorporate the project as an electronic article into the journal. However, two issues arose that made this impossible – the journal could not agree on criteria for refereeing the project, and there were no arms-distance referees with the composite capacities in both history and digital media. A somewhat unsatisfactory compromise was struck – the authors would write an academic article using the traditional genre and criteria of scholarship, and the journal would link to the Virginia website and list it under Electronic Projects (Thomas and Ayers, 2003). As of April 2008, there has not been a new electronic project connected to *AHR* since 2005.

The young and the restless

By the second half of the 2000s, a new generation was moving through the entry-level avenues in tertiary institutions. Young graduate students and recent PhDs were competing for tenure track positions in universities, often with personal histories of creative innovation in media arts, and aspirations to apply their 'digital native' (*http://www*
.digitalnative.org/) orientations to their new work environments. In a 2004 study of six new PhDs employed as assistant professors or lecturers in the humanities at leading Northeastern US universities, I explored the factors in their situations that might explain the disjunction between their aspirations as creative scholars using digital media, and their behaviour as traditional authors of journal articles and monographs.

Two examples help illuminate the issues. Paula (not her real name) had been an ethnographic filmmaker who had undertaken anthropological fieldwork in Latin America. She had a large pool of videos of everyday and ritual life among her field community, and had made one short documentary analysing an aspect of her research. She then faced a critical decision – whether to use the material and develop an interactive research environment based on a digital video database that could be interrogated by a research community – or to process the data in traditional anthropological writing forms, and focus on getting academic tenure. As she reflected on her choice – to follow the tenure track – she identified four key factors that influenced her choice. First, her mentor in her department counselled her to think about her career and the importance of impressing the gerontocracy that ruled the tenure committee. Second, there was no one in the hierarchy of the department who had any understanding of the potential of digital interactivity to whom she could turn for advice. Third, none of the relevant journals at the time were able to consider anything outside the norm. Indeed, it was not until October 2007 that the Open Anthropology (Forte, 2008) project began, spurred by the advent of Web 2.0 (*http://openanthropology .wordpress.com/categories/*), while the first online open source anthropology journal was set up in February 2007 as the *Museum Anthropology Review*. It initially used WordPress (*http://museumanthropology.net/*), then from February 2008 migrated to using Open Journal System (DSpace) through the University of Indiana Bloomington library (*http://scholarworks.iu.edu/journals/index.php/mar/index*). However, it is thus far limited to publishing reviews, and does not make the full use of the multimedia capabilities of Web 2.0. Finally, the technology that might have enabled Paula to more easily incorporate an interactive multimedia component into the concept and design of the paper was not available – instead, assuming it were to be accepted by a journal outside her disciplinary field, such as *Vectors*, she would need to invest significant time, develop high levels of design skills, and build a craft-based website.

Jacques (not his real name) teaches French at a nearby university to Paula. Jacques has the design and creative skills, and indeed was engaged by the university as a language and culture lecturer so that he could research and develop new interactive learning environments. These resources would be built around a dense database of French accents, dialects and cultural minorities drawn from an extensive ethnographic video project that documented diversity in France and its territories. This research is potentially valuable as the basis for further explorations and testing of the idea of 'French culture' in a period of significant social turmoil, and for serving a community of scholars. However Jacques, entrapped in a teaching-only job, aspires to be a researcher and professor, so concentrates on research that can be published in journals and as a monograph. He hopes, he says, to return to his rich data at a later point, once he is embedded and tenured.

The inevitability of change: what will be the paradigm shift that makes it happen?

The argument about the failure of the academic journal in relation to engaged interactive multimedia-based publishing, as either commercial mainstream or collegial open source, is bolstered by the sense of transitional challenge identified by major institutions in a period of rapid globalization (Shah, 2008). A major US report (in part driven by Rosenzweig) has postulated that:

> many who work in the humanities and social sciences (HSS) have come to recognize that the knowledge practices in these disciplines are on the edge of some fundamental changes ... the online world is a new cultural commonwealth (yet there are major constraints including) unsatisfactory tools, incomplete resources, and inadequate access. (ACLS, 2006)

There are the institutional barriers of gerontocratic power, an undeveloped corpus of review criteria, and limited technological capacity, compounded by economic forces seeking to reduce the costs and price of publishing. However, I want to turn here to another issue, that of how the processes of production need to be transformed to enable creative HSS publishing to be more of an industrial process (akin to the word-processing and printing formula) and less one dominated by scarce craft skills (of web design, graphic complexity and interactive scripting). Clearly Web 2.0 opens up some possibilities here, particularly when linked with embedded video (such as YouTube, LiveLeak or CurrentTV), or with audio, or with flash movies and animations. USC History Professor Phil Ethington (see Ethington, 2000, for an early exploration of the multimedia essay, albeit without interactive audience opportunities) has been a key innovator in the application of digital media to the study and communication of historical analyses, especially of urban spaces. He has curated/edited a multimedia companion to the journal *Urban History* that utilizes a spread of Flash animations to explore visual and aural dimensions of urban historical events and locations (Ethington and Schwartz, 2006).

However enabling, audience community engagement needs to go further than this. A model for such a process can be found in the Multimedia Interactive Research Environment (MIRE) based on the metamedia project at MIT. This essentially uses an XML shell with tags, notes and commentaries, including codes drawn from the Dublin Core Metadata Initiative that enable effective open searching on the web. This shell is wrapped around every piece of data, which can then be retrieved, commented on and extended.

If we bring these challenges together, it is possible to model a simple flowchart of the steps involved in a digital research and publishing project. The project is named MIRE in reference to the murky terrain as well as an acronym for the key elements of interactivity, multimedia data and research, and can be stepped out conceptually as is done in Figure 18.1. The workflow models, in skeletal form, an archetypal research project's movement through time. This is an ongoing process where the publication is never 'finished' but always open to continuing discussion, debate and elaboration, as currently occurs in a wiki environment.

The MIRE environment creates a workspace where a researcher or group of researchers can create a project. The project begins by inviting the researchers to specify a broad research topic, either for individuals or for members of the designated research team. The topic has associated metadata, including the research fields and links to the websites of the researchers. Then as the research data are generated (in multimedia forms) they build a digital repository of research materials (using programs such as Portfolio or Aperture), which is tagged to reflect the research framework, while applying Dublin Core and Text Encoding Initiative templates, as well as more elaborate coding. As the project repository expands, it can be searched to build inductive theoretical concepts that can be formed into research questions – or indeed initial research questions can (and usually would) drive the development of the research materials in the database. The repository grows in iterative cycles, as the search pathways are attached to the database items. As the research process intensifies, the researcher or research team would build commentaries and hypotheses around the data, which would remain

Figure 18.1 The MIRE workflow

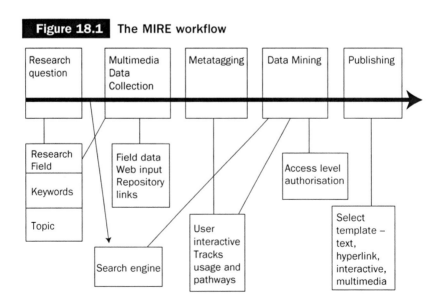

attached for future researchers (and become part of the repository) should they wish to explore them.

The research pathways would be mapped visually, showing which materials were most useful in responding to specific questions, and the way in which different data items are conceptually related to each other. As the researchers begin to 'write' their research results for publication, they would be able to choose one or more of a number of templates that would produce 'texts' suitable for publication in specific environments – online journals (such as the *Electronic Journal of Sociology*) or emerging e-journals and e-print solutions that incorporate peer review, more creative environments such as *Vectors: Journal of Culture and Technology in a Dynamic Vernacular*, web projects (e.g. *American Historical Review* under Rosenzweig's influence) or refereed blog-type publications. The publication would have embedded links to the digital repository used for the research, enabling readers to comment directly on research items, link in to full versions of original documents etc. held in other digital repositories, and view a range of materials (e.g. excerpts of video interviews on a common theme) that underpin the research. Over time another valuable benefit would flow, namely a set of operational reference materials that enable peer reviewers to assess both the academic content and the effectiveness of the communication (as is currently done with the comprehensibility of the text and the interpretation of graphic materials).

Conclusion

The failure of current journal publishing to innovate in a way that utilizes the range of possibilities inherent in digital environments is a consequence, I suggest, of two related factors. First, the political economy of publishing still constrains in an unfortunate and ultimately self-defeating way the capacity of journals to try out risky and experimental options in a systematic and well-resourced way. Second, the industrial technologies are there in the multiple parts but have not yet been brought together, because the problem is usually conceived of as being one of either data collection and storage on the one hand and therefore an issue for museums or galleries, or on the other, of dissemination of completed research findings being the responsibility of publishers and libraries.

We need a journal publishing strategy that understands the scholar as a participant in a community of knowledge-making and testing, in which there are many legitimate stakeholders, and in which truth/insight/ understanding is a function of the interrogations we make of the data we choose. We need to move beyond the current impasse – the issue is which pathway might best take us around the blockages, with their economic, institutional, political and scholarly dimensions.

Bibliography

ACLS (2006) *Our Cultural Commonwealth: The Report of the American Council of Learned Societies Commission on Cyberinfrastructure for the Humanities and Social Sciences*, Washington, DC: American Council of Learned Societies.

Brown, L., Griffiths, R. and Rascoff, M. (2007) 'University publishing in the digital age', *Journal of Electronic Publishing* 10(3), DOI: 10.3998/3336451.0010.301.

Castranova, E., Ross, T., Bell, M., Falk, M., Cornell, R. and Haselton, M. (2008) 'Constructing *Arden*: life inside the machine', *Multimedia IEEE Media Impact* 15(1): 4–8, DOI: 10.1109/MMUL.2008.3

Clarke, R. and Kingsley, D. (2008) 'E-publishing's impacts on journals and journal articles', *Journal of Internet Commerce* 7(1): 120–51.

Davidson, C. (2008) 'More thoughts on e-publishing', available at: *http://www.hastac.org/node/1257* (accessed 13 February 2009).

Dicks, B., Mason, B., Coffey, A. and Atkinson, P. (2005) *Qualitative Research and Hypermedia – Ethnography for the Digital Age*, London: Sage.

Ethington, P. (2000) 'Los Angeles and the problem of urban historical knowledge', *American Historical Review* 105(5), available at: *http://www.historycooperative.org/ahr/elec-projects.html* (links through to: *http://cwis.usc.edu/dept/LAS/history/historylab/LAPUHK/index.html*) (accessed 28 February 2009)

Ethington, P. and Schwartz, V. (2006) (eds) '"Urban Icons," multimedia companion to urban history', *Journal of Urban History* 33(1), available at: *http://journals.cambridge.org/fulltext_content/supplementary/urban_icons_companion/index.htm* (accessed 28 February 2009).

Forte, M. (2008) 'The library as open access publisher, and digital publishing 2.0', *Open Anthropology*, available at: *http://openanthropology.wordpress.com/2008/03/01/the-library-as-open-access-publisher/* (accessed 28 February 2009).

Heath, M., Jubb, M. and Robey, D. (2008) 'E-publication and open access in the arts and humanities in the UK', *Ariadne* 54 (January), available at: *http://www.ariadne.ac.uk/issue54/heath-et-al/* (accessed 28 February 2009).

IEEE MultiMedia Editors (2008) 'Your multimedia community's video blog', *IEEE MultiMedia*, available at: *http://www.computer.org/portal/site/multimedia/* (accessed 28 February 2009).

Jaschik, S. (2008) 'Abandoning print, not peer review', *Insidehighered .com*, available at: *http://www.insidehighered.com/layout/set/print/news/2008/02/28/open* (accessed 28 February 2009).

Kennedy, H. (2003) 'Technobiography: researching lives, online and off', *Biography* 26(1): 120–42.

Khut, G. P. (2007) 'Cardiomorphologies: an inner journey through art', *IEEE MultiMedia* 14: 5–7.

Miller, P. and Berners-Lee, T. (2008) 'Sir Tim Berners-Lee talks with Talis about the Semantic Web', *Talis Podcasts*, 7 February, transcript available at: *http://talis-podcasts.s3.amazonaws.com/twt20080207_TimBL.html* (accessed 28 February 2009).

Nellhaus, T. (2001) 'XML, TEI, and digital libraries in the humanities', *Portal: Libraries and the Academy* 1(3): 257–77.

Neumark, N. and Miranda, M. (2006) 'Talking about the weather', available at: *http://www.scanz.net.nz/weathertalk/* (accessed 28 February 2009).

Research Information Network (2007) *Research and the Scholarly Communications Process: Towards Strategic Goals for Public Policy A Statement of Principles*, London: Research Information Network.

Rosenzweig, R. (2007) 'Collaboration and the cyberinfrastructure: academic collaboration with museums and libraries in the digital era', *First Monday* 12(7), available at: *http://firstmonday.org/htbin/cgiwrap/bin/ojs/index.php/fm/article/view/1926/1808* (accessed 28 February 2009).

Shah, N. (2008) 'From global village to global marketplace: metaphorical descriptions of the global internet', *International Journal of Media and Cultural Politics* 4(1): 9–26.

Sharp, D. and Salomon, M. (2008) *User-led Innovation: A New Framework for Co-creating Business and Social Value Smart Internet Technology*, Melbourne: SmartInternet CRC.

Slane, A. (2007) 'Democracy, social space, and the internet', *University of Toronto Law Journal* 57(1): 81–105.

Smith, J. (1999) 'The deconstructed journal – a new model for academic publishing', *Learned Publishing* 12(2): 79–91 available at: *http://library .kent.ac.uk/library/papers/jwts/DJpaper.pdf* (accessed 28 February 2009).

Smith, J. (2005) 'Reinventing journal publishing', *Research Information*, May/June, available at: *http://www.researchinformation.info/rimayjun05djmodel.html* (accessed 28 February 2009).

Thomas, W. and Ayers, E. (2003) 'An overview: the differences slavery made: a close analysis of two American communities', *The American Historical Review* 108(5); see introduction at: *http://www.vcdh.virginia.edu/AHR/* (accessed 13 February 2008).

Weale, A. (Chair) (2007) 'Metrics and peer review', in *Peer Review: The Challenges for the Humanities and Social Sciences*, available at: *http://www.britac.ac.uk/reports/peer-review/contents.cfm* (accessed 28 February 2009), Chapter 1.

Part VI
Coda

19

'The tiger in the corner': will journals matter to tomorrow's scholars?

Sally Morris

Over recent years, many thousands of words – at meetings, on e-mail discussion lists, and in journals and books (including this one) – have been devoted to the issue of how business models for journals are changing through the possibilities of electronic publishing and dissemination and, in particular, to the perceived threat from open access, in all its manifestations. Yet all of these discussions seem to assume that the basic functions of journals, which Henry Oldenburg and his colleagues described in 1664–65 – registration, dissemination, archiving and certification (Mabe, 2005) – and thus, their form, will continue more or less unchanged. The concerns tend to focus on business models – and open access publishing, at least to my mind, is just another business model.

I would liken this to worrying about the spider in one corner of the room, while in reality there is a tiger in the opposite corner. We need to turn round and face the tiger.

The tiger – the real challenge to all those who are involved in supporting the processes of scholarly communication – is the way that researchers' very behaviour is being utterly transformed by the power of ICT. It is not simply a matter of turning the journal as we know it into a collection of online documents – even one that it enriched by new possibilities of navigation and linking. Nor is it simply a matter of being able to sell access to that collection in completely new ways – from national licences to whole collections of journals, down to 'pay-per-view' access to individual articles or even parts of articles. Rather, we need to understand how ICT is transforming the kinds of research scholars can do, how they do it, and how they communicate with each other about it.

Scholars have access to computing power on a scale unimaginable only a few decades ago. This enables them to carry out completely new kinds of research – collecting vast bodies of data and then processing them, in complex ways, with incredible speed (Borgman, 2008). For example, in the area of ecology, scientists around the world collect, share and use data on climate, earthquakes and many other aspects of our environment; sociologists are able to use vast quantities of population data (the American Sociological Association, for example, includes 'data sharing' in its code of ethics – see *http://www.asanet.org/cs/root/leftnav/ ethics/code_of_ethics_table_of_contents*); similarly, astronomers and astrophysicists collect and analyse data from strategically placed radio-telescopes in many countries (and, indeed, in the 'seti@home' project, have invited the public to put their personal computers at the service of the massive analysis involved to detect any signs of potential extraterrestrial intelligence – see *http://setiathome.berkeley.edu/sah_ papers/woody.php*).

What is more, scholars are able to work in new ways. Where they used to work with a necessarily small group in their own laboratory or university, electronic communications now mean that both the collection and subsequent processing of data can be distributed around the world; more and more research teams are widely spread in different centres and even in different countries, but they can collaborate and communicate perfectly easily. In high-energy physics, for example, where collaborations can involve as many as 290 authors (and over 13 per cent of articles have more than six), they may well come from ten or more different countries (Mele et al., 2006); in one study, multinational authorship of journal articles was found to range from 13 per cent in surgery to 55 per cent in astronomy (Abt, 2007).

How researchers communicate is also changing in very important ways. They are becoming comfortable with a wide range of different ways of communicating. The options used to be limited to discussions within your own lab; presenting your ideas at conferences (first as a poster, perhaps, and later as a full paper), and 'Q&A' and informal discussion with other delegates; distributing preprints to those who requested them; and eventually publishing a paper in a peer-reviewed journal.

But this continuum is changing in fundamental ways. The informal stages are becoming far more important, at the same time that (some would argue) the final, formal stage is being eroded. Preprint databases have long existed in some disciplines, and are now being encouraged (by funders and institutions) more widely. But a preprint is still an early form of a formal article; far more significant, to my mind, are the ways in which the informal and often bi-directional modes of 'chat' through blogs (e.g. Paquet, 2002; Porter, 2002), wikis (e.g. the UK Research Information Network's 'Meta-research Wiki' at *http://www.rin.ac.uk/meta-research-wiki*), bookmarking sites (e.g. CiteULike – *http://www.citeulike.org/*; del.icio.us – *http://del.icio.us/*; Connotea – *http://www.connotea.org/*) and the like are being adopted and adapted by the research community. Here, discussion of one's ideas and one's work is ongoing; others' thoughts and recommendations could sometimes make a real difference to the direction and outcome of that work. The final published article may itself not be a static document – it may be updated or amended as new results or interpretations come to light. The role of the 'expert' – peer reviewer, journal editor – is being rivalled by that of the group as a whole (indeed, this perhaps mirrors a general shift in society at large away from respect for 'authority').

When one brings all these changes together – what researchers do, the way that they do it, and the way that they communicate – it is clear that the formal role of the journal as we currently know it – registration, certification, dissemination and archiving – may become less and less important in the coming decades. Already we find researchers saying that the primary reasons why they publish formal articles in journals include a wish to benefit in career terms from the journal's reputation (Rowlands and Nicholas, 2005), and to ensure long-term preservation of their work (Schonfield, 2005); at the same time, and generally in parallel with formal journal publication, they use other means to disseminate their work to their own peer-group. In some areas, such as computing, different forms of publication – such as conference reports – are already preferred to journals because of their immediacy (see *http://www.cra.org/reports/tenure_review.html*); and in economics, top authors are moving away from top journals altogether (Ellison, 2007).

There are a number of reasons why journals, as we currently know them at least, may not satisfy the evolving needs of researchers in future.

- *Speed*: Because of the (still highly valued) peer-review and editorial processes of filtering, selection and – often – improvement, communication of a research paper is less than immediate, although the widespread adoption of online submission and processing systems, and the growing availability of accepted articles prior to formal publication, has speeded up availability.
- *Static version*: The 'version of record' is often considered (by authors and readers, as well as by publishers) to be of crucial importance

(consider, for example, the NISO/ALPSP 'recommended practice' on Journal Article Versions at *http://www.niso.org/publications/rp/RP-8-2008.pdf*). However, this is not necessarily how researchers operate and how their work develops over time. A scholar's findings may be added to by their own or others' further work; the analysis may develop in the light of comments and discussion. Why, indeed, should a piece of work be set in stone?

- *Single mode of communication*: Journal articles are just one part of the researcher's spectrum of modes of communication. They may talk (in person or via phone and e-mail) with colleagues around the world about the research as it develops; present one or more accounts of work in progress at meetings and conferences, which themselves may be transmitted more widely via web and podcasts; discuss the work in a blog; make data available (and update it periodically); participate in an evolving account of its significance in a wiki; write one or more book chapters; and perhaps even present it to a non-specialist audience on television.

- *Isolation*: The work may also be closely related to other people's work, also being communicated in a similarly wide range of ways. In addition, it may be developed over time through the participation of many other people. The ability to link, and to navigate readily across those links (e.g. using the digital object identifier) has improved enormously, but as Ted Nelson realized as long ago as the 1960s with Project Xanadu (*http://xanadu.com/*), information is not really linear at all – it is a complex, interconnected web.

There are a few publishers – but only a few – who have been very imaginative in responding to these changes, developing all kinds of new features and tools to fit into researchers' new working patterns. Open peer review, where readers' comments on the initially posted version can help to shape the final version, is one area where there has been considerable experimentation: *Electronic Transactions on Artificial Intelligence (http://www.etaij.org/)* was one of the first journals to experiment with this approach. More recently, *Atmospheric Chemistry and Physics (http://www.atmospheric-chemistry-and-physics.net/)* (Pöschl, 2004) now offers public peer review and interactive discussion, while the 'Academic Publishing Wiki' (*http://academia.wikia.com/wiki/Main_Page*) provides a (non-publisher) home for new journals with open peer review. However, recent experiments by *Nature* along similar lines received very little use (*http://www.nature.com/nature/peerreview/debate/nature05535.html*). Linking to and from deposited data, including links to community data repositories (e.g. in crystallography – see Strickland et al., 2008) is becoming increasingly common.

Curiously, although informal communication tools such as blogs and wikis have been adopted by researchers, very few traditional publishers have been involved with these developments – perhaps they are missing a trick? For instance, there is a whole group of subject-related blogs at ScienceBlogs (*http://www.scienceblogs.com*). Wiki tools have also found a place in the scholarly world, for example Sklogwiki (*http://www .sklogwiki.org*) for people interested in simple liquids, complex fluids, and soft condensed matter, and Quantiki (*http://www.quantiki.org*) in quantum information science. Pronetos (*http://pronetos.com*) brings together a whole range of informal community communication tools for a number of different disciplines. Meanwhile, publishers such as Nature (*http://network.nature.com/london/blogs*) and BioMed Central (*http://blogs.openaccesscentral.com/blogs/bmcblog/*) are beginning to look at how they can help the researcher communities they serve by offering a range of communication media, rather than just formal journals.

This may sound like the way to go. But it is more feasible for some publishers than for others. Most journal publishers are small – the average number of journals per publisher is 2.39 (dropping to 1.80 if the four largest publishers are excluded). In addition, the majority of journals are owned (and, in many cases, published) by nonprofit organizations such as learned societies (Morris, 2007). Small and society publishers may not have the necessary financial resources to invest – constantly – in radical development and experimentation; they may also be held back by their own past, by the innate conservatism of their organizations. Unless smaller publishers can find ways of experimenting too – perhaps in collaboration – then there is a danger that, once again, we will see the 'Matthew Effect'[1] stacking the cards in favour of the larger players, and thus pushing small independent publishers either into the arms of larger partners, or out of business altogether. This would be particularly regrettable given that society publishers, in particular, are uniquely placed to be close to their own communities and thus to understand and satisfy the evolving needs of their readers.

But we should never assume that the publishers of today automatically have a role in the scholarly communication of tomorrow. Those who try to understand how researchers work and communicate, and create tools to help them to do so more easily – be they existing players or completely new ones – may well find a growing role and potentially exciting business opportunities in this future landscape of scholarly communication. On the other hand, the traditional formal journal and those who produce it may see themselves increasingly sidelined. Whether these new players, who are willing and able to ride the tiger, are publishers as we currently know them – time will tell.

Acknowledgment

This chapter is closely based on an editorial by the same title which appeared in July 2008 in the journal *Learned Publishing* 21(3): 163–5, available at: *http://dx.doi.org/10.1087/095315108X323901*.

Note

1. Matthew, Chapter 25, verse 29: 'For unto every one that hath shall be given, and he shall have abundance: but from him that hath not shall be taken away even that which he hath'.

Bibliography

Abt, H. (2007) 'The frequencies of multinational papers in various sciences', *Scientometrics* 71(1): 105–15; available at: *http://dx.doi.org/10.1007/s11192-007-1686-z*.

Borgman, C. (2008) 'Data, disciplines and scholarly publishing', *Learned Publishing* 21: 29–38; available at: *http://dx.doi.org/10.1087/095315108X254476*.

Ellison, G. (2007) 'Is peer review in decline?', National Bureau of Economic Research working paper, available at: *http://econ-www.mit.edu/files/906* (accessed 3 March 2009).

Mabe, M. (2005) 'The function of the journal', paper presented at the Research Communications Forum conference, Oxford, 7 March; available at: *http://www.berr.gov.uk/files/file10873.ppt*.

Mele, S., Dallman, D., Vigen, J. and Yeomans, J. (2006) 'Quantitative analysis of the publishing landscape in high-energy physics', *Journal of High Energy Physics* 12: S01; available at: *http://dx.doi.org/10.1088/1126-6708/2006/12/s01*.

Morris, S. (2007). 'Mapping the journal publishing landscape: how much do we know?' *Learned Publishing* 20: 299–310; available at: *http://dx.doi.org/10.1087/095315107X239654*.

Paquet, S. (2002) 'Personal knowledge publishing and its uses in research', available at: *http://radio.weblogs.com/0110772/stories/2002/10/03/personalKnowledgePublishingAndItsUsesInResearch.html* (accessed 3 March 2009).

Porter, S. (2007) 'Science in the blogosphere', paper presented at the ALPSP International Scholarly Communications Conference, London, 13 April; available at: *http://www.alpsp.org/ForceDownload.asp?id=428.*

Pöschl, U. (2004) 'Interactive journal concept for improved scientific publishing and quality assurance', *Learned Publishing* 17: 105–13; available at: *http://dx.doi.org/10.1087/095315104322958481.*

Rowlands, I. and Nicholas, D. (2005) 'New journal publishing models: an international survey of senior researchers', available at: *http://www.ucl.ac.uk/ciber/ciber_2005_survey_final.pdf* (accessed 3 March 2009)

Schonfield, R. (2007) 'Faculty attitudes and perspectives in the transition to an increasingly electronic environment', paper presented at the ALA Conference, Washington, DC, 21–7 June.

Strickland, P., McMahon, B. and Helliwell, B. (2008) 'Integrating research articles and supporting data in crystallography', *Learned Publishing* 21: 63–72; available at: *http://dx.doi.org/10.1087/095315108X248347.*

Index